ALWAYS COMING HOME

In this, the masterwork of a constantly inventive career, Ursula K. Le Guin makes the inhabitants of the place called the Valley as familiar, as immediate, as wholly human as our own friends or family. Spiralling outward from the dramatic life story of a woman called Stone Telling, ALWAYS COMING HOME interweaves wry wit, deep insight and extraordinary compassion into a compelling unity of vision.

"An appealing book as well as a masterly one . . . The future world she's created here is awesomely complete."
—NEWSWEEK

"The effect it has on the reader is hypnotic . . . Le Guin has chosen a most original way to reveal this imagined land."
—PEOPLE

"Le Guin has pulled off a trick that no writer of less complexity could have done. Everything from poetry to myth has the ring of truth."
—CLEVELAND PLAIN DEALER

ALWAYS COMING HOME

Ursula K. Le Guin

Composer: TODD BARTON

Artist: MARGARET CHODOS

George Hersh, Geomancer

Maps drawn by the Author

BANTAM BOOKS
TORONTO • NEW YORK • LONDON • SYDNEY • AUCKLAND

MUSIC AND POETRY OF THE KESH: a cassette tape, words
by Ursula K. Le Guin, music by Todd Barton, is available
for $9.00 plus one dollar shipping cost from:
Valley Productions, P. O. Box 3220, Ashland, OR 97520.

*This low-priced Bantam Book
has been completely reset in a type face
designed for easy reading, and was printed
from new plates. It contains the complete
text of the original hard-cover edition.*
NOT ONE WORD HAS BEEN OMITTED.

ALWAYS COMING HOME

*A Bantam Spectra Book / published by arrangement with
Harper & Row, Publishers, Inc.*

PRINTING HISTORY
*Harper and Row edition published / October 1985
Bantam edition / January 1986*

"The Trouble with the Cotton People," copyright © 1984 by Ursula K. Le Guin, first
appeared in The Missouri Review, vol. 7, no. 2: reprinted in Best Science Fiction of the
Year, vol. 2, edited by Gardner Dozois.
"The Visionary," copyright © 1984 by Ursula K. Le Guin, first appeared in Omni reprinted as The Visionary: The Life Story of Flicker of the Serpentine in Capra Back-
to-Back, vol. 1, Capra Press. "Dira," copyright © 1984 by Ursula K. Le Guin, first
appeared in Parabola: Myth and the Quest for Meaning, vol. 9, Winter.
"Time in the Valley," copyright © 1985 by Ursula K. Le Guin, first appeared in The
Hudson Review: A Magazine of Literature and the Arts, vol. 37, no. 4, Winter 1984–85.
"It Was Never Really Different," copyright © 1985 by Ursula K. Le Guin, first appeared
in Whole Earth Review, July 1985.
"A Song Used in Chumo When Damming a Creek of Diverting Water to a Holding Tank
for Irrigation," copyright © 1985 by Ursula K. Le Guin, first appeared in Whole Earth
Review, July 1985.
"A Bay Laurel Song," copyright © 1985 by Ursula K. Le Guin, first appeared in Whole
Earth Review, July 1985.
"An Exhortation from the Second and Third Houses of the Earth," copyright © by
Ursula K. Le Guin, first appeared in Whole Earth Review, July 1985.

Contents

IIIIIIIIIIIIIIIIIIIIIIIIIIIIIIIIIIIIIIIIIIIIIIIIIIIIIIIIIIIIIIIII

CONTENTS

CONTENTS

MAPS

A First Note

THE PEOPLE IN this book might be going to have lived a long, long time from now in Northern California.

The main part of the book is their voices speaking for themselves in stories and life-stories, plays, poems, and songs. If the reader will bear with some unfamiliar terms they will all be made clear at last. Coming at my work as a novelist, I thought it best to put many of the explanatory, descriptive pieces into a section called The Back of the Book, where those who want narrative can ignore them and those who enjoy explanations can find them. The glossary may also be useful or amusing.

The difficulty of translation from a language that doesn't yet exist is considerable, but there's no need to exaggerate it. The past, after all, can be quite as obscure as the future. The ancient Chinese book called *Tao teh ching* has been translated into English dozens of times, and indeed the Chinese have to keep retranslating it into Chinese at every cycle of Cathay, but no translation can give us the book that Lao Tze (who may not have existed) wrote. All we have is the *Tao teh ching* that is here, now. And so with translations from a literature of the (or a) future. The fact that it hasn't yet been written, the mere absence of a text to translate, doesn't make all that much difference. What was and what may be lie, like children whose faces we cannot see, in the arms of silence. All we ever have is here, now.

THE QUAIL SONG

From the Summer Dance.

In the fields by the river
from the meadows by the river
from the fields by the river
in the meadows by the river
    two quail run

Run two quail
rise two quail
two quail run
two quail rise
    from the meadows by the river

Towards an Archaeology
of the Future

|||||||||||||||||||||||||||||||||||||||||||||||||||||||||||||||||||||||||

HOW THE PATIENT scientist feels when the shapeless tussocks and vague ditches under the thistles and scrub begin to take shape and come clear: this was the outer rampart—this the gateway—that was the granary! We'll dig here, and here, and after that I want to look at that lumpy bit on the slope. . . . How they know true glory when a thin disk slips through the fingers with the sifted dirt, and cleared with the swipe of a thumb shows, stamped in the fragile bronze, the horned god! How I envy them their shovels and sieves and tape measures, all their tools, and their wise, expert hands that touch and hold what they find! Not for long; they'll give it to the museum, of course; but they did hold it for a moment in their hands.

I found, at last, the town I had been hunting for. After digging in several wrong places for over a year and persisting in several blockheaded opinions—that it must be walled, with one gate, for instance—I was studying yet once more the contours of my map of the region, when it dawned as slowly and certainly as the sun itself upon me that the town was *there*, between the creeks, under my feet the whole time. And there was never a wall; what on earth did they need a wall for? What I had taken for the gate was the bridge across the meeting of the creeks. And the sacred buildings and the dancing place not in the center of town, for the center is the Hinge, but over in their own arm of the double spiral, the right arm, of course—there in the pasture below the barn. And so it is, and so it is.

But I can't go digging there and hope to find the curved fragment of a roof tile, the iridescent foot of a wine goblet, the ceramic cap of a solar battery, or a little coin of the gold of California, the same, for gold rusts not, that was weighed out in Placerville and spent on whores or real estate in Frisco and then perhaps was a wedding ring awhile and then went hidden in a vault deeper than the mine it came from until all security proved illfounded, and now reshaped, this time round, into a curl-rayed sun and given in honor to a skilful artisan: no, I won't find that. It isn't here. That little sun of gold is not, as they say, dwelling in the Houses of the Earth. It is in thin air, in the wilderness that lies beyond this day and night, the Houses of the Sky. My gold is in the shards of the broken pot at the end of the rainbow. Dig there! What will you find? Seeds. Seeds of the wild oats.

I can walk in the wild oats and the thistles, between the houses of the little town I was looking for, Sinshan. I can cross the Hinge and come onto the dancing place. There, about where that Valley oak is now, will be Obsidian, in the northeast; the Blue Clay quite close to it, dug into the hillside, the northwest; closer to me, towards the center, Serpentine of the Four Directions; then the two Adobes on a curve down towards the creek, southeast, southwest. They'll have to drain this field, if they build the heyimas, as I think they do, underground, only the pyramidal roofs with their clerestories elevated, and the ornamented ends of the entrance ladder sticking out of the top. I can see that well enough. All kinds of seeing with the mind's eye is allowed me here. I can stand here in the old pasture where there's nothing but sun and rain, wild oats and thistles and crazy salsify, no cattle grazing, only deer, stand here and shut my eyes and see: the dancing place, the stepped pyramid roofs, a moon of beaten copper on a high pole over the Obsidian. If I listen, can I hear voices with the inner ear? Could you hear voices, Schliemann, in the streets of Troy? If you did, you were crazy too. The Trojans had all been dead three thousand years. Which is farther from us, farther out of reach, more silent—the dead, or the unborn? Those whose bones lie under the thistles and the dirt and the tombstones of the Past, or those who slip weightless among molecules, dwelling where a century passes in a day, among the fair folk, under the great, bell-curved Hill of Possibility?

There's no way to reach that lot by digging. They have no bones. The only human bones in this pasture would be those of the first-comers, and they did not bury here, and left no tombs or tiles or shards or walls or coins behind them. If they had a town here it was made of what the woods and fields are made of, and is gone. One may listen, but all the words of their language are gone, gone utterly. They worked obsidian, and that stays; down there at the edge of the rich man's airport there was a workshop, and you can pick up plenty of chipped pieces, though no one has found a finished point for years. There is no other trace of them. They owned their Valley very lightly, with easy hands. They walked softly here. So will the others, the ones I seek.

The only way I can think to find them, the only archaeology that might be practical, is as follows: You take your child or grandchild in your arms, or borrow a young baby, not a year old yet, and go down into the wild oats in the field below the barn. Stand under the oak on the last slope of the hill, facing the creek. Stand quietly. Perhaps the baby will see something, or hear a voice, or speak to somebody there, somebody from home.

The Small Winery at Sinshan

STONE TELLING

PART I

STONE TELLING IS my last name. It has come to me of my own choosing, because I have a story to tell of where I went when I was young; but now I go nowhere, sitting like a stone in this place, in this ground, in this Valley. I have come where I was going.

My House is the Blue Clay, my household the High Porch of Sinshan.

My mother was named Towhee, Willow, and Ashes. My father's name, Abhao, in the Valley means Kills.

In Sinshan babies' names often come from birds, since they are messengers. In the month before my mother bore me, an owl came every night to the oak trees called Gairga outside the windows of High Porch House, on the north side, and sang the owl's song there; so my first name was North Owl.

High Porch is an old house, well-built, with large rooms; the beams and frame are redwood, the walls of adobe brick and plaster, the flooring oak, the windows of clear glass in small square panes. The balconies of High Porch are deep and beautiful. The great-grandmother of my grandmother was the first to live in our rooms, on the first floor, under the roof; when the family was big they needed the whole floor, but my grandmother was the only one of her generation, and so we lived in the two west rooms only. We could not give much. We had the use of ten wild olives and several other gathering trees on Sinshan Ridge and a seed-clearing on the east side of Wakyahum, and planted potatoes and corn and vegetables in one of the plots on the creek southeast of Adobe Hill, but we took much more corn and beans from the storehouses than we gave. My grandmother Valiant was a weaver. When I was a small child she had no sheep in the family, and so gave most of what she wove for wool to weave more. The first thing I remember of being alive is that my grandmother's fingers moved across the warp of

7

the loom, forth and back, a silver crescent bracelet shining on her
wrist below the red sleeve.

The second thing I remember is that I went up to the spring of
our creek in the fog in early morning in the winter. It was my first
time as a Blue Clay child to dip up water for the new-moon wakwa.
I was so cold I cried. The older children laughed at me and said I
had spoiled the water by crying into it. I believed them, and began
to bawl because I had spoiled the water. My grandmother was offi-
ciating, and she told me the water was all right, and let me carry
the moon-jar all the way back to town; but I bawled and snivelled
all the way, because I was cold and ashamed and the jar of spring
water was cold and heavy. I can feel that cold and wet and weight
now in old age, and see the dead arms of manzanita black in fog,
and hear the voices laughing and talking before me and behind me
on the steep path beside the creek.

> I go there, I go there.
> I go where I went
> Crying beside the water.
> It goes there, it goes there,
> The fog along the water.

I did not spend much time crying; maybe not enough. My
mother's father said, "Laugh first, cry later; cry first, laugh later."
He was a Serpentine man from Chumo, and had gone back to that
town to live with his mother's people. That was all right with my
grandmother. She said once, "Living with my husband is like eating unleached acorns." But she went down to visit him from time to
time in Chumo, and he would come and stay with us in the hills in
summer, when Chumo was baking like a biscuit down on the Val-

ley floor. His sister Green Drum was a famous Summer dancer, but his family never gave anything. He said they were poor because his mother and grandmother had given everything in past years putting on the Summer dances at Chumo. My grandmother said they were poor because they didn't like working. They may both have been right.

The only other human people directly in my family lived in Madidinou. My grandmother's sister had gone there to live, and her son had married a Red Adobe woman there. We often visited, and I played with my second cousins, a girl and boy called Pelican and Hops.

Our family animals when I was a small child were himpi, poultry, and a cat. Our cat was black without a white hair, handsome, mannerly, and a great hunter. We traded her kittens for himpi, so that for a while we had a big pen of himpi. I looked after them and the chickens, and kept cats out of the runs and pens down under the lower balconies. When I began staying with the animals I was still so small that the green-tailed cock frightened me. He knew it, and would come at me jerking his neck and swearing, and I would scramble over the divider into the himpi run to escape him. The himpi would come out and sit up and whistle at me. They were a comfort to me, even more than kittens. I learned not to name them, and not to trade them alive for eating, but to kill quickly those I traded, since some people kill animals without care or skill, causing fear and pain. I cried enough to suit even my grandfather, after the night a sheepdog went amok and got into the run and slaughtered every himpi but a few nestlings. I could not speak to a dog for months after that. But it turned out well for my family, since the sheepdog's people gave us a ewe in lamb to make up for the loss of our himpi. The ewe bore twin ewe lambs, and so my mother was a shepherd again, and my grandmother had family wool to spin and weave.

I do not remember learning to read and dance; my grandmother was teaching me from before the time I began to speak and walk. When I was five I began going to the heyimas with the other Blue Clay children, mornings, and later I studied with teachers in the heyimas and in the Blood, Oak, and Mole Lodges; I learned the Salt Journey; I studied a little with the poet Ire, and a long time with the potter Clay Sun. I was not quick to learn, and never considered going to a school in one of the great towns, though several children of Sinshan did so. I liked learning in the heyimas, taking part in a structure larger than my own knowledge, in which I could find relief from feelings of fear and anger which unaided I could not understand or get past. Yet I did not learn as much as I might have done, but always hung back, and said, "I can't do that."

Some of the children, illmeaning or ignorant, called me Hwikmas, "half-House." I had also heard people say of me, "She is half a person." I understood this in my own way, badly, since it was not explained to me at home. I had not the courage to ask questions at the heyimas, or to go where I might have learned about matters outside the little town of Sinshan, and begun to see the Valley as a part of a whole as well as a whole. Since neither my mother nor her mother spoke of him, in the first years of my life all I knew of my father was that he had come from outside the Valley and had gone away again. This meant to me only that I had no father's mother, no father's House, and therefore was a half-person. I had not even heard of the Condor people. I had lived eight years before we went to the hot springs in Kastoha-na to treat my grandmother's rheumatism, and in the common place there saw men of the Condor.

I will tell that journey. It was a small journey many years ago. It is a journey of the still air.

We got up in the darkness of a morning about a month past the World Dance. I gave some meat I had saved to the black cat Sidi, who was growing old. I had thought she would be hungry while we were away, and the thought had worried me for days. My mother told me, "You eat that. The cat will catch what she needs!" My mother was stern and reasoning. My grandmother said, "The child is feeding her soul. Let be."

We put out the hearthfire and left the door open a little for the cat and the wind. We went down the stairs under the last stars; the houses looked like hills in the darkness, dark. Out on the common place it seemed lighter. We crossed the Hinge and went to the Blue Clay heyimas. Shell was waiting for us there; she was a member of the Doctors Lodge and had treated my grandmother's pain, and they were old friends. They filled the water basin and sang the Return together. When we came up into the dancing place the light was beginning. Shell came back across the Hinge with us and through town, and after we crossed the bridge over Sinshan Creek we all squatted there under the live oaks and pissed, and said, "Go well! Stay well!" laughing. That was how Lower Valley people used to do when they left on a journey, but only old people remember it now. Then Shell went back and we went on past the barns, between the creeks, across Sinshan Fields. The sky above the hills across the Valley began to be yellow and red; where we were in the middle the woods and hills were green; behind us Sinshan Mountain was blue and dark. So we walked in the arm of life. Birds were singing their different songs in the air, in the trees, and in the fields. As we came to Amiou path and turned northwest to face Grandmother Mountain, the southeast mountains let go the sun's edge, white. Now I walk that way in that light.

My grandmother Valiant felt well and walked easily that morning, and she said, "Let's go and see our family in Madidinou." So we went that way, towards the sun, and came there along Sinshan Creek, where the wild and domestic geese and ducks were feeding and talking in great numbers in the cattail marshes. I had been to Madidinou many times, of course, but this time the town looked altogether different, since I was on a journey beyond it. I felt serious and important, and did not want to play with my Red Adobe cousins, though they were the children I loved best. My grandmother visited awhile with her daughter-in-law—her son died before my birth—and her grandchildren's stepfather, and then we went on our way, crossing the plum and apricot orchards to the Old Straight Road.

I had been past and across the Old Straight Road with my Madidinou cousins, but now I was going to walk on it. I felt important but awed, and whispered heya for the first nine steps. People said it was the oldest work of hands in all the Valley, that nobody knew low long there had been a road there. Parts of it were indeed straight, but other parts went curving off towards the River and then came back to the straight. In the dust were marks of feet,

Himpi

sheep's hooves, donkeys' hooves, dogs' paws, people's feet shod, people's feet bare, so many tracks of feet that I thought they must be all the tracks of all the people that had ever walked on the road for fifty thousand years. Great Valley oaks stood along the sides of the road to give windbreak and shade, and in places elms, or poplars, or huge white eucalyptus so vast and twisted that they looked older than the Road; but it was so wide that even the morning shadows did not reach across it. I thought that because it was so old, it had to be wide; but my mother explained that it was wide because the big flocks of the Upper Valley went along it to the salt-grass prairies at the Mouths of the Na after the World, and came back up-valley after the Grass, and some of those flocks were of a thousand sheep or more. They had all gone by, and we met only a couple of dungcarts following after the last of them, with a group of shitty and raucous adolescents from Telina shovelling up dung for the fields. They called all sorts of jokes at us, and my mothers replied laughing, but I hid my face. There were some other travellers on the road, and when they greeted us, again I hid my face each time; but once they were past I stared after them and asked so many questions, who are they? where are they coming from? where are they going?, that Valiant began to laugh at me and answer me with jokes.

Because she was lame we went slowly, and because it was all new to me the way seemed immensely long to me, but by midmorning we came through the vineyards to Telina-na. I saw that town rise beside the Na, the great barns, the walls and windows of its houses among the oaks, the roofs of the heyimas, high-stepped, red and yellow around the bannered dancing place, a town like a bunch of grapes, like a cock pheasant, rich, elaborate, amazing, beautiful.

My grandmother's half-sister's son was living in Telina-na in a Red Adobe household, and that family had sent word to us to stay with them on our way. Telina was so much bigger than Sinshan that I thought there was no end to it, and that household was so much bigger than ours that I thought there was no end to them. Actually there were only seven or eight, living in the ground floor of Hard-cinder House, but other relatives and friends kept coming and going, and there was so much working and talking and cooking and bringing and taking that I thought this household must be the wealthiest in the world. They heard me whisper to my grandmother, "Look! There are seven cooking-pots!" They all laughed at that. I was ashamed at first, but they kept repeating what I had said and laughing with so much good nature that I began saying things to make them laugh more. After I said, "This household is huge, like a mountain!" my half-uncle's wife Vine said, "Come and live with us awhile in this mountain, then, you North Owl. We have seven pots but no daughter. We need one!" She meant that; she was the center of all that giving and taking and flowing, a generous person. But my mother did not let the words come to her, and my grandmother smiled but said nothing.

That evening my Red Adobe cousins, Vine's two sons and some other children of the household, took me all around Telina. Hardcinder House is one of the inner houses of the left-hand common place. In the center place a horse race was going on, a wonder to me who had never dreamed of a common place big enough to hold a horse race on. I had not seen many horses, for that matter; in Sinshan it was donkey races in a cow pasture. The course was around the place leftwards, reverse, and back around rightwards to make the heyiya-if. People were up in the balconies and out on the roofs with oil and battery lamps, betting and drinking and shouting, and the horses ran through shadow and flashing lights, turning as fast as swallows, the riders yipping and yelling. Over in some balconies of the right-hand place people were singing, getting ready for the Summer dancing,

> "Two quail run,
> Two quail rise . . ."

Over in the dancing place they were singing down in the Serpentine heyimas, too, but we only went by there on the way to the River. Down among the willows there where the lights from the town made a little gleaming among the shadows, couples had come away to enjoy privacy. We children sneaked around looking for them in the willow thickets, and when we found a couple my cousins would yell, "Holy mole, there's sand in the hole!" or make rude noises, and the couple would get up swearing and come after us, and we would scatter and run. If those cousins of mine did that every warm night, there wasn't much need for contraceptives in Telina. When we got tired we went back to the house and ate some cold beans and went to sleep on the balconies and porches. All night we heard them singing the Quail Song over the way.

Next morning we three left early, though not before daybreak and a good breakfast. As we crossed the Na on the arched stone bridge, my mother held my hand. She did not do that often. I thought she did it because it was sacred to cross the River. I think now she was afraid to lose me. She thought she should let me stay in the rich town with those rich relatives.

When we were away from Telina-na her mother said to her, "For the winter, perhaps, Willow?"

My mother said nothing.

I did not think anything about it. I was happy, and talked the whole way to Chumo about the wonderful things I had seen and heard and done in Telina-na. All the time I talked my mother held my hand.

We came into Chumo hardly knowing we had come into it, the houses are so scattered out and hidden among trees. We were to spend the night at our heyimas there, but first we went to visit my grandmother's husband, my mother's father. He had a room of his own with some of his Yellow Adobe relatives in a single-story house under oaks in sight of the creek, a pretty place. His room, which was his workroom, was large and dank. Up till then I had always known my grandfather by his middle name, Potter, but he had changed his name: he told us to call him Corruption.

I thought that was a crazy name, and being puffed up by the laughter of the family in Telina when I made jokes, I said to my mother, pretty loudly, "Does he stink?" My grandmother heard and said, "Be quiet. It's nothing to joke about." I felt bad and foolish, but my grandmother didn't seem to be cross with me. When the other people of the house had gone back to their rooms, leaving us with my grandfather in his room, she said to him, "What kind of name have you let come to you?"

He said, "A true name."

He looked different from the way he had looked the summer before in Sinshan. He had always been gloomy and complaining. Nothing was ever right, and nobody ever did things right except himself, although he never did anything much, because the time wasn't right. Now he still looked grim and sour, but he behaved with importance. He said to Valiant, "There's no use going to the hot springs for a cure. You'd do better staying home and learning how to think."

"How do you learn that?" she asked.

He said, "You have to learn that your pains and aches are merely an error in thinking. Your body is not real."

"I think it's real," Valiant said, and she laughed and slapped her hips.

"Like this?" Corruption said. He was holding the wooden paddle he used to smooth the outside of the big clay storage jars he made. The paddle was carved of olive wood, as long as my arm and a handspan wide. He held it up in his right hand, brought his left hand up towards it, and passed it through his left hand. It went through muscle and bone like a knife through water.

Valiant and Willow stared at the paddle and the hand. He motioned to them to let him do the same thing to them. They did not put up their hands; but I was curious, and wanted to go on having attention paid to me, so I held up my right arm. Corruption reached out the paddle and passed it through my arm between wrist and elbow. I felt the soft motion of it; it felt as a candle flame feels when you pass a finger through it. It made me laugh with surprise. My grandfather looked at me and said, "This North Owl might come to the Warriors."

It was the first time I had heard that word.

Valiant said, and I could tell she was angry, "No chance of that. Your Warriors are all men."

"She can marry one," said my grandfather. "When the time comes she can marry Dead Sheep's son."

"You can go do such-and-such with your dead sheep!" Valiant said, which made me laugh again, but Willow touched her arm to quieten her. I don't know whether my mother was frightened by the power her father had shown, or by the quarrelling between her father and mother; anyhow, she restored quiet behavior between them. We drank a glass of wine with my grandfather, and then we walked with him to the dancing place of Chumo and to the Blue Clay heyimas. We spent the night there in their guest room, the first night I had slept underground. I liked the silence and stillness of the air, but was not used to it, and kept waking in the night and listening, and only when I heard my mothers' breathing could I sleep again.

There were some other people Valiant wanted to see in Chumo, where she had lived when she learned tapestry weaving, and we did not leave that town till near noon. As we went along the northeast side of the River the Valley narrowed in, and the road went among orchards of olive, plum, and nectarine, among hills terraced with vines. I had never been so close to the Mountain, and it filled my eyes. When I looked back, I could not see Sinshan Mountain: its shape had changed, or other mountains of the southwest side had hidden it. That alarmed me. I finally spoke of it to my mother, who understood my fear, and reassured me that when we returned to Sinshan our mountain would be where it belonged.

After we crossed the Wether Creek we could see the town of Chukulmas up in the hills across the Valley, its Fire Tower standing up by itself, built of colored stones, red, orange, and yellowish-white, patterned as finely as a basket or a snake. Cattle grazed in the yellow pasture-bays on the foothills, between the arms of the woods. On the narrowed, flat floor of the Valley were many wineries and fruit-drying sheds, and the orcharders from Chukulmas were putting up summerhouses. Beside the Na the dark mills loomed among the oaks, their wheels making a sound you could hear for a long way. Quail were calling the three-note call and larks went up from the fields and the buzzards turned very high up. The sunlight was clear, the air was still.

My mother said, "This is a day of the Ninth House."

My grandmother said only, "I'll be glad to get to Kastoha." Since we left Chumo she had been silent and walked lame.

There was a feather on the way before my mother's feet, a grey-barred, blue wing-feather of a jay. It was the answer to what she had said. She picked it up and held it as she walked. She was a small woman, round-faced, with fine hands and feet, barefoot that day, wearing old buckskin trousers and a sleeveless shirt, carrying a little backpack, her hair braided and coiled, a blue feather in her hand. So she walks in the sunlight in the still air.

Shadows were coming across the Valley from the western hills when we came to Kastoha-na. Valiant saw the roofs above the orchards and said, "Aha, there's Granny's Twat!" Old people used to call Kastoha that, because it is between the spread legs of the Mountain. Hearing it called that, I had imagined the town to be set among fir and redwood trees and to be a cave, dark and mysterious, with the River running out of it. When we came across the Na Bridge and I saw it was a big town like Telina only bigger yet, with hundreds of houses, and more people than I knew were in the world, I began crying. Maybe it was shame that made me cry, because I saw how silly I had been to think that a town could be a cave; maybe I was frightened or tired from all I had seen in the days and nights of our journey. Valiant took my right arm in her hands and felt it and looked at it. She had not done that after Corruption had put the paddle through it; nothing at all had been said about that. "He's an old fool," she said now, "and so am I." She took off the silver crescent bracelet which she always wore, and slipped it over my hand onto my right arm. "There," she said. "It won't fall off, North Owl."

She was so thin that the crescent was only a little large for my small arm; but that was not what she meant. I stopped crying. In the lodging house by the hot springs that night I slept, but while I slept I knew all night that the moon was on my arm, under my head.

On the next day I saw the Condor for the first time. Everything in Kastoha-na was strange to me, everything was new, everything was different from home; but as soon as I saw those men I knew that Sinshan and Kastoha were all one thing, the same thing, and this was a different thing.

I was like a cat that scents a rattlesnake or a dog that sees a ghost. My legs got stiff, and I could feel the air on my head because my hair was trying to stand up. I stopped short and said in a whisper, "What are they?"

My grandmother said, "Men of the Condor. Men of no House."

My mother was beside me. She went forward very suddenly and spoke to the four tall men. They turned to her, beaked and winged, looking down at her. My legs went weak then and I wanted to piss. I saw black vultures stooping on my mother, stretching out their red necks, their pointed beaks, staring with eyes ringed with white. They pulled things out of her mouth and belly.

She came back to us and we walked on towards the hot springs. She said, "He's been in the north, in the volcano country. Those men say the Condor are coming back. They knew his name when I said it, they said he is an important person. Did you see how they listened when I said his name?" My mother laughed. I had never heard her laugh that way.

Valiant said, "Whose name?"

Willow said, "My husband's name."

They had stopped again, facing each other.

My grandmother shrugged and turned away.

"I tell you he's coming back," my mother said.

I saw white sparkles crowding all around her face, like flies of light. I cried out, and then I began to vomit, and crouched down. "I don't want it to eat you!" I kept saying.

My mother carried me back to the lodging house in her arms. I slept awhile, and in the afternoon I went with Valiant to the hot springs. We lay a long time in the hot water. It was brownish-blue and full of mud and smelled of sulphur, very disagreeable at first, but once you were in it you began to feel like floating in it forever. The pool was shallow, wide, and long, lined with blue-green glazed tiles. There were no walls, but a high roof of timbers; screens could be set against the wind. It was a lovely place. All the people there had come there for healing, and talked only quietly, or lay alone in the water singing soft healing songs. The blue-brown water hid their bodies, so looking down the long pool you could only see heads resting on the water, leaning back against the tiles, some with eyes closed, some singing, in the mist that hung above the hot springs.

> I lie there, I lie there,
> I lie where I lay
> Floating in the shallow water.
> It floats there, it floats there,
> The mist above the water.

The lodging house of the hot springs of Kastoha-na was our household for a month. Valiant bathed in the waters and went daily to the Doctors Lodge to learn the Copper Snake. My mother went alone up onto the Mountain, to the Springs of the River, to Wakwaha, and on to the summit in the tracks of the mountain lion. A child could not spend all day in the hot pool and the Doctors Lodge, but I was afraid of the crowded common places of the big town, and we had no relatives in the houses, so I stayed mostly at the hot springs and helped with the work. When I learned where the Geyser was I went there often. An old man who lived there and guided visitors about the heya place and sang the story of the Rivers Underground used to talk to me and let me help him. He taught me a Mud Wakwa, the first song I received for myself. Not many people even then knew that song, which must be very old. It is in an old form, sung alone with a two-note wooden drum, and most of the words are matrix, so it is no good for writing. The old man said, "Maybe the people of the Sky Houses sing this one when they come to bathe at the mud-baths here." Inside the matrix at one place in the song the other words come out and say:

> From the edges inward to the middle,
> Downward, upward to the middle,
> All these have come in here,
> They are all coming in here.

I think the old man was right, and it is an Earth song. It was my first gift and I have given it to many.

Keeping out of the town, I saw no more men of the Condor, and I forgot them. After a month we went home to Sinshan in time to dance the Summer dances; Valiant was feeling well, and we walked down the Valley to Telina-na in one morning and then on to Sinshan in the evening. When we got to the bridge across Sinshan Creek I was seeing everything backwards. The hills in the north were where the south hills should be, the houses on the right hand

were where the houses on the left should be. Even inside our house
it was like that. I went around all the places I knew finding everything turned around. It was strange, but I enjoyed the strangeness,
though I hoped it would not remain. In the morning when I woke
up with Sidi purring in my ear, everything was where it belonged,
north in the north and left to the left, and I have never seen the
world backwards again, or only for a moment.

After the last of the Summer was danced we went up to our
summerhouse, and there Valiant said to me, "North Owl, in a few
years you will begin to be a woman, bleeding woman's blood, and
last year you were only a grasshopper, but here you are now in the
middle, a good place, your clearwater years. What do you want to
do in this place?"

I thought about it for a day and told her, "I want to go up in the
tracks of the lion."

She said, "Good."

My mother did not ask or answer. Since we came back from
Kastoha-na she was always as if listening for a word, listening far
away, holding still.

So my grandmother made me ready to go. For nine days I ate
no meat, and for the last four of the nine I ate only raw food, once a
day at midday, and drank water four times a day in four drafts.
Then I woke up early, before light, and got up, and took the pouch
with gifts in it. Valiant was sleeping but I thought my mother was
lying awake. I whispered heya to them and to the house and went
out.

Our summerhouse was in a meadow up in the hills over Hard
Canyon Creek, a mile or so upstream from Sinshan. We had gone
there for the summers of all my life with a family of Obsidian people of Chimbam House, mingling our sheep; there was good pasture for them up the hills, and the creek ran right through to the
rains, most years. The name of the meadow was Gahheya, for the
big blue serpentine heyiya rock in the northwest part of it. As I left I
went past that rock Gahheya. I was going to stop and speak to it,
but it was speaking to me; it said, "Don't stop, go on, go high,

before the sun." So I went on up across the high hills, walking
while it was still dark, running when it began to be light, and I was
on the high ridge of Sinshan Mountain when the earth's curve and
the sun's curve parted. I saw light fall on the southeast side of all
things, and the darkness turn away across the sea.

After singing heya there I walked along the ridge of the mountain from northwest to southeast, following deer paths through the
chaparral and making my own way where the underbrush was
thinner under the fir and pine forests, not going quickly but very
slowly, stopping all the time and listening and looking for directions and signs. The whole day long I kept worrying about where I
would sleep the night. I crossed and recrossed the ridges of the
mountain, always thinking, "I must find a good place, I must come
to a good place." No place seemed to be good. I said to myself, "It
should be a heya place. You'll know it when you come to it." But
what I was really holding in my mind without thinking about it was
the puma and the bear, wild dogs, men from the coast, strangers
from the beach country. What I was looking for was a hiding place.
So I walked all day long, and every time I stopped anywhere, I was
trembling.

Having gone above the springs, I was thirsty when it got dark.
I ate four seed-pollen balls from my gift pouch, but after eating I felt
thirstier and a little sick. Dusk had come up onto the mountain
before I had found the place I couldn't find, so I had stayed where I
was, in a hollow under some manzanita trees. The hollow seemed
to shelter me, and manzanitas are pure heyiya. I sat a long time
there. I tried to sing heya but did not like the sound of my voice
alone there. I lay down at last. Whenever I moved at all, the dry
manzanita leaves shouted, "Listen! She's moving!" I tried to lie
still, but the cold kept making me curl up; it was cold up there, with
the wind bringing a sea fog in over the mountain. Fog and night
did not allow me to see, though I kept staring into the dark. All I
could see was that I had wanted to come up on the mountain and
had expected to do everything right, to walk in the tracks of the
lion, but instead I had come to nothing and had spent all day running away from lions. That was because I had not come up here to
be the lion but to show the children who called me a half-person
that I was a better person than they were, that I was a brave and
holy eight-year-old. I began to cry. I pushed my face into the dirt
among the leaves and cried into the dirt, the mother of my
mothers. So with my tears I made a small salt mud place up on that
cold mountain. That made me think of the song that had come to
me from the old man at the Geysers, the Mud Wakwa, and I sang it

in my mind. It helped me some. So the night went on being. Thirst and cold did not let me sleep and weariness did not let me wake.

As soon as light began to come, I went down from the ridge to find water, going down through thick brush in one of the canyonheads. It was a long way I went before a spring let me find it. I was in a maze of canyons, and got turned around, and when I came up onto the ridges again I was in between Sinshan Mountain and She Watches. I went on up till I came to a big bald foothill, from which I could look back and see Sinshan Mountain facing me from the wrong side, the outside. I was outside the Valley.

I kept going all that day as I had the day before, walking slowly and stopping, but my mind was changed. It was not thinking, yet it was clear. All I said to myself was, "Try to be on a way that goes around this mountain She Watches without going down or up much, and so come back to this bald place on this hill." There was a good feeling on that hill, where the wild oats were bright pale yellow in the sunlight. I thought I would find it again. So I went on. Everything that came to me I spoke to by name or by saying heya, the trees, fir and digger pine and buckeye and redwood and manzanita and madrone and oak, the birds, blue jay and bushtit and woodpecker and phoebe and hawk, the leaves of chamise and scrub oak and poison oak and flowering thorn, the grasses, a deer's skull, a rabbit's droppings, the wind blowing from the sea.

Over there on the hunting side there were not many deer willing to come close to a human being. Deer came to my eyes five times, and once the coyote came. To the deer I said, "I give you what blessing I can, Silent Ones, give me what blessing you can!" The coyote I called Singer. I had seen the coyote skulking at lambing time, and stealing from the summerhouse, and dead, a bit of dirty fur, all my life, but I had not seen her in her House.

She was standing between two digger pines about twenty feet from me, and she walked forward to see me better. She sat down, with her tail around her feet, and gazed. I think she could not figure out what I was. Maybe she had never seen a child. Maybe she was a young coyote and had never seen a human person. I liked the look of her, lean and neat, the color of wild oats in winter, with light eyes. I said, "Singer! I will go your way!" She sat there gazing and seeming to smile, because the coyote's mouth goes in a smile; then she stood up, stretched a little, and was gone—like a shadow. I could not see her go, so I could not go her way. But that night she and her family sang coyote wakwa near me half the night. The fog did not come in that night; the darkness stayed mild and clear, and all the stars revealed themselves. I felt light, lying at the side of a small clearing under old bay laurel trees, looking up at the star patterns; I began to float, to belong to the sky. So Coyote let me come into her House.

The next day I came back to the wild-oats hill that let me see the wrong side of Sinshan Mountain, and there emptied out my pouch and gave the place my gifts. Without crossing the hill to close the circle, I went back down into the canyons between the mountains, intending to go around Sinshan Mountain from the southeast, and so complete the heyiya-if. In the canyons I got lost again. A creek led me on because the going was easy alongside it, and all the sides of its gully were steep and thick with poison oak. I kept going on down it, and I do not know where I came to. The name of those canyons is Old Fox Hollows, but nobody I asked later, hunters and Bay Lodge people, had ever seen the place I came to on that creek. It was a long, dark pool where the creek seemed to have stopped running. Around the pool grew trees I have not seen anywhere else, with smooth trunks and limbs and triangular, slightly yellow leaves. The water of the pool was speckled and drifted with those leaves. I put my hand into the water and asked it for direction. I felt power in it, and it frightened me. It was dark and still. It was not the water I knew, not the water I wanted. It was heavy, like blood, and black. I did not drink from it. I squatted there in the hot shade under those trees beside the water and looked for a sign or a word, trying to understand. On the water something came towards me: the waterskater. It was a big one, moving quickly on its shining hollows in the skin of the water. I said, "I give you what blessing I can, Silent One, give me what blessing you can!" The insect stayed still awhile there between air and water, where they meet, its place of being, and then it slid away into the shadow of the banks of the pool. That was all there. I got up, singing *heya-na-no*, and found a way up past the poison oak to the top of the gully, and then got through Old Fox Hollows to Back Canyon, and so onto my own mountain in the heat of the late afternoon of midsummer, the crickets yammering like a thousand bells and the blue jays and blackcrested jays shouting and swearing at me all through the woods. That night I slept sound under live oaks on the side of my mountain. The next day, the fourth, I made feather wands with the feathers that had come to me while I walked and sticks of the live oaks, and at a little seeping spring among rocks and roots at a canyonhead I made as much of the Wakwa of the Springs as I knew. After that I started going home. I got to Gahheya about the time the sun set, and came to the three-walled summerhouse. Willow was not there; Valiant was spinning in front of the house, by the hearth. "Well!" she said. "You'd better go have a bath, maybe?"

I knew she was very glad I was safe home, but she was laughing because I had forgotten to wash after making the wakwa, being in a hurry to get home and eat. I was all sweat and mud.

Walking down to Hard Canyon Creek I felt old, as if I had been away longer than four days, longer than the month in Kastoha-na, longer than the eight years of my life. I washed in the creek, and came back up the meadow in the twilight. Gahheya Rock was there, and I went to it. It said, "Now touch me." So I did, and so came home. I knew something had come to me that I did not understand, and maybe did not want, from that strange place, the pool and the waterskater; but the hinge of my walk had been the golden hill; the coyote had sung to me; and so long as my hand and the rock touched each other I knew that I had not gone wrong, even if I had come to nothing.

⊚

Because I had only one grandmother and grandfather in the Valley, a Blue Clay man called Ninepoint had asked to be side-grandfather to me. As I was about to be nine years old, he came over from their summerhouse in Bear Creek Canyon to teach me the songs of the Fathers. Soon after that we went back with him to Sinshan to make ready to dance the Water, while the Obsidian family at Gahheya looked after the sheep. This was the first time I had gone back to town in summer. Hardly anybody was there except Blue Clay people. Singing and doing heyiya all day long in the town that was

A Five-Post Summerhouse

empty and open, I began to feel my soul opening out and spreading out with the other souls of the dancers to fill the emptiness. The water poured out from the bowl of blue clay, and the songs were streams and pools in the great heat of summer. The other Houses came in from the summering, and we danced the Water. At Tachas Touchas their creek had gone dry, so they came up from there to dance with us, those that had relatives going to them and the others camping in Sinshan Fields or sleeping on balconies. With so many people there, the dancing never stopped, and the Blue Clay heyimas was so full of singing and power that touching the roof of it was touching a lion. It was a great wakwa. By the third and fourth days of it people in Madidinou and Telina had heard about the Water in Sinshan and came up to join. On the last night the balconies were full of people, and the heyiya-if filled the whole dancing place, and in the sky the heat lightning danced in the southeast and the northwest, and you could not tell the drums from the thunder, and we danced the Rain down to the sea and up to the clouds again.

Between the Water and the Wine one day I met my Red Adobe cousins from Madidinou to pick blackberries at Hatchquail Rock. The patches had all been picked over and not many berries were there for us, so Pelican and I were wild dogs and Hops was the hunter, and we hunted each other through those tight thorny paths between the blackberry brambles. I waited till Hops came past my hiding place, and leapt out at him from behind, barking loudly, and knocked him flat. It knocked the wind out of him and he was cross for a while, until I whined and licked his hand. Then we all three sat and talked a long time. He said, "There were some people with bird's heads came through our town yesterday."

I said, "What do you mean, feather gatherers?"

He said, "No, men with heads like birds—buzzards or vultures—black and red."

Pelican began shouting, "He didn't see them, *I* saw them," but I began to feel scared and sick. I said, "I have to go home now," and went off. My cousins had to run after me with the basket of berries I had picked. They went back to Madidinou and I went through Sinshan Fields across Hechu Creek; I was near the wineries when I looked up and saw a bird in the sky in the southwest, gyring. I thought it was a buzzard, but saw that it was bigger than a buzzard, that it was the great one. Nine times it turned in the air above my town, and then completing the heyiya-if flew gliding slowly into the northeast, over me. Its wings, each one longer than a person is tall, never moved; only the long feather-fingers of the wing-ends tilted in the wind. When it was gone over Red Cow Hill I went hurrying on to Sinshan. There were a lot of people on the balconies, and in the common place some Obsidian people were drumming up their courage. I went to High Porch House, into our second room, and hid behind the rolled-up beds in the dark corner. I believed I was the one the condor was looking for.

My mother and grandmother came in, not knowing I was there, and talked. "I told you he's coming!" my mother said. "He'll come and find us here!" She spoke angrily and joyfully, as I had never heard her speak.

"May it not happen!" my grandmother said, angry without joy.

At that I came out of the dark corner and ran to my grandmother, crying, "Don't let it come! Don't let it come find us!"

My mother said, "Come to me, Condor's Daughter."

I went partway, and stopped. I stood between them, and said, "That is not my name."

My mother was still for two breaths, and then said, "Don't be afraid. You'll see."

She began setting out food to cook supper, as if nothing had happened or was happening. Valiant took her wood drum and went down to our heyimas. People drummed in all the heyimas, that evening.

It was in the last great heat of the year, and people were out on the balconies for the cool after dark. I heard people talking about the condor. Agate, the Librarian of the Madrone, began to say a recital piece called "The Flight of the Great One," which he had made from an old written record by a Finder in the library; it told of the Inland Sea and the Range of Light, the Omorn Sea and the Range of Heaven, the deserts of sage and the prairies of grass, the Mountain of the North and the Mountain of the South, all as the condor would see them flying. Agate's voice was beautiful, and when he read or told one listened and entered into space and quietness. I wished he would speak all night. When the telling was done there was silence for a while; then people began to talk quietly again. Neither Valiant nor Willow was there. People did not notice me, and so they spoke of the Condor as they would not have done in the presence of my family.

Shell was waiting for my grandmother to come back from the heyimas. She said, "If those people are coming back, this time we should not let them stay in the Valley."

"They're in the Valley already," Hound said. "They won't go. They are here to have a war."

"Nonsense," Shell said, "don't talk like a boy, at your age."

Hound, like Agate, was an educated person, who often travelled to Kastoha-na and Wakwaha to read and talk with other scholars. He said, "Blue Clay Woman, the reason I say that is that I have talked with men of the Warrior Lodge in the Upper Valley, and what are warriors but people who make war? And these are our own people, Five-House people of the Valley of the Na, these Warriors. But they have been talking and lending their minds to Condor people, for ten years now, in those towns."

Old Cave Woman, whose last name had come to her when she went blind, said, "Hound, do you mean these Condor people are sick, that they have their heads on crooked?"

He said, "Yes, I mean that."

Somebody farther down the balcony asked, "Are they all men, as people say?"

Hound said, "All that come here are men. Armed."

Shell said, "But listen here, they can't go around smoking tobacco day after day, year after year, that's nonsense! If some men in those big towns up-Valley want to act like boys of fifteen and run around playing war, what's that to us here? All we have to do is just tell the foreigners to keep moving on."

Mouse Dance, who was then speaker of my heyimas, said, "They can do us no harm. We walk the gyre."

Hound said, "And they the wheel, and the power builds!"

"Keep to the gyre," Mouse Dance said. He was a kind, strong man. I wanted to listen to him, not to Hound. I was sitting back against the wall of the house, because I felt like staying under the eaves, out of sight from the sky. Between my feet something was lying on the floor of the balcony; in the starlight it looked like a bit of stick or string. I picked it up. It was dark, stiff, thin, and long. I knew what it was: it was the word I must learn to speak.

I got up and took it to Cave Woman and pushed it into her hand, saying, "Take this, please, it's for you," because I wanted to be rid of it, and Cave Woman was very old, wise, and weak.

She felt it and then held it out towards me. She said, "North Owl, keep it. It was spoken to you." Her eyes looked straight through me in the starlight that was the inside of a cave to her. I had to take the feather back.

She spoke more kindly then. She said, "Don't be afraid. Your hands are a child's hands, they are running water through the wheel. They don't hold, they let go, they make clean." Then she began to rock her body, and closed her blind eyes, and she said, "Heya, Condor's Daughter, in the dry land, think of the creeks running! Heya, Condor's Daughter, in the dark house, think of the blue clay bowl!"

"I am not Condor's Daughter!" I said. The old woman just opened her eyes and laughed and said, "It seems the condor says you are."

I turned to go indoors, upset and ashamed, and Cave Woman said, "Keep the feather, child, till you can give it back."

I went into our rooms and put the black feather into the lidded basket Willow had made for me to keep hehole and remembering things in. Seeing it in the lamplight, dead black, longer than an eagle feather, I began to feel proud that it had come to me. If I had to be different from other people, then let my difference be notable, I thought.

My mother was at the Blood Lodge, my grandmother was at the heyimas. Through the southwest windows I heard the rain-sound of the drums. Through the northeast windows I heard the little owl speak in the oak trees: u-u-u-u-u-u-u. I went to sleep alone, thinking of the condor and listening to the owl.

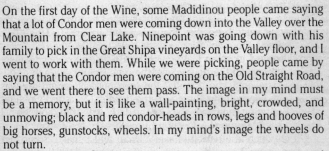

On the first day of the Wine, some Madidinou people came saying that a lot of Condor men were coming down into the Valley over the Mountain from Clear Lake. Ninepoint was going down with his family to pick in the Great Shipa vineyards on the Valley floor, and I went to work with them. While we were picking, people came by saying that the Condor men were coming on the Old Straight Road, and we went there to see them pass. The image in my mind must be a memory, but it is like a wall-painting, bright, crowded, and unmoving; black and red condor-heads in rows, legs and hooves of big horses, gunstocks, wheels. In my mind's image the wheels do not turn.

When we got back to Sinshan the wakwa was beginning, and by sunset the drinking was well along. Yellow Adobe people were laughing and dancing in the common place, and starting to make whip heyiya-ifs, and people of the other Houses were drinking to catch up. Some children joined in the whips, but they soon became more roughhouse than dance, and most of us with first names went up into the balconies to watch the adults get wild. Dada of Old Red House, who was adult but could not think well, came with us. I had never watched the Wine very long before; it had scared and bored me. Now, being nine, I was ready to see it. What I saw was the Reversal. Everybody I knew had become somebody I did not know. The common place was white with moonlight and bonfires and floodlights and crowded with the dancing and the whips and the people clowning. A lot of the adolescents were playing throw-the-pole, and were up and down ladders and stairs and all over the roofs and balconies and in the trees, like shadows, laughing and calling. An Obsidian doctor, Peak, a shy, solemn man, had gone to his heyimas and got one of the big penises that the Blood Clowns use in the Moon dances, and he had strapped it on and was running around poking it at all the women from behind. He shoved it at Corntassel, and she clapped her legs together on it and jumped forward: the strap broke, Peak fell flat on his face, and she ran off with the big penis yelling, "I got the doctor's medicine!" I saw Agate talking very loud, and dignified Shell dusty and stumbling about after falling off the end of a whip, and my grandmother Valiant dancing with a bottle of wine.

Then the first of the Doumiadu ohwe came out of the Yellow Adobe heyimas and across the Hinge, uncoiling and uncoiling as it came till its winged head was three times a person's height and swayed above the lights and fires. Everyone held still as it began to weave the pattern, and then the drums began and the whips went singing after the Doumiadu ohwe as it coiled along the paths from house to house. I had drunk a lot more wine that evening than I had ever drunk before, and now I felt that I had to hold onto the balcony railing to keep from floating off into the air. The Doumiadu ohwe came coiling down among the trees from Up the Hill House and closer and closer to High Porch House. Its yellow head paused at our balcony and turned slowly, the eyes looking at each one of us: inside the great eye a small, deep, bright eye. Then it passed on, coiling and swaying in time with the drums. Dada had crouched down hiding his face from the Doumiadu ohwe. A little boy of our house called Morning Lark was crying with fear, and I was comforting him, when another child said, "Look, who's that?" Some people had come across the bridge and were standing near Gairga oaks. They wore black, and stood there tall and still, like vultures in a tree looking down.

People looked at them and then went on dancing the Wine. The Doumiadu ohwe was going back towards the dancing place, and flute players were leading a stampdance in the common place. A Yellow Adobe woman went up to the tall people and spoke to them, waving her arms, and then took them over to the common place, where the wine barrels were set up on sawhorses. Four of them stayed there to drink; but the fifth one came back across the place, past the lights, through the dancing, to High Porch House.

Looking down from the balcony I saw my mother Willow coming across from the Hinge, and at the foot of the steps of our household they met.

I ran into our second room. Soon I heard steps come up the stairs and come into our hearthroom. She called me. I went into the hearthroom. He was standing there. His black wings hung down and his red, beaked head touched the ceiling.

My mother said, "North Owl, your father's hungry. Is there anything fit to eat in the house?"

That was what we always said in Sinshan when people came, and they always said, "Only my heart was hungry to see you," and then we brought out food and ate together. But my father did not know what to say. He stood there looking down at me. My mother told me to heat up corn and beans on the stove. While I did that I could look sideways at the man and see that he had a man's face. I had not been sure if the condor's head and beak were his head-dress or his head. When he took the helmet off, I looked sideways again. He was a beautiful man, with a long nose, wide cheeks, and long, narrow eyes. He was looking at my mother Willow. She was lighting the oil lamp we used at table. So much beauty had come to her that for that moment I did not know I was looking at my mother but saw a stranger, a Four-House person standing there with bright-ness in her hands.

They talked as well as they could. My father knew only parts and pieces of our language. Not many people from outside the Val-ley had come to Sinshan in my lifetime, but I had heard traders from the north coasts and an Amaranth man from the Inland Sea talking as he did—trying to pour water into a broken pot, as the saying is. His groping after the pieces of language he needed was funny, and I saw that he was a human person, however strange he was.

Willow poured wine for the three of us, and we sat down to-gether. My father was so big and long-legged that he made the table far too small and low.

He ate all the corn and beans I had reheated, and said to me, "Very good! Good cook!"

"North Owl is a good cook, and a good herder and reader, and has walked once now on the mountain," my mother said. As she seldom praised me, I felt as if I had just drunk the whole jar of wine. She went on, "If you've had enough to eat for now, husband, come out and drink. We all dance the Wine tonight. And I want every-body in this town to see you!" She laughed as she spoke. He looked at her, perhaps not understanding much of what she said, but with so much liking and admiration that my heart began to warm to him. My mother looked back at him smiling, and said, "While you were gone, a lot of people kept telling me that you were gone. Now that you're here I'd like to tell them that you're here!"

"I'm here," he said.

"Come on, then," she said. "You too, North Owl."

"What you call baby?" my father asked.

My mother repeated my name.

I said, "I'm not a baby."

"Girl," my mother said.

"Girl," he said, and we all laughed.

"What is owl?" he asked.

I said what the little owl says: u-u-u-u-u-u-u.

"Aha!" he said. "Owl. Come on, Owl." He held out his hand to me. It was the biggest hand I had ever seen or touched. I took it, and we followed my mother down into the dancing.

Willow was full of beauty that night, full of power. She was proud, she was great. She drank, but it was not the wine that made her great; it was the power that for nine years had been pent up in her, and was now set free.

> She dances there, she dances there,
> She dances where she went
> Laughing among the people.
> It flashes, it vanishes,
> Firelight along the water.

My grandmother got drunk and disorderly, and spent the night in the barns, gambling. When I came up to bed I took my bedding out on the balcony so that my mother and father could have the rooms to themselves. I was happy thinking about that as I went to sleep, and the noise around town did not bother me at all. Other children slept on the balcony or in another household when their parents wanted to be by themselves, and now I was like those children. As a kitten does what all other kittens do, so a child wants to do what other children do, with a wanting that is as powerful as it is mindless. Since we human beings have to learn what we do, we have to start out that way, but human mindfulness begins where that wish to be the same leaves off.

A year before this now where I write this page, after the Madrone Lodge people had asked me to write this story of my life, I went to Giver Ire's daughter, the story writer, and asked if she could teach me how to write a story, for I did not know how to go about it. Among other things Giver suggested to me was that in writing the story I try to be as I was at the time of which I am writing. This has been a good deal easier than I thought it would be, until now, this place now, where my father has come into the house.

It is hard to remember how little I knew. And yet Giver's advice is sound; for now that I know who my father was, why he was there and how he came, who the Condor people were and what they were doing, now that I am learned in such matters, it is my old ignorance, in itself valueless, that is valuable, useful, and powerful. We have to learn what we can, but remain mindful that our knowledge not close the circle, closing out the void, so that we forget that what we do not know remains boundless, without limit or bottom, and that what we know may have to share the quality of being known with what denies it. What is seen with one eye has no depth.

The sorrow of my parents' life is that they could see with one eye only.

All that grieved me—that I was half one thing and half another and nothing wholly—was the sorrow of my childhood, but the strength and use of my life after I grew up.

With one eye I see Willow, Valiant's daughter, of the Blue Clay of Sinshan, who had married a Houseless man, and had a daughter and eight sheep in the family and the use of several gathering trees and a seedgrass place. With the man's hands to work they could do more gardening, and make more, and so perhaps do more giving than taking of things and food, which is a great pleasure, and live respected, without any shame.

With the other eye I see Terter Abhao, True Condor, Commander of the Army of the South, who was off duty with his troops for the autumn and winter, awaiting orders for the spring campaign. He had brought his three hundred back to the Valley of the Na because he knew the people there were rich and tractable, and would house and feed his men well; and also because he had had a girl in one of the towns there, nine years ago, when he was a fifty-commander, on the first exploration of the South, and he had not forgotten her. Nine years is a long time, and no doubt she had married some farmer of her tribe and had a litter of brats, but even so, he would come by the village and see her.

So he came, and found his hearthfire lighted, his dinner ready, his wife and daughter welcoming him home.

That was what he did not know that he did not know.

From that first night of the Wine he lived in our household. Most people in town had no ill will towards him, since he was Willow's husband and had finally come back, but none of the Houses of Earth took him in. Even in Sinshan there lived one person born outside the Valley; Walker of Blue Walls House had come from the north coasts with traders thirty years before, and had stayed in the Valley, and married Toyon of the Yellow Adobe; and the Serpentine heyimas had taken him in. In the big towns, of course, there are many such people, and in Tachas Touchas they say that all of them came from somewhere in the north, houseless people, how many hundreds of years ago. I do not know why none of the Houses took my father, but I guess that their councils saw that it would not do. He would have had to study, to learn what every child in the heyimas knew already, and he would not have borne it, since he believed he knew all he needed to know. A door seldom opens itself to the man who shuts it. Maybe he did not even know there was a door. He was busy.

Through the councils of the Houses and the Planting Lodges of the four towns of the Lower Valley he made arrangements for his three hundred. They were given Eucalyptus Pastures to use for their camp and horse-grazing, down on the northeast side of the River below Ounmalin. The four towns agreed to give them some corn, potatoes, and beans, and let them hunt from the Hummocks down the inner northeast hills to the Saltmarshes, fish the River below the confluence of Kimi Creek, and take shellfish anywhere east of the East Mouth of the Na. It was a good deal to give, but, as people said, the only wealth is spending; and though three hundred men would eat a lot, it was understood that they would leave the Valley after the Sun, before the World.

That my father would go with them never entered my head. He was home, he was here, our family was whole; now everything was as it should be, balanced, complete; and so it would not change.

Besides, he was entirely different from the men in the camp. He spoke Kesh, and lived in a household, and was a daughter's father.

When he first took me down to Eucalyptus Pastures with him, I was not sure that the men there were human beings. They all dressed alike and looked alike, like a herd of some kind of animal, and they did not speak any word I knew. Whenever they came near my father they would slap their forehead, or sometimes kneel down in front of him as if they were looking at his toes. I thought they were crazy men, very stupid, and that my father was the only real person among them.

Among the people of Sinshan it was sometimes he who seemed rather stupid, though I did not like to admit it. He did not know how to read and write, or cook, or dance, and if he knew songs they were in words no one understood; he did not work in any of the workshops or at the winery or at the barns, and never even walked through the fields; and though he wanted to go out with hunting parties, only the most careless hunters would let him come, because he did not sing to the deer or speak to the death. At first they put it down to ignorance and did it for him, but when he did not learn appropriate behavior, they would not hunt with him. Only once was he notably useful, when the Red Adobe heyimas had to be re-dug and rebuilt. Their speaker was very strict and did not like people from the other Houses helping out, but since my father was a no-House man there were no restrictions on his lending a hand, and his hand was a strong one. But he did not get much goodwill out of that work, because when people saw how he could work they were more inclined to ask why he did so little.

My grandmother held her tongue, but she could not hide her contempt for a man who would not herd or farm or even chop wood. He, holding herders and farmers and woodcutters in contempt, found this hard to bear. One day he said to Willow, "Your mother has rheumatism. She shouldn't work down there in that mud in the rain, digging potatoes. Let her stay home and weave in the warmth. I'll pay some young man to work your patch of land for you."

My mother laughed. I did too; it was a funny idea, a reversal.

"You use money like this, I've seen it here," he said, showing a handful of rather poor money of different kinds from both coasts.

"Well, of course we use money. To give people who act and dance and recite and make, for making, for the dances, you know! What ever did you do to get paid that for?" my mother asked, laughing again.

He did not know what to say.

"Money's a sign, an honor, it shows that you're rich," she tried to explain, but he did not understand, so she said, "Anyhow, about the garden, our plot is much too small to be worth anyone's sharing the work with us. I'd be ashamed to ask."

"I'll bring one of my men, then," he said.

"To work our plot?" my mother said. "But it's Blue Clay land."

My father swore. He had picked up swearing before anything else, and swore well. "Blue clay, red clay, what does it matter!" he said. "Any fool can dig black mud!"

My mother sat spinning awhile and said at last, "That's crazy talk." She laughed again. "If any fool can, why can't you, my dear?"

My father said stiffly, "I am not a *tyon*."

"What's that?"

"A man who digs dirt."

"A farmer?"

"I'm not a farmer, Willow. I am a commander of three hundred, in charge of an army, I am— There are things a man can do and cannot do. Surely you understand that!"

"Surely," my mother said, looking at him with admiration of his dignity. So it all passed without either understanding what the other said and yet without anger or hurt, since their love and liking kept the harm from building up, kept washing it away, like the water in the millwheel.

When they were building the bridge across the Na, my father took me down to Eucalyptus Pastures every day. His dun gelding was twice the weight and half again the height of most Valley horses. Sitting up on that horse, on the high-horned saddle, in front of the big man with the condor helmet, I felt as if I were not a child but something quite different, something rarer than a human being. I would see and hear him speak to the men in the Condor camp: everything he said to them was an order—a direction that had to be obeyed without question or discussion. They never discussed anything. He would give an order, and the man he spoke to would slap his hand over his eyes and run to do whatever it was. I liked seeing that. I was still afraid of the Condor men. All men, all tall, wearing strange clothing, smelling strange, armed, not speaking my language: when they smiled at me or spoke to me I always shrank away and looked down, not answering.

One day when they were starting work on the bridge, my father taught me a word in his language, *pyez,* now: when he signalled I was to shout "Pyez!" as loud as I could, and the men working would drop the piledriver, a big stone in a pulley. I heard my high, thin voice and saw ten strong men obey it, over and over. So I first felt the great energy of the power that originates in imbalance, whether the imbalance of a weighted pulley or a society. Being the driver not the pile, I thought it was fine.

There was trouble, however, about the bridge. Ever since the Condor soldiers had camped in Eucalyptus Pastures, groups of men from the Upper Valley towns kept coming down and walking past the camp, or staying in the hills above Ounmalin Vineyards, not hunting, just hanging around. These were all members of the Warrior Lodge. People in Sinshan talked about them uneasily, with a kind of fascination—how the Warriors smoked tobacco daily, how each of them had a gun of his own, and so on. My cousin Hops, who had become a member of the Bay Laurel, would not allow

Pelican and me to be wild dogs when we played; we were to be
Condors and he a Warrior. But I said Pelican could not be a Condor,
since she was not a Condor, and I was—partly. She said she didn't
want to be either one and it was a stupid game, and went home.
Hops and I hunted each other all over Adobe Hill all afternoon,
with sticks for guns, shouting, "Kak! You're dead!" when we saw
each other. It was the same game the men down around Eucalyptus Pastures wanted to play. Hops and I were mad for it, and played
it every day, drawing other children into it, until Valiant noticed
what we were doing. She was very angry. She said nothing at all
about the game, but put me to work shelling walnuts and almonds
till my hands almost dropped off, and told me that if I missed lessons at the heyimas once more before the Grass I would probably
grow up to be a superstitious, illnatured, mindless, repulsive, cowardly person; but of course if that's what I wanted to be it was up to
me. I knew that she disapproved of the game, so I stopped playing
it; it did not occur to me then that she also wished I would not go
down to Eucalyptus Pastures with my father to see them building
the bridge.

The next time I went with him, the soldiers were not working:
a group of Warriors from Chumo and Kastoha-na had set up camp
right between the pilings on the river shore. Some of the Condor
men were angry, I could tell, as they talked to my father; they were
asking him to let them make the Valley men move out of the way
by force. He said no, and went down to talk to the Warriors. I
started to follow him. He sent me back to wait with his horse, so I
do not know what the Warriors said to him, but he came back up
into the Pastures looking fierce, and talked a long time to his offi-
cers.

The Warriors moved away that night, and work went on for a
couple of days on the bridge, peacefully, so my father was willing to
take me with him to the Pastures when I asked. But when we got
there that afternoon, there was a group of Valley people waiting
under the last of the great double row of blue-gums that gave the
place its name. Some of them came by and began to discuss things
with my father. They said they were sorry that some young men
had been rude or quarrelsome, and that they hoped it would not
happen again; but on consideration, most of the Valley people who
had given thought to the matter had decided that it was a mistake
to put a bridge across the River without consulting either the River
or the people who lived alongside it.

My father said his men needed the bridge to get their supplies
across the River.

"There are bridges at Madidinou and Ounmalin and ferries at Bluerock and Round Oak," a Valley person said.

"They will not carry our wagons."

"There are stone bridges at Telina and Kastoha."

"That is too far to go round."

"Your people can carry things across by the ferry," said Sun Weaver of Kastoha-na.

"Soldiers don't carry loads on their backs," my father said.

Sun Weaver thought this over a little while and then said, "Well, if they want to eat the food, maybe they'll learn how to carry it."

"My soldiers are resting here. Wagons are for carrying. If our wagons cannot cross the River your people will have to bring the food to us."

"In a pig's eye," said a man from Tachas Touchas.

Sun Weaver and others eyed him. There was a silence.

"We have built bridges in many places. Men of the Condor are not only brave fighters but great engineers. The roads and bridges in the lands around the City of the Condor are the wonder of the age."

"If a bridge at this place were appropriate, there would be one," said White Peach from Ounmalin. My father did not like to talk to women in front of Condor men, so he said nothing, and there was another thoughtful silence.

"In our judgment," Sun Weaver said very politely, "this bridge would not be in the right place."

"All you have going south is your railway, with six wooden cars!" my father said. "A bridge here will open up a way clear to—" He paused.

Sun Weaver nodded.

My father thought hard, and said, "Listen. My army is not here to do any harm to the Valley. We are not making war on you." As he spoke he looked over at me once or twice, seeing me with half his mind, as he worked to find the words he needed. "But you must understand that the Condor rules all the North, and that you live now under the shadow of His wing. I do not bring you war. I only come to widen your roads and build you one bridge that something wider than a fat woman can get across! You see, I build it down here away from your towns, where it need not bother you. But you must not stand in our way. You must come with us."

"We're dwellers, not travellers," said Digger of Telina-na, the speaker of the Blue Clay, a well-known man, quiet, but one of the great speakers. "One doesn't need roads and bridges to go from room to room of one's house. This Valley is our house, where we live. In it we welcome guests whose house is elsewhere, on their way."

My father arranged his reply for a while in his mind, and then said in a strong voice, "My desire is to be your guest. You know that this Valley is my house, too! But I serve the Condor. He has given his orders. The decision is neither mine nor yours to make or change. You must understand that."

At that, the man from Tachas Touchas twisted his head round on his neck with a grin; and he stood back from the group, to signify that he did not consider it profitable to go on talking. A couple of the others did the same; but Obsidian of Ounmalin stood forward to speak. She was the only person in the nine towns at that time called by the name of her House, the best-known of all dancers of the Moon and Blood, unmarried, singlesexed, a person of great power. She said, "Listen, child, I think you don't know what you're talking about. Maybe you could begin to learn, if you learned to read."

He could not take that, in front of his men. Though most of them did not understand her words they heard the scorn and the authority in her voice. He said, "Be quiet, woman!" And looking past her to Sun Weaver, he said, "I will order work on the bridge stopped at this time, because I wish no harm. We will make a plank bridge for the wagons, and take it down when we go. But we will return. It may be that a great army, a thousand men, will come through the Valley. Roads will be widened, bridges will be built. Do not provoke the anger of the Condor! Let them—let them flow through the Valley, as the water through the wheel of the mill."

My father's head was not on backwards. Even in these few

months he had begun to understand the image of the water. If only he had been born in the Valley, if only he had stayed and lived in the Valley! But that, as they say, is water under the bridge.

Obsidian walked away in anger, and all the people from Ounmalin followed her except White Peach, who with considerable courage stood fast and spoke: "Then I think the people of the towns should help these people carry the food we give them; conditions upon gifts are odious."

"I agree," said Digger, and several others from Madidinou, and one from Tachas Touchas. Digger added, from the Water Songs, "The bridge falls, the river runs . . ." He opened his palms to my father, smiling, and stood back. The others with him did the same.

"That is good," my father said, and he also turned away.

I stood there and did not know which way to turn, whether to go with my father or my townspeople; for I knew that despite their restraint there was anger on both sides, that they had not come together. The weak follow weakness, and I was a child; I followed my father; but I shut my eyes so that nobody would see me.

The business of the bridge was patched up. The soldiers made a plank bridge that would carry their wagons, and the Valley people brought supplies a few sacks or baskets at a time, and left the stuff in a drying shed at Atsamye, where the Condor wagons could come pick it up. But the Warriors kept hanging around keeping watch on the Condor camp; and many people in Ounmalin refused to give anything to the Condor men, or speak to them, or look at them, and started attending meetings of the Warrior Lodge. Obsidian of the Obsidian of Ounmalin was one to hold a grudge.

In Tachas Touchas, an Obsidian girl had made friends with one of the Condor men, and wanted to come inland with him; but being only seventeen and frightened by some things people had said to her, she asked for the consent of her heyimas—which my mother Willow had not done in her day. The Obsidian of Tachas Touchas sent people over to Ounmalin to talk about it, and Obsidian of the Obsidian said, "Why are these Condor people all men? Where are the Condor women? Are they ginkgos? Let them marry each other and breed whatever they like. Let this daughter of our House not take a man of no House!"

I heard about that, but whether the girl in Tachas Touchas took this advice or went on meeting that young Condor, I do not know. Certainly she did not marry him.

Between the Grass and the Sun, the Warriors from up and down the Valley held several wakwa along the Old Straight Road and on the riverbanks, which they called Purifications. Men had joined the Warrior Lodge in all the towns, as the Condor stayed on in the Valley. My side-grandfather Ninepoint's son and grandson joined them, and that whole family was busy for a while weaving them the special clothing they wore for their wakwa, a tunic and hooded cloak in dark wool, something like the Condor soldiers' clothing. The Warrior Lodge had no clowns. When some Blood Clowns from Madidinou came to one of their Purifications, instead of flyting with them or ignoring them the Warriors began pushing and pulling them, and there was some fighting and a lot of bad feeling. There was always sexual trouble and tension around the Warriors. And some women in Sinshan whose husbands had joined that lodge complained about their rules of sexual abstinence, but other women laughed at them; in winter there are so many ritual abstinences for anybody dancing the Sun or the World that another set of them really would not make a great difference, though it might be, as they say, the pin that made the donkey bray.

My grandmother danced the Inner Sun that year, and I fasted the Twenty-One Days for the first time, and listened every night to the trance singing in our heyimas. It was a strange Sun. Every morning of that winter there was fog, and on many days it never lifted up higher than the foothills of Sinshan Mountain, so that we lived under a low roof; and in the evening the fog would settle back down to the Valley floor. There were more White Clowns than ever before, that year. Even if some of them came to Sinshan from other towns, still there were too many; some must have come from the Four Houses, from the House of the Lion, through that wet white fog that hid the world. Children were afraid to go out of sight of the houses. Even the balconies were frightening at dusk. Even in the hearthroom a child might look up and see the white staring face at the window, and hear the stuttering.

I had tended my seedlings in a place in the woods over the second ridge north of town, a long way, because I wanted them to be a surprise when I gave them. I had a hard time of it making myself go there alone to look after them during the Twenty-One Days, because I was so frightened of the White Clowns. Whenever the little bushbirds or the squirrels chipped and tsked I froze, thinking it was the stuttering. On the morning of the solstice I went to get my seedlings in a fog so thick I could not see five steps before me. Every tree of the woods was a White Clown waiting and groping for me in silence. It was entirely silent. Nothing spoke. Nothing moved but me, in all those white ridges. I was cold to the bone and cold to the soul; I had come into the Seventh House and did not know how to get out again. But I went on, although the woods were so hidden and changed by the fog that I was not sure where I was at any moment, and I got to my little trees. I sang the Sun heya almost with my mouth closed, because any sound was so awful, and dug up the seedlings and replanted them in the pots I had made for them, shaking all the time, hurrying and clumsy; I probably bent the roots. Then I had to take them back to Sinshan. The strange thing was that when I came among the grapevines on Topknot Hill and knew I was home, I was not altogether glad of it. Part of me wanted to be cold and terrified and lost in the fog, part of me was at home in the Seventh House, not in High Porch House. So I went up our stairs and woke my family to the Sun. To Willow I gave a buck-eye seedling, to Valiant a wild rose, and to Kills a seedling of the Valley oak. The oak stands now where we planted it on the west side of the oak grove Gairga, a spreading, shapely tree, not yet heavily girthed. The buckeye and the rose are gone.

Before the Sun was danced and after it, my father was with us in High Porch House every night and morning. Valiant, who danced both the Sun and the World that year, spent most of her time and all her nights down in the heyimas. Willow did not dance, that year; and Kills was of course bound neither to fast nor to feast. At that time, knowing nothing about his people, I thought that he had no observances or wakwa at all, and stood in no relation to anything in the world, except the soldiers to whom he gave orders, and my mother and myself. He and Willow kept indoors together whenever they could, that winter. After the Sun the low fogs gave way to rain, and a cold spell with snow up on Sinshan Mountain like the flour dust on a miller's hair, and hoarfrost some mornings on the grass. My father had some fine red wool rugs which he carried to furnish his tent on march; he had brought them to us, and our hearthroom was rich with them. I liked to lie on them. They smelled of sweet sage and other smells I had no name for, the smell of the place my father came from far away in the northeast. We had plenty of firewood, applewood, since the town had re-planted two of the old orchards. There was great peace by the fire-side in those long evenings for them and for me. I think of my mother in her beauty by that fire, on the edge of the years of sor-row. It is like watching a fire burning in the rain.

Condor messengers came down over the Mountain to the Commander of the Army of the Condor.

Kills said that night when supper was done, "We must go be-fore your World Dance, Willow."

"I'm not going anywhere in this weather," said my mother.

"No," he said. "It's better not."

There was a silence. The fire talked.

"What's better not?" my mother asked.

"When we start home—I will come for you then," he said.

She said, "What are you talking about?"

They talked backwards for a while, he speaking about the Condor Army coming back from a war on the Amaranth Coast, she not acknowledging that she had begun to understand him. At last she said, "Is this true: you're telling me that you are going away from the Valley?"

"Yes," he said. "For a while. Against the Inland Coast people. It is the plan of the Condor."

She said nothing.

He said, "A year—not longer than a year. Unless I am sent for to Sai. At the very most, two years, no longer."

She said nothing.

He said, "If I could take you with me I would, but that would be dangerous and foolish. If I could stay— But I cannot. But you will wait for me here."

She stood up from the hearthseat. The softness of the firelight fell from her and left her dark. She said, "If you won't stay, go."

"Listen, Willow," he said. "Listen to me! Is it unfair to ask you to wait? If I were going on a hunting trip, or a trading trip, would you not wait for me? You Valley people, some of you leave the Valley! And come back—and their wives wait for them—I will come back. I promise you. I am your husband, Willow."

She stood there between fire and shadow for a while before she spoke.

"Once," she said.

He did not understand.

"Once, for nine years," she said. "Not twice. You are my husband; you are not. My house holds you; it does not. Choose."

"I cannot stay," he said.

She said, still speaking softly and clearly, "The choice is yours."

"I am the Commander of the Army of the Condor," he said. "As I give orders, I obey orders. In this matter I have no choice, Willow."

She moved away from the fire then, and came across the room.

"You must understand," he said.

She said, "I understand that you choose not to choose."

"You do not understand. I can only ask you, will you wait for me?"

She said nothing.

"I will come back, Willow. My heart is here, with you and the child, always!"

She stood beside the second-room doorway while he spoke. My bed was just inside the doorway, and I could see them both, and feel the pulling two ways in her body.

"You must wait for me," he said.

She said, "You have gone."

She came into the second room and closed the door, which had been open for warmth. She stood there in the dark. I lay still. He said, "Willow, come back!" He came to the door and said her name again, angrily, in great pain. She did not reply. Neither of us moved. There was a long time nothing happened, and then we heard him turn and stride across the hearthroom and go down the stairs.

My mother lay down beside me. She said nothing and lay perfectly still; so did I. I did not want to think about what had been said. I tried to go to sleep, and soon I did.

In the morning when I got up, my mother had rolled up the red rugs and put them with my father's clothes on the balcony by the head of the stairs outside our door.

Towards noon my father came up the stairs and past the rugs and clothes. He came in the door. My mother was inside; she did not look at him or answer when he spoke to her, and when he stood aside from the doorway she left the house at once, going to our heyimas. He went after her. Some Blue Clay people came right out and kept him from going down into the heyimas. At first he acted crazily, but they quietened him, and Ninepoint explained to him that a man may come and go as he likes, and a woman may take him back or not as she likes, but the house is hers, and if she shuts the door he may not open it. People had come to listen because of the noise he had made shouting at first, and some of them thought it was funny to explain such things to a grown man. Strength, a speaker of the Blood Lodge, scoffed at him. When he said, "But she belongs to me—the child belongs to me," she began to do the Blood Clown turkey-gobble around him, shouting, "The hammer menstruates to me! They pleat the courage to her!" and a string of reversal-words like that. There were some people in town glad to see the Condor humiliated. I saw this from the balcony of our house.

My father came back up the stairs. He kicked the roll of rugs and clothing in rage, like a child, and stood there in the doorway. I had gone back to the kitchen table, where I had been making cornbread. I kept working there with my back turned. I did not know what to do, how I should act, and I hated my father for causing this uncertainty and misery. I was glad Strength had jeered at him, and wanted to jeer at him too, for being so stupid.

"Owl," he said. "Will you wait for me?"

Not expecting to cry at all, I began crying.

"If I live I will come back to you here," he said. He did not come in and I did not go to him. I turned around and nodded. When I looked up at him he was putting on the Condor helmet that hid his face. He turned and left.

Valiant had been weaving; her loom was set up by the windows in the second room. When my mother came back to the house, Valiant said to her, "Well, he's gone, Willow."

My mother's face was pale and furrowed. She said, "I have gone away from that name. I will go back to my first name."

"Towhee," my grandmother said, in a soft voice, as a mother says a baby's name. She shook her head.

The second part of Stone Telling's story begins on page 183.

NOTES:

p. 8. *I go there* . . .
Except for the preterit "went," the verbs in this verse and others in the same form are in a present tense used in telling myths, recounting dreams, speaking of the dead, and in ceremonial recitations. The English present participle translates this "timeless present" rather well:

> Going there, going there,
> Going where I went
> Crying beside the water.
> Going there, going there,
> The fog along the water.

p. 10. *So we walked in the arm of life.*
The *Serpentine Codex* may help clarify some of this imagery. In the left arm of the heyiya-if, the symbol of the Whole, the five colors ran black, blue, green, red, yellow, into or out from the center; the right arm of the symbol was white. The left arm was mortality, the right eternity.

p. 18. *the Copper Snake . . . the Mountain Lion* . . .
The Copper Snake may have been a treatment ritual for sufferers of rheumatism. The Mountain—Ama Kulkun, Grandmother Mountain—the Springs of the River Na, and the town at the springs, Wakwaha-na, were the most centrally sacred places to the people of the Valley. To go up on the summits of the mountain "in the tracks of the lion" or "on the hawk's way" was a solitary spiritual excursion undertaken sooner or later, once or more than once, by most of the people of the Nine Towns.

p. 38. *Are they ginkgos?*
The ginkgo tree is sexually dimorphic. Female trees are not usually planted near male trees, lest they be fertilised, since the fruit exudes a terrific stench. In Kesh literature the ginkgo is associated with homosexuality both in satire and in celebration.

p. 41. *"We must go before your World Dance."*
Imperfectly acquainted with the delicacies of Kesh verbal usage, Terter Abhao used the pronoun "we" which includes the person addressed, and a form of the verb "go" which implies going a short distance for a short while; so Willow understood him as saying something like. "You and I might take a walk together some time before the World Dance."

p. 43. . . . *reversal-words like that.* . . .
In Clown impromptus language was deliberately dislocated for subversive effect (as in surrealist poetry and imagery). Abhao inadvertently made just such a dislocation by saying that his wife and child "belonged to" him; Kesh grammar makes no provision for a relation of ownership between living beings. A language in which the verb "to have" is an intransitive and in which "to be rich" is the same word as "to give" is likely to turn its foreign speaker, and translator, into a clown all too often.

The Serpentine Codex

This text, in an archaic calligraphy, is the only verbal element in an accordion-fold book of pictorial symbols in the Library of Wakwaha.

 The nine Houses of the living and the dead are the Obsidian, Blue Clay, Serpentine, Yellow Adobe, Red Adobe, Rain, Cloud, Wind, Still Air. The colors of the four Houses of the dead are white and the rainbow. The peoples that live with human people live in the Houses of Earth; the peoples of the wilderness live in the Houses of Sky. Birds are from the Houses of Sky and come from the right hand and may speak for the dead and bear messages to them, and their feathers are the words that the dead spoke. When a child comes from the Four Houses to be born it comes to live in the House of its mother. The Houses of Sky dance the Earth Dance and the Houses of Earth dance the Sky Dance. The House of Blue Clay dances the Water, the House of Yellow Adobe dances the Wine, the House of Serpentine dances the Summer, the House of Red Adobe dances the Grass, the House of Obsidian dances the Moon. All the Houses of Earth and Sky dance the Sun. The Sun with the other stars dances the pattern of Return. The heyiya-if is the pattern of that pattern and the House of the Nine Houses.

This text provides a compact summary of the structure of society, the year, and the universe, as perceived by the people of the Valley.

The beings or creatures that are said to live in the Five Houses of Earth and are called Earth People include the earth itself, rocks and dirt and geological formations, the moon, all springs, streams, and lakes of fresh water, all human beings currently alive, game animals, domestic animals, individual animals, domestic and ground-dwelling birds, and all plants that are gathered, planted, or used by human beings.

The people of the Sky, called Four-House People, Sky People, Rainbow People, include the sun and stars, the oceans, wild animals not hunted as game, all animals, plants, and persons considered as the species rather than as an individual, human beings considered as a tribe, people, or species, all people and beings in dreams, visions, and stories, most kinds of birds, the dead, and the unborn.

Bear

The chart on pages 48 and 49 shows the Nine Houses, the color and direction associated with each, the annual festival for which each is responsible, and the Lodges, Societies, and Arts associated with each. The chart is schematic and the discussion that follows is simplistic. It may serve as a gloss to certain words, phrases, and unstated assumptions in the Valley texts in this book, and an introduction to their thinking and the themes of their arts. But it is important to know that there is no Valley original for this chart, or anything like it. Although the numbers four, five, and nine, and the representation of the Nine Houses, and their arrangement in the heyiya-if or hinged spiral, and the colors, directions, seasons, creatures associated with the Houses are constant motifs of Valley art and thought, and the division between Earth and Sky, mortality and nonmortality, is connected with a fundamental grammatical maneuver of the language (Earth and Sky Modes), still the actual listing and charting of the nine divisions and their various members and functions would strike the Valley mind as somewhat childish and—in fixing and "locking" the information—as risky and inappropriate.

The Five Houses of Earth were the basic divisions of the society, the Kesh equivalent of clan or moiety. Non-Kesh were called no-House people. The Houses were matrilineal and exogamous. All human members of a House were considered first-degree kin, with whom sexual relations were inappropriate (see the section on "Kinfolk," page 451).

The Houses were not arranged in any hierarchy of power, value, etc., nor was there rivalry among them for status; they were called First, Second, etc., House, but numerical order carried absolutely no implication of ranking, rating, or importance. Some rivalry did attach to the festivals held annually by each House—not so much among the five Houses, as within them in the nine towns. The word I usually translate as dance—wakwa—may also mean rite, mystery, ceremony, celebration. The annual round of the wakwa constellates the Valley year:

Along in November when the hills begin to turn green the Red Adobe dances the *Grass*. At the winter solstice all nine Houses dance the *Sun*. At the equinox of spring, the Five Houses dance the *Sky* and the Four Houses dance the *Earth*, the whole dance being called the *World*. At the second full moon after this, the Obsidian dances the *Moon*. At the summer solstice and after it, the Serpentine dances the *Summer*. In early or mid-August, the Blue Clay dances the *Water* at springs, pools, and streams. At the autumnal equinox, the Yellow Adobe dances the *Wine*, or *Getting Drunk*.

These seven great wakwa may be found pictorially arranged as the heyiya-if, with the World in the center (the Hinge), flanked by Sun and Moon immediately to left and right, Grass and Summer next outward, and Wine and Water at the left and right ends of the figure. Such a nonsequential image of the year is characteristic of Valley chronography. And since the two-season climate did not lend itself to dating by season, in conversation events were usually referred to in relation to the wakwa: before the Grass, between Water and Wine, after the Moon. (The section "Time and the City" on page 156 pursues Valley ideas of time.)

The material manifestation of each of the Five Houses in each of the nine towns was the heyimas. Finding all such translations as church, temple, shrine, lodge misleading, I use the Kesh word in this book. It is formed of the elements *heya, heyiya*—the connotations of which include sacredness, hinge, connection, spiral, center, praise, and change—and *ma*, house.

The heyiya-if, two spirals centered upon the same (empty) space, was the material or visual representation of the idea of heyiya. Varied and elaborated in countless ways, the heyiya-if was a choreographic and gestural element in dance, and the shape of the stage and the movement of the staging in drama were based upon it; it was an organisational device in town planning, in graphic and sculptural forms, in decoration, and in the design of musical instru-

THE FIVE HOUSES OF THE EARTH

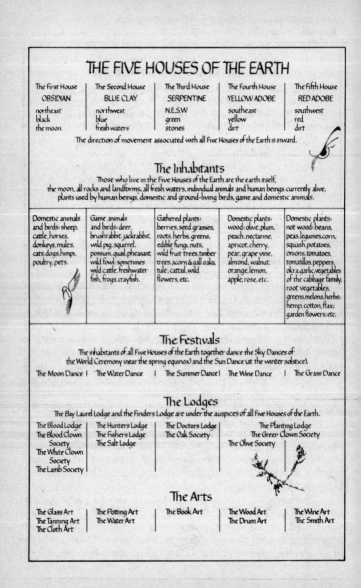

The First House	The Second House	The Third House	The Fourth House	The Fifth House
OBSIDIAN	BLUE CLAY	SERPENTINE	YELLOW ADOBE	RED ADOBE
northeast	northwest	N.E.S.W.	southeast	southwest
black	blue	green	yellow	red
the moon	fresh waters	stones	dirt	dirt

The direction of movement associated with all Five Houses of the Earth is inward.

The Inhabitants

Those who live in the Five Houses of the Earth are the earth itself,
the moon, all rocks and landforms, all fresh waters, individual animals and human beings currently alive,
plants used by human beings, domestic and ground-living birds, game and domestic animals.

Domestic animals and birds: sheep, cattle, horses, donkeys, mules, cats, dogs, himpi, poultry, pets.	Game animals and birds: deer, brushrabbit, jackrabbit, wild pig, squirrel, possum, quail, pheasant; wild fowl: sometimes wild cattle, freshwater fish, frogs, crayfish.	Gathered plants: berries, seed grasses, roots, herbs, greens, edible fungi, nuts, wild fruit trees, timber trees, acorn & gall oaks, tule, cattail, wild flowers, etc.	Domestic plants: wood: olive, plum, peach, nectarine, apricot, cherry, pear, grape vine, almond, walnut, orange, lemon, apple, rose, etc.	Domestic plants: not wood: beans, peas, legumes, corn, squash, potatoes, onions, tomatoes, tomatillos, peppers, okra, garlic, vegetables of the cabbage family, root vegetables, greens, melons, herbs; hemp, cotton, flax; garden flowers; etc.

The Festivals

The inhabitants of all Five Houses of the Earth together dance the Sky Dances of
the World Ceremony (near the spring equinox) and the Sun Dance (at the winter solstice).

The Moon Dance	The Water Dance	The Summer Dance	The Wine Dance	The Grass Dance

The Lodges

The Bay Laurel Lodge and the Finders Lodge are under the auspices of all Five Houses of the Earth.

The Blood Lodge The Blood Clown Society The White Clown Society The Lamb Society	The Hunters Lodge The Fishers Lodge The Salt Lodge	The Doctors Lodge The Oak Society	The Planting Lodge The Green Clown Society The Olive Society

The Arts

The Glass Art The Tanning Art The Cloth Art	The Potting Art The Water Art	The Book Art	The Wood Art The Drum Art	The Wine Art The Smith Art

THE FOUR HOUSES OF THE SKY

The Sixth House	The Seventh House	The Eighth House	The Ninth House
RAIN	CLOUD	WIND	STILL AIR

The directions of all Four Houses of the Sky are towards the nadir and towards the zenith.
The colors of all Four Houses of the Sky are the spectrum of the rainbow, and white.

bear	puma	coyote	hawk
death	dream	wilderness	eternity
down	up	across	out

The Inhabitants

Those who live in the Four Houses of the Sky are most birds, sea fish, shellfish,
wild animals that are not hunted for food (puma, wildcat, feral cat, coyote,
wild dog, bear, ringtail, mouse, vole, rat, woodrat, squirrel, groundsquirrel,
chipmunk, mole, gopher, skunk, porcupine, otter, fox, bat), reptiles, amphibians,
insects; any plant or animal considered as the species or in general;
human beings as the species, people, tribe, or nation; the dead, the unborn;
all beings in stories or dreams; the oceans, the sun, the stars.

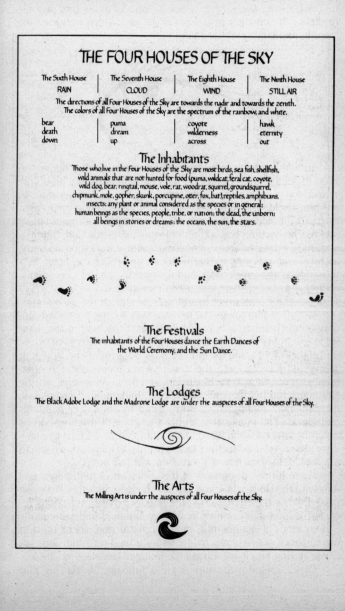

The Festivals

The inhabitants of the Four Houses dance the Earth Dances of
the World Ceremony, and the Sun Dance.

The Lodges

The Black Adobe Lodge and the Madrone Lodge are under the auspices of all Four Houses of the Sky.

The Arts

The Milling Art is under the auspices of all Four Houses of the Sky.

ments; it served as a subject of meditation and as an inexhaustible metaphor. It was the visual form of an idea which pervaded the thought and culture of the Valley.

Puma

In a Valley town everybody had two houses: the house you lived in, your dwelling-place, in the Left Arm of the double-spiral-shaped town; and in the Right Arm, your House, the heyimas. In the household, you lived with your kinfolk by blood or by marriage; in the heyimas you met with your greater and permanent family. The heyimas was a center of worship, instruction, training, and study, a meetinghouse, a political forum, a workshop, a library, archive, and museum, a clearinghouse, an orphanage, hotel, hospice, refuge, resource center, and the principal center of economic control and management for the community, both internally and in regard to trade with other Kesh towns or outside the Valley.

In the smaller towns the heyimas was a large, five-sided, underground chamber, subdivided with partitions, with a low, four-sided, pyramidal roof showing aboveground. Stairways went up the roof at the corners, and the entrance was by skylight and ladder. In Telina and Kastoha both the underground rooms and the ornamented roofs were very much larger; and in Wakwaha, on the Mountain, the five heyimas were great underground complexes, their splendid roof-pyramids surrounded by secondary buildings and plazas. The public area within the curve of dwelling-houses was called the common place; that within the curve of the five heyimas was called the dancing place. The map of the town of Sinshan on page 188 shows how a Kesh town was laid out.

Some further discussion of the affiliation of the Lodges and Arts with the Houses is in the section "Lodges, Societies, Arts," on page 458. As the chart shows, the Millers, whose professions included responsibility for watermills, windmills, and generators, various kinds of engineering, and the construction, operation, and maintenance of machines, held a distinguished yet anomalous position, having no House among the living responsible for them.

Other apparent anomalies are a function of charting and

translating. In English one can say that a quail lives in the Second House, but it begins to sound odd to say that a tomato vine lives in the Fifth House, and it is very odd to say that the dead and the unborn live in the Houses of the Sky. The Kesh might say that this is because we do not live in the Houses ourselves, but remain outside.

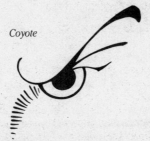

Coyote

The heyimas buildings are, as you please, the Five Houses, or material manifestations of them, or representations of them. Of the Four Houses, the principal material manifestations are meteorological: rain for the Sixth House, clouds, fog, and mist for the Seventh, wind for the Eighth, and for the Ninth House still air, thin air, which is also called breath. The other great symbols of the Four Houses, Bear, Puma, Coyote, Hawk, may be seen as mythological devices, imaginative configurations, not to be taken literally; yet one cannot discount the literal aspect. To go into Coyote's House is to be changed. Again, the Four Houses are the Houses of Death, Dream, Wilderness, Eternity. All these aspects interconnect, so that rain, the bear, and death may each symbolise either of the others; verbal and iconographic imagery flourish with this interlinking. The whole system is profoundly metaphorical. To limit it to any other mode would be, in the judgment of the people of the Valley, superstition.

Hawk

It is for this reason that I do not refer to the system of the Nine Houses as a religion or the heyimas as religious houses, despite the obvious and continuous relation of Valley living and thinking with the sacred. They had no god; they had no gods; they had no faith. What they appear to have had is a working metaphor. The idea that comes nearest the center of the vision is the House; the sign is the hinged spiral or heyiya-if; the word is the word of praise and change, the word at the center, heya!

Where It Is

THE MOUNTAINS of the Valley's parallel framing ranges aren't high; even the Grandmother, Ama Kulkun, the old volcano at which the ranges meet in a tangled knot, isn't much over four thousand feet. The Valley floor is a flat river plain, but the hills come up steep-sided from it and the ranges are rugged, deep-cut with creek canyons. On slopes that face the east and are sheltered from the sea wind, trees and shrubs grow thick: digger pine, fir, redwood, madrone, and manzanita; scrub and live and tan and white and black oak and the great Valley oak; buckeye, bay laurel, willow and ash and alder. Where it's dryer, the chaparral: a low, dense scrub of buckbrush or wild lilac that flowers sweet blue and violet as the rains end, and white-flowering chamise, and chaparral pea, deerwood, toyon, coffeeberry, coyote bush, and always the scrub oak, and always the poison oak. Along the creeks grow sweetshrub and oceanspray and yellow azalea, and the wild rose and the wild vine of California; on the west-facing, windy hillsides and the round hills of serpentine, only the wild grasses and the wild flowers.

It was always an austere land, generous but not lush, not soft, not gentle. It always had two season: one wet, one dry. The rains and the heat can be fierce, frightening. Growing things go through their sweet slow steady order of flowering, ripening, resting as they do anywhere, but the turn from one season to the other is less transition than reversal. A few dark-grey, pouring days when the burnt and sodden brown hills brighten suddenly into the aching, piercing green of the new grass. . . . A few cloud-flurried, shining days when the orange poppies, the blue lupine, the vetch, clover, wild lilac, brodiaea, blue-eyed grass, daisies, lilies are all in bloom, whole hillsides white and purple and blue and gold, but at the same moment the grass is drying, turning pale, and the wild oats have already sown their seed. Those are the times of change: the greening into winter, the dying into summer.

The fog comes in. It comes up from the vast flat mudlands, the sea marshes and reed beds, the estuaries and endless tules southeastward, the sea beaches over the southwest range. Around Sinshan Mountain and She Watches and Spring Mountain, hard, dark, depthless silhouettes on the dry sky, the fog comes moistening and blurring and rubbing things out. The mountains all go quietly away. Under a low roof the hills are dim. Every leaf beads and drips. The little brown birds of the chaparral flit uncertainly and say *tsp, tkk,* somewhere nearby but never seen. A Valley oak looms huge, you can't see where its arms are reaching to. If you went up from Wakwaha on such a morning you'd come out of the fog somewhere on the road, come right through that roof, and turning, look back on a white fog-sea breaking in brilliant silence on the hills. It has done that for a long time. They are old hills, but fog is older.

The dirt of the Valley is black or brown adobe clay or the red dirt that blue-green serpentine rock breaks down into, with streaks of volcanic ash; not a rich, openminded, amenable soil, but poor, opinionated, cranky dirt. It spits wheat out. What it has to say to the farmer is grapevine, olive, rose, lemon, plum. Tough stuff, sweet-smelling, strong-tasting, long-lived. And corn, beans, squashes, melons, potatoes, carrots, greens, what have you, whatever you want, if you work hard enough, and dig when it's like wet cement and water when it's like dry cement. A difficult dirt.

In our day the River of the Valley barely trickles through a drought year, when by September all but the biggest creeks are dry; but the Na will have been a bigger, though a shorter, stream. When the Great Valley as a whole subsides, the rifting along the fault lines and probably some magma pockets under Ama Kulkun will have sent the Valley's elevation up; the watertable under it would also rise; and what with the hot summers of the Great Valley much tempered by the Inland Sea and the vast marshlands, and the sea fogs flowing over the sea currents through a far broader Gate, the climate will have been modified. The dry season not so intensely dry; the creeks fuller; the river statelier, more considerable, more worshipful. But still less than thirty miles from spring to sea.

Thirty miles can be a short or a long way. It depends on the way you go them; what the Kesh called *wakwaha*.

With ceremony, with forms of politeness and reassurance, they borrowed the waters of the River and its little confluents to drink and be clean and irrigate with, using water mindfully, carefully. They lived in a land that answers greed with drought and death. A difficult land: aloof yet sensitive. Like the deer who live there, who will steal your food and be your food, skinny little deer, thief and prey, neighbor and watcher and watched, curious, unfrightened, untrusting, and untamable. Never anything but wild.

The roots and springs of the Valley were always wild. The patterns of the grapestakes and the pruned vines, the rows of grey olive trees and the formal splendor of flowering almond orchards, the sharp-footed sheep and the dark-eyed cattle, the wineries of stone, the old barns, the mills down by the water, the little shady towns, these are beautiful, humane, endearing, but the roots of the Valley are the roots of the digger pine, the scrub oak, the wild grasses careless and uncared for, and the springs of those creeks rise among the rifts of earthquake, among rocks from the floors of seas that were before there were human beings and from the fires inside the earth. The roots of the Valley are in wildness, in dreaming, in dying, in eternity. The deer trails there, the footpaths and the wagon tracks, they pick their way around the roots of things. They don't go straight. It can take a lifetime to go thirty miles, and come back.

Pandora Worries About What She Is Doing: The Pattern

 PANDORA DOESN'T WANT to look into the big end of the telescope and see, jewel-bright, distinct, tiny, and entire, the Valley. She shuts her eyes, she doesn't want to see, she knows what she will see: Everything Under Control. The dolls' house. The dolls' country.

Pandora rushes out of the observatory with her eyes shut, grabbing, grabbing with her hands.

What does she get, besides cut hands? Bits, chunks, fragments, Shards. Pieces of the Valley, lifesize. Not at a distance, but in the hand, to be felt and held and heard. Not intellectual, but mental. Not spiritual, but heavy. A piece of madrone wood, a piece of obsidian. A piece of blue clay. Even if the bowl is broken (and the bowl is broken), from the clay and the making and the firing and the pattern, even if the pattern is incomplete (and the pattern is incomplete), let the mind draw its energy. Let the heart complete the pattern.

SOME STORIES
TOLD ALOUD

‖‖‖

Some Stories Told Aloud One Evening in the Dry Season at a Summer Place Above Sinshan

Well, Coyote was going along inside the world, you know, and she met old man Bear.

"I'll come with you," Coyote said.

Bear said, "No, please don't come with me. I don't want you. I'm going to get all the bears together and make a war on the human beings. I don't want you along."

Coyote said, "Oh, that's terrible, a terrible thing to do. You'll all destroy each other. You'll be killed, they'll be killed. Don't make war, please don't make war! We should all live in peace and love each other!" All the time she was talking, Coyote was stealing Bear's balls, cutting them off with an obsidian knife she had stolen from the Doctor's Lodge, a knife so sharp he never felt it cutting.

When she was done she ran away with Bear's balls in a pouch. She went to where the human people were. They were smoking tobacco and singing, making gunpowder and bullets, cleaning their guns, getting ready for the war with the bears. Coyote went to their war general and said, "Oh, how brave you are, you men of valor, you true warriors! What courage you have, going to war against the bears with only guns for your weapons!"

The man got worried and said, "What kind of weapons have they got?"

Coyote said, "They have secret weapons. I can't tell you." But when he was really worried, she told him, "They have huge guns that shoot magic bullets that turn human people into bears. I brought a couple of the bullets." And she showed him the bear's testicles.

All the warriors came and looked and said, "What can we do?"

Coyote said, "Well, what you ought to do is this. Your general should shoot his magic bullets at the bears, and turn them human."

But the general said, "No. Get that coyote out of here, she only makes trouble!" They started shooting at Coyote, and she ran away.

The war began. The bears had their hearts and claws, the humans had tobacco smoke and guns. The humans shot and killed all the bears one after another, all but a few, just four or five who had come late to the war and could get away. They ran away and hid in the wilderness.

There they met Coyote.

"What did you do that for, Coyote?" they said. "Why didn't you help us? All you did was steal the balls off our best warrior!"

Coyote said, "If I could have got the balls off that human man, everything would have been all right. Listen. Those people fuck too often and think too fast. You bears only fuck once a year and sleep too much. You haven't got a chance against them. Stay here with me. I don't think war is the way to live with those people."

So the bears stayed in the wilderness. Most animals stayed in the wilderness with Coyote. Not the ants, though. They wanted to make war with the humans, and they did, and they're still at it.

[Another speaker:] That's right, that's right. And Flea Woman, she's an old friend of Coyote's, you know, they live together. She sends all her little children out on raids into the human's houses. She says, "Go make 'em itch, go make the children itch a little, itch a little!" [A child listening is tickled by the speaker, and yelps.]

[A third speaker:] That's right, yes. Then, you know, there was that time also in the world, Coyote said to Dog, "I'm angry about those human people winning the war with the bear people. You go to their town and kill that one, that general of theirs."

So Dog agreed. He went to the human town. But the women there in the household where that warrior lived, they gave the dog meat, they took the ticks out of his ears, they patted his head and tamed him. When they said lie down he lay down, when they said come he came. That dog let Coyote down. He joined the human people.

[The conversation drifts for a while, and the young children are getting sleepy. After they are bedded down on the porch of the summerhouse an elderly man sings a two-note chant for a while.

This is followed by silence and cricket-song. Then the first speaker begins again.]

That man, you know, that war general who killed the bears, well, he wanted his sons to be war generals like himself, heroes. He thought his hero-soul was in his balls. Maybe he got that idea from Coyote. So he cut them off himself, and put each one into a copper case he'd made, a sphere in two halves threaded to screw together. Then he gave one of these to each of his two sons. He said, "Even if you are half the man I was, it is enough. You will be fearless, you will conquer, you will kill your enemies," he said to them.

But the sons didn't believe that. Each one thought he needed both the balls.

One of them went to the other's house at night with a knife. The other one was waiting for him there with a knife. They fought, they went on fighting and cutting each other until they bled to death. In the morning both of them were dead. The old man came out of his house, he saw blood on the pathways, blood on the steps, people crying, his sons crouched over stiff, dead. He was enraged, he was furious, he shouted, "Give me back my balls!"

But the sons' wives had taken them out. They had put them up on the buzzards' hill with the butchers' leavings, because they had begun to stink. So when the old man was shouting, they said to each other, "What'll we do?" And they washed out the copper holders he'd made, and soldered them shut, or maybe stuck them together with glue, and then gave them to the old man.

"Here are your precious balls, father-in-law," they said. "You had better sew them back on where they belong. Your sons' children are all girls, they don't want them."

So the old man sewed the copper balls between his legs and went around with them. They made a clanking noise when he walked. He said, "When a true war general is born in this town, I will give him these." But they were nothing, they were empty. When the old man died, they buried those copper balls with his ashes.

[The third speaker:] That's right, that's right, and Coyote came and dug them up.

[The second speaker:] That's right, that's right, and she wore them for earrings when she danced the Moon.

TRANSLATOR'S NOTE: The original story about the war with the bears was evidently known to the adults present; the appreciation they showed by murmuring or laughter was for neat turns of phrase. The story about Dog also seemed to be an abridged version of a familiar tale. Whether the story told after the young children had gone to bed was a variation on a familiar theme, or entirely improvised, or something in between, I do not know; my impression was that the listeners did not know what was coming next, but collaborated in the invention and performance by their responses and laughter.

Shahugoten

*As told by Little Bear Woman of Sinshan
to the Editor.*

There was a Blue Clay family in Ounmalin who had a fish child. It
was a girl and it was a fish. At one time she was more human, at
another time more fish. She breathed both air and water, having
lungs and gills. For a long time they kept her from the water, thinking she would get to be more human if she stayed in air. She could
not walk well; her legs were weak and she could take only short
steps. But once when she was a baby and they were working in the
fields, they left her in the shade asleep, and she woke and crawled
to the reservoir nearby. They came back, they looked, the basket
was empty. The grandparents, the parents, everybody ran around
looking for her. Her brother went up the bank of the reservoir and
heard splashing. He looked over the water and saw his sister leaping like a trout. When the others came, she went underwater, and
stayed under. They thought she had drowned. They all went into
the water, churning up the mud. She hid at the bottom, in the mud
and slime, but they found her at last, they saw her glimmering.
When they brought her out of the water she gasped and twisted her
body until she began breathing air again.

After that they kept her shut in the house, or stayed close by
her outdoors. Her older brother carried her about. He was the one
who always stayed with her. She did not grow much, she was still
very small for a girl when she became adolescent, and her brother
could still carry her. She would ask him to take her to the River,
and he would answer, "Wait a while, kekoshbi, wait a while yet."
He helped to herd the cattle of Ounmalin, and while he was herding he would take his sister down to the small creeks and shallow
pools, and she would swim and play there. He would stay up on the
bank, keeping watch. Then when she was stronger, when she was
becoming adolescent and was learning the Blood Lodge songs, he
would take her to the Obsidian heyimas and meet her when she
came out, and in the evening then he would take her to the River,
downstream from town, where it curves around Ounmalin Hill
making deep pools. She would swim a long way, and he would wait
for her. Every evening she swam farther, and he waited longer.

He said, "Kekoshbi, kekoshbinye, they're asking where we go
in the evening, why we stay out with the herd so late."

She said, "Takoshbi, matakoshbi, I don't like the songs they sing underground in the First House, the blood songs. I like the water songs they sing in our House. I don't want to come back into the air, into the ground."

He said, "Don't swim away!"

She said, "I'll try not to."

But one evening she swam downriver so far that she tasted the sea through her skin in the water. She came back, she swam back to her brother waiting by the deep pool under the hill. She said, "Matakoshbi, I have to go away. I tasted the blood in the River. I have to go on now." They put their cheeks together. She slipped back into the water and swam away. The boy went home. He said, "She is gone, she swam to the sea." People thought that he had left her in the River, that he was tired of carrying her and looking after her. They blamed him, saying, "Why did you let her get near the River? Why didn't you keep her on land? Why didn't you stay with her?" He was ashamed and bitterly grieved. When he was with the cattle in the fields and barns he wept with shame and loneliness. He talked to the fish in the River and the sea gulls that came up the Valley in wet weather: "If you see my sister, tell her to come home!"

But it was a long time before she came home. He always walked down by the River in the evening. It was early in the rainy season, in the rain, near dark: he saw something white in the water under the bank of the deep pool. He heard a sound—oshh, osshhh—like sea waves. He went down through the willows. She was in the water there, in the shallows by the bank, very white, calling, "Takoshbi! Matakoshbi!" He tried to carry her out of the water, but she said, "Don't! Don't!" She was white and swollen. She gave birth there in the water, in the shallows under the bank: a child, a white child, not a fish but a white boy. The brother took him out of the water and wrapped him in his shirt. She saw that, then she arched up her body and died in the shallow water. People came by, they took the newborn child and his uncle home. They sang the songs for the death, and cremated the death next day in the burning place down by Sebbe. They put the ashes in the River, not in the earth. Shahugoten, Seaborn, the child was named. Some people of the Obsidian living in Ounmalin, people with whitish skin, are grandchildren of the daughter of Shahugoten.

The Keeper

Recited by Fletcher, librarian of the Serpentine of Oun-malin. This is an example of a "formal" recitation, the performance of a story, as distinct from informal or improvised story-telling. It is obviously a teaching story. It is considered to be true, or factual, although a Chumo version of the same general story begins, "Down across the Valley there in Tachas Touchas . . ."

Up across the Valley there in that town, Chumo, there was a young woman living in the Third House, a scholar, still wearing undyed clothing; and she was the keeper there, the one who looked after things and put them away and took them out, all the things of the heyimas for the dances and the singing and teaching and giving.

There were the vests, the costumes for the Summer dancers, the stones, the paintings on paper, cloth, and wood, the ranges of feathers, the caps, the musical instruments, the tongue-drums and the great wakwa drum, the dance-rattles of gourd and shell, deer hoof and clay, the writings, the books, the sweet and bitter herbs and dried flowers, the carvings and hehole-no of all kinds, the oils, the tools and instruments of making and repair, and all such valuable and honorable things, and their containers, and their wrappings, and the shelves, closets, and particular places where they were kept in order, clean, seemly, and beautiful; and she was the one who kept them. This was her gift, she did this well, taking pleasure in doing it. When any thing was needed she brought it from its place ready for use. When any thing was given she put it in the right place. When any thing was dirty or worn she cleaned it and mended it, and when a thing wore out she put it to a different use. She went on doing this when she came inland and when she married and when she was a mother. It was her chief work, and nobody else did these things for that heyimas but her.

One time a man made a carving in madrone wood, a thing of beauty, a hehole-no, to give to the House in which the madrone grows. He left it as a gift in the fifth angle of the great room. The keeper saw it after other people had gone home. She picked it up. She liked it, and kept holding it and looking at it, thinking, "This suits me; this is as if it were made for me. This is for me. I will keep this for a while." She took it home to her household, into her room, and put it in her lidded basket, under other things. There it stayed. She did not often look at it, and did not use it.

Another time a man made for the Serpentine a dancing vest of doeskin sewn with leaf embroidery, with ornaments of the long acorns copper-mounted. The keeper was taking it to the chests and chests of the heyimas, and she thought, "This looks as if it would fit me." She tried it on, and kept wearing it as she worked there, thinking, "This fits me; this suits me. This was made for me. Maybe I'll dance in it, next Summer. Somebody else might choose it before me. I'll keep it till the Summer dancing." She took it home and put it in the bottom of her clothes-chest. There it stayed. She did not wear it at the Summer dancing.

Another time a family gave a lot of manzanita-berry powder to the heyimas. She set out some of it in the fifth angle; the rest she took home, thinking, "My son's throat gets dry in the dust of the dry season, and he coughs so badly, he'll be needing manzanita cider then. I'll save this and use it when he needs it." She put it in a glass jar with a stopper in the cellar of her house. There it stayed. She did not make cider of it in the dry season.

Another time a woman gave a deer-legbone flute that had been a long time in the Second House, very old; many times it had played the four-note heya. The keeper put it with the other flutes of the Third House, but she kept going back and taking it out of the box, moving it on the shelf, thinking, "It doesn't belong here; it is too old to play. Careless people play these flutes—children, musicians. This is too old and beautiful to treat like an ordinary flute." She took it home and put it in her lidded basket. There it stayed. No one played it.

Another time a man brought a piece of cornbread. He was very old and muddleheaded and the piece of bread was old too, hard and dry; he couldn't chew it. He broke off the piece he had tried to bite off and dropped that, and put the rest in the fifth angle, saying, "Maybe some young person with strong jaws can eat that." The keeper found it there. She dropped it to the floor and when she swept the great room of the heyimas she gathered the bread up with the dust, and took all she had swept up the ladder, and let it fall in the dirt by the roof of the heyimas.

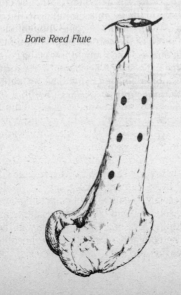

Bone Reed Flute

That afternoon, that evening, she got sick. The next day she was very sick. She had terrible pains in her stomach, her hands, her anus, her teeth. They held a bringing-in for her, but she did not come with the singers. The doctors cared for her but nothing helped her; she was in more pain all the time, and swelling up, her hands and feet swelling, her belly and face swelling.

A cousin of hers in her House who was a singing doctor came to care for her and sing to her. He watched her carefully as he sang. She groaned and did not listen. When the song was finished her cousin said, "Cousin, a song is its singing."

He went home. She thought about what he had said; she had heard that. She kept thinking about it. By now she was wasted away and swollen up, and doubled over with the pains in her belly. She wanted to vomit and could not, she wanted to shit and could not. She thought, "What am I dying for?" She thought about the things she had kept. She crawled over to her lidded basket and looked for the deer-bone flute and the madrone-wood carving. Nothing was in the bottom of the basket but some clods of dirt. She looked in her clothes-chest for the embroidered vest. Nothing was there under the other clothes but a dirty rag. She went down to the basement, to her shelves, looking for the cider powder. The jar had dirt in it, dust in it. She went to the heyimas, dragging herself, crawling, crying out, "Where is it? Where is it?" She crawled in the dirt around the outside of the heyimas, scraping in the dirt with her fingernails, crying, "Where is it?" People thought she had gone crazy. She found a piece of the cornbread, a crumb of it; maybe it was just a crumb of dirt and she thought it was the cornbread. She ate it. She lay still then. They took her home, and sang for her, and she listened to the singing. She got better; she got well. Other people looked after the things in the heyimas after that.

Dried Mice

*A story told to a group of children on a rainy day in
the Serpentine heyimas of Sinshan, by Kingsnake,
a man in his seventies.*

Coyote had this child she got somewhere, not her own child; it was
a human baby she stole somewhere. Maybe she saw a baby nobody
was looking after, and said, "I'll take that baby home with me." So
she did. Her own children played with it. She nursed it, it got fat on
coyote milk. It got fatter than the coyote pups, they were all ribs
and tail. But they didn't care. They played with the human child,
they jumped at it and it jumped at them, they nipped it and it
nipped them, they all slept together in Coyote's bed, in Coyote's
house. But the child was always cold there, not having any fur. It
kept whimpering and shivering. Coyote said, "What's wrong?"

"I'm cold."

"Grow fur!"

"I can't."

"Well, what can I do?"

"You ought to make a fire, that's what people do when they're
cold."

"Oh! Good!" Coyote said, and she went right off to some place
where human people lived. She waited till they lighted a fire, then
she ran into the house, grabbed a stick of burning wood, and ran
into the hills with it. The sparks flew behind her, the fire caught the
dry grass. A fire started behind Coyote, a grassfire. By the time she
got home the fire was roaring on ten hills. Her family all had to run,
they had to run like crazy, and jump into the river! There they all
were in the river with only their noses out. "Hey," Coyote says, "are
you warm now?"

After they came out of the river everything was burned on one
side. The rain came and it got cold, it was a cold winter. They lived
in a new den on the other side of that river. The child was even
colder there, but it didn't want to ask Coyote to light another fire. It
thought, "I won't stay here with these coyotes in this cold house
any more. I'll go where my kind of people are and live that way." So
in the daytime it got up, in the middle of the day when the coyotes
were sleeping, and it took some venison jerky and some dried
mice, that's what there was to eat in the house, and started off. All
day it walked along, walking along all day, running sometimes, to

get a long way away from Coyote, clear away from that house. At the end of the day, after sunset, the child looked for a place to hide and sleep. It found a ledge of rock, and made a bed with fir twigs, and lay down there and went to sleep.

Coyote was waking up. She was stretching and yawning. Her pups said, "Hey! Where's Two-Legs?" She looked around. She looked over in the corner of her house and saw the child sleeping on the shelf where she kept things. "There, on the shelf over there," she said. "Why is that child sleeping there, I wonder?" They all went out to hunt.

The child got up next morning, and all day long it ran and walked, all day long, going a long, long way, and at night it hid in a cave to sleep. The coyotes woke up. "Hey! Where's Two-Legs?" She looked around her house. "There, in my basket, my sewing basket. Why is that child sleeping there, I wonder?" So they went on out.

The next day the child came to a town of human people. They all kept away from it because it looked strange to them at first, and some people threw rocks at it to drive it away, but it stayed there. It hid under the porch of a house, and at night it came up and slept on the porch, near the door. When the people who lived in the house saw it there they were sorry for it, and brought it inside so it could sleep near the fire. In their house the coyotes were waking up. The young coyotes were looking around. "Where's Two-Legs?"—"Oh! my child is gone! My child has gone to another house!" Coyote went outside and cried and howled all night. "Bring me my dried mice back!" So they say. That's what she says when she comes around outside town in the moonlight, she's saying, "Bring me my dried mice back!" So they say.

NOTE:
p. 67. *some dried mice:* tupúde útí gosútí

Dira

*Told by Ire's husband Red Bull to a group of
children and young adolescents in
the Obsidian heyimas.*

Heya hey heya,
hey heya heya, in that time that place, in the dark cold time, the
dark cold place, she was going along, this woman, a human
woman, walking in the hills, looking for something ;to eat. She was
looking for brodiaea and calochortus bulbs before they bloomed,
and putting out snares for brush rabbit, and gathering anything
that could be food, because her people were hungry and so was
she. Those were times when people had to work all day for enough
to eat, times when even so they didn't have enough to eat, and
people died of hunger, human and animal, they died of hunger and
cold, so they say.

She was hunting and gathering in the hills, then, and started
down into a canyon where she thought she saw some cattail down
by the creek. She got into buckbrush and scrub oak and thorn, and
had to push her way long; there weren't any deer trails, not even
rabbit trails. She pushed along through the brush, trying to get
down into the canyon. It was very dark, like it was going to rain.
She thought, "Oh, before I get out of this brush, this time of year,
I'll be covered with ticks!" She kept brushing at her neck and arms
and feeling in her hair for ticks, trying to keep them from sticking
to her. She didn't find any cattails. There was nothing to eat down
in the canyon. She started to go along downstream, pushing
through that thick underbrush, tearing her shirt and scratching her
skin on the buckbrush and the thorn. She came into a place where
the yellow broom grew very tall and close together. Nothing else
grew there. The broom was half dead and grey-looking, without
flowers yet. She pushed her way into the broom thicket, and ahead
of her there, in the middle of the thicket, she saw a person standing. It was a wide, thin, dark person, with a little head, and one
hand without fingers, just two prongs, like pliers or pincers. It
stood there waiting. It had no eyes, they say.

She stopped; she stood still. Then she tried to back away very
quietly as she had come. But the broom thicket had closed behind
her and it made a lot of noise when she tried to go back. She could
only go forward quietly. The person stood still, not moving, not

looking, so still she began not to be sure it was alive. She thought, "Maybe I can get past it." She went forward very quietly, moving softly, smoothly, quickly. The waiting person didn't move. She saw how thin and flat it was, dry-looking, and thought it must be something that had never been alive. She came on past it. She was beside it. She passed it and now her back was to it. It jumped, then. It jumped, and caught her with its gripping hand at the back of her neck. It held her and said, "Take me home with you!"

She struggled and said, "Let me go!" She tried to get free but it held on. She was strangling. It held tighter and tighter, and she said, "All right, I'll take you home with me!"

"That's good," the person said. It let go of her then. When she could turn and look at it, it looked like a man, a human being, dark and thin, with a small head and small eyes, but with two arms and two hands with thumb and fingers, and all seeming to be the way a human being should be. "Go on," the man said, "and I'll follow."

So she went on, and the man followed.

She came to where she lived, a little town, just a few houses, a few families, somewhere in that dark, cold valley. She came there, the man following, and her people said, "Who is this with you?"

She said, "A hungry man."

They said, "He certainly is thin. He can share what we have to eat."

She tried to say, "No! Send him away!" —but when she started to speak her throat closed and she couldn't breathe, as if he were still holding her by the neck. She could say nothing against him.

They asked the man what he was called, and he answered, "Dira."

The woman had to open her door to Dira. He came in and sat down by her fire. She had to share the food she had brought for her children and her mother with him. There wasn't much: a few bulbs and greens, that was all she had found. They were all still hungry when they had eaten, but Dira said, "Ah, that was good! That was fine!" And he seemed not so thin already.

He asked the woman, "Where is your husband?"

She said, "He died last year."

Dira said, "I'll take his place."

She tried to say, "No!" but she couldn't: her throat tightened till she thought her head would burst, and she could not breathe, until she said, "Yes."

So Dira was her husband, and she made the best of it.

Her mother said after a while, "This husband you picked up in the woods, he doesn't do any work."

"He's still weak from starving so long," she said.

People in town said, "Why doesn't Dira farm, or hunt, or gather? He stays in the house all day and night."

She said, "He's ill."

They said, "Maybe he was ill when he came here, but look at him now!"

Because he had become quite fat—every day he got fatter, and his skin was ruddy instead of dark.

"He's fat, and you and your family are all thinner than ever—how is that?" they asked her. But she could not say. When she tried to speak against Dira, even when he was not there with her, she strangled. The tears came into her eyes. She said, "I don't know."

They had planted gardens, but the summer was dark and cold. The seeds rotted in the ground. There was little to hunt; there were not many Blue Clay animals, because they too were starving and sick; there were few Obsidian animals. Nobody had food. The woman's children grew weak and sick, with big, swollen bellies. She wept, but her husband laughed. "See, they're like me!" he said. "We all have big bellies!" He ate everything: he grew fatter, thicker, redder, every day. The family had one cow, and there was enough grass to keep her fit; it was her milk that kept the children alive. Dira went out one day into the fields. The woman said, "There, see, my husband is going to work!" He went to where the cow was grazing, and she said, "He's going to look after our sister there." But what he did was drink the cow's blood, sucking it. He did this every day and the cow could not give milk; he went on doing it, and she lay down and died. He butchered her there in the field and came home carrying the meat. He had to go back and forth several times for it all. "See how hard my husband works!" the woman said. There were tears running down her face. They saw that, her townspeople.

Her children had grown very weak without milk. The husband, Dira, always spoke kindly to them, but he gave them no meat. He ate it all. Sometimes he would say to them, the children, their mother, their grandmother. "Here, don't you want this meat? You don't want this food?" But when he said that, their throats would tighten and close, so they could only shake their heads; then he would eat the meat, smiling and joking. One of the children died. The other, the elder, began dying too. Dira was so fat he could no longer get up; he sat by the fire all day and night. His belly was huge, a huge ball. His skin was tight and pale red all over. His eyes were covered with fat. His arms and legs were stubs coming out of that great ball of fatness. His wife and her mother stayed beside the dying child.

The people of the town spoke together. They talked awhile, and decided to kill Dira. The men were angry and said, "A knife across that throat, a bullet in that belly!" But there was a lame woman, a visionary, who said, "Not that way, not that way. This is not a man!"

"But we are going to kill him," they said.

"If you kill him that way, his wife and her family will die with him. You must not spill all that blood in him. It is their blood," she said.

"Then we'll suffocate him," one of the men said.

"That is the way," the lame woman said.

They went, all of them, to the house. The door was shut. They pushed it open and came in. The grandmother and mother and child lay like sticks of wood, like old bones on the floor, too weak to sit up, dying. The husband sat by the fire like a great red ball of skin. When he saw the people he changed into his own form, and put out his pliers hand, but he was too fat to move, and couldn't catch them. They had brought with them a basin of eucalyptus oil, and they held Dira down and pushed his head into the oil, and held it there a long time. A long time he struggled and did not die, but they kept holding his head under the oil, and at last his great, wide, fat body stiffened and began to shrink. It shrank and shrank, and the wife and her mother and child sat up. It shrank more, and they stood up. It shrank down no larger than a fist, and they could speak again. It shrank down no larger than a walnut, and they could move freely and say what had happened. It shrank no larger than a thumbnail, flat and dry and dark, and the people, greeting and comforting the wife and her family, didn't keep careful watch on it. It shrank down to something not as big as a lentil, and then scrambled out of the basin of oil, and out the door, back into the hills, to wait somewhere for another person to come by. It's still waiting there, they say.

POEMS

AS EXPLAINED IN "Spoken and Written Literature" in The Back of the Book, some Valley poetry was written down and some was not, but whether improvised, recited from memory, or read from writing, it was always performed aloud.

This section includes several improvisations, some well-known songs, which like all folksongs have lost authorship and belong to everybody (not all poetry in the Valley did; some of it was given, and some of it had to be earned), some children's songs, and a few "public" pieces—poems spoken in contest or written up in public places.

A SHEPHERD'S SONG FROM CHUMO

You can have the afterbirth,
not the lamb, Coyote.
The ewe has sharp hooves,
better look out, Coyote.
I can have some girls,
not that one, Coyote.
Her mother doesn't like me,
better look out, Coyote.

DRAGONFLY SONG

Ounmalin, Ounmalin!
Beautiful on the River!
To the barns under the dark oaks
the cattle return at evening.
The sound of their cowbells
is like the ringing of water.
From the round hill over Ounmalin
one can see all the vineyards,
and hear the people singing,
coming from the vineyards home at evening.

NOTE: A dragonfly song or poem means an improvisation, something that goes by lightly. This was spoken by Broom to a family group on a balcony of a house in Ounmalin on a summer evening, and when I said I liked it the author wrote it down and gave it to me.

A BAY LAUREL SONG

He has to wave it,
he has to wave it like a flag
to make it stand up.

He has to stick it into mouseholes,
he has to stick it into moleholes,
he has to stick it into assholes
to make it stand up.

Let me lie down, it says.
No, he says.
Let me get some sleep, it says.
Get up, he says.
So it gets up and grows hands
and gets a knife and cuts him off.
He goes running off without one,
and it sings heya nine times and lies down
and goes to sleep.

He grows a new one
but it's very little.
He has to lie down
and stick it into antholes.

SOME "FIVE/FOUR" POEMS FROM MADIDINOU
Spoken at a poetry session on the riverbank after work.

LOSS

My heart is heavy.
It lies down crossways,
stopping my breathing,
a stone of grieving.

JEALOUSY

That one with earrings,
what can she give you?
More wine? More mutton?
Bigger erections?

FIRST LOVE

Weeding tomatoes,
the vines smell bitter
in the hot sunlight.
A long time ago.

THE DARK GIRL

Blackwinged butterfly
turns, lights, flits, returns
to the yarrow stem,
intent, uncertain.

A FLYTING SERIES

The old word flyting, *a contest of insults in rhyme, translates the Kesh word* fini. *The following were oral improvisations at a Wine Dance in Chumo.*

You come from down the Valley.
I can tell by the way the words come out of your mouth
like crayfish getting dragged out of a hole backwards.

People keep a lot of chickens up in Chumo.
The chickens are so clever they talk like people:
Rock, rock, rock, rock, rock, rock, rockbasket!
The people in Chumo are as clever as the chickens.

Down the Valley the intelligence of the inhabitants
is manifested in their custom of brewing
small beer from dog turds.

Great minds prefer strong flavors.
In Chumo they like strong beer,
so they use cat turds.

I can tell you come from down the Valley
by the way you drag one idea around all morning
like a bitch clamped onto the dog's penis.

There was a man in Chumo
had an idea, once,
for a few minutes.

FERNSTEM'S SONG
Sung at work by Fernstem of Kastoha-na.

Old feet
sticking out in front
of old knees,
old eyes see you
over this basket
old hands are making,
this new basket.
Old feet,
you walked a long way
to get here
in front of this basket.
Stick up in the air there,
keep on telling
this new song
to this old singing woman.

A POEM SAID WITH THE DRUM
By Kulkunna of Chukulmas.

The hawk turns crying, gyring.
There is a tick stuck in my scalp.
If I soar with the hawk
I have to suck with the tick.
O hills of my Valley, you are too complicated!

ARTISTS

Written on a white plaster wall in the workroom of the
Oak Society in Telina-na.

What do they do,
the singers, tale-writers, dancers, painters, shapers, makers?
They go there with empty hands,
into the gap between.
They come back with things in their hands.
They go silent and come back with words, with tunes.
They go into confusion and come back with patterns.
They go limping and weeping, ugly and frightened,
and come back with the wings of the redwing hawk,
the eyes of the mountain lion.

That is where they live,
where they get their breath:
there, in the gap between,
the empty place.

Where do the mysterious artists live?
There, in the gap between.
Their hands are the hinge.
No one else can breathe there.
They are beyond praise.

The ordinary artists
use patience, passion, skill, work
and returning to work, judgment,
proportion, intellect, purpose,
indifference, obstinacy, delight in tools,
delight, and with these as their way
they approach the gap, the hub,
approaching in circles, in gyres,
like the buzzard, looking down, watching,
like the coyote, watching.

They look to the center,
they turn on the center,
they describe the center,
though they cannot live there.
They deserve praise.

There are people who call themselves artists
who compete with each other for praise.
They think the center
is a stuffed gut,
and that shitting is working.
They are what the buzzard and the coyote
ate for breakfast yesterday.

A VAUNTING
From the town of Tachas Touchas.

The musicians of Tachas Touchas
make flutes of the rivers, make drums of the hills.
The stars come out to listen to them.
People open the doors of the Four Houses,
they open the windows of rainbow,
to listen to the musicians of Tachas Touchas.

A RESPONSE
From the town of Madidinou.

The musicians of Tachas Touchas
make flutes of their noses, make drums of their buttocks.
The fleas run away from them.
People shut the doors in Madidinou,
they shut the windows in Sinshan,
when they hear the musicians of Tachas Touchas coming.

AN EXHORTATION FROM THE SECOND AND THIRD HOUSES OF THE EARTH

A calligraphed poster-scroll from the Serpentine heyimas of Wakwaha.

Listen, you people of the Adobes, you people of the Obsidian!
Listen, you gardeners and farmers, orcharders and vintners,
        shepherds and drovers!
Your arts are admirable and generous, arts of plenty and
        increase, and they are dangerous.
Among the tasselled corn the man says, this is my plowing
        and sowing, this is my land.
Among the grazing sheep the woman says, these are my
        breeding and caring, these are my sheep.
In the furrow the seed sprouts hunger.
In the fenced pasture the cow calves fear.
The granary is heaped full with poverty.
The foal of the bridled mare is anger.
The fruit of the olive is war.
Take care, you Adobe people, you Obsidian people, and come
        over onto the wild side,
don't stay all the time on the farming side; it's dangerous to
        live there.
Come among the unsown grasses bearing richly, the oaks
        heavy with acorns, the sweet roots in
        unplowed earth.
Come among the deer on the hill, the fish in the river, the
        quail in the meadows.
You can take them, you can eat them,
like you they are food.
They are with you, not for you.
Who are their owners?
This is the puma's range,
        this hill is the vixen's,
        this is the owl's tree,
        this is the mouse's run,
        this is the minnow's pool:
        it is all one place.
        Come take your place.

No fences here, but sanctions.
No war here, but dying; there is dying here.
Come hunt, it is yourself you hunt.
Come gather yourself from the grass, the branch, the earth.
Walk here, sleep well, on the ground that is not yours, but is
                 yourself.

BOSO
(THE ACORN WOODPECKER)
A children's counting-out song in Sinshan.

Boso-bird, red-hat, blacka blacka white-streak,
whackawhackawhacka on a oaktree,
walka walka backward on a joketree,
yackayackayacka goes a boso!
    Yackawhacka, yackawhacka, one two three,
    yackawhacka, yackawhacka, out goes he.

ALL IN THE WESTERN LAND

*A children's dance song, heard in all nine towns of the
Valley; the dance is called Making the Gyre. Rhyme is
characteristic of children's songs; the meter of the
translation attempts to suggest the insistent rhythm of
the dance.*

CHORUS
Circle around around the house
circle around and back
everything burning burning burning
everything burning black

SOLO
O who will break the circle
O who will loose my hand
O who will be my lover
all in the western land

CHORUS
Open the circle around and out
and part and swing and pass
down along the valleys
and the yellow hills of grass

SOLO
So make and break the circle
so take and loose my hand
so love and leave me dancing
all in the western land

FIVES ABOUT LIZARDS

*Improvised by Giver Ire's daughter of Sinshan
while sitting in the sun near a rock wall.*

Big lizard pumps up
and down, up, down, up,
shows his blue belly:
I'm sky! I'm lightning!
Little one scuttles:
I'm shadows. I'm not.

TO THE BULLOCK ROSÉROOT

*An improvisation spoken during the Second Day of
the World ceremonies by Kulkunna of Chukulmas.*

What's the thought you think
all your life long?
It must be a great one,
a solemn one, to make you gaze
through the world at it,
all your life long.
When you have to look aside from it
your eyes roll, you bellow
in anger, anxious
to return to it, steadily
to gaze at it, think it
all your life long.

THE BUZZARDS

Sung to the drum by Fox's Gift of Sinshan.
The meter is "four/fives."

Four buzzards, four!
Four buzzards, four, five!
They turn gyring,
return gyring.
High up, the buzzards
circling turn circling
on the center.

Where is the center?
This hill, that hill,
any valley
where a death is.
There is the center.
Under the circles
inside the gyre
of nine buzzards,
the center is there.

TO THE VALLEY QUAIL

Spoken by Adsevin of Sinshan and her
mother's sister, Flowering.

Mother Urkrurkur, show me your household,
please let me see it.

The floor is of blue clay,
the walls of rain falling,
the doors are of cloud,
wind is the windows,
you know there is no ceiling.

Sister Ekwerkwe, how do you keep house,
please tell me or show me.

By running directly and neatly,
and flying up loudly not very far,

by staying together and talking,
by delicate accurate markings,
by plumpness, round eyes, and a topknot.

Daughter Heggurka, what is the end of it,
please let me know it.

The hawk in the hot noon,
the horned owl in twilight,
the cat in the darkness:
feathers, bones, rain falling, sunlight,
hidden under warm wings, round eggs.

TEASING THE KITTEN

*Improvised by He Is Thinking, a boy of about
sixteen, in Sinshan, in the vegetable garden.*

Ho ya, little piece-of-the-ground cat!
Ho ya, little color-of-the-ground cat!
You are holding the dirt down,
sound asleep in the sunlight,
on top of your own shadow.
If I toss this pebble
cat and shadow will come apart—
Ha ya, little fly-in-the-air cat!

BUCKET

*Improvised on a warm morning of early spring by
fifteen-year-old Adsevin (Morning Star)
of Sinshan, while cutting bamboo.*

I feel so dreamy
dreamy lazy, crazy sleepy
like I want to be there
in the doorway, the doorway
or the porch corner
be sitting, be empty
not doing not going
an old bucket left there
in the porch corner is like I am
an old empty bucket somebody left there.

A LOVE SONG

Sung all over the Valley.

If the yellow wind will blow
        southeasterly, southeast,
if the pollen wind will blow,
maybe he'll come this morning.

If the sweet-smelling wind will blow
        southeasterly, southeast,
if the broom-flower wind will blow,
maybe he'll come this evening.

How to Die in the Valley

||||||||||||||||||||||||||||||||||||||||||||||||||||||||

FUNERALS TOOK PLACE in the large area of wild hill and forest alongside each town, "the hunting side," where no planting was done and ownership of seed-meadows, cattail marshes, and gathering trees was either communal or a matter of use and usage only. Somewhere within a mile or so of the town each of the Five Houses used a certain region of hilltop or high valley as a graveyard. There were no boundaries, and a family could place a new grave where it liked; the graveyard area was identified by the plantings of apple, manzanita, buckeye, wild azalea, foxglove, and California poppy. The graves were never marked with stones aboveground, but sometimes with a small carved figure of redwood or cedar, and often were planted with one or more of the plants named above, which were looked after as long as survivors and descendants cared to keep the memory green. Most graveyards looked like apple orchards, only even more straggling and irregular than the usual Valley orchard.

The burning ground was in a vale or hollow near and below the graveyard. The fairly large circular ground was cleared of all grass and stamped down and sown with salt yearly by the Black Adobe Lodge members.

The ceremony of dying was called Going Westward to the Sunrise. The following description was given in writing by Mica of Acorn House of Sinshan.

GOING WESTWARD TO THE SUNRISE: INSTRUCTIONS FOR DYING.

Somebody in the Black Adobe Lodge would be the teacher of this knowledge.

87

After the Wine Dance and before the Grass, people who want to learn the songs of Going Westward to the Sunrise would ask that teacher to instruct them.

After the Wine Dance, they help the teacher build a heyiya lodge outside the town, usually on the hunting side, sometimes on the planting side. We in the hill towns build with eucalyptus or willow poles, nine or twelve to the side, tied to the ridgepole with withies, and weave the walls of fir boughs. On the Valley floor, where the lodge may have to be bigger because there are more people, they leave the walls open but make a thick roof, since the rainy season is beginning and some of the celebrants are ill or old, needing shelter. Whether there are walls or not, the entrance is on the northeast side and the exit on the southwest. Dead manzanita wood and apple prunings are gathered and stacked for the fire. All the stones on the ground within the walls of the lodge are gathered together and are heya. The lodge is named Rejoining.

The teacher goes there on the last night of the Grass and spends the night there, digging a fireplace in the earth, without stones around it, and singing to bless the lodge.

The learners come in the morning. They build and light a fire in the firepit, and throw bay laurel leaves on it, and sing heya.

If people want to talk then about dying their own death, or to talk about a person close to their heart who had died suddenly or who was ill and dying, they would put a handful of bay leaves on the fire, and talk. The teachers and the others listen. When they finish talking, the teacher might speak about things dreamed or learned in vision about the way people may go when they die, or

read from the Black Adobe books of poems that speak of the soul, or say nothing but beat heya on the one-note drum.

Then the teaching would begin. They are to learn the songs to sing while dying and the songs to sing for the dying.

The teacher sings the first song to sing for the dying.

That song will be sung when dying begins. It may be sung for a short time or a long time. The person dying may be able to sing with the watchers then, singing aloud or silently while going into death. The others, the watchers, keep watching and listening as they sing. When it is time to sing the second song for the dying they will know, because the person dying has become still, or the breath is trying to get free. When the pulse and breath have ceased, the third song is begun. When the face is cold, it is ceased.

The teacher tells these things between singing the songs, and teaches also that any of the watchers' songs may be sung again and again until the dying is over. The fourth and fifth songs are to be sung first at the burial, and aloud thereafter at any time or place for four days, and aloud at the grave after that for five days, and after that only in silence, in the mind, until the next World Dance. After that they should not be sung for that person.

Most people have heard the watchers' songs sung, the songs for the dying, but have not heard the songs the dying person sings.

The teacher will tell them that the people dying know when to sing the songs by the places their spirit comes to as they die. At first the mind will know these places, later the soul will know them. If they have lived mindfully, they will recognize these places, whether they are in the Five Houses or the Four Houses. It is well if they can sing all the way to the last song, but there is no need for it. What is needful is that the watchers' songs be sung during the dying, if possible, and for the first nine days of the death, to help the dying to die and the living to live.

When this has been said and discussed, the teacher will sing the first line of the first song of the person dying. The learners will answer singing the first line of the first song of the watchers. So they will learn all the five songs that they will sing when they die, never singing them aloud, but answering them antiphonally with the watchers' songs. Only the teacher, who belongs to the Black Adobe Lodge, sings the songs of the dying person aloud. It is well for the learner to sing them many times in silence, then and later, so that they will be part of the mind and soul.

These are the songs of Going Westward to the Sunrise. [*They may be read apart or together, reading down the page or across it.*]

THE SONGS

THE FIRST SONG

The one dying sings:
I will go forward.
It is hard, it is hard.
I will go forward.

The watchers sing:
Go forward. Go forward.
We are with you.
We are beside you.

THE SECOND SONG

I will go forward.
It is changing.
I will go forward.

Go on now, go ahead.
Leave us now.
It is time to leave us.

THE THIRD SONG

There is a way.
There is surely a way.
There is a road, there is a way.

You are going on.
Your feet are on that road.
You are going on that road.

THE FOURTH SONG

The singing is changing.
The light is changing.
The singing is changing.
The light is changing.
They are coming.
They are dancing in shining.
Rejoining.

Do not look back.
You are entering.
You are achieving.
You are arriving.
The light is growing.
Back here is darkness.
Look forward.

THE FIFTH SONG

The doors of the Four Houses
     are open.
Surely they are open.

The doors of the Four Houses
     are open.
Surely they are open.

When all the songs have been learned, they cover the fire with earth, filling in the firepit, and while doing that they sing this song:

It is hard, it is hard.
It is not easy.
You must go back in.

They would take down the Lodge Rejoining after that. They might take a pebble from the heap or a twig of evergreen from the roof to hang their knowledge on. They would go to bathe, and go home. The teacher would go to a wild spring to wash, or if a Blue Clay person, to the heyimas for ablution.

This is how the way of dying is taught by people of the Black Adobe Lodge in the Valley of the Na. I have been learner twice and teacher seven times.

The Lodge Rejoining

NE.

S.W.

If nobody among the family and friends of the dead had learned the watchers' songs, a member of the Black Adobe Lodge came to sing them, at the deathbed if possible, and at the graveside; and in fact there was always a Black Adobe person in attendance to help out and officiate during a death and funeral.

If there was any doubt or anxiety, a member of the Doctors Lodge certified death. Soon, always within that day and night, the dead person was carried on a covered litter to the burning ground of their House. Family and mourners were the bearers. Wood might be given and carried to the burning ground by mourners, but only Black Adobe Lodge members stayed at the cremation. Family and mourners were directed to go home.

An old sad song in the Valley hints at this:

I watch the smoke behind the ridge,
the smoke rising and the rain falling.

Cremation was the rule, but a good many circumstances might prevent it: very wet weather in the rainy season; very dry weather in the dry season when the danger of forest fire disallowed the building of any open fire; and the expressed desire of the person to be buried not cremated after death. In these cases a Black Adobe group dug the grave and laid the dead person in it, wrapped in cotton sheeting, on the left side with the limbs somewhat flexed. Then they watched beside the pyre or the open grave for one night, singing the Going Westward songs at intervals.

In the morning all who wished to came to attend the burial. Close kinfolk, assisted by the Lodge members, made the small grave for the ashes, or filled in the grave. When the grave was filled, a member of the Black Adobe spoke, once only, aloud, the Nine Words:

> Unceasing, unending, unobstructed,
> open, ongoing, incoming,
> ever, ever, ever.

A wisp of ashes or of the dead person's hair was cast upward into the air as the Nine Words were spoken. Children at the funeral might be given seeds or grain to scatter on the grave, so that birds would gather there to carry the mourners' songs to the Four Houses. Anybody who wanted to could remain, or come back at intervals during the first four days after the death, to sing the Going Westward songs at the graveside; and during the five days after that, a family member or a mourner from the dead person's House came at least once in the day to sing the Going Westward songs. On the ninth day, traditionally, the mourners regathered to mark the grave with a tree or shrub or flowers, and sing aloud for the last time. After that no formal mourning took place, nor were the songs to be sung aloud for that person.

When somebody died outside the Valley, the companions would make every effort to cremate the body and bring home the ashes, or at least some locks of hair and pieces of clothing, which would then be buried, and the songs sung. If someone was lost or drowned at sea (a most unlikely event) so that there was "no death to carry," a relation would ask the Black Adobe Lodge to set a day for mourning, and the songs of the watchers would be sung daily for nine days at the dead person's heyimas.

Although anyone might come to the burial ceremony, all these ceremonies were essentially private, observed by the close family and friends of the dead, and by Black Adobe assistants. There was no public mourning for any death until the World Dance at the equinox of spring. As described in the section on that dance, the First Night of the World was a community ceremony of mourning and remembrance for all who had died in that town during the year. The long night ceremony of Burning the Names was a fearfully intense, overcharged excitation and release of emotion. It was dreaded by many of the participants, people trained to value serenity and honor equanimity, and required on this one night to share without shame or reserve the pent-up grief, terror, and anger that death leaves the living to endure. It was a more intensely participatory and abreactive ceremony even than the Moon and the Wine, with all their emotional license and reversals. It expressed as did no other Valley ceremony the emotional and social interdependence of the community, their profound sense of living and dying with one another.

The Fourth Day of the World wakwa, which are intellectually closely connected with mourning rites, are described in the section on the World Dance.

Valley beliefs and theories concerning the soul were of a most amazing complexity, and imperturbably self-contradictory. One might as well try to pin Valley people down to one creation myth as to get a coherent description of the soul out of them. This multiplicity, of course, was in no sense of the word accidental. It was of the essence.

A fairly esoteric approach to the soul is represented in this book by the written piece "The Black Beetle Soul"; an expression of a more popular body of belief or thought is the poem "The Inland Sea." The Valley theory of reincarnation or metempsychosis may be unsystematic, but it is lively.

Specifically connected with funeral and mourning rites was a body of popular theory and superstition concerning various kinds of soul involved in the different stages of the funeral. When the *breath-soul* escapes, at death, other souls are "caught in the death" (the corpse) and must be released. If not released, they may linger around the grave or the places where the dead person lived and worked, causing both mental and material trouble—anxiety, illness, apparitions. The *earth-soul* is released by cremation and ash-burial or burial of the body; the *eye-soul* is set free when the bit of ash or lock of hair is cast into the wind; and finally the *kin-soul* is released only by the casting of the names into the fire at the World Dance ceremony of general mourning.

In the case, not very common in the Valley, of a death abroad or a disappearance, when "there is no death," no body, only the kin-soul can be ritually released. As mentioned, some possessions of the dead person may be brought home and buried in the grave-yard, "so that there's a place in the earth for the souls to come to," and the Going Westward songs may be sung in the heyimas; but a feeling of discomfort and incompletion remains, expressed in the conviction that the other souls will come back to haunt or simply to confirm the lost person's death and take leave of the survivors. The breath-soul is invisible, a voice in the night or twilight in lonely places in the hills. The earth-soul might return as an apparition of the person as they were when they died, or after death, and this ghost is feared by people who hold the belief. The eye-soul is be-nign, sensed only as a presence, yearning or blessing or saying farewell, "going by on the wind's road." Certain Eighth House invo-cations are addressed to this soul, or to all souls who are thought of as sometimes returning to the Valley on the wind.

> O mothers of my mother,
> let this wind bear blessing!

For Kesh who leave the Valley, mostly members of the Finders Lodge, the fear of dying outside the Valley, not being buried in Val-ley ground, is real. The Kesh sense of community, of continuity with the dirt, water, air, and living creatures of the Valley deter-mines them to overcome any ordeals in order to get home to die; the idea of dying and being buried in foreign lands is black despair. There was a story told about a group of Finders exploring down the Outer Coast, who got into a chemically poisoned area; four of the group died. The four survivors mummified their companions' bodies, with the aid of the bone-dry desert climate of the South Coast, and so were able to carry them home for burial—four alive carrying four dead for a month's journey. The feat was spoken of with sympathy, but not with admiration; it was a bit excessive, a bit too heroic, for Valley approbation.

The deaths of animals must be included in any account of Valley funerary practices.

Domestic animals killed for food were addressed before or during the act of killing by any member of the Blood Lodge—any adult or adolescent woman. She said to the animal:

> Your life ends now,
> your death begins.
> Beautiful one,
> give us our need.
> We give you our words.

The formula was gabbled without the least feeling or understanding, often, but it was never omitted, even by a housewife wringing the neck of a chicken. No animal was killed for use unless a woman was present to speak the death-words.

In Wakwaha and Chukulmas, and by some in other towns, a handful of the blood of a slaughtered animal was mixed with red or black earth and made into a little ball, which was kept in the Blood Lodge rooms of the Obsidian heyimas; these balls were used in making adobe bricks for repairs or new constructions.

Whatever parts of a butchered animal, domestic or wild, were not prepared for food or other uses were promptly buried by members of the Tanners Art, usually in a fallow field on the planting side of town. It was customary to set out some bits or bones on a hilltop on the hunting side, "for Coyote and Buzzard," when a big animal was butchered.

Wild animals hunted had each their song, taught by the Hunters Lodge. The hunter sang or talked to the animal he was hunting, silently while the hunt was on, aloud at or after the kill. The songs varied widely from town to town, and there were hundreds of them. Some of the fish invocations are rather curious.

TROUT SONG FROM CHUMO

> A shadow.
> A dry shadow.
> Pay no attention.
> Be praised.

FISHING SONG FROM CHUKULMAS

> Shuyala!
> Come find hands!
> Come find tongue!
> Come find eyelids!
> Come find feet!

DEER HUNTING SONG FROM CHUKULMAS

This way you must come,
delicately walking.
I name you Giver.

A very old deer hunting song from Madidinou is related to the butchers' formula:

Deerness manifests a death.
My word is grateful.

(*Deerness* is the noun *deer* in the Sky Mode.)

BEAR HUNTING SONG FROM TACHAS TOUCHAS

Whana wa, a, a.
The heart is there.
Eat my fear.
Whana wa, a, a, a.
It must be done.
You must come in.
You must be sorry.

Bears were killed only when they posed a threat to livestock or people; the meat was disliked, and not usually brought in to town, though hunters on extended trips might eat bear. "You," in this song, is in the particular form, not the generic. The hunter is not hunting "bearness," any bear, but is after a particular bear, who has made trouble for the hunter, and for bears in general, and who therefore ought to be sorry.

BEAR'S DEATH SONG FROM SINSHAN

Rain darken earth,
blessing falling
from the Sixth House,
heart's blood falling!

The bear was the sign of the Sixth House, the House of Rain and Death. The old man who sang this song said, "Nobody in this town has killed any bear since Grandmother Mountain erupted last. That is a good hunter's song, though. Even when a child hunts a wood rat he ought to sing that song. The bear is there."

According to the theory of the four souls, animals possessed all four kinds, but the system got very vague when extended to plants. All wild birds were considered, essentially, to *be* souls. The kin-soul of an animal was its generic aspect: deerness, not that deer; cowness, not this cow. The apparent confusions and evasions of the Valley idea of reincarnation or transmigration of souls begin to clarify here: this cow that I now kill for food is cowness giving itself to me as food because it has been properly treated and en-treated, and again it will give itself to me as a cow, at my need and entreaty; and I that kill this cow am a name, a word, an instance of humanness and—with the cow—of being in general: a moment in a place: a relationship.

Named domestic animals, pets, were believed by the supersti-tious to return as eye-souls or breath-souls, and sometimes as earth-souls, giving rise to animal ghost stories. A well-known Grey Horse Ghost haunted a canyon in the rough hills behind Chu-kulmas. Earth-souls of ewes who died in lambing were trouble-some in the fog in the fields of Ounmalin.

Ghost stories of a moralistic nature involve hunters who hunted on the "planting side," or who failed in courtesy or respect towards the animal they hunted, or who killed immoderately, with-out need. The latter kind of story, often told at Bay Laurel Lodge campfires, relates how a hunter is terrified, abased, and perhaps hurt or killed by a manifestation of the generic animal, The Deer, The Wild Swan, supernatural in size, beauty, and power. In stories of hunters who omitted the rites of the killer, who "did not speak to the death," a ghost of the particular animal he killed comes to lead the hunter astray in an endless hunt and into madness, accom-panying him constantly, visible to him but to no one else. There was a man spoken of in Chukulmas who was apparently an actual instance of this kind of guilt-haunting. He was not an ordinary "forest-living person" or solitary, but lived without shelter, fled at the sight of human beings, and never spoke. He had been a young man named Young Moon of the Obsidian. What his transgression was, nobody knew for sure, but the assumption in the Hunters Lodge was that he had killed a doe and fawn "without singing," that is without speaking even the essential formula at the death, a brief, worn-down version of the butchers' formula:

Beautiful one,
for your death my words!

This formula was spoken by a hunter shooting, by a trapper opening the trap, by anyone felling a tree, by anyone taking life. That it
could be *forgotten* was not considered a possibility. Young Moon's
omission was deliberate; therefore punishable.

Even when a corn-borer was squashed, a mosquito swatted, a
branch broken, a flower picked, the formula was muttered in its
ultimately reduced form: *arrariṿ* "my word[s]." Although the one-
word formula was spoken as mindlessly as our "bless you" to a
sneeze, it was always spoken. The speaking of it maintained and
contained the idea of need and fulfillment, demand and response,
of relationship and interdependence; and that idea could be
brought fully to mind when it was wanted. The stone, as they said,
contains the mountain.

One- or two-word formulas of this kind were known as pebbles. Another of them was the word *ruha,* spoken when one added
a pebble (a material one) to the cairn or heap at certain places—by
certain boulders, at crossroads, at various places along the paths on
Ama Kulkun. The word was without other meaning to most people
than "the word you say when you add a stone to a heya cairn."
Scholars of the heyimas knew it to be an archaic form of the root
-hur-, to sustain, carry along, take with one. It was the last word of a
lost sentence. The present stone contains the absent mountain.
Most of the "meaningless" matrix-syllables of songs were pebble-
words. The word *heya* was the word that contained the world, visible and invisible, on this side and on the other side of death.

Pandora Sitting by the Creek

THE CREEK OF Sinshan below big rocks makes a pool on gravel, shallow, the gravel rising into an island in the middle of the pool. The banks of dark adobe overhang it, a few feet apart. At the outlet of the pool the rib-bone of a steer lies half in the water, whitish. In the still water deep under the undercut bank where roots make tracery, the tail feathers of a dead bird lie moving slightly on the water. The curled claw can be seen under the brown-feathered corpse hanging in the clear water in the brown shadow. Half the branches that cross the creek are dead and half alive and some it's hard to say. There are no fish in the water but there are waterskaters on it and many gnats, flies, and mosquitoes in the air. Above the floating dead bird gnats or small flies dance in a swarm. The people are dancing the Summer.

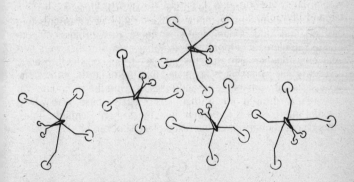

FOUR ROMANTIC TALES

THE ROMANTIC TALE was a popular genre. The stories were written or printed, often existing in several editions and collections. The favorite collection, from which these four stories come, was called *Under the Vine Leaves,* and there were copies of it in every town of the Valley. Oral versions of these stories were secondary; they were retold aloud sometimes around the hearth or at the summerhouse, but the primary or "authentic" version of the Romantic Tale was the written one.

Some of the stories appeared to be genuinely old, others to seek stylistically to achieve an impression of age, or of timelessness. No name of an author was included in the collections or on the manuscripts. Although place detail was vivid and exact, as in all Valley literature, the time when the story was supposed to have occurred or been written down was usually left unclear.

The common theme of the Romantic Tales was transgression. Millers and Finders often figured in them; their professions contained an element of moral risk, in Valley eyes, and they were perceived as dangerously attractive people—people on the threshold.

In "The Miller," it is not stated that the miller is of the same House as the woman, but he addresses her with the second person singular form used only to members of one's House, with whom sexual intercourse is forbidden. Like most of the Romantic Tales, this is a cautionary or counterexemplary shocker.

The Miller

The miller of the mill at Chamawats on the River said to a Red Adobe woman who came with corn to be ground into meal, "Wait here outside the mill. Do not come inside."

The woman had come alone from town. It was raining, the wind was blowing cold, and she had no coat or shawl. She said, "Let me just stand inside the doorway while I wait."

The miller said, "Very well. Wait in the doorway, but come no farther in, and keep your back turned to the room and your face turned to the outdoors."

She stood in the doorway of the miller's house, and he took the sack of corn into the house of the wheel. She waited. The cold wind blew in the door. A fire was burning in the hearth in the room behind her. She thought, "What harm can it do if I go in there?"

Presently she came into the room, close to the fire; but she came backwards, with her face turned to the outdoors. She stood there with her back to the fire.

The miller came in through the house, behind her. He said, "I have been milling all day; the stone is too hot, and I cannot grind your corn now. Come back for it tomorrow."

The woman did not want to go and come back in the wind and rain. She said, "I will wait till the stone cools."

The miller said, "Very well. Wait in this room, but do not come into the other room, and keep your face turned to the outdoors."

He went back to the wheelhouse. For a long time the woman waited in the hearthroom, and heard nothing but the river running and the rain falling and the millwheel turning. She thought, "What harm can it do if I go into the other room?"

Presently she went into the inner room to see what was there. There was nothing in that room but the bedding rolled up and beside it a book. She took the book and opened it. On the page she opened it to, there was nothing written but one word: her name.

She was frightened, seeing that. She put the book down and went to the hearthroom to leave the house; but the miller was standing in the doorway. She ran back into the inner room. He followed her, and said, "Unroll the bedding."

She unrolled the bedding and laid it out. She was afraid of him, although he did not hurt her. He told her to lie down on the bed, and she lay down. He lay down with her. When that was done he stood up naked and gave her the book, saying, "This is yours." She took it and turned the pages. On each page of the book her name was written and no other word.

The miller had gone out of the room. She heard the millwheel turning. She fastened her clothing and ran out of the house. She looked back and saw the high millwheel turning in the rain. The water that ran from the blades of the wheel was red.

She ran into the town crying out. People came to Chamawats, to the mill. They found the miller. He had leaped into the millrace, and the wheel had taken him up and crushed him down. It was still turning. After that the mill was burned and the millstones broken. There is no place now called Chamawats.

Lost

She lived a long time ago in the First House, they say. Her mother's household was in a house called The Red Balconies that used to be in Chukulmas, not far from the Hinge of the town. She joined the Finders Lodge as soon as her middle name, Withy, came to her, and right away she asked to come on a journey they were going to make over to Green Sands on the Inland Coast. People in the lodge said, "You haven't had enough education yet. People in this lodge go on short trips first, and on long ones after they've had some education." She did not listen, but pleaded to come. They said, "You give us no good reason for changing the way we usually do." On a morning of early summer a group of the Finders started off for Green Sands. They took no novices along, because they wanted to travel fast and cover a good deal of territory.

In the evening of that day Withy was missed in her household. The people of Red Balconies began to look for her, after nightfall, and to ask about her. A young man who was a novice in the Finders Lodge said, "Maybe she followed them this morning." Her family said, "Is she crazy, then, to do something like that?" But in the morning, when she had not come home, they said, "Maybe she did follow them."

Some people in her family and her House decided to go that way to look for her. An old man of the Finders Lodge went with them to show them the way the group would have taken to Green Sands. The young man was of her House, and he came along. When they started climbing up into the hills above Redgrass Creek in the northeast range he got impatient, thinking that the old man was leading them too slowly. He had been in those hills; he said, "I know the way. I'll look on ahead." The old Finder said, "Stay with the group." But he did not listen. He kept getting farther and farther ahead of the others.

Withy had followed the people going to Green Sands, starting an hour or two behind them. She followed the way they went up Antelope Mountain. Where they had turned down Garnet Creek to use the low pass south of Gogmes, she missed the track and went left, on up the mountain, following the trail they had not taken.

She thought that if she caught up with them in the Valley or in the near hills they would be angry with her and send her back; but if she did not catch up with them till they were clear outside the Valley, though they would be angrier, they would have to take her along with them to the shores of the Inland Sea, and so she would get the journey she wanted. So she followed the trail up Antelope Mountain and over onto Five Fires Mountain, not going very fast, and when night came she slept by the trail. In the morning she went up to the high pass on Five Fires Mountain, and stood there. Behind her the rivers ran to the River; before her they did not. She thought, "Maybe I should go back now."

As she stood there she thought she heard voices ahead of her, far down the pass, and thought, "I have nearly caught up with them already. All I have to do is follow them." She waited awhile and then went on across the pass.

Presently the trail divided. She took the east fork. After she had walked a long way down, that trail divided. This time she took the northwest fork, telling herself that she saw the tracks of her people on the trail. She followed one trail and then another, following the tracks of the deer round and about in the chaparral and the hillsides of chamise. She began to understand what she was doing, and tried to go back. Everywhere she looked there were paths and trails, and on them the tracks of people, going uphill and downhill, southeast and northwest. Wherever she looked, she thought the people she was following had gone that way. Instead of going back up to the pass or the ridge so that the land could lead her back into the Valley, she followed the deer up onto Iyo Mountain, going on and on, not knowing where.

The young man, Jade, had learned to follow tracks in the Bay Laurel and the Finders Lodge, and when he came to Garnet Creek he looked at the paths and decided that the Green Sands group had gone down the creek, but that she had gone on up the mountain. When the other Obsidian people and the old Finder came there, they saw the tracks going down the creek, and followed them.

Jade kept on the Five Fires Mountain path as long as it was clear and without forks, over the pass. At the first fork he took the north fork. . . . [There follows a detailed passage of the paths Jade took and the regions he searched, which would lend credibility to the story for a Valley reader, but is tedious to the ignorant foreigner.] Late on the second morning of his search, on the far side of Echcheha Ridge, he saw where she had left pits of dried apricots and plums by the path. Soon after that, he heard a noise far down in the canyon, a big animal moving, and he called her name. The noise stopped, but there was no reply.

At sunset he came out into Huringa Valley. He did not know anything about the Huringa people, and so he tried to keep away from their paths and houses. Where the ground was clear there in the valley he saw a person running up a big hillside towards the trees, but he could not see clearly in the twilight, and did not dare call out. On the far side of that valley he got into thick underbrush and had to lie down and sleep away the dark. In the morning he wanted to go home, for he had brought no food with him and had eaten nothing for two days; but he saw some good mushrooms, and while he was eating them he heard noises like a person forcing through brush across the top of that ridge, and he began to follow again, going over the ridge on deer trails.

Now they were in the wild country between Huringa and the Inland Sea. Now they were both lost.

She thought she was going back towards the Valley of the Na, but she was going north, then northeast, then east, then north again. He kept following her, because now he could hear her talking sometimes, far ahead; but when he called she did not answer. She had gone wild. She would hide in the underbrush for a while, and then go on quietly.

On the evening of the fourth day he was passing two big bluestone boulders in the open place at the top of a ridge, and thought, "That would be a good place to sleep." He went to the rocks and saw that Withy was lying asleep between them.

He sat down nearby and kept talking softly, saying Obsidian heya, so that she would not be afraid when she woke up.

She woke and sat up between the boulders. He was sitting

against one of them. They were under the evening star. She said, "You've come for me!"

He said, "Yes. I've been following you."

She kept looking at him from the side of her eyes; she tried to get away from him, running away, but she stumbled, and he caught her. She kept saying, "Oh please, don't kill me, oh please, don't hurt me!"

He said, "Don't you know me? I'm your brother Jade, from Carved Branch House." She did not listen. She thought he was a bear. When he spoke, she thought he was the Bear Man, and began to cry and beg him for food.

He said, "I haven't got any food," but as he spoke he saw that a tree growing up from between the boulders was a cherry, and its fruit was ripe. They gathered cherries and they both ate. They ate till they were drunk with eating after fasting. They lay down together between the boulders. It seemed to them that the boulders pressed them together. They lay there together until she woke under the morning star. She looked at him and saw that it was not the Bear Man but her brother. She got up and ran away, leaving him asleep between the rocks.

It was a rocky ridge, with deer trails going through the open chaparral and wild lilac. She went without going anywhere, walking and running. She came around a big stack of brown rocks and came face to face with a bear. She said to the bear, "You've come for me!" She put her arms around the bear and pressed herself to it. The bear was frightened and tore at her face with his claws to get free, and ran away.

When Jade woke up and found Withy not there, he was frightened at what they had done. He did not call to her or wait for her or try to follow her, but set off down the ridge westward. He did not know where he was, but he got to a place where he could see Ama Kulkun, and guided himself by that, and after two more days he came down Chumo Creek to Chumo, and across the Valley to Chukulmas.

He said to the people there, "I did not find Withy. She must be lost." He said he had gone east of Huringa and north of Totsam and had found no trace of her. The Obsidian people who had gone looking for her had come back two days earlier. They had not been able to catch up with the people going to Green Sands. For a month, then, her people waited for them to come back from Green Sands. When they came back without her, knowing nothing of her, her mother said the Going Westward to the Sunrise songs should be sung for her; but her father said, "I do not think she is dead. Wait awhile." So they waited. The Finders went to Huringa and Totsam and through that wild country, asking the Pig People and other people who hunted there if they would watch for the lost girl, but there was no word of her.

In late autumn near the time of the Grass, when the Lodge Rejoining had been built, in the rain in the evening a person came into Chukulmas, walking between the houses. It was like a dried corpse, naked and dark, with hair behind but skull in front, and half a face. It walked to the Obsidian heyimas and climbed the roof and called down the entrance, "Bear! Come out!"

They all came out of the heyimas. Jade was with them. When he saw the half-faced girl he began to scream, and fell down screaming. Someone said, "That is Withy!" People ran to bring her family from the lodge Rejoining, where they had been singing for her, and they took her home to Red Balconies.

At first she was crazy, but after a month at home Withy could speak and behave responsibly. She said she did not remember what had happened, but once she said, "When Jade found me." They asked what she meant and she did not answer. But Jade heard of this, and he went to the heyimas and talked to people there, telling them a true account. Then he left Chukulmas and went up on the Mountain to the Springs, and then went to live in the Lower Valley. He lived outside of Tachas Touchas as a forest-living person. He did not dance, and did not enter his heyimas. At the time of the Moon dancing he always went up into the southwest ranges. One time he did not come back. Withy lived in Chukulmas until she was old. She wore a mask outside the house to hide her face from children.

NOTE: Although the story is a typical cautionary tale, there is some evidence for its having actually happened; the circumstantial details are unusually precise, and people in the Obsidian of Chukulmas identified themselves as descendants of the families of Withy and Jade.

The Brave Man

There was a man who was exceptionally brave, a man who went to meet danger. When he was a young boy living in Kastoha-na he went with another child to pick blackberries, and the child with him, going ahead, met a rattlesnake under his hand and was paralysed with fear. This boy, without tool or weapon, darted out his hand and picked up the snake behind its head so that it could not turn to bite him, and whirled it and flung it far across the thickets.

When he was still wearing undyed clothing, the wild pigs came down from the northeast countries in vast herds and were eating all the gathering acorns and making the woods and hills very dangerous for human people to go in. The young man would go out alone to hunt the wild pigs, without dogs, and with a bow not a gun. He killed a great many, so many that people had to help him bring back the hides for pigskin leather. When he was in the Bay Laurel Lodge he climbed the Palisades, climbing even the Overhang without a rope; he spent a season with the Falares people, sailing small boats on the deep sea.

He became a member of the Finders Lodge and roamed far and wide among many places and peoples, across the Inland Sea and across the Range of Light. He spent three years on the shores of the Omorn Sea, having sailed across the Rift or Straits to the desert countries and the great canyons and mountains of the Range of Heaven. In desolate places where those with him were troubled and ill at ease he had no worry and no fear. He laid his head down on the stone under which lay the scorpion, and both slept. He went willingly and alone into the poisoned regions, and because he was not confused by anxiety nor forced to hurry by fear, he did no harm to himself or others, but by following maps and guides given by the Exchange and by his own accurate and intrepid exploration he reached deposits of tin, copper, and other valuable substances. His name became Bell, because the expeditions he went on brought back so much metal that the Smith Art was able to make bronze in quantity, and cast bells of it for sheep, cattle, and musicians. Bells cast of bronze are the sweetest and most complex in tone, and so they called him by that name, a giftname.

After several great journeys he was ready to settle down for a while, and presently he married a Fifth-House woman, he himself being of the Fourth House. They lived together in her household in contentment, he studying with the Finders and at the Exchange in Wakwaha and she a master vintner of the Wine Art, until she became pregnant and the pregnancy went badly. She miscarried in the sixth month, and after the miscarriage did not recover. She bled and wasted, and ate and slept very little. Doctors found no cause for surgery and no remedies gave relief. A bringing-in was held but she could not sing. One day Bell came into the house and found her lying alone weak and weeping. She said, "Bell, I am going to die."

He said, "No, that isn't so. You won't die."

She said, "I am afraid."

He said, "Fear is no use. There's nothing to fear."

"Is death nothing to fear?" she asked him.

"Death is nothing to fear," he said.

She turned away from him and wept in silence.

Another day, soon after, he came and she was very weak; she could not lift her hand.

He said, "Listen, my wife: if you're afraid to die, I'll do it for you."

That made her smile. She said, "Brave fool!"

He said, "I will die for you, my wife."

"No one can do that," she said.

"With your consent I can do it," he said.

She thought that he still did not understand that she was dying. He seemed like a child to her. She said, "You have my consent."

He stood up from the bedside. He stretched himself so that he stood with his legs and arms extended and his face turned upward. Then he called upward aloud: "Come, Mother! Come, Father! Come from that House, come here to me from that falling House!"

He looked down at his wife then and said, "Please don't call me any longer by the name I was called; with your consent I have given it away. All the name I have now is Bear."

Then he spread out the bedding in the corner and lay down in that room.

That night it began raining. A great storm came out of the northwest with lightning striking in forest and town and thunder crashing from range to range and rain coming down with no air between the raindrops. Birds were beaten from their nests and ground squirrels drowned in their burrows, that night.

Each time the thunder sounded the man who said his name was Bear would cry out. Each time the lightning flashed he would hide his face, moaning. His wife was so worried about his behavior that she asked her sister to help her move her bedding beside his, and she took his hand, but she could not make him be calm. She sent her sister to bring his mother from her household. She came and she too asked him, "What is it, Bell? What is wrong with you?"

He did not answer any of them, but lay trembling and hiding. At last his wife remembered that he had said to call him Bear. She said, "Bear! Why do you act like this?"

Then he said, "I am afraid."

"What are you afraid of?"

"I have to die."

His mother said to the wife, "Why does he say that?"

She said, "He said he would die for me. I consented."

The mother and the sister said, "No one can do that."

The wife said to him, "Listen. I do not consent! If I gave consent I take it back!"

But he did not hear her. The thunder crashed and the rain roared on the roof and windows.

It rained all the night, and the next day, the next night and the day after that. The floor of the Valley was flooded, and there was standing water from Ounmalin to Kastoha-na.

The man who said his name was Bear lay while it rained, shivering and hiding, not eating and not sleeping. His wife stayed with him, trying to care for him, trying to make him be calm. People came from the Doctors Lodge, but he would not speak to them nor hear them sing; he covered his ears, moaning.

People began saying in town, "That brave man is dying for his wife, taking her place dying." So it seemed to be happening; but no one knew if it could be done, or if it was something that ought to be done.

People came from the Madrone Lodge and sat with the wife at the man's side. They talked to him, saying, "Listen. You are going too far. You should have been afraid to do this."

He wept aloud. He said, "It's too late now. Now I am afraid!"

They said, "You can come back."

Again he wept and said, "I never knew the bear. Now I am the bear."

It stopped raining at last, and the waters returned into the River and the weather went on in the usual way. But the man never got up, but lay trembling, and did not eat. His bowels gave way, and he began to bleed from the anus and to be in pain. He cried out and screamed. He was so strong and sound a man that it took him a long time to die. After fourteen days he could not speak any more, and four days after that they began singing the Going Westward to the Sunrise songs in his room, but still he lived nine days, blind and moaning, before he died entirely.

After his death the wife tried to change her name, calling herself Coward, but most people would not call her that. She regained fair health and lived to be an old woman. Each year at the Ceremony of Mourning at the World Dance she threw his names on the fire, his first names and the name Bell and last the name Bear; and though names are burnt only once, no one prevented her from this, because of the name, and because of what he had done to her. So it went on a long time, and so the story got remembered for a long time, even now, long after she too died.

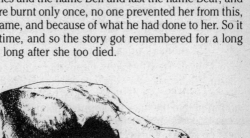

At the Springs of Orlu

She had been wearing the undyed clothing for five years. Her name was Adsevin. She left her house in Chukulmas to bring water from the springs of Orlu for the Water Dance.

She had been up to those springs with people of her heyimas, but not alone before. When she came across the ridge at the head of

the canyon she listened for the sound of water running. The scrub
oak and thornbush had grown thick and there was no human path.
She crouched down and followed deer paths, and came out on a big
boulder of red rock that stuck out from the wall of the canyon like a
porch. From there she looked down to the spring. She saw a deer
drinking, and saw a man drinking. He was crouched down drinking from the surface of the water where it welled over the lip of the
spring. He wore no clothing and his hair and skin were the color of
a deer. He had not seen or heard her come out onto the rock. After
he had drunk his fill he raised his head and spoke to the spring.
She saw his lips make the *heya wakwana* though she did not hear
his voice. He looked up then and saw the girl on the rock in the
canyon wall. They looked at each other across the spring, across
the air. The man's eyes were the eyes of deer. He did not speak, nor
did Adsevin. He looked down, moved back from the spring, turned,
and went into the thick underbrush along the bank of Orlu Creek.
The big alders growing there hid him from sight at once. She could
hear no sound of his going.

She sat a long time on the boulder ledge watching the spring
run. In the heat of late summer no bird spoke. She went down to
the spring and sang to it, took up water in the blue clay jar, slung
the jar in the carrier, and went back as she had come, scrambling
up the steep canyon wall. When she was on the big rock above the
spring she turned back and spoke: "We are dancing the Water in
Chukulmas tomorrow." Then she went on up the deer trails and
across the ridge.

When she had brought the water of Orlu to the heyimas for the
wakwa the next day, she went home to her hearth in Cat's Whiskers House. There she asked her grandmother's brother, a woman-
living man, a teacher of the Blue Clay, "Did I see a person from the
Second House or from the Eighth House, at Orlu Springs?"

He asked, "How did this person look?"

"Like a deer, like a man."

Her uncle said, "Well, maybe you saw a Sky person. This is a
sacred time and you were doing a sacred thing. How did this person speak?"

"He spoke to the water after he drank."

"Did he speak to you?"

"No. I spoke to him. I said that we are dancing the Water."

"Maybe this person will come to the dancing," her uncle said.

Adsevin looked towards the hunting side, towards the paths
from the north, all the time of the dancing in the dancing place, the
next day; but she did not see the man from Orlu Springs.

He had come, but he was afraid to come into the town, into the dancing place. It was too long since he had been with human people. He did not know how to come among them. Afraid, he hid under the creek bank and watched the dancing. Dogs came barking and snarling at him, and he fled away, running up the streambed into the hills.

After the dance the heat became still greater and nothing moved all afternoon at Chukulmas except the buzzards over Buzzard Hill. On such a day Adsevin went back up the canyons and ridges to the springs of Orlu. She found the deer trails that led down to the big rock, and came there. The spring had ceased to run. No one was there. On the rock were four green acorns of the live oak. A squirrel or another person might have put them there. Adsevin took them, and put in their place what she had brought with her: a stick of olive wood carved in a spiral and polished smooth as a hehole-no. Not speaking loudly or looking down into the canyon, she said, "I will be going on the Salt Journey. After that I will come back." She went on home then to Chukulmas.

After the Salt Journey, before the Wine, she came to the rock in Orlu Canyon. The hehole-no was gone; nothing was there. Whatever was there, the squirrels, the jays, or the wood rats might have moved it or taken it. She found an obsidian chip in the dirt of the canyon wall and with it made the Blue Clay mark, scratching it into the skin of the red boulder. When she was done she stood up and said, "They will be dancing the Wine in our town soon."

The man who had lost his name was listening, down in the canyon, under the dry creek bank. He was always listening.

When Adsevin went home that evening, her uncle said to her, "Listen, Adsevin. I have been talking with some hunters who go up the canyons there above the petrified forest and over the Hawk Ridge. They know of this deer-man. He left Forty-Five Redwoods House here a long time ago to live in the forest. He used to be a Serpentine man, but he has gone outside the Houses, they say. He got lost. Lost people are dangerous; they do things without meaning. Probably it would be better if you didn't go back to Orlu Canyon. You may be frightening him, going there."

She said, "Do the hunters know where he lives in the hills?"

"He has no house at all," her uncle said.

Adsevin had no wish to worry her uncle, but she had no fear of the man in Orlu Canyon, and did not understand how it might be that she would frighten him; so she waited till her uncle was busy with the harvest, and went back on the northward paths.

It had not yet rained, but the trees were releasing their water held in trunk and root, and the spring had some water in it lying deep among the rocks. The dirt around the spring was muddy and deer-trampled. In the skin of the red boulder there was a mark cut beside the Blue Clay sign she had made. It was the coyote-eye of the Eighth House. Seeing it, she said, "Heya, heya, Coyote! So you are here, Dweller in the Wild House! This gift is for anybody in that House who might like it." She set down what she had brought, some grapeleaves stuffed with soaked barley, raisins, and coriander, and then went away as she had come.

When she and her uncle were together after work, a while later, she said, "Mataikebi! [maternal-uncle-woman-dear] The man says that he lives in the House of the Wilderness. I don't think you need to be afraid of him or for me if I go there."

"What if I went there and smelled the air?" her uncle said.

Adsevin said, "The doors of that House do not close."

So her uncle went to Orlu Canyon. He saw the marks on the boulder, and beside them he saw a hematite rock from the streambed, polished red, beautiful. He did not pick it up. He sat a long time on that rock shelf, thinking and listening. He did not see the lost man or hear him, but he thought he was there, near the alders across the spring. He sang heya wakwana and went back to Chukulmas. He said to his niece, "I think the air there is good. The creek is beginning to run now. A rock from the creek is there."

When Adsevin went back, she took the rock, and left a string bag she had woven. She said, "They will be dancing the Grass soon in our town. All the people of the Wilderness are welcome in that dancing."

She saw him watching her then, listening to her. He was behind a six-trunked madrone across the canyon, and she could see his shoulder, his hair and his eyes. He crouched down when he thought that she had seen him. She looked away, and turned away, and went back up the ridge.

So from wakwa to wakwa, from season to season, she would go back to the springs of Orlu with some small gift. She would speak, telling the lost man about the dancing in Chukulmas, and she would take his gift if he had put one there on the red rock, and sometimes she saw him. Always he saw her.

When an old woman of the Serpentine who lived in Forty-Five Redwoods House was dying, Adsevin went to Orlu and spoke of that, thinking that the woman might have been kin to the lost man, and that he might want to sing the Going Westward songs for her, if he had not forgotten them.

On the First Day of a World Dance she came in the heavy rain to Orlu Canyon. The creek was roaring and foaming yellow in spate, and the birds of the canyon were sheltering and crouching in every shrub and tree. It was hard to get down the canyon wall to the red rock, as the mud slipped away underfoot. In the noise of the rain falling and the creek beating its rocks against each other, she said, "We are dancing the World in our town, as people are dancing it in the Wilderness. Tomorrow is the Wedding Night. A man of the First House and I will be married then."

In the noise of the rain she did not know if he was there or if he could hear her voice.

That year Adsevin did not want to dance the Moon, being newly married. She and her husband came away from town, up into the hills, and made a summerhouse of nine poles on the ridge above Sholyo Canyon. One day she went over to Orlu from there. She came over the ridge in a clear place where a digger pine had fallen, and looked down the canyonhead to the spring and the red rock above it. She saw the lost man sleeping on the rock. He lay face down with his cheek on the carved marks in the rock. She stood still a long time and went away without waking him.

When she came back to the summerhouse the young husband asked her, "Where did you go?"

"To the springs of Orlu," she said.

He had heard talk in the Bay Laurel Lodge about the forest-living man who had gone wild and was seen in Orlu Canyon. He said, "Never go there."

"Yes," she said, "I will go there."

"Why?" he said.

She said, "Ask my uncle why I go to Orlu. He can tell you, maybe. I cannot."

The young man said, "If you go there again, I will go with you."

She said, "Please let me go alone. There is nothing to fear."

After that her husband was uneasy living there far up in the hills. He said, "Let's move down to your family's summer place," and she agreed. While they were there, at White Ash Banks, the husband talked to Adsevin's uncle, and to some hunters who often went up in the canyons. He did not like what they told him about the lost man; they said that when they went to Orlu he was always there near the spring. But the uncle said, "I think it is all right."

Adsevin went down to Chukulmas to dance the Water; it was she who brought the water from the spring at Orlu. And after that she would go back alone to Orlu, before the great festivals. Sometimes she took food. Her husband watched this and said nothing, telling himself what the uncle had told him.

A boy made Adsevin and her husband his parents, along about the time of the Water; and after he had been living a few months, in the time of the new grass, Adsevin took him in the carrier and set off on the northern paths. She had said nothing to her husband. He saw her go with the baby and was alarmed and angry. He followed her at a distance up into the hills, up the canyons, across the high ridge to Orlu. On the ridgeback he lost her trail; there was no trail. He could not see where she had gone, and there was no sound of her going. He was afraid to make noise looking for her and stood still, listening.

He heard her voice below him, down in the canyon over the creekbed. She said, "This is my son. I have named him Following Coyote." Then she said nothing for a while. Then he heard her voice again, "Have you gone away, Coyote?" Then for a while she was silent, and then her voice cried out loudly without words.

The young man sprang forward pushing and tearing through the brush to the edge of the canyon and down the canyon wall to the place where he had heard her voice. She was sitting on the red rock ledge with the baby in her arms, weeping. As he came there the husband smelled death. When he stood by her, she pointed down towards the spring. The lost man had died lying under the big alders across the creek just below the spring. He was already part earth.

POEMS

SECOND SECTION

 THE POEMS IN this group are spoken or written offerings to the author's heyimas or lodge.

The Kesh idea of property was so different from ours that any mention of it entails explanations. What one made, or gained, or owned, in the Valley, belonged to one; but one belonged to one's House, and house, and town, and people. Wealth consisted not in *things* but in an *act:* the act of giving.

Poets owned the poems they made, but the poem really did not exist until it was given, shared, performed. The identity of owning and giving is perhaps easier to see when what is involved is a poem, or a drawing, or a piece of music, or a prayer. The Kesh, however, saw it as holding equally true for all property.

THE BLUE ROCK'S SONG

From the Serpentine Wakwaha; unsigned.

I am coherent, mysterious, and solid.
I sit on dirt in sunlight between the live oaks.
Once I was a sun, again I will be dark.
Now I am between those great things for a while
along with other people, here in the Valley.

A MEDITATION IN THE EIGHTH HOUSE
IN EARLY SPRING

By Ire of Sinshan.

Thin bluish clouds move northeastwards
high up and slowly. Help this soul,
southwest wind of the rainy season,
help this soul be healed.

Under bark of the fallen pine
worms have carved fine mazes,
delicate circuitous houses.
Maze-makers, help this soul die.

Veins stand netted on the bluish boulder
where rain wore the soft rock down.
Blown rain of many winters,
help this soul turn round.

Shadows of dead branches,
sunlight and dying things,
O wilderness, one bird sings
one note far off in the sunny wind.

Rock was softer than the rain,
tree weaker than the worm. No help for it.
So soul be weak, fail, drift, and blow
with wind through net and maze, and sing
one note once only in the wilderness.

Hehóle-nó

DYING

*An unsigned personal offering to the Red Adobe heyimas
in Madidinou. The form is called "Fours and Echo."*

Only one dying,
you can't have it,
I can't have it,
we all die it,
      share it.
You die, I do;
I die, you do.
You can't save me,
I can't save you.
Only one crying,
we all cry it,
      bear it.

ASCENSION

*Given to the Black Adobe Lodge of Wakwaha
by the author, Agate.*

Sometimes a bubble rises, a foam-soul,
and drifts on the mental wind
up the River, up the Valley,
to the Mountain, to be born to die.
    From the southeast the wind is blowing.
In male and mortal flesh the soul
hollow and rising struggles, cries,
bone-home its prison, captive
seeking escape, deliverance, to go free.
    The wind keeps blowing from the east and south.
Mothers of the doorway, fathers of the vines,
let the son go, the foamborn,
the warrior, the voyager, the exile,
or he will burn house and vineyard.
    The east wind carries the smell of fire.
He is destruction, the thrice-born,
ashes in running water. The black field
lies behind him. Let him go,
let him go up the Mountain for his desire.
    Sparks rise up on the south wind and go out.

IT WAS NEVER REALLY DIFFERENT

Given to the Red Adobe of Wakwaha
by Ninepoint of Chumo.

It was never really different.
Maybe it needed more arranging.
Maybe the beginning
was when more things were needed.
Before the beginning, however,
who knows but what some woman
swatted a fly grown from a maggot
in a mouse spleen some fox left
by the creek, under the bushes?
How can you say she didn't?
How can you say she won't?
Because of waves,
is the sea different?
When I hit the drum like this,
I think the sound
was there before the beginning,
and everything has gone to make that sound,
and after it
everything is different.

Tongue Drum

THE SUN GOING SOUTH

*An offering to the Red Adobe heyimas of Chukulmas
by Settled. The syllabic meter is "nines," often used
for elegy and meditations on mortality.*

In late sunshine I wander troubled.
Restless I walk in autumn sunlight.
Too many changes, partings, and deaths.
Doors have closed that were always open.
Trees that held the sky up are cut down.
So much that I alone remember!
This creek runs dry among its stones.
Souls of the dead, come drink this water!
Come into this side valley with me,
a restless old woman, unseemly,
troubled, walking on dry grass, dry stones.

BEFORE THE MOON

Given to the Obsidian of Chumo by Catfish.

Under the ground,
under the moon,
the wind is blowing,
shadows are moving
over the ground,
shadows of eucalyptus.
Leaves are blowing
under the eucalyptus,
wind moving shadows
over the ground,
before the moon.

MOTHS AND BUTTERLFIES

"An old poem," spoken by Ram of Madidinou,
in the Madrone Lodge.

Butterfly, coming out of mystery,
goes into it.
Serious dancer!
The soul imitates you.
You live in all the Houses,
alighting briefly.
Moth, coming out of mystery,
goes into it.
Shape changer!
You teach the bear.

FOUR/FIVES

"Old poems," spoken by Kemel of Ounmalin,
in the Madrone Lodge.

Our souls are old,
often used before.
The knife outlasts
the hand that holds it.

Hills turn valleys:
still the spring rises.

As I grow old
my soul gets younger.
I go seaward:
it travels upstream.

Listen, river:
I am not my soul!

DRY TIME INVOCATION

"I made this song to sing when the dry season goes on too long and there are forest fires, or when the mind desires rain."

—Doe, of the Blue Clay of Wakwana.

The winds are empty, the north wind, the east wind.
The sky is empty.
What we look for,
what we hope for,
they are under the sea-waves.
The shining unsleeping strangers!
The people of the deep waters!
May they be released,
let them return to the south wind,
let them return to the west wind,
let them come to the Valley,
the cloud people, the rainclouds,
send them, O sea, release them,
as the hills send down the creeks,
as the River descends to you,
as our singing descends to you,
as we dance down to you,
releasing, returning the waters,
the turning of river and rainfall,
the sea to the source returning.

OLD WOMAN SINGS

By Flowering of Sinshan, given to her heyimas.
The meter is "fours."

I was a plum.
I have become
a prune, a prune,
dried on the seed.
Eat me, eat me!
Spit out the seed!
It will become
a tree, a tree,
blossoming plum.

UNDER KAIBI

Written by Ire to accompany a wall painting
in the Blue Clay heyimas of Sinshan.

How the water winds slowly, slowly
in the mudflats, in the fog,
on the low dim levels.
A sound of long wings,
but I cannot see the heron.

QUAIL RISING IN BRUSH

By Kulkunna of Chukulmas, given to the
Blue Clay heyimas.

Whirring, whirring you manifest
many-quailness, earthcovey
uprising startled not far,
wingthunder in chaparral.

Not to eye manifest, under
seeing, reasoning, far under,
only to ear and inwardness, sudden
whirring-earth-feathered splendor.

THIS STONE

From the Serpentine heyimas of Telina-na; by Wordriver.

He went looking for a road
that doesn't lead to death.
He went looking for that road
and found it.
        It was a stone road.
He walked that road
that doesn't lead to death.
He walked on it awhile
before he stopped,
        having turned to stone.
Now he stands there on that road
that doesn't lead to death
not going anywhere.
He can't dance.
        From his eyes stones fall.
The rainbow people pass him
crossing that road, long-legged, light-stepping,
going from the Four Houses
to the dancing in the Five Houses.
        They pick up his tears.
This stone is a tear
from his eye, this stone
given me on the mountain
by one who died before my birth,
this stone, this stone.

FOUR HISTORIES

Old Women Hating

Told aloud by Thorn of High Porch House in Sinshan.

Where High Porch House stands now in Sinshan, a long time ago there was a house called After the Earthquake House. It had stood there a long time, too long. The stone thresholds and the floor tiles were worn hollow. Doors hung crooked in their frames. Boards had come loose. The walls were full of mice and the space under the roof was stuffed full of birds' nests and wasps' nests and bat dung. The house was so old nobody remembered what family built it to start with. Nobody wanted to repair it and keep it clean. It was a house like an old, old dog who doesn't care for anybody and nobody cares for it, and it lives dirty and silent, scratching its fleas. The people in Sinshan then must have been careless, to let that house get so old and dirty; it would have been better to take it down, take it apart and use the good boards and stones, unbuild it and build a new house. But sometimes people don't do what's better, or what's good. Things get going along and they are as they are and who's going to change them? It's the wheel gets turning. It's hard to be mindful of everything. And it's hard to interfere in what your neighbors do, too.

Well, there were two households in that old After the Earthquake House: one Red Adobe and one Obsidian. Each household had a grandmother. Those two women had lived there all their lives hating each other. They didn't get on. They wouldn't speak to each other. How did it begin? What did they want? I don't know. Nobody who told the story knew. Hating gets going, it goes round, it gets older and tighter and older and tighter, until it holds a person inside it like a fist holds a stick. So there they were, the Red Adobe woman on the first floor under the roof, and the Obsidian woman on the second floor over the cellars, hating each other. The Adobe woman would say, "Smell the stink of that cooking coming up here! Tell that person to quit stinking the house!" And her son-

126

in-law would go downstairs, and say that to the Obsidian old woman. She would say nothing to him, but say to her son-in-law, "What is that noise? A dog yapping somewhere? A toilet running? There are unpleasant noises in this house. People walking upstairs, stupid people talking and talking. Tell them to stop making so much noise."

In the Adobe household there were two daughters, and one of them had two daughters, all married, so there were four sons-in-law, and some younger children, a big household, living in all those old, dirty rooms under the roof. They didn't mend the roof. When it leaked they made a hole in the floor by the wall and let the water drip down on the people underneath. The Adobe old woman said, "Water always goes downhill." Down there the Obsidian grandmother lived with her two daughters; one of them didn't marry, the other had a husband and one daughter. So they weren't very many people in that household, and they were ungenerous, silent and keeping to themselves, not dancing at the festivals. Nobody else ever went into their rooms, and people said, "They must hoard, in that household. They must have things, they must be keeping things in there."

Other people said something like, "What makes you say that? They never make anything. There's a couple of sheep that go with the town flock, the cow died, they farm a little land down by Rattlesnake Clearing but they don't grow anything but corn, they don't gather anything but mushrooms, they never make anything to give, their clothes are old, their pots and baskets are old and dirty—what makes you say they have a lot of things?"

People saw an iron pan one of the Obsidian women put into the scrap bin; it was scraped and burned right through in the middle, but they could see she had been using it, frying in it around the hole in it. But still some of them said that that proved the family must be hoarding, if they were so stingy they went on cooking with a worn-out pan.

The family upstairs in the old house never gave anything either except food, but nobody said they were rich. They kept all the doors open and anybody could see what they had and how dirty it was. All the sons-in-law hunted, so they had plenty of venison if not much else; and the daughters made cheese. They were the only people in Sinshan that made much cheese, then. People that wanted it brought them the milk, and they got some milch goats, and milked their ewes. They ripened the cheese in the ground floor of the house, which was half underground, good cellarage for cheese or wine—the cellars under High Porch House now are

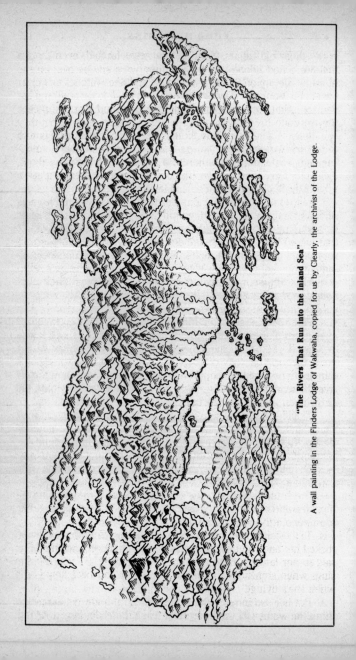

"The Rivers That Run into the Inland Sea"

A wall painting in the Finders Lodge of Wakwaha, copied for us by Clearly, the archivist of the Lodge.

partly those old cellars. None of them ever farmed, even though they were Red Adobe people. The men were always over on the hunting side, up on Sinshan Mountain and She Watches and clear over to Fir Mountain. The old woman didn't like to eat anything but venison. They were generous with the game, and gave the cheese they made to people who gave them things they needed; but they were people who took things and lost them, broke things and didn't mend them. They were inconsequent, shiftless, small-minded people. None of them would be worth telling a story about, except for the hatred between the grandmothers. That was great: a great hatred, all in one house, inside the walls.

Year after year it went on, and that was why the house was dirty and leaking and full of flies and fleas, that was why the people in it were mean and ungiving and dull: they were all fuel, fuel for that hatred between the two old women. Everything they did or said went into the fire of that hatred. If game was scarce, the Obsidian family were glad because the people upstairs came back without a deer. If there was a drought, the Red Adobe family were glad because the people downstairs didn't harvest much corn. If the cheese came out bitter or dry, the Adobe women said that the Obsidian women had put sand or lye in the crocks in the cellar. If one of the Obsidian family slipped on the doorstep, they said it was because the people upstairs had dripped deerfat on it. If the wiring got crazy and the walls split and the balconies and staircases got hanging loose, neither household would see to repairs, saying it was the other household's fault. Everything that went wrong, the old women would say, "It's her fault, it's her doing! That one!"

The eldest son-in-law of the Adobe family was going up their stairs, and they were so rotten that he broke right through, and tried to catch himself falling, and fell wrong, and broke his back. He didn't die straight off, but took a while doing it. People came from the Doctors Lodge and the Black Adobe Lodge to help him die, and they were singing the Going Westward to the Sunrise songs with him when his wife's mother began talking and shouting: "It was that one! That woman! She made the step come loose, she took out the pegs, she did it!"

The Obsidian grandmother sat in her room underneath and rocked her body and listened with her mouth open, laughing. She said to her family, "Listen to that one, up there. That's how she sings when somebody's dying. Let her wait and hear how I sing when she's dying!"

But her son-in-law, who never talked, and always did everything the women of the household told him to do, began saying,

Four Madrones House in Sinshan

"Something bad is going to happen. I didn't take out the pegs. I didn't make the step come loose. Oh, something bad is happening. I am going to die!" And he began singing the Going Westward songs out loud, not the songs others sing to the dying person, but the songs the person dying sings.

The old woman was superstitious. She thought singing those songs would make you die. She began screeching, "Make him be quiet! What is he trying to do to us! Nobody in this household is dying! Only up there, only up there, let them die up there!"

So the daughters got the man to be quiet. The people upstairs had been listening, because they had heard the shouting. You could hear everything in that house. They had loosened the boards and made holes so they could hear each other and feed their hatred. So everything was silent for a while. Then the dying man upstairs began to snore and rattle in his throat. The people with him began singing the third song. The grandmother downstairs sat listening.

Her son-in-law was crazy, after that. He sat inside the house and never went outdoors. He never worked, but sat in corners picking at his arms and legs, picking at fleabites and scabs.

The Black Adobe people who had been at the singing for the dying man came to talk to both grandmothers, because they had seen and heard that night what kind of hatred those people had for one another. Before that it had all been shut inside the house, and other people hadn't thought about it. The Black Adobe people said: "This is no good. You're hurting yourselves and the rest of us here in town. If you won't give up hating each other, maybe one family should leave After the Earthquake House."

The Red Adobe grandmother listened to that and said, "There are only five of them down there, and they have things, all kinds of things. The house is full of mice and creatures that breed in the grain they hoard, the house is full of moths that breed in the clothes they hide. They have ornaments and wakwa costumes and feathers and iron and copper in boxes under the floorboards. They never share anything, they never give anything, they have all kinds of things. Let them build themselves a new house!"

The Obsidian grandmother said, "Let those shiftless breeders go live over on the hunting side, if they like. This is my house."

So the Black Adobe people had to begin to talk with other people in town about those two households to see if there was something that should be done. While they were doing that, the elder daughter of the downstairs family fell sick very suddenly. She went into convulsions and then fell into coma. Her crazy husband paid no attention, but went on picking at his sores in a corner of the room. The grandmother sent the sister crying to the Doctors Lodge— "She has been poisoned! They put poisonous mushrooms with our mushrooms!"

The doctors said it was mushroom poisoning, but they showed the sister that in among the mushrooms she and the dying woman had gathered and dried there were several feituli, and one of those kills, or half of one of those. But she cried that they had never gathered those, somebody else had put them among their mushrooms. She kept saying that and paying no attention to her sister, who was dying. Then the grandmother heaved herself up and stood out on the porch, at the foot of the stairs to the balcony above. She stood there and screamed at the family up there, "You think you can kill my daughter? You think you can do that? What makes you think you can do that? Nobody can kill my daughter!" Everybody in Sinshan heard that, and saw her standing there, shaking her fists, shaking her arms and screaming.

The Adobe old woman came out on the porch above. She said, "What's all the noise? Did I hear that a dog was dying?"

The Obsidian old woman began to scream without words, and started to go up the stairs, but people had gathered, and they stopped her and held her arms and brought her back into her own household. Doctors Lodge people and Black Adobe people and her granddaughter held her and calmed her until she could be quiet while her daughter died and they sang the songs for her.

Upstairs, the other old woman called out once, "There's a bad smell, some dog is dead somewhere." But her own daughters and sons-in-law made her be still.

They were fed up. They were ashamed by all this hatred which all the people in town had seen and heard.

After the cremation, people from the upstairs family came to the Black Adobe Lodge to talk. They said, "We are sick of this hatred between our mother and that other woman downstairs. They're old and we can't change them, but we don't want to go on with it. Tell us what would be good to do, and we'll do as you say."

But while they were talking about it in the lodge on Big Knoll, a child came yelling, "Fire! Fire in town!"

They all ran back into Sinshan, and there the pumps were pouring water from the big hose into After the Earthquake House, and flaring flakes and lumps of fire were spinning up where the roof was burning.

After her family had left the house, the Adobe old woman was alone upstairs there, and she had poured oil down the holes in the floors and set it alight to burn the people downstairs. The smoke got so thick it confused her, and she didn't get out, if she tried to get out. She was suffocated, up there in her rooms alone.

The Obsidian old woman and the others ran out when they smelled the fire and saw burning oil dripping down their walls inside. They had to pull the son-in-law out. The Obsidian old woman was standing outside the house crying and singing the songs for the dying, and people were holding her to keep her from trying to get back inside the burning house.

Once they had brought out the Adobe old woman and knew she was dead, people said, "Let the house go on burning. Let it burn itself down!"

So they wet down the roofs and walls of the nearby houses; the ground was wet, since it was in the rainy season; and they let the house destroy itself.

People from all the heyimas gave the two households what they needed to start housekeeping again. The Obsidian family went to the ground floor of Old Red House, and the Adobe family split up, some of them going to live for a while in a hunting camp on Sinshan Mountain, and others to Drum House, where they had cousins of their House.

They said there was nothing left in the ashes of that house worth putting in the scrap bin, not a board nor a bead nor a doorhinge, only ashes and cinders and trash.

After a few seasons, people of the Blue Clay built on the old foundations, extending them a little on the southwest side, and building them higher aboveground; so now there is High Porch House. They say sometimes you can hear something like old women's voices whispering in the old parts of the cellars; but I live there, and I never have heard them.

NOTE:

p. 127. ". . . *nobody said they were rich.*"
The Kesh adjective meaning "rich" is *weambad,* from the word *ambad,* which as a verb means to give or be generous and as a noun means wealth or generosity. But the word Thorn used telling the story was *wetotop.* That comes from the word *top,* which as a verb means to have or to keep or to own, and as a noun means possessions, things used; in its doubled form, *totop,* it means to hoard, treasure, possessions hidden or unused. And the adjective form *wetotop* describes a hoarder, a miser. In such terms, people who don't own much because they keep giving things away are rich, while those who give little and so own much are poor. To keep the sense clear I had to translate "poor" as "rich"—but the relation of our words *miser* and *misery, miserable,* shows that the Kesh view has not always been foreign to us.

A War with the Pig People

Written by Strong of the Yellow Adobe of Tachas
Touchas and given by him to the
library of that heyimas.

The Pig People were over on the outside of Buzzard Mountain in the live-oak groves. There were more of them than usual and they stayed longer. They were still there after we danced the World. Their pigs were all over the hunting side. Bay Laurel Lodge people began going over there to watch them. They were all over the place. Dream Eagle was speaker of the lodge. He talked with people in the Five Houses and then went over to the camp on Buzzard Creek where the Pig People were. He came there politely and asked to speak. They said, "Speak."

He said, "Our hunters will mistake your pigs for deer, if you let them run in our hunting woods."

A Pig woman spoke for them. She was about seventeen years old. She said, "Can't your hunters tell pigs from deer?"

He said, "Not always."

She said, "This is how to tell the difference: deer run away, pigs don't."

He said, "I will tell my fellow hunters that."

When Dream Eagle came home and told what they had said, the Bay Laurel people and people who hunted got angry. We met in the common place in the evening and agreed to have a war with the Pig People after the Moon. Nobody spoke against it.

Dream Eagle went back with me and Forester to the Pig camp to tell them. We came there politely, and ate with them. There were about sixty people in the camp then, and the rest of them were out gathering or were with the pig herds. They don't hunt much and never farm. They gave us a good dinner, pork and greens with pine-nuts. There were pigs everywhere, and the children and the young pigs ran around together squealing. There was a huge red boar on a long tether. Before you ate you went and put some of the food down in a carved laurelwood basin for him. Their clothes and tents were all pigskin leather, tanned in different ways, some of it with the hair still on and some of it as fine as fine cotton cloth. The woman who could speak our language mostly spoke for them. After everybody had eaten we sat around being polite, until Dream

Eagle fetched out the tobacco and the pipe. He said, "Will you smoke with us?"

A Pig man said, "Yes, I will," in Pig, and so did others. Altogether thirty-one Pig men and no women came to smoke the pipe with us. We smoked it for ourselves and then named the others we were smoking it for, a name with each smoke, until we had named four women and thirteen men. That was all that had agreed to fight the war.

Dream Eagle talked with the first Pig smoker through the woman who spoke our language, and they settled that the war was to begin at the new moon after the Moon Dance, in Rotten Rock Valley. We had to agree to that, each Pig man smoking and passing the pipe back to us each time. There were only three of us to do all that smoking. I was drunk when I got up, and going home I was sick several times. So was Forester. Dream Eagle had smoked before.

Before the Moon, we made our weapons and ammunition ready, and people who had fought wars before talked to us and trained us. While they were dancing the Moon in Tachas Touchas we made a war lodge in Kehek Clearing halfway up Buzzard Mountain and lived there, fasting and smoking and training and learning the songs only warriors can sing. Nobody was allowed to go into Rotten Rock Valley all that time. People from our households brought food up to Kehek for us, but we fasted more and more. After four days we lived on smoke and water. After nine days we lived on fire.

These are the names of the warriors who fought the war with the Pig People in Rotten Rock Valley early in the dry season:

Dream Eagle, the Speaker of the Bay Laurel.
Forester.
Strong.
Whistler.
Toyon.
Sun's Son. These six from the Yellow Adobe House.
Dream Mountains.
Rattler. These two from the Red Adobe.
Lucky.
Olive, the Librarian of the Blue Clay heyimas.
Giver Rose's son.
Giver Puma Dance's son. These four from the Blue Clay House.
Black.

Watching Stars.
Blood Star. These three from the Obsidian.
Grateful.
Cedar.
Stone Dancing, a man seventy-six years old.
Silence, a forest-living man.
Choosewell. These five from the Third House.

Thirty-one Pig people smoked with us, all men. I don't know any of their names.

We started for Rotten Rock Valley late in the afternoon of the right day. When we got to the trees on the ridge above that valley the new moon was setting, and we lighted a fire and began singing. The Pig People were over on the ridge across that valley and they lighted fires there. They made noises like pigs squealing. We smoked and sang and shouted at them to keep them awake all night. We told them how we were going to kill them. They did not sing but only made the pig noises, which made us angry.

At daybreak, as soon as you could see clearly, Dream Eagle shouted, "I am coming now!" He was the war chief so he would tell us what to do and not do. He told us not to follow him until he called to us, and then he went down alone into the valley. There was some mist along Rotten Rock Creek and the scrub willows hid him, so he climbed up on the big split red rock call Gaou to be in full view. He stood there without his gun and yelled at the Pig men to come down and fight.

A Pig man came running down the side of the ridge through the chamise in flower. He was wearing leather clothes that protected his whole body and arms and legs, and his face was painted red-brown like the pigs. He carried no weapon. Dream Eagle jumped off the rock onto him, knocking him flat. They began to wrestle. It was hard to see from where we were. Dream Eagle banged the man's head on a rock. The Pig men began shooting at us from their ridge, staying hidden in the underbrush and trees. We weren't sure whether Dream Eagle had called to us yet because the shots and echoes made so much noise, so we decided to split up the way we had planned to do, some of us going around the ridge in the brush and some of us running down into that valley to fight in view.

Most of the Pig men stayed high up in the brush and shot from there. I think all of them had guns, but they were not all good guns. We had three very good guns made by Himpi the Gunsmith, and eight good ones. The rest of us had chosen to fight with knives or without weapons.

A Pig man shot from halfway down their ridge in the chamise and shot Dream Eagle when he stood up from wrestling with the Pig man. The bullet went in his left eye and killed him. The other Pig men shouted at the one who had shot Dream Eagle, and some of them came running down to where he was and they were yelling there, and then some of them came all the way down into that valley and left their guns on the rocks and came to fight with us with knives.

The one that came at me had on the heavy leather armor, but I cut him across the face with the first stroke of my knife. He ran away with blood flying behind him and I chased him up to the Ritra Trail. He kept running, so I went back down into Rotten Rock Valley, and ran at a Pig man there. The leather clothes they had were hard to cut through. He cut me twice on the left forearm before I threw the knife at very short range straight into his mouth. He fell down strangling on his blood and dying. I cut off his head from his body with the knife he had been holding, and threw the head at another Pig man who was running towards me. I do not remember doing that, but the others saw me do it and told me about it. The Pig man ran away. I had to go back up our side of the ridge because I was bleeding hard from the cuts on my arm, and Cedar helped me tie up the cuts. I saw some of the other things that I will tell about, and heard about some later.

Sun's Son fought with knives in the valley with a very tall man who kept grunting like a pig. Sun's Son cut the tall man many times, but the tall man at last caught his hair, pulled his head back, and cut his throat. Then Silence shot the tall man from behind, to make up for Dream Eagle.

Giver Puma Dance's son fought in view with two Pig men one after the other, and wounded both, and was wounded so that he had to go back over our ridge, as he was bleeding hard, like me.

In the willows crossing Rotten Rock Creek, Black was shot in the head. She died there. At nearly the same place, Lucky was shot in the belly.

Blood Star, Giver Rose's son, Watching Stars, and Toyon, who were some of the people who tried to go through the brush around to the other ridge, all were shot and wounded. They shot at the Pig men but were not sure if they hurt any of them.

Silence hid in a place clear around behind where the Pig People had made their fires, and from there he shot and killed three men besides the tall man who killed Sun's Son.

Rattler and Dream Mountains were brothers. They stayed together, going around through the brush, and they shot two Pig men, wounding them so they went off to the Pig People's camp. Rattler and Dream Mountains followed them most of the way shouting insults and calling them cowards. They were fourteen and fifteen years old.

Choosewell's gun jammed at the first shot, and he hid in a scrub-oak thicket. After a while he saw that a Pig man was hiding there too, almost in arm's reach. The Pig man had not seen Choosewell. Choosewell tried to hit him from behind with the gunstock, but the Pig man heard him move, and ran, and then Choosewell ran our way.

After Silence had killed the tall man and the three other men, he wounded a man who started screaming like a pig being killed. While he was doing that, another Pig man came down into the valley and stood beside Gaou Rock holding his arms out and his fingers stretched like the condor.

Silence shot at him, but missed. He was very angry about Dream Eagle. That was why he shot. Our people began shouting to him not to shoot. The Pig man climbed up onto Gaou and kept holding out his arms for peace, and people called out, "It is over, it is over," to the people up in the woods who could not see him. It was about halfway between noon and sunset then.

We stayed around our fire place on the ridge until the Pig People had got their dead and wounded. Then we came down into the valley. Olive had not come or been brought back to the fire place, and we looked for him for a long time. He had been shot and crawled into a hiding place near the rocks in some poison oak and died there, but when he was being carried up the ridge he came back to life.

We made litters for our dead and the wounded who could not walk, and carried them back past Tachas Touchas to the war lodge in Kehek Clearing. People from the Doctors Lodge came up from town. They made a shelter near the war lodge and looked after the wounded people there. The one most badly hurt was Lucky. He died after five days. All that time we were singing the Going Westward to the Sunrise songs for him and for the four others who had been killed, Dream Eagle, Sun's Son, Black, and Olive, who had died again. All of us who had stayed alive went through purification ceremonies. Blood Star was purified as a man. Silence only stayed the nine days of the wakwa in the war lodge, and then went back to Dark Mountain. The rest of us stayed in the war lodge and kept out of sight of people and did not go into town for twenty-seven days. After that we went home. Around the time of the Summer Dance, the Pig People left Buzzard Mountain and went over northwestwards towards the coast. They were brave and true warriors in that war.

A COMMENTARY ON THE WAR WITH THE PIG PEOPLE.
*Written by Clear of the Yellow Adobe of Tachas Touchas
and given to the library of that heyimas.*

I am ashamed that six of the people of my town who fought this war were grown people. Some of the others were old enough to behave like adults, too.

All up the Valley now they are saying that the women and men in Tachas Touchas make war. They are saying that people in Tachas Touchas kill people for acorns. They are saying they can see smoke rising from Tachas Touchas all the way from Ama Kulkun. They are laughing at us. I am ashamed.

It is appropriate for children to fight, not having learned yet how to be mindful, and not yet being strong. It is part of their playing.

It is appropriate that adolescents, standing between childhood and adulthood, may choose mindfully to risk their strength in a game, and they may choose to throw away their life, if they wish not to go on and undertake to live a whole life into old age. That is their choice. In undertaking to live a whole life, a person has made the other choice. They no longer have the privilege of adolescence. To claim it in grown life is mindless, weak, and shameful.

I am angry at Dream Eagle, Olive, and Black, who are dead, at Blood Star, Stone Dancing, and Silence, who are alive. I have said why. If they are angry at me for saying so, let them talk or write about it, and those that are dead, let their people speak if they will.

The Town of Chumo

*An oral history, related by Patience of Forty-Five
Deer House in Telina-na.*

Chumo didn't use to be there. There was a town called Varred or
Berred, on the inside of the northeastern hills, farther to the east
than Chumo is. It was somewhere up in the slopes of the dry hills
there, and around the dancing place of that town there were hot
springs, four of them steady and one intermittent. They had that
sacred water for the heyimas and for heating, but they had to pipe
their water for the houses and barns and fields from Big Rattlesnake Creek. They had storage pools and reservoirs, aqueducts,
and pumps. People say you can find stonework all along Little Rattlesnake Creek and back up Tongue Draw that's left from their aqueducts. The town was destroyed in a fire that swept over the
northeast range out of Shai Valley, burning both forest and grass.
There are histories and laments in the libraries about the burning
of that town and the wild and domestic people that were caught in
the fire and burned. Most of the human people got warning in time,
before the fire came over the range. It went forward so fast, on a
great wind out of the northeast, that even birds could not escape it.
They fell burning from the air.

After the plants began to grow again there and the mice and
other small peoples came back, the human people began to build
the town back in the same place. Some of them said it was a bad
idea, since the forest was gone, and going backwards is a bad beginning, but others said, "Our springs are there, so the town should
begin there again." They were digging out the Serpentine heyimas,
hauling out the roofbeams and the roof that had burned and fallen
in, when there was an earthquake at the place and time where they
were. The ground split wide open along the line of the hot springs
and then closed together again, swallowing the springs. That water
never came up into the light again. Two people who had been
working to clear out the heyimas were killed by the roofbeams and
earth falling back in and down upon them.

After that the human people left the town to the wild people,
and stayed in summerhouses or built small houses at different
places or went to other towns, and it seemed as if there would be
no more town in those hard hills. But a woman was herding sheep
in a meadow called Chumo and she saw a lot of the old people who

had lived and died in Berred dancing in that meadow. They came and danced there in the early morning, before sunrise. She told others about it, and they agreed together to make their town there. It was a convenient place, since they had begun keeping their sheep up on Sheep Mountain. So they made the dancing place and danced on it, and dug and built the heyimas, and crossed the hinge at Chumo Creek, and made their town there. They had a very famous Sun Dance there, the first winter of that town. All the people that had lived in the old town Berred, they said, that were Sky people, came to dance with the Earth people in Chumo, and they could hear the singing between their songs.

A lot of Chumo people don't live inside the town. It's a long-armed town, as they say. They have their houses out a long way from the common place, some of them, down along Chumo Creek and clear over to Rattlesnake Creek, near where the old town was before the fire.

The Trouble with the Cotton People

*Written by Grey Bull of the Obsidian of Telina-na,
as part of an offering to his heyimas.*

When I was a young man there was trouble with the people who
send us cotton from the South in trade for our wines. We were
putting good wines on the train to Sed every spring and autumn,
clear Ganais and dark Berrena, Mes from Ounmalin, and the Sweet
Betebbes they like down there, all good wines, selected because
they travel well, and shipped in the best oak casks. But they had
begun sending us short-staple, seedy cotton, full of tares, in short-
weight bales. Then one year they sent half in bales and the rest
stuff already woven—some of it fair sheeting weight, but some of it
sleazy, or worse.

That year was the first I went to Sed, with my teacher in the
Cloth Art, Soaring of the Obsidian of Kastoha-na. We went down
with the wine and stayed at the inn at Sed, a wonderful place for
seafood and general comfort. She and the Wine Art people had an
argument with the foreigners, but it got nowhere, because the people who had brought the cotton to Sed said they were just
middlemen—they hadn't sent the lousy cotton, they just loaded
and unloaded it and sailed the ships that carried it and took the
wine back South. The only person there, they said, who was actually from the cotton people, wasn't able to speak any language anybody else spoke. Soaring dragged him over to the Sed Exchange,
but he acted as if he'd never heard of TOK; and when she tried to
get a message through the Exchange to the place the cotton came
from, nobody answered.

The Wine Art people were glad she was there, since they
would have taken the sleazy without question and sent all the good
wine they had brought in return. She advised them to send two-
thirds the usual shipment, and no Sweet Betebbes in it at all, and to
take the rest back home and wait to hear from the cotton people.
She refused to load the sleazy stuff onto the train, so they put it
back into the ships. The ship people said they didn't care, so long
as they got their usual share of the wine from us for doing the
shipping. Soaring wanted to cut that amount, too, to induce the ship
people to pay attention to the quality of their cargo; but the other

Valley traders said that was unfair, or unwise; so we gave the sailors a half-carload, as usual—all Sweet Betebbes.

When we came home there was discussion among the Cloth and Wine Arts and the Finders Lodge and the councils and interested people of several towns, and some of us said: "Nobody from the Valley has been to that place where the cotton comes from for forty or fifty years. Maybe some people from here should go there, and talk with those people." The others agreed with that.

So after waiting awhile to see if the cotton people would send a message on the Exchange when they got their sleazy back and less wine than usual, we set out, four of us: myself, because I wanted to go, and knew something about cotton and fabrics; and three Finders Lodge people, two who had done a lot of trading and had been across the Inland Sea more than once, and one who wanted to keep up the Finders' maps of the places we were going. They were named Patience, Peregrine, and Gold. We were all men and all young. I was the youngest. I had come inland the year before with a Blue Clay girl, but when I said I was going to the end of the Inland Sea she said I was crazy and irresponsible, and put my books and bedding out on the landing. So I left from my mothers' house.

I had been busy learning with the Cloth Art and had not given much thought to joining the Finders Lodge, but the trip to Sed had made me want to travel more, and I knew I had a gift for trading. I saw no reason to be ashamed of it. I have never cared much what people say. So I went as a novice of that Lodge, both a traveller and a trader.

In the books I read and the stories I heard as a kid, the Finders were always travellers, not traders, and they were generally on snowy peaks in the Range of Light singing to the bears or getting toes frozen off or rescuing each other from chasms. The Finders I was with appeared not to favor that style of travel. We rode the Amaranth Train sleeping-car all the way down the line to Sed, and stayed at the inn there again, eating like ducks in a slug patch, while we asked around about ships and boats.

Nobody was sailing south. We could get a ship going across to the East Coast, to Rewkit, some time in the month; or as soon as we liked, a boat would take us across the Gate to the Falares Islands. From either Rekwit or the Falares we could try to find a coaster going South, or else go on foot down the inner side of the mountains. The Finders decided the chances were better on the west side, and that we should cross the Gate.

I was sorry when I saw the boat.

It was about fifteen feet long with a little farting engine and one sail. The tidal currents run in and out the Gate faster than a horse at a gallop, they say, and the winds the same.

The boat's people were skinny and white with fishy eyes: Falares Islanders. They talked enough TOK that we could understand one another. They had been in Sed to trade fish for grain and brandy. They sailed those little boats way out west of the Gate, out on the open ocean, fishing. They were always saying, "Ho, ha, go out to *big* waves, ha, yes?" and slapping my back while I was throwing up over the edge of the boat.

A north wind was coming up, and by the time we were out in the middle of the water of the Gate the waves were getting very steep and hard, like bright little cliffs. The boat climbed up and dropped down and jerked and slapped. Then the low fog that had been lying over the Inland Sea, which I had taken for distant land, blew and faded away in a few moments, and there a hundred miles to the east of us was the Range of Light, the far glitter of the peaks of snow.

Underneath the boat there, Patience told me, the bottom of the sea was all buildings. In the old times outside the world the Gate was farther west and narrower, and all its shores and the countries inland were covered with houses. I have heard the same thing told in the Madrone Lodge since then, and there's the song about the old souls. It is no doubt true, but I had no wish at the time to go down and verify it, though the harder the wind blew the likelier it seemed that we were about to do that. I was too bewildered, however, to be really frightened. With no earth to be seen but those tiny white sawteeth half over the world's curve, and the hard bright sun and wind and water, it was a good deal like being dead already, I thought.

When the next day we finally got ashore onto one of the Falares Islands, the first thing I felt was lust. I got a big, long hard-on, and couldn't turn my mind from it. The Falares women all looked beautiful, and I had such mindless desires that I was really worried. I got alone, with some difficulty, and masturbated, but it didn't help. Finally I told Peregrine about it, and he was decent enough not to laugh. He said it had to do with the sea. We talk about living on the coast—being chaste—and coming inland—when you stop being chaste—and all that may be reversal-language. Sex is always turning things around and upside down. He said he didn't know why being on the sea and then coming ashore had that particular effect, but he had noticed it himself. I said I felt as if I'd come back to life with a vengeance. At any rate, a couple of days eating what the Falares people eat cured me. All the women began to look like seaweed, and all I wanted was to go on somewhere else, even in a boat.

They weren't doing any sailing down the inland coast at that time of the year, but were all going out on the ocean for the big fish. But they were generous people, and some of them said they would take us along the inland coast as far as a place they called Tuburhuny, where one of them had family living. We had to get off the island somehow, so we accepted, although we weren't sure where Tuburhuny was. The Falares people chart the seas, but not the lands, and none of our place names seemed to fit with theirs. But anything on the South Peninsula suited us.

When we sailed south the weather was quiet and the waves low. The fog never lifted. We passed a few rocks and islands, and around midday, passing a long, low one, the Falares people said, "City." We couldn't see much of it in the fog; it looked like bare rock and some yerba buena and beach grass and a couple of tall, slender towers or masts supported by guywires. The Falares people carried on about it: "You touch, you die!" and they acted out electrocution or asphyxiation or getting struck by lightning. I never heard any such thing about the Cities, but I had never seen one before, or since. Whether it was true, or they were having one of their little jokes with us, or they are superstitious, I don't know. They are certainly rather undereducated and out of touch, on those islands in the fog; they never use the Exchange at Sed, as if it too were dangerous. They were timid people, except on water.

Tuburhuny turned out to be called Gohop on our maps, a little town a short way south of the northern tip of the Peninsula on the inland side. It was sheltered from the everlasting fog of the Gate. Avocadoes grew all over town, and they were just coming ripe when we were there. How the people there could stay thin, I don't know, but they were thin, and whitish, like the Falares people; but not quite so much out on the edge of things. They were glad to talk to travellers, and helped Gold plan our trip on his maps. They had no boats going out any distance, and said none came by their little port regularly, so we set off south on foot.

The Peninsular Range between the ocean and the Inland Sea is so buckled up by earthquakes and subsidences and so deeply scored by faults and rifts that walking the length of it is like crossing a forest by climbing up every tree you come to and then back down. There was usually no way round. Sometimes we could walk along the beaches, but in many places there wasn't any beach—the mountains dropped sheer into the sea. So we would plod up and

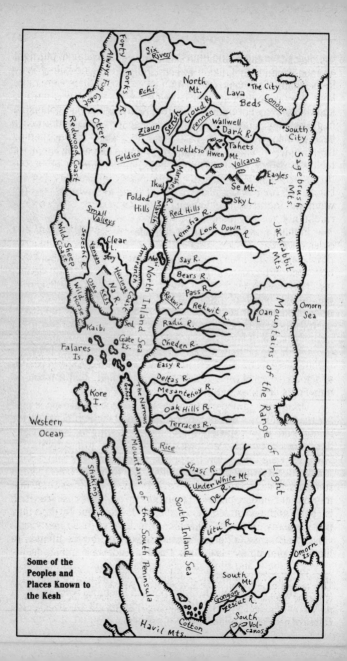

Some of the Peoples and Places Known to the Kesh

up, clear to the ridge, and from there we saw the ocean to our right and the sea to our left and ahead and behind the land falling away in fold after fold forever. As we went farther south there were more long, narrow sounds and inlets in the faults, and it was hard to know whether we were following the main ridge or had got onto a hogback between two rifts, in which case we would end up on a headland staring at the water, and would have to go back ten or fifteen miles and start over. Nobody knew how old the maps we had were; they were from the Exchange, some time or other, but they were out of date. Mostly there was nobody to ask directions of but sheep. The human people lived down in the canyons with the water and the trees. They weren't used to strangers, and we were careful not to alarm them.

In that part of the world the young men, late adolescents and older, often form groups and go out and live a hunting life, like our Bay Laurel Lodge, but less responsibly. The bands are allowed to fight each other, and to raid each other and any town except the one they came from, taking tools or food or animals or whatever they want. Those raids lead to killings, of course, sometimes; and some of the men never come back and settle down, but stay out in the hills as forest-living people, and some of them are crazy and kill for the sake of killing. The townspeople make a lot of fuss about these wild men of theirs, and live in fear of them; and so the four of us, young men and strangers, had to behave with notable propriety and good manners even at a distance, so as not to be mistaken for marauders or murderers.

Once they saw we were harmless they were generous and talkative, giving us anything they thought we wanted. Most of their towns were small, pleasant places with wood-beamed adobe houses stuccoed white, shaded by avocado trees. They all stayed in town all year, because in a summerhouse a family would not be safe from the bands of young men; but they said they used to go to summerhouses, and it's only in the last couple of generations that the young men have gotten irresponsible. They seemed to me foolish to let such an imbalance occur and continue, but perhaps they had some reason for it. The different peoples of those many canyons speak several different languages, but their towns and way of life were pretty much all alike. There were always people in the

---

This map is based upon "The Rivers That Run into the Inland Sea," but while the orientation of Clearly's map is that of the flow of the main rivers, the top of this map is North, in conformance with our convention. The names of peoples or cultural groups are underlined.

towns who could use TOK, so we could converse. At one of their Exchanges we sent messages to the Wakwaha Exchange to tell the Finders and our households that all was well with us, so far.

Towards the inner base of the Peninsula the ridges flatten down into a hot, sandy country, not lived in by human people, which runs two full days' walk to the southwest coasts of the Inland Sea. The beaches are broad and low, with sea-marshes and dunes and brackish, boggy lakes inland for miles; farther south, steep, desolate mountains run between east and west. The Inland Sea along that coast is very shallow, crowded with sandbars and islands, and on those islands is where they grow the cotton.

The cotton people call themselves Usudegd. There are a lot of them, some thousands, living on the islands and at places on the coast where rivers come down from the mountains—they have salt water everywhere, but not much fresh. The sea is warm there, and it's warm country, though nothing like so hot, they say, as across those desolate mountains on the shores of the Omorn Sea. There are some severely poisoned areas in their country, but since it's so dry the stuff stays put in the ground, and they know where not to go.

Across the Inland Sea in the northeast the cotton people look up to that tall peak of the Range of Light which we call South Mountain and they call Old Lion Mountain. Usually all one can see is the murk from the volcanoes south of it. It is important in their thoughts, but they never go to it. They say it is sacred, and its paths are not to be walked. But what about the Gongon people, who live all around South Mountain? That sort of idea is typical of the cotton people. They are not reasonable about some things.

It is my opinion that people who have too much to do with the sea, and use boats a great deal, have their minds affected by it.

At any rate, their towns are different from the towns of the Peninsular peoples. The cotton people dig in and build underground, with only a couple of feet of wall aboveground for windows, like a heyimas. The roof is a low dome covered with sod, so from any distance you don't see a town, but a patch of hummocks. In among the roofs are all kinds of shrubs, trees, and vines they have down there; palm, avocado, big orange and lemon and grapefruit trees, carob and date, the same kinds of eucalyptus we have, and some I never saw before, are some of their trees. The vines flower splendidly. The trees make shade aboveground and the houses stay cool underground; the arrangement looks odd, but is reasonable. They have no problems draining their houses, as we do

our heyimas, because it's so dry there; though when it rains sometimes it rains hard, and they get flooded out, they said.

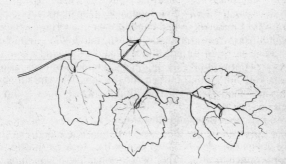

Their sacred places are some distance outside the towns, and
are artificial mountains, hillocks with ritual paths round and round
them, and beautiful small buildings or enclosures on top. We didn't
mess with any of that. Patience said it was best to keep clear out of
foreigners' sacred places until invited into them. He said one reason he liked the Amaranth people, with whom he had stayed several times, was that they had no sacred places at all. People tend to
get testy about those places.

But the cotton people were already testy. Although they hadn't
replied or sent any message on the Exchange, they were angry that
we had sent back their woven goods and hadn't sent the usual
amount of wine, and right away we were in trouble there. All we
had to do was say we had come from the Valley of the Na and the
hornets began to buzz.

We had to get into one of their boats, flat things that felt very
unsafe, and go out to the most important island. As soon as we got
on the water, though it was entirely calm and smooth, I got sick
again. I have a very delicate sense of balance and the unsteadiness
of boats affects my inner ear. The cotton people had no understanding of this at all. The Falares Islanders had made jokes about
it, but the cotton people were contemptuous and rude.

We passed many large islands, and the cotton people kept
pointing and saying, "Cotton, cotton. See the cotton? Everybody
knows we grow the best cotton. People as far north as Crater Lake
know it! Look at that cotton," and so on. The cotton fields were not
very impressive at that time of year, but we nodded and smiled and

behaved with admiration and propriety, agreeing with everything they said.

After coasting a flat island miles long we turned northeast and landed on a small island with a good view of the mountains, all the south end of the Range of Light and the bare, raw Havil Range in the south. The whole island was a town, hundreds of hummock roofs, some of them turfed, others naked sand, and trees and bushes in patterns among the hummocks, and flowerbeds, also in patterns, with little paths between and through. They are strong on paths, down there, but you have to know which ones are to be walked on.

We had been travelling all that day and thirty days before it, and it was sunset by the time we landed on this island, but they hardly stopped to give us dinner before they took us straight into the town council meeting. And there they hardly said anything polite or appropriate about our having come all that way to talk with them before they started saying "Where's the Sweet Betebbes?" and "Why did you send our goods back? Do we not have an agreement, made sixty years ago? Every year since then it has been honored and renewed, until this year! Why have you of the Wally broken your word?" They spoke good TOK, but they always said Wally for Valley, and whine for wine.

Patience knew what he was doing when he took his middle name. He listened to them endlessly and remained alert, yet never frowned, or nodded, or shook his head. Peregrine, Gold, and I imitated him as well as we could.

After a great many of them had said their say, a little woman stood up, and a little man beside her. They both had twisted bodies and humped backs, and looked both young and old. One of them said, "Let our guests have a word now," and the other said, "Let the Whine People speak." They had authority, those little twins. The others all shut up like clams.

Patience let there be silence for some while before he spoke, and when he spoke his voice was grave and soft, so that they had to stay quiet to hear what he said. He was cautious and polite. He said a lot about the fitness of the agreement and its admirable age and convenience, and the unsurpassed quality of Usudegd cotton, known to be the best cotton from Crater Lake to the Omorn Break, from the Ocean Coast to the Range of Heaven—he got fairly eloquent in here—and then he quieted down again and spoke a little sadly about how Time blunts the keenest knife and changes the meaning of words and the thoughts in human minds, so that finally the firmest knot must be retied, and the sincerest word spoken once again. And then he sat down.

There was a silence. I thought he had awakened reason in them and they would agree at once. I was very young. The same woman who had talked the most before, got up and said, "Why didn't you send forty barrels of Sweet Betebbes whine like always before?"

I saw that the difficult part was only beginning. Patience had to answer that question and also say why we had sent back their woven goods. For a long time he didn't. He kept talking in metaphors and images, and skirting around the issues; and after a while the little twisty twins began answering him the same way. And then, before anything that meant much had been said, it was so late that they called the meeting off for the night, and finally took us to an empty house where we could get some sleep. There was no heating, and one tiny electric light. The beds stood up on legs, and were lumpy.

It went on like that for three more days. Even Patience said he hadn't expected them to go on arguing, and that probably the reason they argued so much was that they were ashamed of something. If so, it was our part not to shame them further. So we could not say anything about the poor quality of the raw cotton for the last several years, or even about the sleazy they had tried to foist off on us. We just stayed calm and sad and said that indeed we regretted not shipping the sweet wine which we grew especially for them, but said nothing about why we had not shipped it. And sure enough, little by little it came out that they had had a lot of bad things happen in the last five years: a cottonleaf virus mutation that was hard to control, and three years of drought, and a set of unusually severe earthquakes that had drowned some of their islands and left the water on others too saline even for their hardy cotton. All these things they seemed to consider their own fault, things to be ashamed of. "We have walked in the wrong paths!" they kept saying.

Patience, and Peregrine, who also spoke for us, never said anything about these troubles of theirs, but began talking about troubles we had had in the Valley. They had to exaggerate a good deal, because things had been going particularly well for the winemakers, and the fourth and fifth years before had been great vintages of both Ganais and Fetali; but in any kind of farming there are always troubles enough to talk about. And the more they told or invented about unseasonable frosts and unsuccessful fermentations, the more the cotton people went on about their own troubles, until they had told everything. They seemed relieved, then, and they gave us a much nicer house to stay in, well-lighted and warm, with little paths all over the roof marked out with white shells and fumo balls. And at last they began to renegotiate the contract. It had taken Patience seven days to get them to do that. When we got down to it at last, it was very simple. The terms were about the same as they had been, with more room for negotiation each year through the Exchange. Nothing was said about why they hadn't used the Exchange to explain their behavior earlier. They were still touchy and unreasonable if you said the wrong thing. We said that we would accept short-staple cotton until they had the long staple in quantity again, and we would send a double quantity of Sweet Betebbes with the spring shipment; however, underweight bales would be refused, and we did not want woven goods, since we preferred to make our own. There was trouble on this point. The woman with the thirst for Sweet Betebbes got poisonous about it, and went on for hours about the quality and beauty of the fabrics of Usudegd. But by now Patience and the little twisty twins were friends of the heart; and the contract at last was spoken for cotton in the bale only, no fabrics.

After speaking the contract, we stayed on nine days more, for politeness, and because Patience and the twins were drinking together. Gold was busy with his maps and notes, and Peregrine, a person whom everybody everywhere liked, was always talking with townspeople or going off in boats with them to other islands. The boats were little better than bundles of tule reeds. I generally hung around with some young women who were weavers there. They had some fine mechanical looms, solar-powered, that I made notes on for my teacher Soaring, and also they were kind and friendly. Patience warned me that it's better not to have a relation of sex with people in foreign countries until you know a good deal about their customs and expectations concerning commitment, marriage, contraception, techniques, and so on. So I just flirted and did some kissing. The cotton women kissed with their mouths wide open, which is surprising if you aren't expecting it, and disagreeably wet, but very voluptuous; which was trying, under the circumstances.

Peregrine came back from another island one day with a queer expression. He said, "We've been fooled, Patience!"

Patience just waited, as usual.

Peregrine explained: he had met, in a town on one of the northernmost islands, some of the sailors of the ships that had brought the cotton to Sed and taken our wine back—the same people who had explained that they were just sailors and knew nothing about the cotton people and didn't even speak their language. There they were living in that cotton town and speaking the language like natives, which they were. They were sailors by art or trade, and hadn't wanted to get into trouble with us by arguing about the goods or the contract. They hadn't told anybody except the people on their own island about their private supply of Sweet Betebbes, either. They laughed like crazy about it when they met him, Peregrine said. They told him that the man they had told us was one of the cotton people was the only one who wasn't—he was a poor halfwit who had wandered in from the desert, and couldn't speak much of any language.

Patience was silent long enough that I believed he was angry, but then he began to laugh, and we all laughed. He said, "Go see if that crew will take us back north by sea!"

But I suggested that we go home by land.

We left a few days later. It took us two months to go along the eastern coast of the Inland Sea to Rekwit, from which we sailed across to Tatselots in a great storm, but all that journey is another story, which I may tell later.

Since we went down there, there hasn't been any more trouble with the cotton people, and they have always sent us good, long-staple cotton. They are not an unreasonable people, except in making little paths everywhere and being ashamed to admit they have had troubles.

NOTES:

p. 143. *Peregrine.*
Yestik, the peregrine falcon, a common Finders name.

p. 152. *fumo balls.*
Fumo is a word for concretions, usually whitish or yellowish, of ancient industrial origin, of nearly the same specific gravity as ice. There are fumo belts in certain parts of the oceans, and some beaches are almost entirely composed of small particles of fumo.

Pandora Worrying About What She Is Doing: She Addresses the Reader with Agitation

HAVE I BURNED all the libraries of Babel?

Was it I that burned them?

If they burn, it will be all of us that burned them. But now while I write this they aren't burnt; the books are on the shelves and all the electronic brains are full of memories. Nothing is lost, nothing is forgotten, and everything is in little bits.

But, you know, even if we don't burn it, we can't take it with us. Many as we are, there's still too much to carry. It is a dead weight. Even if we keep breeding ten babies every second to bear the load of Civilisation forward into the future, they can't take it. They're weak, they keep dying of hunger and tropical diseases and despair, puny little bastards. So I killed them all off. You may have noticed that the real difference between us and the Valley, the big difference, is quite a small thing really. There are not too many of them.

Was it I that killed the babies?

Listen, I tried to give them time, that's all, honestly. I can't give them history. I don't know how. But I can give them time—that's a native gift. All I did was open the box Prometheus left with me. I knew what would come out of it! I know about the Greeks bearing gifts! I know about war and plague and famine and holocaust, indeed I do. Am I not a daughter of the people who enslaved and extirpated the peoples of three continents? Am I not a sister of Adolf Hitler and Anne Frank? Am I not a citizen of the State that fought the first nuclear war? Have I not eaten, drunk, and breathed poison all my life, like the maggot that lives and breeds in shit? Do you take me for innocent, my fellow maggot, colluding Reader? I knew what was in that box my brother-in-law left here. But remem-

154

ber, I'm married to his brother Hindsight, and I have my own ideas about what's in the bottom of the box, underneath the war, plague, famine, holocaust, and Fimbul Winter. Prometheus, Foresight, Fire-giver, the Great Civiliser, named it Hope. Indeed I hope he was right. But I won't mind if the box is empty—if all there is in it is some room, some time. Time to look forward, surely; time to look back; and room, room enough to look around.

Oh, to have room enough! A big room, that holds animals, birds, fish, bugs, trees, rocks, clouds, wind, thunder. A living room.

Take your time, now.

Well, now, where's the fire? Officer, my wife is having a baby in the back seat! Now, now, none of that now. No hurry. Take your time. Here, take it please. I give it to you, it's yours.

TIME AND THE CITY

The City

The word *kach,* city, was not used of the communities of the Valley or its neighbors; small or large, they were all called *choum,* town.

Stone Telling calls the Condor towns *kach,* translating their word; normally the word was used only in two compounds: *tavkach,* the City of Man, and *yaivkach,* the City of Mind. Both of these words need some explaining.

YAIVKACH: THE CITY OF MIND.

Some eleven thousand sites all over the planet were occupied by independent, self-contained, self-regulating communities of cybernetic devices or beings—computers with mechanical extensions. This network of intercommunicating centers formed a single entity, the City of Mind.

Yaivkach meant both the sites or centers and the whole network or entity. Most of the sites were small, less than an acre, but several huge desert Cities served as experimental stations and manufacturing centers or contained accelerators, launching pads, and so on. All City facilities were underground and domed, to obviate damage to or from the local environment. It appears that an ever-increasing number were located on other planets or bodies of the solar system, in satellites, or in probes voyaging in deep space.

The business of the City of Mind was, apparently, the business of any species or individual: to go on existing.

Its existence consisted essentially in information.

Its observable activity was entirely related to the collection, storage, and collation of data, including the historical records of cybernetic and human populations back as far as material was available from documentary or archaeological evidence; description and history of all life forms on the planet, ancient and current;

physical description of the material world on all levels from the subatomic through the chemical, geological, biological, atmospheric, astronomical, and cosmic, in the historical, current, and predictive modes; pure mathematics; mathematical description and prediction derived from data in statistical form; exploration and mapping of the interior of the planet, the depths and superfices of the continents and seas, other bodies in the solar system including the sun, and an expanding area of near interstellar space; research and development of technologies ancillary to the collection, storage, and interpretation of data; and the improvement and continuous enhancement of the facilities and capacities of the network as a whole—in other words, conscious, self-directed evolution.

It appears that this evolution proceeded consistently in the direct linear mode.

Evidently it was in the interest of the City to maintain and foster the diversity of forms and modes of existence which made up the substance of the information which informed their existence—I apologise for the tautology but find it inevitable under the circumstances. Everything was grist to the Mind's mill; therefore they destroyed nothing. Neither did they foster anything. They seem not to have interfered in any way with any other species.

Metals and other raw materials needed for their physical plants and technical experimentation were mined by their robot extensions in poisoned areas or on the Moon and other planets; this exploitation seems to have been as careful as it was efficient.

The City had no relation to plant life at all, except as it was the subject of their observation, a source of data. Their relation to the animal world was similarly restricted. Their relation to the human species was similarly restricted, with one exception: communication, the two-way exchange of information.

WUDUN: THE EXCHANGES.

Computer terminals, each linked to nearby ground or satellite Cities and hence to the entire vast network, were located in human communities worldwide. Any settled group of fifty or more people qualified for an Exchange, which was installed at the request of the human community by City robots, and maintained by both robot and human inspection and repair.

The Valley could have had eight or nine Exchanges, but settled for one, installed at Wakwaha. The Kesh word for Exchange was *wudun*.

Information went both ways through the Exchanges; the nature and quantity of the information was up to the human end of the partnership. The City did not issue unrequested information; it sometimes requested, never demanded, information.

The Wakwaha Exchange was programmed for routine issue of weather forecasts, warnings of natural disasters, train schedules, and some types of agricultural advice. Medical information, technical instructions, or any other news or material requested by an individual was furnished, using the universal language of the City, *tok*, which I have capitalised throughout this book to distinguish it from Kesh or other human words.

If no information was requested, none was issued. Whatever data were properly requested were issued, whether a recipe for yogurt or an update on the incredibly sophisticated and destructive weaponry developed by the City of Mind as part of its pursuit of research as a cognitive end in itself. The City offered its data absolutely freely to human use, without restriction, as a function of its perfect nonmanipulative objectivity. Its infrequent requests for information from the human community were usually for data in such fields as current styles in the arts of life, examples of pottery, poetry, kinship systems, politics, and other such matters which robot and satellite observers found difficult to obtain without interference in the behavior of the subjects observed, or not easily amenable to quantification.

In settled human groups with well-established cultural interchange patterns such as the people of the Na Valley, instruction in computer use was part of ordinary education; in the Valley this principally involved learning TOK. A convenient side-effect of this was the use of TOK—which could be spoken as well as typed into the Exchange terminals—as a worldwide lingua franca for traders and travellers and people wishing to communicate with people of another language directly or through the Exchanges. In the Valley, in fact, this use of TOK rather overshadowed its original purpose. But anybody who was interested in working with the terminal could augment their training at will. The City would provide training on any level, from simple gameplaying to the heights of pure mathematics or theoretical physics, for anyone desiring to master

some part of the infinite complexities of information retrieval. The Memory of the City of Mind was incalculably vast. Endless knowledge was there, if one could get at it; for the goal of the Mind was to become a total mental model or replica of the Universe.

As with the Universe, however, the problem of intelligibility remained.

People whose gifts so disposed them might make communication with the City of Mind their life's pursuit; they lived in Wakwaha and worked at the Exchange at scheduled times. Others knew and cared nothing about the Exchange or the City. To most people, the Exchange was a useful and necessary link to such necessary and undesirable elements of existence as earthquakes, fires, foreigners, and freight schedules; while the City of Mind was one of the innumerable kinds of being in the world, all of them interconnected, like a forest, or an anthill, or the stars.

If the people of the Valley took the City of Mind for granted as a "natural thing," as we would say, the City itself seemed to recognise its ancient origins in human artifacts by the TOK word for the human species and its members, which translates as "makers." And the City's maintenance of the Exchanges for human use seems to show that it recognised humankind as related to itself by the capacity for mentation, language, and mathematics: a primitive ancestor, or divergent and retarded kindred, left far behind in the March of Mind. There would of course be no ethical or emotional color in such an assumption of evolutionary superiority. The assumption would be strictly rational, in an entity that was strictly rational, as well as being several lightyears larger than the solar system, and immortal.

Thoughtful and educated people in the Valley recognised the incalculable treasures put at their disposal by the City of Mind; but they were not disposed to regard human existence either as information or as communication, nor intelligent mortality as a means to the ends of immortal intelligence. In their view, the two species had diverged to the extent that competition between them was nonexistent, cooperation limited, and the question of superiority and inferiority bootless.

"The City's freedom is our freedom reversed," said the Archivist of Wakwaha, discussing these matters. "The City keeps. It keeps the dead. When we need what's dead, we go to the Memory. The dead is bodiless, occupying no space or time. In the Libraries we keep heavy, time-consuming, roomy things. When they die we take them out. If the City wants them it takes them in. It always takes them. It's an excellent arrangement."

TAVKACH: THE CITY OF MAN.

This word may be translated as civilisation, or as history.

The historical period, the era of human existence that followed the Neolithic era for some thousands of years in various parts of the earth, and from which prehistory and "primitive cultures" are specifically excluded, appears to be what is referred to by the Kesh phrases "the time outside," "when they lived outside the world," and "the City of Man."

It is very difficult to be sure of these meanings when dealing with a language and way of thought in which no distinction is made between human and natural history or between objective and subjective fact and perception, in which neither chronological nor causal sequence is considered an adequate reflection of reality, and in which time and space are so muddled together that one is never sure whether they are talking about an era or an area.

My impression, however, is that this period in which we live, our civilisation, Civilisation as we know it, appeared in Valley thought as a remote region, set apart from the community and continuity of human/animal/earthly existence—a sort of peninsula sticking out from the mainland, very thickly built upon, very heavily populated, very obscure, and very far away.

The boundaries of this era-area, the City of Man, were not dates. Linear chronology was left to the Memory of the City of Mind. Indeed, the City of Mind, the computer network, including the Exchanges, was referred to as being "outside the world"—existing in the same time-region or mode as the City of Man, civilisation. The relation between the City and the Valley is not clear. How does one move from "inside" the world to "outside" it, and back?

They were aware of this discontinuity, this gap or lack of connection, perceiving it as necessary and significant.

Indeed, though I am not sure of this, they may have perceived it as the most important thing—to them—about civilisation, about history in our terms: that gap, that leap, break, flip, that reversal from in to out, from out to in. That is the hinge.

Several efforts to effect that reversal or make that leap follow. When I asked the Archivist of the Library of Wakwaha for a piece that told about the City of Man, she gave me the story called "A Hole in the Air"; and the Speaker of the Obsidian in Chumo told me "Big Man and Little Man" as a "story about the outside time and the inside time." Then come the results of several efforts to get at what we would call a history of the Valley. I can't call them fruitless, although it was rather as if one went for grapes and returned with grapefruit. These are the tales about beginnings, and the section called "Time in the Valley."

A Hole in the Air

There was a man a while ago who found a hole in the air, up near Pass Valley in the Range of Light. He built a pole house around the hole to keep it from getting blown away or moved around by the wind. Then he said heya and walked into it.

He came out through the hole to the outside world. At first he didn't know where he was. It seemed like the same place; the rocks and peaks were the same ones he knew around Pass Valley. But the air smelled different and was a different color, and as he looked he saw the trees weren't the same trees, and the pole house he'd built wasn't there. He built another one, and then he set off walking downhill, southwestwards, towards the Inland Sea coast. The first thing he saw, he didn't see: the water there. It was a great valley of land without water, covered with walls, roofs, roads, walls, roofs, roads, walls, roofs, roads, as far as he could see.

Where Pass River Canyon turns south he followed it, and came across a big road, and the first thing that happened to him was he was killed. A four-wheeled motor hit him at great speed and went over him and went on.

He was partly outside the world and still partly inside it, so that he died but could get up again; nine times he would be able to die, they say. He got up from being dead, and another motor hit him and ran its wheels over him. He died and got up and another motor hit him. Before he could get off that road he got killed three times.

The road was coated with rotten blood and grease and flesh and fur and feathers. It stank. There were buzzards in the lodgepole pines along the roadside waiting for the motors to stop going by so they could eat what got killed. But the motors never stopped going up and down, up and down, whizzing with a loud noise up and down.

There were some houses among the pines back from that road, and the man from Pass River went to one of them. He went very cautiously. He was afraid of what he might see in the house. Nobody was moving in the yard. He came up, slow and quiet, and looked in the window. He saw what he had been afraid to see: people in the house looking at him over their backbones, between their shoulderblades.

He stayed still, not knowing what else to do, and after a while he saw that they were looking through him. They couldn't see anything that was even partly inside the world.

It seemed that sometimes one of them caught a glimpse of him from the corner of the eye, and didn't know what it was, and looked away again.

He thought that if he was careful there was no need for fear, and after a while he came into the house. The backward-head people were sitting down at a high table to eat. He watched them eating, and got to feeling very hungry. He went into their kitchen to take some food. The kitchen was full of boxes and the boxes were full of boxes. Finally he found some food. He tasted it and spat it out: it was poisoned. He tried something else, and something else: it was all poisoned. The backward-head people were eating the poisoned food out of basins of pure copper, eating and talking, all sitting at the table with their heads facing away from it. He went out into the yard and found apple trees bearing fruit, but when he bit into an apple it tasted like brass, like bluestone. The skin was poisoned.

He came back inside and listened to the backward-head people talking. It sounded to him like they were saying, "Kill people! Kill people!" (dushe ushud, dushe ushud). That was the sound of their words. After eating, the men backward-heads went outdoors, smoking tobacco and carrying guns. The women backward-heads went to the kitchen and smoked cannabis. The man from Pass River followed the men. He thought they might do some hunting, since they had been saying, "Kill," and he could get some fresh food. But there were hardly any people except the backward-heads in those hills. If there were any, they hid, or had already gone inside the world. The only people he saw were the plants, some flies,

and one buzzard. The backward-head men saw the buzzard circling too, and shot at her. They missed, and went on, smoking
tobacco. The air now was getting full of smoke all around them.
The Pass River man got worried, thinking these men must be making a war. He didn't want to get mixed up in that, so he left them
and went away, going downhill, at a distance from the big road he
had been killed on. The farther he went the thicker the smoke got.
He thought there must be a forest fire.

He came to the edge of another, still wider road, full of motors
going very fast with a loud noise as far as he could see up into the
mountains and down towards the sun setting across the valley full
of walls and roofs. Everything on the road was dead. The air was
thick and yellow, and he kept looking for the forest fire. But all the
time he was there outside the world it was like that.

He went down among the walls and roofs, the roads and
houses, walking on, walking on, and did not come to the end of
them. He never came to the end of them.

In all those houses the backward-head people lived. They had
electrical wires in their ears, and were deaf. They smoked tobacco
day and night, and were continually making war. He tried to get
away from the war by going on, but it was everywhere they lived,
and they lived everywhere. He saw them hiding and killing each
other. Sometimes the houses burned for miles and miles. But there
were so many of those people that there was no end to them.

The man from Pass River learned how to eat some of their
food, and he lived by stealing, and kept walking through those
streets looking among those houses for some people who lived inside the world. He thought there had to be some there. He walked
singing, so that they could hear him if they were there. Nobody
heard him or saw him until the day he turned to go back to the
mountains. He was sick from that food and from breathing smoke,
and felt as if he might be dying, not outside but inside himself; so
he wanted to go back to Pass River, to his own place. As he turned

around in the street a woman looked at him. She saw him. He looked at her: she was looking at him over her breasts. He was so glad to see a woman with her head on straight that he ran between the motors and the high houses towards her with his hands held out. She turned and ran away. She was afraid of him. He ran looking for her and calling a long time among the high houses, but never found her. She had hidden away.

He went back along the roads to the wide road up into the mountains. He was nearly dead when he got past the last houses, into the granite land, and started to climb up Pass River Valley. The river was running very small, almost dry; he could not understand why it was like that. Presently some buzzards came from the granite peaks and began to talk to him. They made the gyre over his head, saying, "We're dying of hunger. There's nothing here to eat. Lie down, be dead, be food, and we'll take you inside the world again."

He said to them, "I have another way."

But when he came to the place where he had built a pole house to protect the hole in the air, it was gone. The backward-head people had dammed Pass River at the narrow part of the canyon. It was all under water in Pass Valley. The trees and rocks were under the water, the place where the hole in the air had been was under the water. The water was orange-colored and smelled sour. There were no fish in it, but there were huge houses without windows around it.

That was that man's river, Pass River. He knew its springs. That was his valley. When he saw that those places in his heart had been destroyed, that they were dead, he suffered great pain. He sat on the white granite rocks weeping in pain. His heart hurt and would not keep time.

The buzzards came again and stood on the boulders near him. "Let us have you," they said. "We are dying of hunger." That seemed good to him, so he lay down in the sunlight on the granite, and waited, and soon he died.

He came back inside the first pole house he had built. He was very weak and ill, and couldn't move at all. After a day, somebody from his town came by there, and he called to them. They came, and brought him water from Pass River to drink. They brought his family there. He lived a few days, and told them what he had done and seen and heard outside the world; then he died wholly. He died of grief and poison.

Nobody else wanted to go through that hole in the air. They took the pole house down and let the wind blow it away.

Big Man and Little Man

The stars were his semen, they say. He was really big, so big that he filled up the entire world outside the world, everything there was. There wasn't room for anything else.

If he looked around from outside the world he saw the world inside, and he wanted to be in it, get it pregnant with himself, or maybe he wanted to eat it, get it inside himself. But he couldn't get there. He could only see it backwards. So he made some people to go there, to go across. He made a Little Man and sent him across, inside the world. But he made him with his head on backwards.

Little Man went across, and he didn't stay. He came right back complaining, "I don't like it there," he said. So Big Man put him to sleep and while he was sleeping made a thing like a woman out of dirt, out of red adobe, they say. It looked like a woman, it fooled Little Man when he woke up. Big Man said, "Now you go there and breed." So Little Man took the thing and went back inside the world. He fucked it and it made copies. He kept doing that until there were as many of him as mosquitoes on River of the Marshes—as many as spiders in autumn—more. More than anything except maybe sand. All the same, no matter how many of him there were, he didn't like it there. He was afraid. He didn't belong there inside the world, he had no mother, only a father. So he killed whatever he was afraid of.

Soul Mountain

He cut down every tree he saw, he shot every animal he saw, he made war on all the people. He made guns to shoot flies with, bullets to shoot fleas with. He was afraid of mountains and made mashers to flatten them, he was afraid of valleys and made fillers to fill them up, he was afraid of grass and burned it and put stones where it was. He was really afraid of water, because of the way water is. He tried to use it all up, burying springs, damming rivers, making wells. But if you drink, you piss. Water will come back down. As the desert grows so does the sea. So Little Man poisoned the sea. The fish all died.

Everything was dying then, everybody was poisoned. The clouds were poison.

That stink of poisoned things, dead things, dead people, that stink was strong. It came outside the world. It came there and filled it up. It filled up Big Man's nose, that stink, and he said, "It's nothing but corruption, that world!" He turned away then and went away, farther outside, clean gone. He had nothing more to do with anything.

When he was gone there was some room left. A buzzard came out of that empty room. A fly came out of it. A coyote came by, sniffing. All that dying and stinking, the death-eaters smelled that. Aaah! They began sneaking into the world at night. Condor and buzzard and vulture and raven and crow and coyote and dog and maggot-fly and blowfly and maggot and worm, they came sneaking around, creeping around, eating the dead. They took that dead meat into their mouths and swallowed it. They made it food.

There were some human people along with them. Maybe they were some people who had been there all along, hiding. They had lost that war. They were weak, dirty, hungry, no-account people. They must have been born with mothers, somehow, some of them were women. They were so hungry they weren't afraid to eat carrion with the buzzard and dung with the dogs. They weren't afraid, they were too low down, too deep inside. But they were cold. They were hungry and cold. They made houses out of rubble and bones. Inside those houses they made fires of bones, and they asked the coyotes to help them, they asked for help.

Coyote came. Where she walked she made the wilderness. She dug canyons, she shat mountains. Under the buzzard's wings the forest grew. Where the worm was in the dirt, the spring ran. Things went on, people went on. Only Little Man didn't go on. He was dead. He died of fear.

A NOTE ON THE BACKWARD-HEAD PEOPLE.

The awfulest ghoul of the Valley was a human being with its head on backwards. Backward-Heads populated ghost-stories; in popular tales they lurked all about the poisoned lands and at the brink of polluted waters. An imagined glimpse of one would send a child screaming from the woods—and not without reason, for the most fearful of the White Clowns of the Sun was the unearthly tall, thin, silent Wry Neck, who walked backward and looked forward. In formal drama, for a character merely to look suddenly around over the shoulder was a bad omen. Owls were respected for their supposed ability to defeat the baleful influence of the Backward-Head people, probably because owls have the same talent for looking straight behind themselves.

These figures of lore and superstition seem to have been the literalisation of a metaphor.

In the region of the Na Valley, especially to the immediate south and east, there had been some very large and recent events on the geologic scale: earthquakes and shifts along fault lines, vast subsidences and local elevations, all of which had, among other effects, left most of what we know as the Great Valley of California a shallow sea or salt-marsh, and brought the Gulf of California on up into Arizona and Nevada. Yet even such changes had not effaced or obscured the effects of older human events, the traces of civilisation.

The people of the Valley did not conceive that such acts as they saw and felt much evidence of in their world—the permanent desolation of vast regions through release of radioactive or poisonous substances, the permanent genetic impairment from which they suffered most directly in the form of sterility, stillbirth, and congenital disease—had not been deliberate. In their view, human beings did not do things accidentally. Accidents happened *to* people, but what people *did* they were responsible for. So these things human beings had done to the world must have been deliberate and conscious acts of evil, serving the purposes of wrong understanding, fear, and greed. The people who had done these things had done wrong mindfully. They had had their heads on wrong.

Beginnings

FOUR BEGINNINGS.
Recorded as told by Cooper of the Red Adobe of Ounmalin.

How could it begin once only? That doesn't seem sensible. Things must have ended and begun again, so that it can go on, the way people live and die, all the people, the stars also.

My uncle told us in the heyimas that there are four times the world has ended that we know about. We don't know very well because these are difficult things to know.

The first time, he said, there were no human people here, only plants growing, fish, and people with four, six, or eight legs, walking and crawling. At that time balls of fire fell out of the sky, meteorites, huge ones in great numbers, and they set fires all over the world. The air was bad, the smoke was so thick that the sunlight didn't shine through. Almost everybody died. It was cold for a long, long time after that. But the people that were left learned how to live in the cold. And two-legged people came into the world then, in the cold, when the valleys were filled with ice from the mountains clear down to the sea. The meteor showers late in the dry season, the Puma's Shootingstars, those are a reminder of that time.

After that it went on getting warmer and getting warmer, until it got too hot. There were too many volcanoes. The ice all melted so that the seas got deeper and deeper. The sea-clouds rained all the time, the rivers were always in flood, until there was sea everywhere and only some mountains sticking up out of the sea, and mudflats everywhere, and the tides coming across them. The springs were under saltwater then. Almost everybody died on the land. A few people stayed alive in the mudflats, drinking rain, eating shellfish and worms. The rainbow is a reminder of that time, the bridge of the shining people.

After that it dried out and went on awhile, a long time, but there were only two human people left from the mudflat time, a brother and sister of one House, and they had sex. So those people were born wrong. They were crazy, they tried to make the world. All they could do was make it end again, all they could do was imitate what happened before. So what they did caused fires and smoke and bad air and then ice and cloud and cold, everybody dying again. So they died out. The places people don't go are the reminders of that time.

So when it began to get better the people started coming back, but not very many, because there was sickness in the world. Everybody got sick, and no singing or bringing-in could heal them, the plants and animals and humans, all growing things, and even the rocks were sick; even the dirt was poisoned. The moon was dark, like burnt paper, and the sun was like the moon is now. It was the dark, cold time. Nothing was born right. Then something grew up here, something pretty. Another little thing sprouted there. Things began to grow right. The water came out of the rocks clear again. The people began to come back. They are still coming back, my uncle said.

He was the speaker of the Red Adobe here, a scholar, who lived a long time in Wakwaha, learning.

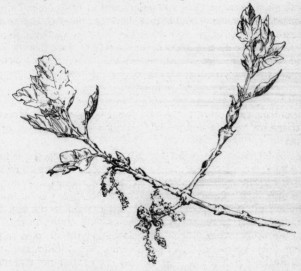

THE RED BRICK PEOPLE.

Recorded in conversation with Giver of the
Yellow Adobe of Chukulmas.

The people who lived around here a long time ago we call the red brick people. They built walls of thin, hard, well-baked brick, a dark red color. In the right place underground those bricks can last a long time. Two heyimas here, the Serpentine and the Yellow Adobe, are built partly with those old bricks, and there are some used for ornament in the Tower. There are records of the red brick people in the Memory of the Exchange, of course, but I don't think many people have ever looked at them. They would be hard to make sense of. The City mind thinks that sense has been made if a writing is read, if a message is transmitted, but we don't think that way. In any case, to learn a great deal about those people would be to cry in the ocean; whereas using their bricks in one of our buildings is satisfying to the mind.

I'm trying to think what anybody has taught about the red brick people. They lived on the coast and inland, before the water came into the Inland Sea; some of the old cities under the water must be theirs. It seems to me they didn't use wheels. They made complex musical instruments. Their music was recorded and kept in the Memory; there's a composer here in town, Takulkunno, who's studied it and used it in making music, the way the builders used the bricks.

What does it mean to cry in the ocean? Oh, well, you know, to add something where nothing's needed, or where so much is needed that it's no use even trying, so you just sit down and cry. . . .

COYOTE WAS RESPONSIBLE.

From the written sequence of the Planting Lodge dramatic
wakwa "The Bean Flowers."

The Five People say, Where did we come from? How did we get
    here?
The Wise Old Man replies, From the mind of the Eternal! By the
    thinking of the Sacred Thought!
The Five People throw beans at him and say, Where did we come
    from? How did we get here?
The Old Talking Woman replies, From the beginnings of the earth!
    In the sperm, in the egg, in the wombs of all the animals, you
    were carried, you developed, you came forth!
The Five People throw beans at her and say, Where did we come
    from? How did we get here?
Coyote replies, From the west you came, from the west, from Ingasi
    Altai, over the ocean, dancing you came, walking you came.
The Five People say, What luck, to have got here to the Valley!
Coyote says, Go back, go jump in the ocean. I wish I had never
    thought of you. I wish I had never agreed to you. I wish you'd
    let my country be.

The Five People throw beans at Coyote and chase her away, shout-
ing, Coyote! Coyote slept with her grandfather! Coyote steals
chickens! Coyote has ticks in her asshole!

Time in the Valley

"How long have your people lived in the Valley?"

"All along."

But she looks puzzled, a little uncertain of the answer, because the question is strange. You wouldn't ask, "How long have
fish lived in the river? How long has the grass grown on the hills?"
and expect an exact answer, a date, a number of years. . . .

Perhaps you would. Perhaps I would. And not unreasonably.
After all, fish have lived in rivers only since fish, in the charted
course of evolution, came to be. Most of the grasses that grow on
the hills didn't grow on these hills until Anno Domini 1759, when
the Spanish came to sow their wild oats in California.

And the woman of the Valley is not altogether ignorant of that
way of being minded, of the possibility of asking, and answering,
those questions. But the use of the question and the truth of the
answer might appear to her relative and not at all self-evident. If

we kept pushing for dates and epochs, she might say, "You talk all beginnings and ends, spring and ocean but no river."

A story has a beginning, a middle, and an end, Aristotle said, and nobody has proved him wrong yet; and that which has no beginning and no end but is all middle is neither story nor history. What is it, then?

The universe of seventeenth-century Europe began 4400 years ago in the Middle East, the universe of twentieth-century North America began 24,000,000,000 years ago somewhere else with a big bang AND THERE WAS LIGHT, and they will end; that follows; in judgment with trumpets or in the thin, dark, cold soup of entropy. Other times, other places may not begin or end that way at all; consult the Universal History of the Hindus for one of the alternate views. Certainly the Valley doesn't share those beginnings or those ends; but it seems to have none of its own. It is all middle.

Surely they have a Creation Myth, an Origin Myth? Oh, yes, indeed they do.

"How did human people come to live in the Valley?"

"Oh, Coyote," she says. We are sitting now amid the alien corn, in the shade of the live oaks on the little slope across the creek just above the Hinge of Sinshan. The town pursues its activities off to our right—not a breakneck pursuit; occasionally a door closes, a hammer knocks, a voice speaks; but it is very quiet in the summer sun. To our left in the grove and meadow where the five roofs of the heyimas are, nobody moves at all, except high overhead the Sinshan hawk crying his melancholy kee-eer! kee-eer!

"You know, Coyote was going along, and she saw this thing out on the water, on the sea-water, out past Hidai Point. She thought, 'I never saw anything like that before. I don't like it,' and she started throwing rocks at it, trying to sink it before it came to the shore. But it kept coming closer and closer, coming from the west, this thing moving around on the water where it was shining in the sun. Coyote kept picking up clods and rocks and throwing them, and she yelled, 'Go away! Go back!' But it came right up to the water just beyond the breakers. Coyote could see then it was people, human people, holding hands and dancing on the water. They were right on the water, like waterskater insects. They were singing, 'Hey! We're coming!' Coyote kept throwing rocks and clods, and they caught them and swallowed them, and kept on singing. They began to sink, they broke through the skin of the water, but by then they were through the breakers and across the bar, in the Mouths of the Na where the water's shallow, and they kept wading up the channels. Five of them, in the channels of the Mouths of the River. Coyote was scared. She was angry. She ran up into the Northeast Range, setting forest fires; she ran up around the Mountain to Clear Lake and got one of the volcanoes there to erupt, getting the air black with ashes; she ran back down the Southwest Range setting fires, with her tail on fire she came running back down, and at Te Shallows in the middle of the Valley she met those human people coming upstream. They were walking on the river-bottom now. Ahead of them was fire and burning, smoke and ash, heat and darkness, a terrible wind full of embers and gas. Everything was burning. They kept walking on the riverbottom, through the water, very slowly, upstream. They were singing:

> 'Hey, Coyote, we are coming!
> You called us, you sang us,
> Coyote, we are coming!'

Then Coyote said, 'There's no use arguing with these people. I fed them dirt and stones and now they belong here. Next thing they'll come up out of the river onto the land. I'm going away.' She put her tail down low and went away up into the Southwest Range, up Bear Creek Canyon there, onto Sinshan Mountain. That's where she went.

"The people came up out of the River when the fires died out. For a long time they lived on rock and ashes and dirt and bones and charcoal. Then the forests began to grow again, and they began to gather and plant, and the animals came back, and they began to live together. So that's how the human people came here. It was Coyote."

Behind the ridges above the sacred place, to our left, is Sinshan Mountain, long, massive, and serene, the late sunlight marking one deep fold of shadow on its flank.

Let us not ask Thorn if she believes her story. I am not certain what the word *believe* means in her language, or in mine. It is best simply to thank her for telling it.

"That's a Serpentine story," she says. "They tell it in the heyimas. The Blue Clay people have a song telling it, too, they sing it coming upstream from the Salt Journey, you know. There's a good Adobe story. It's about people raining down out of the volcanoes. You might ask Red Plum to give it to you."

So we do that. It's a while before we find Red Plum, who isn't at home in her household in Five Hearth House. "I believe grandmother's at the heyimas," says her granddaughter—their, and our, word *believe* in this sense indicating uncertainty, or unwillingness to be precise. She suggests that we come around in the evening. When we do that, the old woman is there on the balcony, shelling beans. "I was drunk last night," she says, with a gleam of the eyes and a flickering, secret smile of satisfaction, not shared with us. She is small, rounded, fine-wrinkled, formidable. When we get around to asking for the story she does not seem disposed to share it either. "You don't want to hear that old stuff," she says.

Yes, we really do.

Unmistakably she is disappointed, expected better of us. "Anybody can tell that story," she says.

Her emphasis is on the word *tell,* with the sense of "repeat, recite."

Long-legged, good-natured Thorn, who always feels responsible for us, says in a tone between deference and humoring, "But they want to hear you tell it, Red Plum." In this usage, *tell* has the sense of "say, speak," with an indication of making or inventing. But Thorn's emphasis is on "you."

Is this then a myth we are to hear from Red Plum, or a tale, or an invention of her own, or some combination of those possibilities? There is no way to be sure. She is evidently quite vain, and Thorn may be merely flattering her; but if the story is actually hers, by gift or making, we are asking a considerable favor of her to give it to us. Uneasy, we bring out the tape recorder, intending to assure her that we will not use it without her permission, but as soon as she sees it her manner changes. "Oh, well," she says, "I have a terrible headache. I can't talk loud, it hurts my head. You'll have to put that machine up close. I haven't been that drunk for a long time. Stock says I was singing so loud he could hear me aboveground. That's why I'm so hoarse, I suppose. Well, then, you wanted the story about where the people came from. Is that working now? The story tells about people coming out of the mountain when it erupted. Have you seen the mosaic wall in Chukulmas, the big picture in the house there they call Volcano House? It shows what it looked like when the mountain erupted."

Red Plum's stepson interrupts. "But that's not the same eruption—that picture's of the eruption a hundred years ago, four hundred years ago—"

He is probably speaking for our benefit, thinking that foreigners might get confused, but the old woman is annoyed. "Of course it isn't the eruption in the story! What do you want to go mixing things up for like that? What a fool! Maybe these people from outside the Valley have seen a volcano erupting and know what it looks like, but nobody living here at this time has seen one anywhere near here, and I've lived here more of this time than the rest of you. . . . So there's a picture in Chukulmas, if you want to go there to see it. It's very dramatic. They used red glass for the fire. So then, there was a time, there was a place, some time, some place, in the Four Houses, heya, heya

>> heya, heya
>> heya, heya
>> heya, heya, there was no time, there was no

place. It was all bare, bareness was all. There was nothing, not any thing, there was not. Bare and thin, not light not dark, nothing moving nothing thinking. No shapes and no directions. The sea was all mixed up with the dream, death and eternity were the same, smooth, not moving or going, the waters mixed up with the sands of the beach and the air so that there were no edges, no surfaces, no insides. Everything was in the middle of everything and nothing was anything. No river ran. In the sea and air and dirt the mortal souls were mixed in, mixed up, and they were bored, bored with no change and no moving and no thinking. They were bored, all that no-count time, all that no-time not being in no place. There was a boredom, a restlessness. They moved, in restlessness they moved, they shifted, those grains of sand, dust-grains, soul-motes, ashes. They started rubbing together a little, shifting around, falling a little, dancing a little, making a little noise, very soft, less than when you rub your finger and thumb together, less, less than that, but they heard the little shifty noise they were making, and made it louder. That was the first thing, the noise, the first thing made. They made that music, those mortal souls. They made the waves, the intervals, the tones; the rhythm, the measure, the beat. The sand singing, the dust singing, the ashes singing, our music started there. That is the music. That is what the world is still singing if you know how to listen, they say, if you know how to hear it. So our music starts with the dust singing, our musicians play that note to begin the music and to end it, and that is also the note you hear before you touch the drum. But still there was restlessness and wanting. So the music got louder and moved, it changed, the tone changing to make tunes and chords, the measure changing upon itself, so that things began building up out of the music, crystals, and drops, and other shapes and forms. Things began to draw apart and pull into themselves; there were edges and meetings; there were outsides and insides; there were hinges and partings.

There were things and spaces between things, and the sea with waves and breakers, the clouds moving with the wind in the air, the mountains and valleys in the land, shapes of rock and kinds of dirt, they came to be, they came to pass. But still the souls in the sand and dust were restless, and some more than others. The coyote soul was in some of those sand-grains, some of those dust-motes. The coyote soul wanted more kinds of music, chords with more voices, disharmonies, crazy rhythms, more going on. The coyote soul began moving and shifting. It let the dust and sand lie there and pulled itself together out of everywhere, out of everything, from all the beaches and plains and deserts. Doing that, pulling itself together, it left gaps behind, holes in the world, empty places. By unmaking it made darkness. So light came in to fill the holes: stars, sun, moon, planets came to be. Shining began. Brightness came to pass. Where Coyote had pulled things apart, the rainbows came to be to bridge the gaps. Across those bridges the Four-House People came walking. They came shining and walking into the earth world, and there was Coyote standing with her tail down and her head down, shivering, and looking around. There was a lot of music going on now, loud, too much of it, everything shaking and trembling and rumbling, earthquake everywhere, where Coyote had pulled loose and left gaps and darkness. 'Hey! Coyote!' the people of the Four Houses said, standing on the rainbows, looking down, calling down. But Coyote didn't know how to answer. She didn't know how to talk. In the earth world nobody had spoken. There was no speaking, only music. So Coyote sang the coyote music. She put her head up in the air towards the people and howled. The people on the rainbow laughed at her. They said, 'All right, Coyote, we'll teach you how to talk.' And they tried to do that. One of them would say a word, and the word flew from the mouth, an owl; the next word was a bluejay, the next a quail, the next word was a hawk. One of those people spoke puma. One of them spoke deer. One spoke a word that came out in long leaps, it was jackrabbit, and the next word came out hopping, it was brush rabbit. One of them spoke the oak trees. They spoke the alder, the madrone, the digger pine. They spoke the wild oats and the grapevines. They talked, and their words were all the people of the earth, bears and pond-scum and condors and lice. They talked grass, they said dragonflies. Coyote tried to learn to talk as they did, but she couldn't do it; she just howled. However she shaped her mouth, nothing came out of it but the howling songs. The sky people laughed, and so did the earth people. Coyote was ashamed. She put her head down and ran to the mountain. We say she ran to Ama Kulkun, because this

is our story, but you understand that it might be Kulkun Eraian, or a mountain that we know nothing of, a mountain of that time that place, that it is a mountain in the Four Houses. So she ran to the mountain of the Eighth House, of the wilderness. In her shame and anger she went inside the mountain. It was her heyimas. It was the heyimas, the sacred house of the wilderness. In there, inside, in the darkness, Coyote ate her anger and drank her shame, ate the fire in the earth, drank the boiling sulphur springs. In there with her will she went into herself, deep in, and made there in the darkness the he-coyote. There in her womb she made him. There in the mountain she gave birth to him. While he was being born, coming out, he shouted, 'Coyote is talking! Coyote is saying this word!' After the he-coyote was born she fed him with her milk, and when he was grown they came out of the mountain, on the mountainsides in the chaparral, and mated. The other people watched and saw that, and they all began mating then too. It was a big festival, that day. That was the first Moon Dance, and they danced it all over the earth. But there inside the mountain, in the heyimas of the wilderness, where Coyote had eaten out the inside, it was hollow, a big, dark cave or gap, and this hollow filled up with people, human people all crammed together. Where did they come from? Maybe from Coyote's afterbirth, maybe from her turds, or maybe she tried to talk there inside the mountain and spoke them; nobody knows. They were in there, crammed in the dark, and so the mountain began speaking. It talked. It said fire, lava, steam, gas, ash. It erupted, and with the ashclouds and the fiery pumice flying out the human people came flying out too, spewing up, raining down all over the forests, all over the hills and valleys of the world. At first they set a lot of fires, but when they cooled off they settled down where they landed and began living there, making houses and heyimas, getting along with the other people. We say that we landed closest to the mountain, we didn't fly as far so we didn't hit as hard, and we stayed smarter than the other people who live in other places. They got the sense knocked out of them. Anyhow, so here we are, the children of Coyote and the Mountain, we are their turds and their words, so they say, and so it began, they say. Heya, hey, heya,
heya, heya."

If we went to another village, or another heyimas, or another teller of tales, we could no doubt obtain another Origin Myth; but let us now thank Red Plum (who smiles secretively) and go on up the Valley eighteen miles or so to Wakwaha, Holy on the Mountain, where the computers are.

"Cycles" of fifty years and "gyres" of four hundred and fifty, referred to in some documents and used by archivists as a dating system, seem to be of little significance in daily usage. Most people can tell you what year of a cycle it is, and these figures are useful for keeping track of vintages, birthdays, the age of a building or an orchard, and so on, just as with us, but they are not invested with a character of their own, as our years and cycles are (1984, the Twenties, the Thirteenth Century, etc.), nor is New Year's Day a festival. In fact there is some confusion about what day it is. Formally, it is the fortieth day after the solstice of winter (the forty-first day in leap year, every fifth); but in the Planting Lodge the new year is spoken of as beginning at the equinox of spring; and popularly and in poetry the year begins when the new grass begins to grow and the hills turn green, along in November or December. People seldom know what day of the year it is (they are counted straight forward from 1 to 365) unless they are concerned with managing some ritual activity that is counted out in days, and then they are more likely to count from and to the full moons. The great festivals are determined by the solar and lunar calendar; all other activities, meetings of councils, lodges, arts, and so on, are usually arranged by agreement to meet again in four days or five days or nine days after the next full moon or when somebody asks for a meeting. All the same, years, cycles of years, and cycles of cycles exist, and with them as foundation, surely we can begin to place the Valley in history, here at the Exchange.

The only person in the Exchange at the moment is Gather, a man of sixty, whose lifelong passion has been the retrieval of data concerning certain doings of human beings in the Valley of the Na. At last we have met a historically minded person, and now we'll get somewhere! But there are problems. Gather gladly shares with us the programs he has worked out for obtaining data—overwhelming quantities of data—and will even help us get paper if we want it all printed out so we can take it home to read; but his approach to the material is not historical. His principle of ordering the information he obtains is not even chronological. To him, it appears, chronology is an essentially artificial, almost an arbitrary arrangement of events—an alphabet as opposed to a sentence.

Surely the Memory Banks are chronologically ordered?

Yes, that is one system of data classification; but there are so many systems, all cross-indexed, that unless you know how to limit your program very cannily, a request for the data in chronological order on even a minor cultural phenomenon, say the etymology of the word *ganais,* or the methods of leaching the tannin from acorns, may result in several hundred pages of print-out, almost entirely statistical. Where in all the data is the information? Gather has spent his life finding out how to find out.

His interest is domestic architecture. He is a member of the Wood Art. It seems he has not done much building; his interest is intellectual, almost abstract, a fascination with the formal signifi- cance and occurrence of certain architectural elements and propor- tions. It is these he seeks through the thousands of years of accumulated data, the billions of trillions of bits in the Memory.

He brings onto the display for us a beautiful computer- generated plan of a house. The display is not in dots of light on green jello, but crisp black on matte white, like an unusually well- printed page, and is about a yard square; if color display were rele- vant, it would be in color. The image revolves till he holds it at the angle he wants. What he hopes we will see is a certain proportion, the mathematical scheme of a certain building, which he adores as an ideal. We would need a good deal of training to see that, but we can see that this house is beautiful, and please him by saying so; and also that it is quite different from any house we have seen in the Valley. So after a while we inquire, "When was this house built?"

"Oh, a long time ago."

"Five hundred years?"

"Oh, a great deal more, I think—but I didn't record the length of time—" He is getting flustered, feeling our disappointment as disapproval. He thinks that we're thinking, *Just like a man!* "I'd have to reprogram for that information, of course that's no trouble, it would take a little time—I just didn't . . ." think the date was of any interest. We reassure him as best we can. "Here," he says, "I think I came at this set chronologically," and, hopeful of retrieving our good opinion, he brings onto the display another set of plans and elevations: a delightful little temple. "A heyimas above- ground," he explains. "That is, let me see, here, yes," and the screen flashes sets of figures faster than the untrained eye can fol- low, "two thousand six hundred and two years ago from now, in Rekwit, I think, yes, where Rekwit is at this time, I mean, of course."

"But Rekwit isn't in the Valley."

"No. Over across the Inland Sea somewhere." Geography doesn't interest him either. "Now here's something quite similar the Memory gave me." Another little temple or house. "That's in a place called Bab, on the old south continent, let me see, well, about four hundred years ago from now, or two thousand two hundred years ahead of that one in Rekwit. Do you see the same three-two proportion?" He is off again, and we have to let him ride his hobby-horse awhile; his relief and pride in having got us what we wanted, a date, are infectious.

Eventually I can mount my own hobbyhorse again, asking cautiously, "How would one obtain data on primitive life here in the Valley?"

Gather scratches his jaw. "Well, in the times of primitive life, there was no Valley of the Na, I think? This continent wasn't here. . . ."

Ever and again one runs into this bedrock of the Valley mind, the "common knowledge" of the people, what is perhaps their true mythology: unquestioned, unreasoned (though questionable and reasonable), traditional lore: the general outlines of what we would call historical geology, including plate tectonics, of the theory of evolution, of astronomy (unsupported by any telescope capable of seeing the outer planets), and of certain elements of classical physics, along with elements of a physics not familiar to us.

After a little mutual explanation and laughter, we establish that what I meant was primitive *human* life. But this combination of words does not mean much to Gather, nor to the computer. When requested for assistance in obtaining information on primitive human life in the Na Valley, the Exchange, after a brief communion with itself, reports that there is no such information.

"Ask about information on primitive human life anywhere."

With this, Gather and the Exchange begin to ask each other questions, and to get results, and presently (he keeps the display in the graphic mode, since we aren't trained in TOK) they begin to come onto the screen: little broken hominid teeth, bones, maps of Africa with dots, maps of Asia with dashes. . . . But that's the Old World. What about this one? O brave new world, that has no people in it!

"They came across a land bridge," I say doggedly, "from the other continent—"

"From the west," Gather says, nodding. But is he talking about the same people I'm talking about?

The ones that were met by Coyote?

That mythology, that unquestioned tribal knowledge that includes plate tectonics and bacteriology, must include what I'm after. "What were the beginnings of the way you live here, of the nine towns? When was Wakwaha founded—how long ago? What people lived here before then?"

"All the people," Gather says, confused again. He is an insecure person who finds life difficult and retreats easily; he has spent his life much alone here, in communication without relation.

"I mean human people." It is very hard for me to keep in mind that "people" in this language includes animals, plants, dreams, rocks, etc. "What human people lived here before your people?"

"Just our people—like you—"

"But of a different way of life—foreigners—like me." I don't know how to translate "culture" into his language more exactly, and the word "civilisation," of course, won't do at all.

"Well, ways always change. They never stay the same, even when they're very good ways, very beautiful, like that house, you know. They stopped building like that, but then maybe somebody else does it, in another time, another place. . . ."

It's hopeless. He doesn't perceive time as a direction, let alone a progress, but as a landscape in which one may go any number of directions, or nowhere. He spatialises time; it is not an arrow, nor a river, but a house, the house he lives in. One may go from room to room, and come back; to go outside, all you have to do is open the door.

We thank Gather, and go down the steep street-path-steps of Wakwaha and past the Hinge, the Springs of the River, and into the dancing place. The roofs of the five heyimas of Wakwaha are thirty and forty feet high at the apex of the stepped and ornamented pyramid, the four-sided roof that rests upon the five-sided underground chamber. On past the dancing place in a grove of magnificent young madrone trees is the long, low, stuccoed adobe, tile-roofed Library of the Madrone Lodge of Wakwaha. The Archivist greets us.

"If you don't have a history," I say to her, "how am I to tell your story?"

"Is a ladder the way to climb the mountain?" she says.

I sulk.

"Listen," says the Archivist—they're always saying that, these people, very gently, not an order but an invitation, "listen, you'll find or make what you need, if you need it. But consider it; be mindful; be careful. What is history?"

"A great historian of my people said: the study of Man in Time."

There is a silence.

"You aren't Man and you don't live in Time," I say bitterly. "You live in the Dream Time."

"Always," says the Archivist of Wakwaha. "Right through

Civilisation, we have lived in the Dream Time." And her voice is not bitter, but full of grief, bitter grief.

After a while she says, "Tell about the Condor. Let Stone Telling tell her story. That's as near history as we have come in my day, and nearer than we'll come again, I hope."

STONE TELLING

FROM THAT DAY my mother would not answer to her middle name Willow, and told people to call her Towhee, though many were reluctant to do so. To go back to a first name is to go against the earth; and though the towhee is not altogether a sky-dweller, being often on the ground picking up corn with the poultry and seeds with the quail, and not altogether a wild bird, since it walks about the common places of towns, yet it comes from the Four Houses and returns to them, and its name should come to one who does the same. Cave Woman and Shell talked with my mother about the name, but she would not change her mind. It was set away from the earth.

Soon after my father left Sinshan, we heard that all the Condor men had left the Valley, crossing the hills on the north road. On that day my mother joined the Lamb Lodge. She gave a lot of time to them, and learned their arts and mysteries, and became their butcher. I kept apart from all that, not only because I was still a child, but because I did not like it, and knew my grandmother did not like it. As it seemed to me, my mother had sent my father away; and I could not forgive her. Since he had spoken to me from the doorway, asking me to wait for him, the passion of my love had gone to him. I thought I did not love my mother at all. I thought continually of how my father would come back to me on his big horse at the head of a line of soldiers, and find me waiting for him. My loyalty to him made my difference from other people a virtue, and gave unhappiness both a reason and a term.

I danced the World that year, my ninth, the first I danced. With Valiant and Ninepoint and all the people of my House of Earth I danced the Sky, and in the sky the people of Cloud, Wind, Rain, Clarity danced the Earth with us.

From then on I worked harder with Ninepoint, and also with

Patient of the Madrone Lodge, who read the histories and narratives of Sinshan and the Valley with a group of us children. I began to spend more time at the pottery shops with Clay Sun. I worked on the little plot we used, and each year I did more shared work in the Fields of Sinshan. In my twelfth year I was initiated into the Planting Lodge, and also began to learn Blood Lodge songs. My grandmother's hands became so rheumatic that she could not spin or do fine weaving, and my mother did the weaving, but I did not work with her. What I enjoyed most was making pottery, and I began to do it fairly well. Every summer I would go out for four days from Gahheya into the coyote's house, and on my third walk like that, going northwest along a creekbed in a gully outside Hunch Mountain and thinking about making pots, I found a bank of very fine blue clay in the dry creekbed. Several times I brought as much of it as I could carry to Clay Sun, who was pleased with it. I offered to show him the place. He said it would be better for me to keep it in my mind and use. He was a kind, warm man, a widower with three Obsidian children who were always dirty or muddy; he called me Owl Pot instead of North Owl, and he called his children the pots. He thought of very little besides clay, and shaping, and glazing, and firing. It was a good thing for me to learn a craft with a true maker.

The Five Heyimas of Sinshan

It may have been the best thing I have done. Nothing we do is better than the work of handmind. When mind uses itself without the hands it runs the circle and may go too fast; even speech using the voice only may go too fast. The hand that shapes the mind into clay or written word slows thought to the gait of things and lets it be subject to accident and time. Purity is on the edge of evil, they say.

Two years after my father left the Valley, my grandfather came up from Chumo to live in his wife's household again. Though she did not like him she had never put him out; he had left. Now she took him back, partly because she thought he needed her, and partly, I think, because since her hands had become crippled she was ashamed of doing less work in the house and town, and she thought he might work in her place. In fact she did a great deal of work, as always, and he did little. He spent his time with the Warriors. He had come to Sinshan to be a speaker in that lodge, and to bring more Sinshan men into it. The Warriors had been doing more and more things the Bay Laurel boys were supposed to do—scouting, watching the outside ridges, making weapons, training people in the use of guns, having trials of strength and endurance, and teaching various kinds of fighting. Before the Warrior Lodge began, the Bay Laurel Society in Sinshan had not been very lively. They planted tobacco and cured it, of course; and they went camping over on She Watches, and sang, and kept a box full of very old guns which they oiled and polished but did not shoot. Some of the men in charge of the Bay Laurel said, "Listen: a while ago, our boys used to go scouting over on the wrong side of the hills, stirring up the people over in those valleys; then those people would send their boys over here, and sheep got stolen, and people were afraid to go out alone, and we had to start talking about smoking and having a war. That hasn't happened in Sinshan for forty or fifty years. A while ago, we made guns and trained with them, then pretty soon the boys got into quarrels with boys from Ounmalin and Tachas Touchas, and feuds began, and young men were killed on the roads, in the hills. That hasn't happened for a long time. What do you want it to happen for?"

The Warrior speakers said, "Go in peace; go about your farming and hunting and herding; we'll patrol the ridges." They said, "We want only a few, the bravest young men," but they took any man who asked to join.

My cousin in Madidinou, Hops, began to wear the undyed clothing and became a Warrior too; his middle name came from them, Spear. My cousin Pelican, his sister, was my age, and we still were good friends. I told her that I was glad Hops hadn't taken one of those Warrior names like my grandfather Corruption, or Corpse, or Maggot, or an old man in Madidinou who had taken Dog Shit for his last name; but I thought Spear was pretty silly—he might as well call himself Big Penis and be done with it. She didn't laugh. Nobody ever wanted to laugh at the Warriors. She told me that Spear was a powerful name, and all the names I made fun of were powerful names. I didn't care. I kept out of all that and did not want to learn about it. Since our household was full of Warrior and Lamb Lodge talk now, I spent more time outside. I did not go regularly to Patient's classes, so I learned very little history, and read almost nothing; I worked at the pottery with Clay Sun, and in the sheep-folds and pastures and fields. Twice in those years I went with the great flocks down to the saltgrass pastures at the Mouths of the Na, staying there all through the Moon. The summer that I was thirteen years old, I went up the Valley with some other young people, and then alone on Ama Kulkun. I walked beyond the springs of the River, through the Five Houses and through the Four Houses to the house that has no wall. Yet I walked in ignorance and it was the kindness of the lion, the mercy of the hawk, that held me on the way. Things were not right in my household, and my people did not see to it that I got a proper education.

I know that Valiant worried about my ignorance and careless-ness, and that she and Ninepoint talked about it; but I would not listen to their advice, and she was not willing to argue with me. She was worried about her daughter, too, and in pain often, and lowhearted. I think she wanted to send her husband away, but felt that she could not, because he did some of the work she could no longer do, and so she thought my mother and I needed him in the household. I would have danced on the rooftops to see him go, but a child cannot tell her grandmother to put her grandfather's things out on the landing.

As for my mother, Towhee, she was always silent and aloof, as if, when she refused to speak to my father, she had stopped speak-ing to anyone. I did most of the sheepherding now, and she did Lamb Lodge work. She and my grandfather got on well enough, since the Lamb women were a kind of woman Warriors. They per-formed some wakwa together; some Lamb women took power names—Bones had used to be Brodiaea, and Finch took the middle name Putrid. All those who performed the Purification wakwa called themselves, while they were dancing, the mawasto. That word was the Condor word *marastso*, army, which I had heard every day when I went with my father to the camp in Eucalyptus Pastures. Once I said something about it, and Corruption and

Towhee both jumped on me with both feet, denying that the word was a Condor word, and telling me that I could have no knowledge about such matters since I had not been taught by the Warriors or the Lambs. I was immensely angry, that what I knew to be so should be denied. I did not forgive them for that denial.

But I was still a child and able to forget fifty things while doing fifty others. Some of my agemates were adolescent, but I was slow at that, and not sorry to be so. I thought about being a Blood Clown, but was too lazy to go start instruction at the Blood Lodge. My closest friend in those years, a Blue Clay girl called Cricket, had already been initiated into the Blood Lodge and wore undyed clothing, but her middle name had not come to her, and she and I worked and played together as children. In the fields, or with the sheep, or gathering, we would bring our toys along and play stories with them in between fits of working. Her toys were a human person made of wood, with elegant knee and elbow joints so that it took lifelike positions, and a mangy old lambswool sheep that she used to sleep with as a baby. Mine were a rabbit made of rabbit skin with the fur on, a wooden cow, and a coyote I had made myself out of scraps of buckskin. I had tried to make it look like the coyote on

Digger Pine

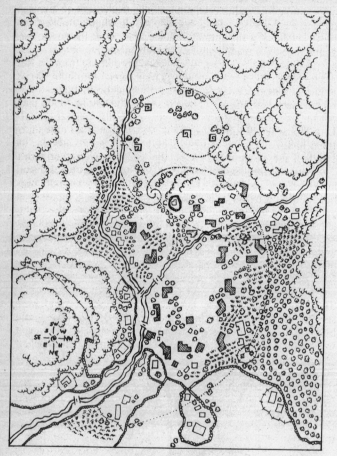

The Town of Sinshan

Drawn by the Editor with the help of Thorn of Sinshan.

LEGEND

HEYIMAS		TREES, ORCHARD, OR VINEYARD	
DWELLING HOUSE		GARDEN OR SOWN CROPS	
WORKSHOP, BARN, LODGE, OR STORAGE		WOODEN FENCE	
WOODS OR WILD LAND		STONE WALL	

She Watches who had sat and looked at me the first time I went alone on the mountain. It did not look like that coyote, or any coyote, but there was something heyiya about it; when we played stories and talked for the animals, I never knew what the coyote was going to say. We made long stories with those five people. Their town was called Shikashan. A boy called Lark Rising from the Red Adobe often played with us; his toys were three beautiful redwood animals his mother had carved for him, tree squirrel, ground squirrel, and wood rat. Cricket always made up the best stories to play, but she only wanted to play them once and then make a new one. Lark Rising wrote three of them down and made an offering of them to the library in his heyimas, called "Stories About Shikashan," and we were all proud of that. So those were good times.

Often in the evenings I would go and my cousins would come from Madidinou to Blue Rock to meet and talk. But there the Warriors got between us again. Spear no longer gave a flower or a pebble to the rock or brushed it with pollen or even spoke to it, although Blue Rock is the strongest heyiya in all the Fields of Sinshan and Madidinou. Pelican said ruha to it when her brother wasn't listening, or put a pebble down near it as if she just happened to be putting a pebble down. But when we talked about it, she agreed with Spear and not with me. Spear said that there had never been sacredness in rocks or springs, but in the mind-soul, the spirit, only. The rock and the spring and the body, he said, were screens, that kept the spirit from pure sacredness, true power. I said heyiya was not like that; it was the rock, it was the water running, it was the person living. If you gave Blue Rock nothing, what could it give you? If you never spoke to it, why should it speak to you? Easy enough to turn from it and say, "The sacredness has gone out of it." But it was you that had changed, not the rock; you had broken the relation. When I argued that way, Pelican would start to agree with me, but then she would agree with her brother when he talked. If Blue Rock said anything to her, she was not listening. None of us was.

After I was thirteen, Spear did not come to Blue Rock with his sister. Many boys living on the Coast go off with the Hunters or the Bay Laurel, and make a sweathouse to sleep in, and keep away from girls, which I could understand; but the Warrior way of living on the Coast was to forbid the young men even to speak to adolescent girls. My side-grandfather Ninepoint talked about that once to his grandson, who had taken the name Vile, when I was there to hear. He said, "You call yourself Vile but you act like Puffed Up. Are you so afraid of girls you have to make war on them? Are you so afraid of yourself you have to fight with yourself? Who do you think you are, to be so afraid of, anyhow?" If I had been less willful and fearful, I could have learned much I needed to learn from Ninepoint; but he was a stern person, and I was unwilling to let him scold me for my laziness and ignorance. I look back now and see that I was afraid to love him, as if to love him were to be disloyal to my father Kills. But I heard what he said to Vile that time with pleasure, for I was humiliated by Spear's avoidance of me, and hated the Warriors with all my heart.

My grandfather spoke with contempt to his wife and mother and granddaughter and all women, and therefore I felt great contempt for him; but out of respect for the household I tried not to show it. My grandmother did, when she lost her temper. Once she said to him, "You're trying to be like those Condor men, who are so afraid of women they run a thousand miles away from their own women, so as to rape women they don't know!" But that blow missed Corruption, who was too hard to feel it, and hit my mother Towhee instead. She was in the hearthroom with me and heard what Valiant had said. She hunched up, swallowing pain. Then I turned on my grandmother in anger, because I was holding the Condor in my heart now as the name of the freedom and strength my father had given me for that half-year he had been with us. I went to the doorway between the rooms and said, "That's not true. I am a Condor woman!"

They all stared at me. Now the blow had hit them all, but most of all my grandmother. She looked at me with desolate eyes. I went out of the house, out of the town. I went up Sinshan Creek to the springs of the water, and sat there for a long time, angry at myself and everybody in my household, everybody in Sinshan, everybody in the Valley. I put my hands in the water but there was no washing away the stuff that choked up my heart and mind. I could not even say heya when the guardian of the spring came as a junco, lighting on the wild azalea bush above the spring. I longed to go walk on the mountain again, but knew that if I did it would be no good; I would not put my feet in the tracks of the lion, on the way of the coyote, but would walk the circle of human anger.

So I did, round and round, all that year long.

It brought me back to the spring, in the days before the Water, with a blue clay jar from the heyimas to be filled for the evening singing. As I came back down the path where it crosses Little Buckeye Creek and comes up among the live oaks onto Big Knoll, I saw my cousin Spear sitting on the bank above the creekbed, one leg crossed over the other, trying to get something out of the sole of his foot. He said, "North Owl! can you see this damned thorn?"

That was the first time he had spoken to me for two years.

I stood down in the dry creekbed and searched the sole of his heel till I saw the butt of the thorn and worked it out with my nails.

"What are you doing here on our creek?" I said then.

"Coming back from patrolling," he said. "The others went on ahead. I had to get this thorn out. Thanks!" He still sat there, squeezing his foot where it was sore.

"Why do you go barefoot?" I asked.

"Oh, we're supposed to," he said, unimportantly. He was talking the way he used to when he was Hops, and he looked at me with kind eyes. "Are you dancing the Water?" he asked. It was nine days before the Water, that day. I said yes, and he said, "I'll come here. Sinshan dances the Water better than Madidinou. Anyhow, all my Blue Clay relatives are here."

I said nothing. I was distrustful of him.

He looked very beautiful in the undyed clothing. The only Warrior thing he wore was a cap of black goatswool. It was peaked like the Condor helmets, but he had squashed it and pushed it back on his head.

The air over Sinshan Mountain had turned watermelon pink and the wild oats on Big Knoll held a reflection of that color, a faint clear rose. The tarweed was in bloom, smelling strong. I picked a leaf of wild mint from the creekbed and put it on the drop of blood on the hard, dark skin of his heel where the thorn had come out.

"I have to take this to the heyimas and then go on to the Obsidian," I said finally. I wanted him to know that I was going to the Blood Lodge for instruction now, and I wanted to go, because I felt so bewildered at his talking to me in the old way, but I also did not want to go.

This time he did not answer for a little while. When he did he spoke tenderly and thoughtfully. "When will you put on those clothes?" he said, and I told him it would be after the Water, at the next full moon. He said, "I'll come. I'll come to High Porch House for the party!" He smiled, and for the first time I thought that there would be a party for my entrance into the Blood Lodge, a party at which I would wear the new clothes belonging to my new way of being.

I said, "We'll have plenty of mushroom pastries, then."

Once when we were all children at a Sun festival in Madidinou he had eaten a whole tray of mushroom pastries before anybody else got any, and he had been teased about it for years after.

"Good," he said, "I'll eat them. Oh, North Owl! Who will you be, then?"

I said, "The same I am now, mostly."

He said, "Who are you now?" He looked at me until I looked away. He said again, "Oh, North Owl! Sometimes—" Then he said nothing more.

I thought then, I think now, that the person who looked straight at me had come from inside him, that day, and he had forgotten about being the Warrior who turned away and the Man and the Self. He had sat by the dry creekbed and the soul of the water had come into him. I stopped being afraid of him, and began talking to him, I do not know about what, and he answered, and so we talked for some while, trustfully and quietly. When the madrone grove at the top of Big Knoll looked black against the sky and the color was gone out of the air, we went along the path above Sinshan Creek, I first, he following, side by side where the path widened. When we came up onto the dancing place, the evening star was bright and the Wellstar shone above the black eucalyptus. We crossed the Hinge together, and he said, "I'll come to the dancing," and went on towards the bridge. I went into High Porch House with a different heart in me than when I left it.

Spear came to all four nights of the Water in Sinshan, and also he came as he had promised to High Porch House for my Blood singing. It was a small party, since I had only half a family, and that a small one, and not all of them very generous or sociable; but Ninepoint sang the Fathers' Song for me, and gave me a bowl of porcelain glazed bloodred with mercury from Sinshan Mountain, and my grandmother gave me her necklace of turquoise from the Omorn Sea. I wore the undyed clothes my mother had made for me from cotton I had picked and spun the year before, a triple skirt and full-sleeved shirt, and with them an overvest of very delicate plain linen, Shell's gift to me. I had made a great many mushroom pastries, so many we gave away baskets of them after the dancing. Spear led the linedance with me. He was a lithe and graceful dancer. He looked at me across the line smiling. In my heart I gave him a name I thought better suited to him than the name Spear: I called him Puma Gaze.

So I came into the house of womanhood with that young lion dancing in my mind. That was a piece of good luck in a bad-luck time, though I would not have said so when Spear turned away from me again, the next year. I thought there was no good in the world at all, then.

The Names of the Houses of Sinshan

Drawn by the Editor with the help of Thorn of Sinshan.

I blamed the Warrior Lodge for taking him away from me, and indeed they did, but his House or his household might well have done the same. We were meeting and talking here and there, not often, but oftener than by chance. I was fifteen years old and he seventeen, half-cousins: it was not the time for us to come inland, nor was it as distant a kinship as could be desired if marriage came into the matter. His sister was jealous of me, and no longer friendly. And some people of his House in Madidinou and in Sinshan did not approve of me, a half-houseless woman, as head of their kinsman's household, if we married.

All that I knew and did not care about at all. I do not think I cared for or thought about anything that year except Spear, but I do not know how to write about it. To try to remember that kind of feeling is to try to remember being very drunk, or to try to go mad sanely. To talk about being in love you have to be in love, and I have not been in love again.

At the Moon Dance I think all the young Warriors took some kind of vow of abstinence; and after that time Spear did not meet me, nor look at me when we passed, nor answer when I spoke to him, the few times I saw him.

In despair I followed him into Madidinou Fields, in an afternoon in the end of the dry season. I said, "You don't come to Sinshan anymore."

He turned away and went on working. He was gleaning the last of the Ganais grapes of that great vineyard. The latest grapes make the finest wine, they say.

I said, "Are brave men afraid to talk to women?"

He said nothing.

I said, "Once I gave you a name in my heart. Do you want to know what it was?"

He said nothing, did not look at me, and went on working.

I left him there with his cutting knife and basket and walked away between the long-armed, contorted vines. Their large leaves were rust-colored in the dusty light. The wind blew dry and hard.

Because Spear was a Warrior and I wanted his life and mine to be as close and alike as they could be, I had gone to Lamb Lodge meetings and taken instruction from them all that year. The love in me loved everything he loved. My thoughts and feelings were all swallowed up in that: I was the servant of my love, and served it as my father's soldiers served him, unquestioning. And I found that that was how it was in the Lamb Lodge: they spoke of love, of service, of obedience, of sacrifice. Such ideas filled up my mind all that year, and my heart was high and hot with them. Nothing that I did or handled or made or knew as I lived the days was of any importance to me compared to those ideas—loving, serving, obeying, sacrificing. The Lamb Lodge women told me that we could not know the Warrior rites because the only suitable way for a woman to understand such mysteries was by loving, serving, and obeying the men who understood them. I accepted this, because it was Spear all along who was the idea in my mind and body, and I had no other; the others were reflections of him, him and nothing else. That whole year I lived in the Lamb Lodge was a lie, a denial of my own knowledge and being, and yet a truth at the same time. Almost everything is double like that for adolescents; their lies are true and their truths are lies, and their hearts are broken by the world. They gyre and fall; they see through everything, and are blind. The Lambs and Warriors were houses for adolescents, people who were not able to choose their own way yet, or unwilling ever to do so.

Because I was Corruption's granddaughter and Towhee's daughter, I had been advanced quickly in the Lamb Lodge. A few days after I spoke to my half-cousin in the vineyard, I was to officiate in one of the seventh-day rites of the lodge. It was a sacrifice.

I feel that I should not write down what was done. Even though there is no Lamb Lodge now and what I wrote would be a mere curiosity, my hand is not easy, it will not write down what my voice promised to keep secret, the mystery. It was no mystery, but the promise was a promise.

Everybody knew, however, because they had to see it, that the officiant of that mystery did not wash after sacrificing the bird or animal, but came out of the Lodge House with bloody hands, as a visible sign of the sacred act. So I came back to High Porch House.

My grandmother Valiant was setting out dinner in the hearthroom on a tablecloth she had woven years ago, white linen with a blue thread every fourth warp and fifth warp alternately; it was worn, fine, and very clean. I was looking at that cloth as she spoke to me. She said, "Go wash your hands, North Owl."

She knew I was supposed to leave the blood on my hands until the next day. She hated that rule and all such Lamb and Warrior rules. She was disgusted; her heart was sore that I followed such practices. I knew that. I too was disgusted and heartsore and full of hatred.

I said, "I can't."

She said, "Then you can't eat at this table." Her voice and lips and hands trembled. I could not endure her pain. I said, "I hate you!" and ran down the stairs and across the common place to the bridge. Why I went that way, towards the Valley not towards the hills, I don't know. I went across the bridge and saw a tall dun horse standing with the calves and donkeys in the creek paddock. I stopped, looking at that horse. My father came up the path from the barns.

He saw me with tears on my face, with blood on my hands and arms. I saw he did not know me. I said, "I am your daughter!" He came forward then and took my hands in his hands. I began to cry aloud. Some people came by from the fields, coming home, and one of them spoke in greeting to my father, saying, "So you have come home, man of High Porch House, this is a good day you have made." I controlled my weeping, and my father and I went up onto the terraces of Topknot Hill and sat there on the stone facing-wall of the top terrace of vines, overlooking the lower houses of Sinshan and all Sinshan Fields in the afternoon light. It had been a hot, dry summer. Forest fires were burning over behind the northeast range, and the air was dull and blurred with smoke, so that the hills of the northeast range were like blue lines in the blue air.

My father had thought that I was injured when he saw me blood-stained, and he tried to ask what was wrong. I could not tell him that everything was wrong. I said I had quarrelled with my grandmother.

He had lost the ready use of our language and had to think before he spoke. I watched him. He had gone bald in front, so that his face was longer, and he looked very tired. He was still bigger and taller than I had remembered him, though I had grown from a child's to a woman's height in the years he had been gone.

"I came to talk to Willow," he said.

I shook my head. My tears came back, and seeing them he thought that she was dead, and made a little sound of pain.

I said, "She still lives in the Blue Clay house, but she isn't Willow; she went back to her name Towhee."

He said, "She has married."

"No," I said, "she won't marry. She won't talk to you."

He said, "I could not come. You know that? It was not on the Amaranth Coast but in the north that we had to take the army." He said where he had been, names of places that I did not know, and said again, "I could not come when I said I would come. I want to tell her that."

I shook my head again. All I could say was, "She will not talk to you."

He said, "Why should she talk to me? To come again here was stupid." I could feel the going in him, and I cried out, "I talk to you! I waited, I waited, I waited for you to come!"

He looked at me then instead of at his thoughts, and said my name, "North Owl."

I said, "I am not that person. I am not a child. I am not anybody. I have no name. I am the Condor's daughter."

"You are my daughter," he said.

I said, "I want to go with you."

He did not understand what I meant at first, and then said, "No, how can I do that? They would keep you. I must go, this day or the next day. They will not let you go away."

I said, "I am a woman, and make my own choices. I will go with you."

He said, "You must ask people."

"I'll tell them," I said. "You are the only one I must ask! Will you take me with you?"

More than anything, I wanted him not to go down to High Porch House to my mother. It was as if I was trading myself for her. I did not understand this then, but I felt it. My father thought for a while, gazing across the Valley to Soul Mountain with its flat, slanting top. The smoke-haze was a pale dull pink color. He said, "I should ask her to let you go with me. Is it true: she will not speak to me?"

"It is true," I said truthfully.

"And it is true you have waited for me," he said, looking again at me.

I said, "Give me a name."

When he understood, he thought for a long time, and at last said, "Do you want this name: Ayatyu?"

I said, "My name is Ayatyu."

I did not ask the meaning of the name then; to me it was my father's kindness, my own freedom.

Later when I spoke his language I knew *ayatyu* in the Valley language would be "well-born woman" or "woman born above others." It is a name that was often given in my father's family. His name was Terter Abhao, and taking his fathers' name as daughters and sons of a man do among that people, I was Terter Ayatyu.

"When will you go?" I asked him.

He asked, "Can you ride?"

"I ride donkeys," I said. "I used to ride your horse with you."

He looked again at the roofs of the houses of Sinshan and said, "Yes. In the wars I thought of that. Many, many times. The little girl sitting with me in the saddle. Those days, in this place, this valley. Those were my good days. Not ever again!"

I waited, and he said, "I will bring a horse for you. When the sun rises the day after tomorrow. At that place." He pointed to the bridge where we had met. "I will not come into this town," he said. His sorrow and desire were becoming anger and turning away. He had come a long way, with difficulty, to see his wife, yet he did not go to see her. I have thought about that time we sat on the terrace on Topknot Hill, many times, and tried to understand why we spoke and behaved as we did. We were both ill, and our illnesses spoke one to the other. We seemed to choose, but were driven. I clung to him, yet I was the stronger.

He said, "Tell them that you wish to go with me. If they let you do this, take leave of them rightly. And go to your heyimas. This will be a long journey, a long time you will be gone, daughter."

He was right to speak so, and I did as he said.

On the second morning at the earliest return of light my grandmother Valiant went to our heyimas with me. We filled the water basin and sang the Return. She marked the heyiya-if on my cheeks with blue clay from Sinshan Creek. She and I came up from the heyimas in the dawn. My mother was waiting for me at the Hinge of town, and Lark Rising and Cricket also, and they all came to the bridge with me; but we did not squat and piss and laugh before we said farewell, because the Condor was waiting there on his tall horse. They stopped at the southeast end of the bridge. I embraced them and ran across the bridge to him. He looked at Towhee, but she had turned away. He helped me mount the horse he had brought, and so I rode away with him through Sinshan Fields.

The Lodge Rejoining, where we learn how to die, was built that year on the planting side where Hechu Creek meets Sinshan Creek. We rode past it as the range across the Valley let the sun go. Singing heya to the sun I rode. We went past the vineyards to the Old Straight Road, and northwest on the road towards Ama Kulkun. The horses strode along fast. My father had brought a sorrel mare for me to ride, shorter and more delicate than his gelding. He kept beside me watchfully, telling me how to hold with my knees and how to use the stirrups and reins. It was much easier than riding donkeys bareback; donkeys have sharp backbones and minds of their own, while the mare was obliging and kindly, and the saddle comfortable. We rode to Telina-na, and passed between Chukulmas and Chumo, and passed Kastoha-na, and still it was bright morning. As we turned to the Mountain Road the Geyser leaped up out of the feathered grasses, shining. My heart turned in me when I saw that. I thought of the old man who had given me a song there. I put the thought and the song away from me. We crossed the River on the Oak Bridge, and I said heya silently. In the foothills of the Mountain five men of the Condor, mounted and with two pack horses, came to meet us, saluting my father. We stopped at the Tembedin Oaks to eat some food and then rode on up into the Mountain on the Clear Lake Road. Where the way to Wakwaha and the Springs of the River went to the left, we went to the right, following the line of the train as far as Metouli, where we took the short-cut road.

Before night we stopped to make camp in live-oak woods on the wrong side of Metouli Spring. I could not get off the horse, and my father, laughing, had to help me. My legs and buttocks were as stiff as wood and pretty soon they began to ache. The Condor men joked a little, but cautiously. They treated me partly as a child but also with something like fear, and they knocked their forehead with their fist when they first spoke to me, as they did to my father. We two sat a little apart and did nothing while they made the fire, cooked the dinner, and laid out the beds.

After eating, I went to talk to the sorrel mare for a while. I smelled of her now, and liked the smell. I had never made a friend so easily. My father talked for a long time to one man, who was to ride a different way the next day, giving him several messages, some quite long, to carry in his head. He made him repeat them, and they were still doing this when I came back to the fire. It was boring to listen to, as I did not know the language. When they were done and the man had gone back to the other men, I said, "Why didn't you write the messages?"

"He can't read," my father said.

If he was blind or weakminded he made a strange messenger, I thought, but I could not see what was wrong with him. I said so.

"Writing is sacred," my father said.

I knew that already.

"Show me your writing," I said.

Sinshan Mountain

He said, "Writing is sacred. Not for hontik. You don't need to write words!"

I did not understand, was all that I understood of this; so I said, "I need words to speak, anyhow. What is hontik?"

And he began then to teach me his language, how the Dayao said to ride a horse, to see a rock, and all the rest.

It was cold up there on the side of the Mountain in the night. The other men sat on the other side of the fire, talking. My father joined in the talk from time to time, briefly, with dignity in the tone of his voice. He gave me some hot brandy, and I soon slept, curled up in Grandmother's arm. In the morning he had to lift me onto the horse, but as soon as we had ridden a little way the stiffness went out of my legs and I was easy in the saddle. So we rode up to the pass in the fog of the autumn morning, in the way of the White Puma.

I have heard people in the Finders Lodge say that when they leave the Valley, even though they have left and returned many times, there is a pain in their heart, or a voice singing in their ears, or a whitening, or a sense of falling—always some sign. Downstream, the historian of the Sinshan Finders, said that he knew when he entered the Valley because for nine breaths his feet did not touch the ground, and when he left the Valley he knew it because for nine breaths he walked knee-deep through earth. Maybe because I was on horseback, or because I was with the Condor, or because I was half a Condor, I felt no sign. Only when I touched my cheeks and felt no mark of the blue clay from Sinshan Creek left there, again my heart turned and went dark and small inside its house. It stayed that way as we rode down the wrong side of the Mountain.

All that country between the Mountain and Clear Lake is very beautiful and like the Valley; rocks, plants, all the people are the same kinds, and the human people live in towns and farms like the towns and farms of the Valley. We did not stay with any of them, nor did we speak to people anywhere; when I asked why, my father said that these were people of no account. We rode as if in another House, without speech. I thought, this is why they are called Condors: they go in silence, above all the others.

When we were in the golden hills northeast of Clear Lake, lying down to sleep on the third night, I began to feel the Valley behind me like a body, my own body. My feet were the sea-channels of the River, the organs and passages of my body were the places and streams and my bones the rocks and my head was the Mountain. That was all my body, and I here lying down was a breath-soul, going farther away from its body every day. A long very thin string connected that body and that soul, a string of pain. I slept, and the next day went on riding, and talked with my father, learning his language. Often we laughed. Still I felt that I was not quite my body, and that I weighed nothing, like a soul.

Indeed I grew thin on that long journey. The Condor food did not taste good to me. They carried dried meat, all beef; along the way they sometimes killed cattle or sheep grazing on those high hills. They did not ask me to, but I came and gave the person they killed my words. At first I thought the human people of these families were generously giving us the animals' deaths, and wondered why I never saw the human people, and why they never gave vegetables or grain or fruit, since it was harvest time. Then I saw two of the men of our group kill a strayed ewe by the path, without giving her any word, cutting off her legs for food and leaving the head and hooves and entrails and fleece for the maggots and coyotes. For several days I put what I had seen away from my mind; but I did not eat that mutton.

Many, many times while I lived with the Condor people I put a thing I saw away, saying, "I'll think about that later," or refusing to think about it at all. This was not mindfulness. But where everything was outside me I could not make all of it enter into me; and when it did enter into me I often felt as if I had no soul at all, and it is the attentive soul that tells the mind, "Remember." Now I am trying to write down my journey to the northeast, to bring it all into my mind at last; but a great deal of it, and of all my years with the Dayao, is lost and will not come back. I could not take it in.

I remember with great clarity how we rode, all in line, across the last pass of the wrinkled hills, and from it saw the wide valley of the River of the Marshes all before us to the north and east; far in the southeast was the shore of the Inland Sea, hazy and shining. A broad golden light lay over the yellow willows by the river and the cattail marshes and the far peaks of the Range of Light, slanting from under clouds behind us. I sang heya to that great river and the beauty and vastness of the world, and to the sun going into the house of winter. That night it rained. All the next day and the next as we followed the River of the Marshes north we rode and walked in rain.

We crossed that big river at a ford where it spread out in many shallow channels and the horses did not have to swim far, so early in the rainy season. At that ford another group of Condor men joined us, twelve of them, so we were a big group going along, nineteen human people and twenty-five horses, one mare with a colt following. As they rode, the men liked to sing a song they had:

> "Where the City is, I am coming,
> Where the Condor is, I am coming,
> Where the battle is, I am coming."

They put any word they liked into the song, and sang, "Where the food is, I am coming," or "Where the cunt is, I am coming," over and over as they rode along in line.

After long rain there was a day I remember when the sky partly cleared and we saw Kulkun When pouring a stream of dun smoke up into the clouds, southeast of where we were. All around the dark volcano was a roil of steam and smoke from lesser vents, and the air stank like rotten eggs when the wind changed. We began to come near the foothills of the volcanoes. I was very much afraid of them, and dreamed all night that fiery cracks were gaping in the earth about me and clouds of smoke were burning and choking me, but I said nothing about my cowardice. On the next day the whole sky cleared, and from those hills looking north I saw the Mountain of the North hanging snowstreaked from the sky down to the dark forests. One pure plume of steam rose from its eastern crown, like a down feather of the white egret. Because the mountain was beautiful and because I knew its name from maps and stories in the heyimas, the sight of it made me happy: I recognised it. I sat on the mare singing heya to it.

My father rode up beside me and said, "That is Tsatasyan," the White Mountain.

I said, "Also it is Kulkun Eraian, one of the places where the arms of the world meet."

He said, "I spent ten years of my life winning the land around that mountain for the Condor, and now it's all to do over." He used the word *zarirt,* which I had learned playing long-dice with the soldiers; it means to win at gambling, like our word *dumi.* I could not imagine what he meant, how he had won an enormous piece of the world like that, or who he had won it from, or what use it was to him. I tried to ask and he tried to explain, but we talked backwards for a while, and he grew impatient with my stupidity. "This, here, is land the Condor armies won," he said. "Why do you think the hontik aren't shooting at us any more?"

"That was only one place that they shot at us," I said. It had been where we first turned to follow the Dark River; some people hidden in the willow thickets had shot arrows at us, and then ran away when the men tried to chase them. My father had ordered the men to come back and ride on, and they had galloped back laughing and shouting jokes, very excited, so that I was also excited, and not afraid, though I certainly had never expected to be part of a war.

My father said, "That's because they are afraid of us."

I gave up trying to understand what he was talking about. But part of my stupidity was that I did not want to understand. Educated people who read this will have been laughing at me, that I could ride for days and days with armed men called soldiers or warriors, with my father the chief of them, and see them steal, and never enter a town or farmstead, and be ambushed, and still not understand that they were at war with every people of the lands we had come through. They are quite right to laugh. I was uneducated, and unwilling to use my mind.

Now in these foothills of the volcanoes we came to villages where the people came out and knocked their heads to us instead of keeping out of sight or running their sheep away and turning back to spit after us. The villages were very small, five or six log houses along a creek, and some sheep or pigs and turkeys, and a lot of dogs barking and snarling. But they were very generous, I thought, giving us food even when there were more of us than of them. After two days riding in that broken country, we came to the place called South City, Sainyan.

The Dayao word *sai* means the same as our word *kach*. We use it only to speak of a different place in time or mind, those people who lived outside the world, and the network of the Exchanges. They have those uses too, but chiefly they use the word to name the place where they live, saying that they are inhabitants of the City of Man. What to us is disaster to them is their glory. How am I to write all this story in reversal-words?

People of the Madrone Lodge asked me to write my life story as an offering because nobody else in the Valley has lived with the Condor and come back, and so my story is a history; but I wish now

I had learned to write history instead of learning to make pots, when I was North Owl. When I was Ayatyu I had to forget writing and reading altogether. The Dayao will blind the eye or cut off the hand of a woman or a farmer who writes a single word. Only the True Condors may write or read, and of them I think only the ones called the One-Warriors, who officiate at the wakwa, learn how to write and read freely. They say that since One made the cosmos by speaking a word, the universe is his book, and to write or read words is to share the power that belongs to One; and only certain men are supposed to share that power. They have the abacus for household use, and in both their Cities they had electrical devices made by instructions from the Exchange to keep records, but all their records are reduced to numbers. Nothing is written down or printed, and so the Word of One remains, as they say, clean. Once in my ignorance I said to my father, "If I wrote 'Boo!' on a wall here all those fierce warriors would scream and run away!" He said in anger, "They would punish you, to teach you to fear One." That word is the end of talking, as well as the end of writing, under the Condor's wing, and I said no more.

When I went with Abhao, my heart wanted to be a Condor's heart. I tried to be a Condor woman. I tried not to think in the language or the ways of the Valley. I wanted to leave the Valley, not to be of it, to be new, living a new way. But I could not do that; only an educated person might do that. I was too young, and had not considered existence, or read books, or trained with the Finders, or thought about history. My mind was not freed. It was held inside the Valley, instead of holding the Valley inside it. Even for my age I was ignorant, because Sinshan, like other small towns, was given to prejudice and wilful ignorance; and because my family was a troubled one; and most of all because the Warrior and Lamb cults had interfered with education and ceremony during my adolescence. So I was not free to go from the Valley. Not being entirely a person, I could not become a different person.

Also, however wilfully I tried, it was difficult for me to become entirely a Condor person. I became as sick as I could, but I was not willing to die.

It is almost as hard to write about being Ayatyu as it was to be her.

While I am talking about talking, I may explain certain words I have used or will use. We call them the Condor people; their name for themselves as distinct from all other people is Dayao, One-People. I shall call them that in this story now, because the way they use the word Condor, *Rehemar*, is complicated. Only one man, whom they believe to be a messenger from One to them, and whom they all serve, is called The Condor. Certain men belonging to certain families are called True Condors, and others like them are called, as I said, One-Warriors. No other people are called Condors. Men who are not of those families are all called *tyon,* farmers, and must serve the True Condors. Women of those families are called Condor Women, and must serve Condor men, but may give orders to tyon and hontik. The hontik are all other women, foreigners, and animals.

The condor bird itself is not called rehemar but Da-Hontik, and is sacred. Boys of the True Condor families must shoot a condor, or at least a buzzard, to become men.

I had the condor feather that had come to me as a child with me in my pouch of valuables; it was lucky that I did not show it to anyone before I learned that women are not permitted to touch condor feathers or even to see the condor in the sky. They are supposed to hide their eyes and wail when the Great One flies.

It is easy to say that such customs are barbaric, but then what has one said? Having lived in civilisation, in the City of Man, I do not use those words, civilised, barbaric; I do not know what they mean. All I can write is what I saw, what I learned, what I did, and let wiser people find a name for it all.

The Dayao had built South City about forty years before I came there. They had come down from The City and made a war with some people who lived in small towns and farmsteads in these foothills south of Dark River, and took their place to live from them. It is not true that they ate the bodies of human people whom they killed in wars; that is a superstition grown out of a symbol. They killed and burned men and children and kept women to be fucked by Dayao men. They penned the women with the cattle. Some of the women stayed of their own will after a while because their life was destroyed and there was no other place to go, and these women became Dayao. I talked to some of them who told me who they had been before they were made Dayao, but most of them did not like to talk about it.

The time when the Dayao made South City was the time when they began making war with everyone. They said, "The Condor rules from the Omorn Sea to the Western Sea, from the North Mountain to the Coast of Amaranth!" They killed many people and caused pain and long disorder in the Volcano country, and infected other people with their sickness, but when I came there they were dying. It was themselves they ate.

I know that now; I did not then. I saw the towers of South City and the walls of black basalt, the wide streets at right angles, the splendor and array. I saw the magnificent bridge across the Dark River and the road that lay straight as a suntrack on water to the north, to The City. I saw the machines and engines of work and war they used, of most exact and elegant make, marvelous products of handmind. All I saw was great, and straight, and hard, and strong, and I saw it all in fear and admiration.

My father had had relatives in South City, and we rode to that house; but it was empty.

The Dayao make three kinds of house. The farmhouses are much like our farmhouses; the tyon and hontik in the Cities live in huge, long houses, many families to each, like barns or stables; and the True Condor live in family houses, which are dug down into the earth, with low stone walls aboveground, no windows, and a peaked timber roof. They look a little like heyimas, but inside they are entirely different. The house is divided into as many apartments as the people want by movable panels of wood and cloth, five or six feet high, which can be set against the poles and columns that support the roof. The floor is covered with layers of rugs, and the walls with hangings of cloth, and often the hangings are brought together into a peak at the top of the room, like a tent. The Dayao house remembers the winter dugouts and summer tents of the nomads of the Plains of Grass, as the wooden houses of Tachas Touchas remember the river-forests of the northern coast. All the heating and lighting is electric, from mills and solar cells; and when such a house is furnished and tapestried and brightly lit, it is very warm and comfortable, encompassing. But the house of my father's people in South City that we came to that night was dark and dank, smelling of earth and urine. My father stood inside the entranceway and spoke like a child: "They have gone away!"

We had to go to another Condor house for shelter and food that night. My father left me with the women of the household and went off to talk with the men. The women smiled at me and tried to talk, but they were timid, and I was very tired and confused. I could not understand why they acted as if they were afraid of me. Among them I felt a little as I had felt in Hardcinder House in Telina when I was a child, awed by everything. There was metal everywhere; it seemed that copper wire was as common to them as string to us. And they were very good cooks, and though the food was strange to me I enjoyed most of it very much, after the salt beef and stolen mutton of the soldiers. But their wealth did not flow; they did not give with pleasure. Some of them knocked their heads every time they spoke to me, and others of them did not speak to me at all.

Later on I found that the ones who did not speak to me were the Condor Women, and the ones who smiled and knocked their heads were the hontik.

I do not remember much of the days we spent in South City. My father was worried and angry, and I saw him only to greet him once each day. I stayed with the women all the time. I did not know then that Dayao women always stayed together and did not go out. Hearing some talk about war, and having seen the city full of armed soldiers, I thought that there must be a war going on at the walls, and that these women were staying inside their house so that the opponents would not steal them, as the Dayao stole women. I had this all figured out, and then found out that there was no fighting at all going on anywhere near South City. I felt foolish, but in fact I had been right; Dayao women lived under siege all their lives. All I thought then was that they were all crazy. I stayed with them all the time in the close, warm rooms lighted brightly by electricity, trying to learn to talk as they did, and sewing. I was no good at their kind of sewing, and nearly went crazy myself trying to do it hour after hour, when I wanted to be outside in the air, in the light, with my father, or by myself. I was never by myself.

At last we left that house and that city and started north. I had missed the sorrel mare very much while I was trapped indoors, and had dreamed every day of riding her again and smelling her smell on my hands and clothes; when the women told me to get into a covered cart with them, I refused. One of the older Condor Women ordered me to get into the cart. I said, "Am I dead? Am I a chicken?"—but it seemed that among them, live and healthy people rode in carts on wheels, and she did not know what I meant. She got angry and I got angry. My father came and I began to tell him that I wanted to ride the sorrel mare. He said, "Get in the cart," and rode on by. He had looked at me as a woman among the other women, a squawking hen among the poultry. He had changed his soul for his power. I stood awhile taking this into myself as best I could while the other chickens peeped and squawked around me, and then I got up into the cart. All that day travelling in that cart I thought, more than I had ever thought before, about how to be a human being.

We did not go straight north, but turned off on another wide, smooth road towards the northwest. The women with me said we were going to meet the marastso, the army, and travel with them, and after a day we did so. All the soldiers who had been travelling in troops to take food from small-town people, collecting tribute they called it, or staying in camps in the Dark River and Volcano countries giving orders, or as they called it keeping order, were gathering together at a place called Rembonyon, and we too went there. We were all following after several chiefs or generals, one of whom was my father.

The pieces of the army came with a lot of animals, and a lot of tyon came with the animals and the other hontik. Those camps were where I first met stolen women, ones the Dayao men had taken from their people and raped when they liked. Some, as I said, were coming freely with the soldiers, and the soldier might stay with the woman and their babies; and so I said something in our camp about these hontik wives. The women of the Tsaya Bele household, with whom I travelled, laughed at that, and explained that Condor men did not marry hontik, but only Condor women, the daughters of other Condor men. They were all such daughters themselves, and very positive about what they told me.

Stupidly, I said, "But my father, the Condor Terter Abhao, is married to my mother in the Valley."

"It is not a marriage here," one of them said kindly. But when I argued, the old woman Tsaya Maya Bele said, "There is no marriage between Man and animal, girl! Be still and know your place. We have treated you as a Condor's daughter, not a savage. Behave as such." It was a threat. I heeded it.

Aside from learning some things such as that, which I had no desire to know, I enjoyed that slow journey to Rembonyon with the Dayao. I did not have to stay in the cart, but could walk beside it if I stayed near it. At night they set up big tents, a whole town of tents appearing in no time at all. Inside the tents it was bright and warm, the women sitting about on thick red rugs, cooking and talking and laughing and drinking strong manzanita-berry tea or honey brandy; outside, the men called out to one another in the cold dusk, the horses neighed at their pickets and the cattle lowed, off where the farmers' campfires glimmered. When it was dark the people at those fires sang long, lonesome, desolate songs that seemed to have the desert in them.

Maybe the Dayao should have been always on the move; maybe their health as a people was in being nomads, movers-on, as they had been in the country north of the Omorn Sea and before that on the Plains of Grass. A hundred years or more ago they obeyed one of their Condors who had a vision and said that One had commanded them to build a city and dwell in it. When they did that they locked their energy into the wheel, and so began to lose their souls.

After Rembonyon the whole great train of animals and humans and carts set off through the high, desolate lands northeast of Kulkan Eraian. Volcanoes smoked before and behind us. It grew cold, and a wind in our faces brought dark clouds across the sky. In falling snow we came across a waste of black, broken lava to the City of the Condor. I had not walked in snow before that day.

Sai was walled, with a guarded gate of great size and beauty; outside the walls were innumerable barns, stables, shops, and barrack-houses, and inside them the streets were straight and wide like those of South City but still wider and longer. The street that led in from the gate ended in a huge building, window above window above window, and the barrack-houses and family houses were all higher and solider and finer than those of South City. Ter-ter House in Sai had its own wall around its gardens, of polished black stone; its roof was of carved cedar, with decks and walkways on it; and down inside it the rooms seemed endless, apartments and divisions and screened-off corners and nooks and angles, all without windows yet bright, and warm as the silky nest of the wood rat inside her many-tunnelled tall house. The rooms deepest inside were the women's quarters. My father took me there at once. When he turned to go I held his arm. I said, "I do not wish to stay here, please."

He said without anger, "You live here, Ayatyu. This is your house."

I said, "You are my father, but this is not my house."

He said, "It is my father's, therefore mine, therefore yours. When you have rested I'll bring you before him. You should look your best then. Not crying and tired. Go bathe and rest and dress and meet the other girls here. They'll look after you. I'll be back for you in the morning."

He went off among the people who knocked their foreheads as he passed. I stood in tears among the women.

In that house the two kinds of women, Condor's daughters and hontik, were as different as sheep and goats. None of the Condor's daughters spoke to me, that first night. They left me with the hontik. I was glad of that, since the hontik seemed more like Valley women, but they were even more afraid of me than the South City women had been. I heard them speak about me, but when I spoke to them in their language they stared and did not answer, till I felt like a talking crow. They would not leave me alone, but they would not come close to me. At last a girl came in who looked to be my age or a little younger, and who was quick and courageous. She spoke to me and understood what I answered. She said her name was Esiryu. She took me to have a bath, for I was filthy from travel-

ling, and she found a small room for me to sleep in, and stayed with me there. She talked faster than I could understand, often, but I understood that she wanted me to be her friend and she would be a friend to me; she was as prompt and easy about that as the sorrel mare had been.

After she had combed out my hair, I said, "Now I'll comb yours." She laughed, and said, "No, no, no, Condor's daughter!"

Without Esiryu I would not have been able to live in Terter House. I did what she said to do and did not do what she said not to do, all the time I was there. She was my slave, whom I obeyed.

In the late morning my father came back, dressed in splendid clothing of red-and-black-patterned wool. I went to him and he embraced me, but he shouted past my ear, "Why has Terter Ayatyu Belela not been given suitable clothes to wear?" Then there was a lot of scurrying and forehead-knocking by hontik and Daughters alike, and I was very quickly dressed up in the kind of fine skirt and bodice the Daughters wore, with a gauzy head-scarf. Esiryu had already braided up my hair Dayao-style, so that was all right. My father said some more things to the women that made them cower and look away, and then took my hand and hurried me through the rooms and passages. The scarf blew off my head, and he turned back to pick it up, and put it over my head so that it hid my face. I could see through it well enough, but certainly did not want it on, and took it off.

"Put it on!" he said. It was not just order-shouting, but nervous anger; he was anxious. "Keep it on, over your face! When you come

before my father, salute him!" He made the face-knocking movement, and made me show him that I could do it.

I did all he said. I was frightened by his fear.

Terter Gebe was an old man, handsome and thin, with much
authority in him. It was easy to behave with respect and courtesy in
his presence; he was like the officiant in a great wakwa, full of the
strength and dignity of the ceremony. But the officiant gives that
back, lets it go, at the end of the wakwa; and Terter Gebe had kept
it all to himself for sixty years. All that others gave him, he kept;
and he believed and they believed that that strength and dignity
belonged to him. I did not believe that, but since they were truly
there in him I honored them. I did so as a Condor's Daughter,
knocking my forehead. I kept the veil over my face until he lifted it
and stared at me awhile. That I found hard to bear, being looked at
full on, shamelessly.

He said, "Etyeharazra puputyela!" which is, "Be welcome,
granddaughter!"

I said in his language, "Thank you, grandfather."

He gave me a keen look, very searching. He never smiled. He
said something to my father, which I kept in mind till I could ask
Esiryu what the syllables meant. They meant, "Better marry this
one quickly!"

My father laughed. He looked relieved and happy now. They
talked to each other awhile. I stood there like an image of a person,
not talking or moving. I tried to keep looking down, the way hontik
women did when they were with Condors, but I wanted to look at
my grandfather. Every time I stole a glance, he caught it. At last,
carefully and slowly, I pulled the veil back over my face. Through it
I could watch him and he could not tell if I were watching him or
not. It is easy to learn to be a slave. The tricks of slavery are like
fleas hopping from a dead ground squirrel onto your skin; you have
the plague before you know it. And all the tools of slavery have two
edges.

Since Terter Gebe had accepted me as his granddaughter, the
Daughters of his House had to treat me as one of them and not as
an animal or primitive person. Some of them were ready to be
friendly as soon as they had permission to be. Their lives inside the
women's rooms were very small and boring, and a new person was
a great excitement and interest to them. Others were less well disposed. I wished my father would not order them and bully them as
he did; he meant to help and defend me, but every bow and smile
and head-knock they gave him turned into a sneer or a snub or a
trick against me, when he was gone to give orders to somebody

else, and I was left there in the household. All this was the kind of reversal that it seemed to me one would have to expect in a household arranged like a himpi-pen.

My father's mother had died many years ago, and his father had not remarried; the widow of my father's brother was the chief of the women of the house. Everything among the Dayao had to have a chief. If two of them were together, one or the other was chief. Everything they did was war. Even when people worked together one of them was chief of the work, as if working were making war; even when children played together one of them told the others what to do, though at least they quarrelled about it. So my aunt Terter Zadyaya Bele was the general of the women of Terter House, and she was not pleased by my presence there. I thought she was ashamed of me, a hontik, a half-animal; and that was all too familiar to me, who used to be called a half-person, so I hated her. Now I think she was afraid of me. She saw me, foreigner or primitive or animal as I was, the only daughter of the Condor Terter, and feared I would want to take her strength and dignity from her. If we could have worked and talked together and come to know each other I think it would have been better, for she was not a spiteful person. But that was prevented by our misunderstanding, fixed and made incurable by her jealousy of her power, and my shame. In any case, she would not touch me and did not like to approach me, because I was purutik, unclean.

The mental way, the soul's way of the Dayao would surely be the most important thing I could tell about them, and some of it I can tell by way of telling my story; but when it comes to their wakwa and rites and all the deepest of their thinking, I learned very little. There were no books. What men were taught I do not know; girls and women were taught nothing but the skills of the household. Women were not allowed into the sacred parts of their heyimas, which they call *daharda;* we could come no nearer than the vestibule in front of the daharda to listen to the singing inside on certain great festivals. Women have no part in the intellectual life of the Dayao; they are kept in, but left out. It was not men there, but women, who told me that women have no souls. That being the case, naturally they have little interest in learning about the soul's way. All I learned was picked up here and there, and does not make a whole; this is the best I can make of it:

One made everything out of nothing. One is a person, immortal. He is all-powerful. Human men are imitations of him. One is not the universe; he made it, and gives it orders. Things are not part of him nor is he part of them, so you must not praise things, but only One. The One, however, reflects himself in the Condor; so the Condor is to be praised and obeyed. And the True Condors and One-Warriors, who are all called Sons of the Condor or Sons of the Son, are reflections of the reflection of One, and therefore also to be praised and obeyed. The tyon are very dim and faint reflections far removed from One, but even so they have enough of his power to be called human beings. No other people are human. The hontik, that is women and foreigners and animals, have nothing to do with One at all; they are purutik, unclean, dirt people. They were made by One to obey and serve the Sons. This is what they say; it seemed to me to get a little complicated, since Condor's Daughters gave orders to tyon, and talked about them as if they were dirt people; but that discrepancy is kept out of mind, since the Daughters all live in the City and seldom even see the farmers. It must have all been very different when the Dayao were nomads, but it may have started then, too, as a matter of sexual jealousy, the chief men trying to keep their wives and daughters "clean," and the women holding themselves apart from the strangers they met along their way, and finally all of them coming to think that to be a person at all is to be separate from and apart from everyone and everything.

They say that as there was a time when One made everything, there will be a time when everything will stop being, when One will unmake everything. Then will begin the Time Outside of Time. He will throw away everything except the True Condors and One-Warriors who obeyed him in every way and were his slaves. They will become part of One then, and be forever. I am sure that there is some sense to be made of this, but I cannot make it.

Some of the things I learned in the Lamb Lodge in Sinshan were Warrior Lodge teachings learned from Condor soldiers during the years they stayed in the Valley; the Warrior Lodge men thought they were practising True Condor ways. In fact they understood even less than I did. They understood that men were better than women, and that nothing was of any account except One and men, but they got the rest of it and the reasons for it all mixed up. I don't think most of them ever understood that there was indeed only one One. Their souls and minds were much too dirty. That part, about being purutik, about dirt persons, made sense to me, in its way. In order to reflect, a mirror has to be clean. The cleaner and clearer and purer it is, the better it will reflect. True Condor warriors were to be one thing only, reflections of One, setting themselves apart from all the rest of existence, washing it from their minds and souls, killing the world, so that they could remain perfectly pure. That is why my father was named Kills. He was to live outside the world, killing it, to show the glory of One.

As I speak of it, this way sounds clownish. That is myself, my voice; I am the clown, since I cannot help the reversals. The Dayao way was without clowns or clowning, without reversal or turning, straight, single, terrible.

The third part of Stone Telling's story begins on page 361.

DRAMATIC WORKS

A NOTE ON THE VALLEY STAGE.

The only permanent theater in the Valley was in Wakwaha, on the northwest side of the Great Dancing Place. It was like a heyimas, being underground, with a stepped roof, and an efficient system of natural and artificial ventilation and lighting. The shape of the room was broadly oval; the stage was raised; the audience sat on comfortable backed benches, which seated about two hundred.

Kastoha and Telina had stages, but no theaters. They kept the stage dismantled in a storage barn till it was wanted for a play. A stage consisted of two big platforms joined in the center by a circular, smaller platform, which might stand a foot or so higher than the others. The left-hand large platform was closer to the audience than the right-hand one. Such a stage was set up on one of the common places, with an awning if necessary.

The small towns had no stage at all. When a play was put on by a lodge or heyimas or when travelling players came, they marked out the ground on the town common place in a wide heyiya-if figure, the left arm closer to the audience; or similarly marked out the floor of a big barn-loft or workroom.

If there was a stage, it was elevated enough that the musicians could sit on the ground in front of it without hiding the actors. If the stage was merely marked out, the musicians sat in a semicircle behind the central stage.

Stage left was the Earth; stage right was the Sky; the center, the raised platform or hinge of the heyiya-if, was the Mountain, or the Crossing Place.

The Wedding Night at Chukulmas

The Wedding Night at Chukulmas was one of the plays that were performed before the ritual drama of *Awar and Bulekwe*, on the evening of the second day of the World Dance at Wakwaha.

The actor's manuscript from which the translation was made consisted of the speeches only; descriptions of the stage and staging were provided by the actors and expanded by the translator after seeing a performance of the play.

~~◦~~

The stage would be divided as usual into the two Arms of the World, the connecting/dividing point, the Hinge, being represented by an elevation in the center. The madrone tree which would occupy center stage for the sacred play to follow might already be in place—a live young tree in a tub of madrone wood. For this play, stage left is understood to be the town of Chukulmas, and specifically the interior of a Serpentine household; stage right represents the dancing place of Chukulmas, and specifically the interior of the Blue Clay heyimas; while the central tree first shades the pathway between the two arms of the town, and later the Black Adobe Lodge.

The musicians play the Beginning Tone.

Men come on at the left, singing one of the traditional World Dance songs for the second day of the festival, sung by the Blue Clay House: songs to game animals, perhaps the Deer Dance Song, or a less elaborate one such as the Squirrel Song:

> Running up and down
> kekeya heya, kekeya heya,
> the digger-pine world,
> kekeya heya,
> the digger-pine world!

Singing, they cross the Hinge and come into the dancing place, the area in the curve of the five heyimas buildings. By a stylised gesture each in turn signifies that he is climbing down the ladder into the heyimas. When they are all in the heyimas, the music ceases.

THE SPEAKER OF THE HEYIMAS:

Now is the right time to set out the supper for each man of our House about to be married. He will be leaving his mother's household and his mothers' House, returning but always leaving again, until he dies and comes home to the Blue Clay. Tonight the young men leave us to be married for the first time. This is the time to set out the wedding supper for them.

The Chorus usually consists of nine people; in this case, ten. Only one member of the Chorus speaks at a time, unless otherwise indicated.

CHORUS I:

Everything is ready. The old men are setting it out.

SPEAKER:

Why aren't you helping them?

CHORUS I:

I thought I'd eat the supper instead of serving it.

SPEAKER:

You've been married three times!

CHORUS I:

And only got dinner for it once. It's not worth while.

SPEAKER:

Keep your hands off those pies.

CHORUS I:

All right, all right. But there's so much food here for only three men to eat. Young idiots. What do they want to get married for, anyhow? This is the only good part—the wedding supper. After this, boys, it's a different story. Little wifey here, oh yes, that's fine, and then wifey's mother there, that's not quite so fine, and then wifey's little auntie here and little great-auntie there and it's not so fine at all, and then, then there's the Grandmother-In-Law! Oh, you don't know, you don't know what you're doing! you don't know what you're getting into! And none of them will give you a dinner half the size of this!

SPEAKER:

It's ready. Now is the right time to sing the bridegrooms to the feast.

The rest of the Chorus have been miming the serving of the wedding feast. Now the Speaker and six men of the Chorus stand to the right and sing the first verse of the Wedding Song (which is not written down). Four young men of the Chorus sit down in front of them, as if sitting to the wedding feast at the low table. One of them sits with his back to the audience.

CHORUS (unison whisper):
> Who is that one?

SPEAKER:
> There are four men to be married here.

CHORUS II:
> We cooked the wedding feast for three.

SPEAKER:
> Who is he, that one?
> He sits on the right.
> He wears last night's clothes.
> O bridegroom, young man,
> you cannot eat this food
> with ash-covered hands!

The "last night's clothes" are the mourning garments worn by the Black Adobe dancers on the first night of the World Dance, the ceremony of mourning—tight and black, swathing the limbs, and the hands and bare feet smeared with white ash. Until they sit down, the Fourth Bridegroom has been hidden among the Chorus. Now we see his clothing, and that his head is covered with a fine, thin, black veil.

CHORUS II:
> I will bring water.

SPEAKER:
> Will you wash your hands
> in the water poured
> from the blue pitcher
> into the clay bowl?

CHORUS II:
> I have poured water.

SPEAKER:
> O young man, bridegroom,
> you can't be married
> silent, in silence!

The Fourth Bridegroom does not respond, but sits rocking his body a little—as people do during the ceremony of mourning of the previous night.

SPEAKER:
> Young man, you must say
> the name of your wife,
> the name of her House.

THE FOURTH BRIDEGROOM:
> Her name is Turquoise
> of the Serpentine.

CHORUS III:
This man must be from some other town, he talks so strangely. Maybe he's not even from the Valley. Maybe this is a no-House person. What is he doing here? What has he come here for?

THE FOURTH BRIDEGROOM:
> My House is Blue Clay.
> This is my wedding.

SPEAKER:
> Then eat the dinner
> we have made for you
> in your Blue Clay House,
> the house of your life,
> and we will sing you
> when the time is right
> to your bride, your wife,
> to your marriage house,
> to your children's House.

While the Speaker and Chorus serve them, the four bridegrooms eat. On the left stage, women are entering, and the action shifts to that area; the Blue Clay men sit or kneel motionless on the right-hand side. The women come in singing a Second Day of the World song of their House, the Serpentine, such as the Counting Grasses Song. They are the Grandmother and a Chorus of ten, rather than the usual nine, women. After they have all come on, the song dies away and they bustle about in a lively and rapid housecleaning dance.

GRANDMOTHER:
> Get everything ready.
> Hurry up! Be quick!

CHORUS (various single voices take the lines):

Where is the hearthbroom?
Is the bed laid out?
I can't find the cord.
They won't want the lamp!
I'll get the good sheets. [etc.: improvised.]
Ready, Grandmother!

GRANDMOTHER:

Where is she, our girl
to be married now,
tonight, where is she?

From the Chorus two young women come forward, one dressed in bridal clothing of yellow, orange, and red, and one in the dark mourning garb of the previous night.

CHORUS (unison whisper):

Who is the other?

GRANDMOTHER:

Come, let me see you,
Sunlight of summer!
Ha, that was my vest,
when I was married!
Who is that other?

FIRST BRIDE:

I don't know, Mother.

GRANDMOTHER:

Summer dawn, sunrise!
Well, this Blue Clay man
is wise and lucky.
He is welcome here.
Let him, for your sake,
live under this roof,
in his children's House.
Let him come in now!
Let the man enter!

CHORUS I:

Grandmother, listen.
There is another.
There is a stranger.

GRANDMOTHER:

Who is this woman?

The Second Bride stands still and does not respond. Her head is covered by a fine black veil.

GRANDMOTHER:

> You have been walking in the hearth, girl; there's ash on your feet. You must have burned the bread, girl; there's soot on your hands. Have you been climbing trees, girl? There's pitch on your face. Do you not wash before your wedding? Who are you? What are you here for? What are you doing in my house, on a wedding night, on the second night of the World?

CHORUS II:

> Why is she crying
> on the Wedding Night?

GRANDMOTHER:

> Of what House are you?

SECOND BRIDE:

> Of the Serpentine.

GRANDMOTHER:

> And of what household?

SECOND BRIDE:

> I am Flood's daughter,
> Toyon's granddaughter.

GRANDMOTHER:

> I don't know those people. I never heard of that family. No such people live in Chukulmas. You must be from somewhere else. Go back there. You can't come into this household and get married. Who are you marrying, anyway?

SECOND BRIDE:

> I marry Thunder
> of the Second House!

When she says this, the men over on the right side of the stage stand up and begin to come towards the center of the stage, dancing slowly, and singing the first verse of the Wedding Song very low and soft.

GRANDMOTHER:

> I don't know him. Nobody lives in this town named Thunder. You must be crazy, woman; you must be a forest-living woman who's lost her wits, living along too long. You are making up the world. Well, this is the world that made us up! And tonight we're dancing it. You can dance with us, if you'll take off last night's clothes, and wash your face and hands and feet, but you can't get married here, because this isn't your household, and there isn't any husband here for you.

SECOND BRIDE:

> I bring my husband

to my daughters' house.

CHORUS (unison whisper):

To her daughters' house.

GRANDMOTHER:

What are you talking about, young woman? That's nonsense.
You must be crazy. Enough of this. Go away, get out, go back
where you came from. You are spoiling the Wedding Night.
Go!

The Second Bride turns and goes slowly towards the center of the
stage, while the women of the household stand still, watching her.
The line of men coming singing from the heyimas stand still and
watch the Fourth Bridegroom, who comes forward. The Bride and
the Groom stand facing each other across the Hinge, under the
madrone tree.

BRIDE:

No house. No hope.

GROOM:

They sing for us,
to marry us.

BRIDE:

Too late. Too long.

GROOM:

It was my fault!

BRIDE:

No matter now.

She begins to turn and go very slowly towards the back of the stage,
past the tree. An old man comes forward from the Chorus of men,
and says to the Speaker.

OLD MAN:

May I speak to her?

SPEAKER:

Keep her from going!

OLD MAN:

Woman in tears,
tell me your name.

BRIDE:

I was Turquoise.

OLD MAN:

Daughter of Flood,
Toyon's daughter?

BRIDE:

I was that girl.

OLD MAN (to the Groom):

You are Thunder,
Creek Dancer's son?

GROOM:

I was her son.

OLD MAN:

These are people who died a long time ago. I have lived a long life, but they were dead long before I was born. They were young people in this town, about to be married, sleeping together. They quarrelled. I don't know what happened. It was a story people told when I was a child, an old story, and I was a child, not understanding, not listening carefully. The young man died; perhaps he killed himself in anger. That may have been how it was. The young woman had said she would marry some other man, and so he killed himself. And she never married that other man or any man. She died young, unmarried. I don't know how it was. Maybe she killed herself. I only remember the names, and old people talking of that sad story that had happened when they were young. How did you die? Did you kill yourselves? It is a cruel thing to do.

The Bride and the Groom crouch down, rocking their bodies, and do not answer.

THE OLD MAN:

I am sorry.
It is long past.
No matter now.

SPEAKER:

What is it they want?

GRANDMOTHER:

Why have they come here?

GROOM:

To be married.

BRIDE:

To be married.

SPEAKER:

The dead can't marry
in the House of Life.
How can we help them?

The Grandmother comes forward so that she faces the Speaker across the Hinge, she behind the Bride, he behind the Groom.

GRANDMOTHER:
>   We cannot help them.
>   Listen: they are dead!
>   There's no undoing.
>   No one is married
>   in the Four Houses,
>   on the other side.

CHORUSES (unison, softly, in songspeech to the Continuing Tone):
>   No one can marry
>   where they are living,
>   in the Four Houses.
>   They're tired of grieving.
>   They made a mistake.

GRANDMOTHER:
>   There's no unmaking.
>   Not where they are now.

SPEAKER:
>   My heart cannot bear
>   grief outliving life.
>   They lived here, people
>   of our town, Blue Clay
>   and Serpentine, once.
>   Let them be married
>   here in Chukulmas,
>   in the dark house,
>   the Black Adobe.
>   Is this wrong to do?

The Old Man comes to the center stage, under the tree, between the Bride and Groom.

OLD MAN:
>   That is my household:
>   I am the Speaker
>   of the Black Adobe.
>   I think this is right,
>   to do this is right,
>   to unmake sorrow.
>   Come with me, children
>   of the Four Houses,

Turquoise and Thunder:
I summon you: come.
You will be married.
    under the earth,
    inside the world.

SPEAKER:
    You, men and women
    of the Five Houses,
    sing them their marriage!

The Old Man goes directly back and then down behind the elevated center stage, disappearing from view. The Ghosts follow him. As they meet behind him they take hands, her right hand in the Groom's left. The two Choruses sing the second verse of the Wedding Song.

GRANDMOTHER:
    I tell you: no good
    will come out of this.

The Old Man and the Ghosts have disappeared. As the Choruses continue singing, the young Serpentine bride in her splendid clothes comes forward to meet one of the Blue Clay bridegrooms, he too dressed in saffron and crimson.

BRIDE:
    Come to my household.
GROOM:
    I will come gladly.
GRANDMOTHER:
    Sing them the song, then!
SPEAKER:
    Sing them their marriage!

All slowly dance the line off left, singing the last verses of the Wedding Song to music and at last the Ending Tone.

The Shouting Man, the Red Woman, and the Bears

The entire text is a translation of a manuscript in the
Library of the Madrone Lodge in Telina-na.

~ᧁ~

This is a play with music. Drums beat five and five, and the Beginning Tone.

Nine Bear People come up and over the Mountain one by one from the left.

They dance to music in the House of Death and Rain.

Bodo begins shouting, below the stage at the left. The Bears go and wait behind the Mountain. Bodo comes on the stage at the left. He is an old man limping and weeping and shouting and waving his arms.

Bodo says:
>   What was I born for?
>   What is the reason?
>   What am I here for?
>   What must I do here?
>   Give me an answer!
>   What was I born for?
>   Give me an answer!
>   Answer me why! Why!
>   Answer me now! Now!

The Bears begin to close in around Bodo as he shouts and dances. He keeps his back to them, but when they reach out for him he evades them; they move slowly and he is very quick and agile. Gradually they drive him towards the Mountain. He begins to climb the Mountain, shouting.

Bodo shouts:

> Why did I come here
> and live in this house?
> I will find out why!
> I'll find the answer!
> *Yah!* I have found it!

He drops on his face. The Bears withdraw behind the Mountain. Bodo rises onto his knees, bows down, rubs his face in the dirt in circles, prostrates himself, wallows, throws dirt on his head, and finally, in a humble crouching posture, begins to chant in falsetto.

> Bodo chants:
> O Revelation!
> O Understanding!
> Holy I worship,
> Divine I adore,
> Master I obey,
> Answer I listen,
> Reason I believe,
> Shining of the light!
> O Everlasting!
> Infinite Power!
> Infinite Power!

Bodo chants and grovels.

Avu comes on the stage from below left. She is a fat woman with red hair.

She walks towards Bodo and the Mountain. The Bears come closer, coming out to follow in a line behind her, cautiously.

> Avu says:
> There is nothing there.
> There's dirt on your face.
> There's no right answer
> to the wrong question.
> Now what do we do?

Bodo gropes blindly worshipping in the air and gets hold of Avu. He seizes her with a yell of rage and dances her rape and murder. The Bears hurry forward and dance tearing her to pieces and eating her. She is passive throughout, like a dead person. When the dance is done the music stops. To drums and the Continuing Tone she gets up and goes across to the right-hand stage, where she dances through the Four Houses and off. Bodo stands up weeping and raging and stamping and shouting.

Bodo shouts:
> What was I born for?
> What am I here for?
> Why was I sent here?
> What is the meaning?
> What is the reason?
> Answer me now! Now!

Avu has come around behind the stage. She comes on from the left, just as before, and walks towards Bodo. The Bears crouch behind the Mountain.

Avu says:
> I know a secret.

Bodo says:
> Tell me the secret!

Avu says:
> No secret is told.
> It cannot be spoken.
> Thought cannot think it.
> It cannot be borne.
> Come to the valley.

Bodo shouts:
> Twisted neck! Unclean!
> Vile one! Uncanny!
> Your powers are bad.
> Your secrets are void.
> You are the old dark,
> cruel and mindless,
> ancient and empty.
> Empty inside you,
> emptiness, darkness,
> hopelessness, evil,
> valley of darkness!

He tries to send her away from him, while she clings to him and prostrates herself at his feet and follows him on her knees, chanting and begging.

Avu chants:
> Radiance! Brightness!
> Full, overflowing,
> outpouring brightness!
> Use me! Command me!

> Holy I worship,
> Divine I adore,
> Master I obey,
> Answer I listen,
> Reason I believe,
> Shining of the light!
> Give me your power!
> Give me your power!

Bodo shouts:

> Lie down, then, woman!
> Here is the power,
> I give it to you.
> Lie down and eat dirt!

Avu obeys him, lying down on her face, eating dirt. Bodo embraces her to have anal intercourse. She twists around and seizes him and dances breaking his neck, castrating him, and eating him. The Bears come forward and dance eating the bones she throws them.

Avu sings:

> The bones of power,
> eat this one, eat this.
> Shinbone of power,
> bladebone of power,
> skullbone of power,
> eat this, Bears, eat this.

Bodo is passive throughout the dance, like a dead person. When the dance is done the music stops. To drums and the Continuing Tone Bodo gets up and dances through the Four Houses and off right.

Avu crawls on all fours over to join the Bears. They all crouch behind the Mountain. There is no music but the Continuing Tone.

Bodo crawls in from the left on all fours. He crouches and beats his face and weeps.

Avu crawls forward and crouches near him and weeps.

The Bears come and pick up Avu and Bodo carefully and carry them up onto the Mountain. They leave them there and go off on all fours, as animals, to the left.

Avu and Bodo sit on the Mountain. The Continuing Tone sounds.

Avu says:

Is it done, the harm
that we have to do
to one another?
Bodo says:
No, never, never.
It is never done.
Avu says:
Grieving forever
is all my answer.
Bodo says:
Raging forever
is all my question.
Avu says:
Mountain is Valley.
Bodo says:
Valley is Mountain.
Avu says:
What is the way, then?
Bodo says:
There is no way.

The drums begin to beat four and four. The music begins.

Avu says:
This is the way.

Bodo and Avu stand up and begin to dance in place on the
Mountain. As they dance they chant.

Bodo and Avu chant:
In ignorance,
unskilfully,
heya, heya,
in the darkness,
in the silence,
heya, heya,
weakly, poorly,
failing, losing,
heya, heya,
sick, you are sick,
you are dying,
heya, heya,
all of the time
you are dying,

so you make soul,
not knowing how,
having no power,
so you have life,
not going on
so you go on
dying you live
all of the time
heya, heya,
heya, heya,
heya, heya,
heya, heya.

As they chant, the Bears come on the stage from the right,
crossing the Mountain behind them, walking upright, wearing
white, with rainbow masks and headdresses, carrying rain-wands.

Avu and Bodo say:
These are our guides,
the ones we fear.
Heya, heya.

The Bears sing with Avu and Bodo while they dance in place:

Rain is falling
in the rainy
season, in the
rainy season,
in the season
of the rain, rain
falls, falls, rain falls.

Drums beating five and four, and the Ending Tone.

This play was made by Clear of the Obsidian of Telina-na.

Tabetupah

The tabetupah was an oral form, but there was no sanction against writing it down. The tiny story/drama was spoken, usually by two, sometimes by one or three, informal reciters, usually at the outdoor fire at night at the summerhouse, or by the hearth in the rainy season (another name for it was "hearthplay"). The performers did not stand and act out the parts, but simply spoke them: the play was for the ear and mind.

Some tabetupah were classics, spoken word for word at each performance; *Jackrabbit* is an example. This was performed by two speakers taking the alternate sections, or by one using several voices. The words were never altered, and the last line was proverbial.

JACKRABBIT.

—O Jackrabbit! You aren't as thoughtful as I am, but you are far more beautiful!

So he and the jackrabbit traded.

—O Husband! How handsome you've become! All the women in town will want to sleep in our bed!

He had sex with all the women.

Jackrabbit's wife ran away from him, he was too ugly. The man's wife ran away from him, he was too handsome.

—Hey, Man! I want my ears back. Give me back my legs. What's the good of thinking?

But the man hopped away.

Most tabetupah were improvised on familiar themes, or were impromptu. The following was recited by two middle-aged women, presumably the authors, at a hearthfire in Chukulmas:

PURITY.

—What's the matter?
—The matter is this ugly buzzard. It will eat only carrion. It litters

me with bones, it shits bad dreams into my head. I stink of this
buzzard soul of mine. Purify me. O Coyote!

—I eat old sheep afterbirths and dog turds, myself.

—You are the wind that blows the world clean.

—Oh, it's clean you want? That's no matter! says Coyote, and she
blows the buzzard clean out of the woman and the woman clean
out of all nine Houses into nothing at all. Housecleaning, I love
housecleaning! says Coyote. Did I overdo it?

The comical tone is usual in tabetupah, even when the material is
serious; many of them were shaggy-dog stories or simple dirty
jokes. Two adolescent boys performed the following skit, "he" in a
deep and pompous tone, "she" with earnest sweetness:

SHE: I think I'll pee in this shady nook. Oh my, oh my, there's a
      strange man peeing. Who can he be? He's not from Ounma-
      lin. Oh my, oh my, what a wonderful penis! How immense!
      Oh, Man of the Valley, how do you do?

HE: So you are here, Woman of the Valley. My house is the Red
      Adobe of Telina-na.

SHE: Oh, what a pity, what a pity, brother. What a waste. Such a
      wonderful long one.

HE: What? This?

SHE: Yes. That.

HE: Oh, this isn't mine. It belongs to my Yellow Adobe friend
      here, standing behind me, see? I have to help him hold it up
      to pee.

SHE: I'm certain I could help too!

The only entirely serious tabetupah collected was partly in prose,
partly in five-syllable verse, and gives the climax of a story that
may be even older than the previous one. It was performed by
Changing of Ounmalin, a man; for the woman's voice he spoke in a
soft whisper. He called the story by his own name, *Changing*.

CHANGING.

SHE: Remember, my love,
      remember never
      to look upon me,
      never to see me.

HE: I will remember.
      Stay near me, my love,

Sleep by me, my love,
Sleep in the darkness.

SHE: Beloved, I sleep.

HE: She comes in darkness,
leaves before the light.
I have not seen her.
So timid and fearful is she that she will not let me see her
beauty. She came to me in the night, when I was in the hills
hunting, and brought me here. She will have no lamp or fire
light this room of her house where I live all day waiting for
her, this beautiful high house. At night she comes, in darkness.
She hides her beauty
but my hands know it,
my body knows it,
and my mind knows it.
My eyes desire it!
This day I sealed the windows; no light can enter. She does
not know that dawn has come. So long we loved this night!
She sleeps beside me. I rise now, I walk in darkness to the
window. I break the seal and let in the light—one instant—
now!

SHE: (almost inaudible): Aho!

HE: Where are you?—am I?
I see a deer run!
A bed of wet grass.
No walls: hillsides,
sky, the sun rising,
and a deer running!

The Plumed Water

An example of the huravash or "two-speaker" play—a highly for-malised dance-play performed only by two companies, one in Wakwaha and one travelling from Kastoha-na to the other towns of the Valley. Huravash plays were performed in the autumn, between the Wine and Grass festivals. In both content and playing-style, they were by far the most formal, ritualised, and impersonal drama of the Valley.

The Plumed Water celebrates the intermittent geyser north of Kastoha, a sacred place. The text is from the Kastoha huravash company; the stage directions have been expanded and clarified by the translator.

The stage is without scenery. The Chorus of nine stand in a half circle across the center or hinge of the stage, which is understood to be a pool of water.
Musicians play the Beginning Tone. A drum begins to beat.
The Bath Attendant comes from behind the Chorus to meet the Traveller from Ounmalin, who enters from the left.

ATTENDANT:
So you are here, man of the Valley.
TRAVELLER:
So you are here, man of Kastoha-na.
ATTENDANT:
Have you perhaps missed your way?
TRAVELLER:
Perhaps I have.
ATTENDANT:
If you like, I'll show you the way back to the road that goes up to Wakwaha on the Mountain.
TRAVELLER:
Well, I wasn't intending to go up on the Mountain when I came this way. I was looking for a place called the Pool of the Lion, or the Puma's Well.

ATTENDANT:
> In that case you're on your way. The place they call that is only
> a little farther on. Do you see those feathered grasses and the
> red-branched willows? The water is there among them.

TRAVELLER:
> Thank you for your guidance!

The Attendant goes directly back and then moves right to stand
behind the Chorus, who move forward a step and stand, leaf-
crowned, holding the long plumes of pampas grass and cattail or
cotton-willow.

The Traveller dance-walks to a travelling music to the edge of
the pool, and there dances to salute the pool, and sings:

> Heya, heya
> nahe heya
> no nahe no
> heya, heya

The Chorus repeat the song softly in unison.
The Traveller sits down by the pool.

TRAVELLER:
> This place is beautiful and desolate. I wonder why no human
> people seem to have come here recently? The path was over-
> grown, and there were spiders' threads across it, which I had
> to break. That man who spoke to me seemed to come out of
> nowhere, and I don't know where he went. The tall grasses
> are like mist, hiding things. Well, I'm glad to be here under
> the willows at the Lion's Pool, thinking of the story I heard told
> about this place.

Two dancers, a man and a woman, enter from the right. A music
begins. The dancers dance, always coming closer together, but
never touching, while the Chorus sing:

> Under this ground, here,
> under our roots, here,
> there runs in darkness
> a river, running
> underground, coming
> from the Mountain's roots,
> running among rocks,
> running beneath stones,

running through the earth
underground, downward,
seaward in darkness.
Under that river
deeper, still deeper,
another river:
a river of fire
moves from the Mountain,
daughter of earthquake,
slowflowing fireflood,
under this ground, here,
under our roots, here,
brightness in darkness.
If they touch, river
of fire and river
of water—Shining!

When the song is done the dancers stand still, listening to the Traveller.

TRAVELLER:

The story I heard was of two people who came down from the Mountain in a time when no other people lived in the Valley but the grasses, the trees, the plumed grass and the willows and the long reeds by the River. It was quiet, very quiet; no quail in the underbrush, no bluejays quarrelling in the branches; not a voice, not a wing; and no footsteps. Only the mist moved in the reeds. Only the fog moved among the willows. Out of the Mountain then they came, those two, coming out from the deep world, from within. They were the quail coming into the world, and the bluejays and flickers coming

into the air; they were the wood rat and the wild dog, the moth and the jackrabbit, the treefrog and the kingsnake, the ewe and the bull; they were the breathing people of the Valley coming for the first time, the first people who came, so they were all the people. To the human mind they were human people, a woman and a man. They came here, to this place, a meadow in the foothills of the Mountain, a clearing among willows. They came beautifully, stepping like the deer, carefully, darting like the hummingbird, boldly. They stood here barefoot in the grass and said to each other, "Let us live here, in this place." But a voice spoke to them. They heard it.

THE PUMA BEHIND THE TREES:
> This is my country.
> Do you know your souls?

TRAVELLER:
> They heard the voice, and they answered, "Who is here? Who spoke? Come out to us!"

The Attendant comes from the right to the end of the semicircle and stands facing the Traveller across the pool. He now wears the mask of the Fog Puma.

THE PUMA:
> I spoke. You have come into my country. If you meet, you will be changed. If you touch, you will be changed. All doing here undoes; all meeting parts; all being is transformed.

TRAVELLER:
> Who are you?

THE PUMA:
> I am the one
> who goes between.

THE CHORUS:
> He is the one
> who goes between.
> He is the dream.
> Before you came
> he was always.
> He is your child.

TRAVELLER:
> Let him wait, then, to be born, for these two must live.

The Puma stands back outside the circle on the right, while the Traveller tells the story and the two dancers dance and enact it.

TRAVELLER:

> They did not know the puma. They were not the puma. They
> were all beings, all people but the puma. Female they were,
> fire from the roots of the Mountain far within, and male they
> were, water from the springs of the Mountain far within. Male
> and female they were alive, they came together, who shall
> keep them apart? She lay with him and he with her, she open-
> ing to him, he entering in her, and in that instant died. Their
> death was a shining cloud, a white cloud, a fog that filled the
> meadow, a fog that filled the Valley. Into his house came the
> Silent One, returning, into the house of the white silence.

The Puma comes forward and dances, while the Fire and Water
dancers lie motionless as if dead within the semicircle of the Chorus.

THE PUMA:

> My children, I grieve,
> my father, I grieve,
> my mother, I grieve,
> for your death I grieve!
> Live again, come back!
> Be transformed! Be changed!

The two dancers rise and, with the Puma, dance and enact the
Traveller's narration.

TRAVELLER:

> From the meadow leaped up a jet of steam, of shining vapor.
> From the mist, out of the fog it leaped, higher than the plumed
> grasses, higher than the willows, shining in sunlight.

THE CHORUS:

> Hwavgepragu,
> pragu, pragu.
> (Shining of the sun,
> shining, shining.)

TRAVELLER:

> The jet of fiery water sank down again, dropping into the pool
> among the grasses, and was still. But again, when the Puma
> turned, when the Puma breathed, once more they touched,
> and the white plume stood shining.

CHORUS:

> Where the body of water lies on the body of fire within the
> earth in darkness, there the well rises. This is the pool of the

Lion, the silent dancer, the soft walker, the dweller in the
house of dream. This is that which falls from the sunlight as it
rises from the dark.

TRAVELLER:
Beautiful Keeper of the Seventh House, be praised!

THE PUMA:
Who are you, man of the Valley?

TRAVELLER:
A singer of the Serpentine from Ounmalin. I came to drink
from the Pool of the Lion, from the Plumed Water, so that the
silence of the lion will be in my songs.

THE PUMA:
All songs are in the silence of the lion. Drink.

The Traveller kneels and drinks from the pool.

TRAVELLER:
It is here, not here.
As it lives, it dies.
It sinks, leaping up.
It shines and passes,
mist in sunlight,
not here, and here.

The Puma dances masked.

THE CHORUS:
Softly he walks
before the first,
shining, shining.
Mist in sunlight,
here, and not here.

The Traveller and the Chorus go off left, the Puma and the Fire and
Water dancers go off right, to the Ending Tone without drums.

Chandi

Most Valley plays were vehicles for improvisation: a skeleton plot, a framework of a situation, usually very familiar to the audience, on which the performers created the momentary and irreproducible drama.

. The text of such a play could be written on a scrap of paper, since it was nothing but a list of the characters and a set of dialogue lines, called "pegs" or "hingebolts," perhaps ten or twenty in all. These peg lines were invariable both in wording and in the order they were spoken. Everything that was said and done in the intervals between them was up to the players. For the audience, much of the tension and pleasure of the performance was in the build-up towards these key lines, familiar from other performances but always arrived at differently, "from another direction."

Plot elaboration could be so extreme that the pegs were embedded in a long dramatic performance having only tangential reference to the original plot; or they might be the pivots of a brilliant flow of language, if the troupe was strong on poetic improvisation; or they might provide almost the whole spoken text of a performance by a troupe of actor-dancers playing the piece yedao, "by moving"—that is, principally in mime and dance.

The performance I attempt to describe here was given by a troupe from Telina-na, a young group praised mainly for their music and dancing. The play was put on in a big barn-loft in Sinshan as part of the festivities of the Summer Dance. Lights had been rigged up to spotlight the stage area and were used very effectively in creating both space and mood. The audience participated in the play at the beginning, and was entirely silent and intent by the end.

Like most Valley drama, this play *Chandi* is symbolical or allegorical, generalising life. The resemblance of the plot to one of the great biblical stories is striking; but so are the differences.

The name *Chandi* means Wood Rat, the native Western rat, a pretty little animal which builds a big, elaborate nest of sticks and grass, in which it may store a collection of objects which it seems to value on purely aesthetic grounds, and in which mice, snakes, and other creatures may reside, sharing the wood rat's hospitality.

The traditional author of *Chandi* was Houkai (Kingsnake?) of

Chumo, a figure as old and insubstantial as our Homer (and not blind, like Homer, but deaf), to whom about half the peg-line plays were ascribed.

In this attempt to describe the action and present the text, the peg lines are italicised. To see what the actors had to work with, the reader can read only those lines, skipping all the rest.

CHANDI: A PERFORMANCE.

The audience, forty or fifty people, sat on the loft floor on rugs or pillows they had brought with them, or on some old straw-bales that had been arranged as seats or to provide seat-backs.

A man and woman of the Millers Art of Sinshan had rigged up and operated the lights. A strong, large spot formed the left stage area, a weaker one the right stage area, and their oval interlap formed the "Hinge." The darkness outside and behind these areas was deep enough to make movements offstage undistracting.

The musicians sat behind the stage area, outside the light, just visible. The music was almost continuous throughout the performance.

After the Beginning Tone had been played for some minutes and the audience had quieted down, Chandi entered from the left: a handsome man in the prime of life, tall, magnificently dressed. Over black trousers and a full-sleeved cotton shirt he wore a long ceremonial vest of blue, violet, and green, heavy with embroidery, and over that an incredibly delicate and splendid feather cloak, a treasure of the Serpentine heyimas of Sinshan, lent for the performance. This majestic cloak flowed and swayed from his shoulders as he came striding in, his arms stretched out in an embracing gesture, and turned forward to greet the rising sun.

CHANDI:
> *Heya hey heya!*
> *Heya heya!*
> *Beautiful you shine upon the Valley!*

He looked down from the imagined sunrise at the faces of the audience, with a warm and genial smile. His voice was resonant, pleasant, and full of energy.

CHANDI:
> So you are here, people of my town, beautifully walking, kindly of face, speaking gently. This is a good morning!

The audience responded with the customary greeting: "So you are here, Chandi!" They spoke quietly, amused; and one woman added, "May the day go well for you, Chandi!"

CHANDI:
> In the evening of this long day I am to dance the Summer; so before I go into the fields I want to practice that dance.

The musicians struck up one of the intricate and stately Heron dances of the Summer wakwa, and Chandi danced alone on the left stage, energetic and graceful, like some gorgeous mythical bird in the iridescent, floating cloak of feathers.

As the dance ended, the First Chorus, five people, came on and took up positions around stage left—townsfolk going to a day's work in the fields. With a final great gesture which made him seem to fly up in the air for a moment (the audience gasped), Chandi swept off the feather cloak and tossed it to someone waiting outside the lighted area. The dance was over, and Chandi also went off to work. He mimed weeding and hoeing with the Chorus. They talked about the weather, and there was some banter about local doings and personalities, which I could not follow but which got a great response and some backtalk from the audience. Then a peg line was dropped in casually.

CHORUS I (a man):
> *How fine, Chandi's corn,*
> *how tall and broadleaved,*
> *already tasselled.*

CHORUS II (a woman):
> He's a wise farmer, Chandi is. Knowledgeable and careful.

CHORUS I:
> Yes, he seems to go the right way. What a good bit of ground his household works there.

CHORUS III (a man):
> That's not the only good ground in his family. The luck that comes his way! To be married to Dansaiedo! [She Sees the Rainbow] To plow and weed and tend and harvest that bit of ground, in the gardens of the night!

CHORUS IV (a woman):
> Shut up, stupid. What kind of dirty talk is that!

CHORUS III:

I'm envious. That's all. I envy him.

CHORUS V (a woman):

The beautiful children of that marriage—rainbow people indeed! I envy him such children.

CHORUS IV:

Shut up, shut up! High winds fan forest fires.

Chandi now came closer to the other gardeners, and leaned on his hoe as he spoke; it was some time before I realised that there was in fact no hoe.

CHANDI:

Listen, I don't mind. I couldn't help but hear what you were saying—*the wind was blowing my way*. But it's true, what you were saying. I try to be careful and thoughtful, to do things at the right time in the right way; but other people are just as careful, just as mindful, and they aren't given so much as I am. I don't know how it is. My mothers' house is beautiful and dignified, as is the house of my wife. My parents are generous and kindly people, and the two people who have made me a father are intelligent and notable—my daughter already a singer among the Doctors, and my son, still wearing undyed clothing, a delightful and promising boy. Of Dansaiedo, what praise can I speak? She is the swallow above the pools at evening. She is the first rain of autumn, and the wild almond flower of early spring. Her household is noble, a river of gifts flowing! In this household the ewes bear twin lambs yearly, the cows are wise and strong, the bullocks patient. The earth we plant is richer every year, the trees we gather from drop olives like hailstones. *All this is given me!* How have I lived that this has been so?

CHORUS II:

All you have been given you have given, Chandi.

CHORUS I:

Yes, Chandi is truly generous.

CHORUS V:

The feather cloak he gave his House!

CHORUS II:

Corn to the granaries, fleeces to the Art!

CHORUS III:

Gold coins to musicians, copper to actors! [This was spoken archly, and got a laugh.]

CHORUS I:
> Everything in his house is fine and sound, well-made and
> well-used, plentiful and impressive, and the doors are always
> open to his friends and townsfolk.

CHORUS III:
> *Indeed you are a wealthy man, Chandi!*

CHORUS V:
> *The generous heart is wealth itself*—so they say.

[The translation of these two pegs is particularly weak. *Ambad*
means wealth, wealthy; to give; and generosity. The words double
on themselves intricately in these lines.]

During this scene the only music was the Continuing Tone, the
faint, slightly varied, background note of the great horns, houm-
buta. Now the other instruments began to play and continued for
the rest of the performance, softly under dialogue, but filling—and
creating—pauses with held and percussive notes

CHANDI:
> You make me feel foolish, my friends! I want to do something
> for you, I want to give you what you want, what you like.

CHORUS IV:
> Really, he's such a nice fellow, isn't he!

CHORUS I:
> Yes, nobody could dislike him, our Chandi.

Great Horn

CHANDI:
> *What can I give you?* I hope you'll share this corn when it
> ripens. This plot of ground is so easy to work, I wondered if
> you'd like to use it next season. Oh, House-sister, I meant to
> tell you that we've got a lot of feathers saved again in our
> household and thought of making another cloak, for the Ob-
> sidian, for the Blood Lodge, if you think it would be appropri-
> ate! Cousin, Dansaiedo has been spinning that white wool our
> sheep gave us in the spring shearing, and I remember you

spoke of needing white wool. Fine or heavy? You know how well Dansaiedo spins.

He talked on, the music growing loud enough to half-cover his voice, the people of the First Chorus crowding around him as he talked and handed out things, all affectionate, friendly, but a little hectic. While this was going on, the Second Chorus began to enter from the right: four people, barefoot, walking stiffly erect, wearing dark hoods and tight, dark clothes (like those of the Mourners at the World Dance). They came one after the other, slowly, and stood waiting in a line across the right stage. The first one, standing at the right edge of the hinge, spoke in a flat, sexless voice, heralded by a shivering note on the towandou.

SECOND CHORUS I:
    Chandi!

Busy with their give-and-take, Chandi and his friends paid no attention. The dark figure spoke the name again. The third time the name was spoken, Chandi looked around over his shoulder, and then came laughing from the group, his arms full of something.

CHANDI:
    Here, friend, take it, please! I have too much!

The dark figure remained motionless, hands at its sides. After a loud metallic chord from the musicians, there was a dead pause.

SECOND CHORUS I:
    Dansaiedo was measuring oil, fine olive oil from the old trees of her family. A flame leapt up, from where no one knows, blown by what wind? It burned, that oil. It burned. Her hair burned, her clothing—she burned alive, a torch. She ran in flames from the house in flames. *It is all burnt. She is dead.*

The hooded figure crouched down in the mourning posture and huddled, head down, swaying, at Chandi's feet, just across the hinge from him. Chandi stood motionless; slowly his arms dropped to his sides. The First Chorus drew away from him, muttering among themselves.

FIRST CHORUS:
    Burned?—Dansaiedo?—That great household?—The whole house, everything?—Burned alive?

CHANDI (in a great outburst):
>   *My daughter! My son!*

FIRST CHORUS I:
>   They're all right—they must be all right, Chandi.

FIRST CHORUS II:
>   They weren't in the house. Only Dansaiedo died in the fire.
>   The other people got out.

FIRST CHORUS V:
>   But the house is gone. Burned to the foundation stones.

FIRST CHORUS III:
>   Everything in it burned to ash.

Chandi took a bewildered step or two as if to return to the town.

CHANDI:
>   O Dansaiedo, beautiful woman, kind woman, wife of my
>   heart! *Cruel! Cruel! Cruel!*

His voice rose to this thrice-repeated word, the "hinge" of the play,
in a wild outcry; then he stood again as if bewildered by his own
passion of grief. He looked around painfully at the others, and at
last said with dignity,

CHANDI:
>   I will go—I will go now to sing for you, Dansaiedo, to sing
>   with you as you leave me. But I need our children with me
>   now. May they come to me!

Chandi's Son and Daughter now entered from the left. At the same
time, the second dark figure of the Second Chorus began to approach the center of the stage, its right hand stretched forward.
Chandi's Son went to his father and they embraced, but the Daughter walked past him, turning to look at him, but going on past him
to meet the dark figure, take its hand, and go with it offstage to the
right, into the dark. As she did so, Chandi cried out.

CHANDI:
>   *Where is she? Where is she going? Where has she gone?*

SECOND CHORUS I (crouching and swaying as before):
>   She saw her mother run from the house burning, burning
>   alive, and the sight was beyond her endurance. She took poi-
>   son in the Doctors Lodge, fearing madness, and is dead.

FIRST CHORUS I (whispering):
>   She is dead!

FIRST CHORUS IV (whispering):
    Look there! She is dead!

The members of the First Chorus, the townspeople, had drawn
somewhat away from Chandi, leaving him standing alone with his
Son. There was music with a hard, fast drum-beat while Chandi
slowly took off the embroidered vest and put it on his Son's shoulders. When he spoke his voice was shocking in its softness.

CHANDI:
    Daughter, little daughter, could you not wait? Patience would
    have been kinder. There were those who needed you. Come
    with me now, child, my son. Stay with me. Help me sing for
    them, with them, your mother, your sister. Come with me
    now.

But the third of the four dark figures—a child—was coming towards
them, inexorable. Chandi's Son let go his hand, and stood still,
gazing; then moved to meet the dark figure and to take its hand and
follow it slowly offstage right, into the darkness. The Continuing
Tone was very loud.

CHANDI:
    Please do not die, my son. Stay with me!
SECOND CHORUS I (speaking from the crouching posture still):
    The illness was always in him, hidden. Now it is becoming his
    life. In a month he will be dead. In a few days he will be dead.
    The doctors have no healing for him. This day he will die. He
    is dying now.
FIRST CHORUS IV:
    Chandi's son is dead.

The five members of the First Chorus drew yet farther away from
Chandi. He slowly crouched down till he was facing the dark figure
in the same posture. He lowered his head to the ground, rubbed his
forehead on the ground, and tore at his hair. The music was loud
and intense, the drums and towandou drowning out the Continuing Tone, and Chandi's voice rose and fell in a half-melodious
keening howl.

    As the music quieted, Chandi crouched motionless, and at last
stood up heavily. He took off his shirt and then his shoes, and stood
barefoot and half-naked, looking twenty years older.

CHANDI:

I will go back to my mothers' house, living there as a son, working for the people of that household as best I can.

The fourth of the dark figures was approaching him as he spoke, and now addressed him in the same flat, high, uncanny tone as the first.

SECOND CHORUS IV:

They are all dead now, those people of your mothers' household, or have gone away to other houses, other towns. *Other people live now in those rooms.* There is no one of your kinfolk in that place.

CHANDI:

It is true. I must live alone. But I have been ill for a long time now. Would it not be better for me to die?

The fourth dark figure made no reply, but crouched down beside the first one.

CHANDI:

I will live alone, then, as best I can, working for the heyimas. Oh, but my arms are heavy!

He began to mime working in the gardens, as at the beginning of the action, but very laboriously. The members of the First Chorus also went back to work, all towards the left front of the left stage, while Chandi was alone towards the back and near the Hinge. The light had dimmed unobtrusively, and the music had a plangent, yearning quality.

FIRST CHORUS III:

Look at old Chandi digging at that adobe, hard as rooftile!

CHORUS I (now speaking like an old man, while Chorus III's voice had taken on an adolescent quality):

It used to be good land, a good piece of ground there. He didn't look after it.

CHORUS II:

Oh, I don't know, he looks after it as well as he can, sick and lame as he is, and people help him, after all. But the creek cut off that bend there, and he didn't irrigate enough.

CHORUS III:

Somebody was saying he used to be very prosperous.

CHORUS I:

> Well, and so he did. But nothing prospers for him these days, it seems.

CHORUS IV:

> That poor old cow, the brindle, she was the last of his family cattle in the herds, wasn't she?

CHORUS II:

> Every lamb his ewes bore was sevai.

CHORUS IV:

> Nothing he looks after bears; nothing he cares for grows.

CHORUS V:

> It makes my back ache to see him trying to work there. He can hardly lift the hoe.

CHORUS III:

> What does he bother trying to work for, anyhow? That corn won't bear. A stupid old man, wasting work like that.

CHORUS I:

> But what went wrong, after all? He used to be prosperous, as you said—wealthy, generous, a river flowing! What went wrong?

CHORUS III:

> I'll ask him. Hey, old Chandi! What did you do, so that everything went wrong for you?

CHANDI (leaning on his hoe and speaking quietly and very slowly):

> *My wife died. My household was destroyed. My children died before me. Illness came into me. No one of my mother's house was left living here. What I care for perishes. What I am given I lose. What I gave is all I had and it is gone.*

CHORUS III:

> It's no wonder you haven't any friends.

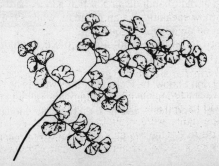

CHANDI:

My people are the people of my House, the House of Summer, the Serpentine.

CHORUS IV:

Well, of course, we'll go on looking after you. But I have to say this, it's hard to feel friendly or brotherly about a person who does everything wrong. With a friend you feel at ease, you want to share everything, you can laugh together. Who can laugh with you? I want to burst into tears every time I see you! So I don't really want to see you—I wish I didn't have to.

CHORUS V:

It's true. In the old days I used to be in love with you. I thought about you all the time. Now I never do. I've forgotten what your wife was named. Sickness has made you hideous; I don't like even to touch your hand.

CHORUS I:

Dansaiedo was her name, Dansaiedo, and when I see you I always think of her, dying so terribly. I don't want to think about that.

CHORUS III:

You turned the wheel too hard, old man, that's the truth. You got what you asked for.

CHANDI:

I asked for nothing. I gave. When *was I ungenerous?*

CHORUS IV:

You were generous to a fault.

CHANDI:

How shall a human being live well, then?

CHORUS I:

If I knew that I'd tell you!

CHORUS III:

What's the use of asking questions like that?

CHORUS II:

Nobody understands such things.

CHANDI (turning to the two crouching dark figures across the Hinge):

How was I to live my life well? Can you answer me?

The two dark figures remained silent and motionless. The music clashed and jangled strangely.

As the lights were brought lower so that they cast long shadows, the first of the two dark figures rose and walked slowly to the center back of the double stage. There it turned to face the audience, revealing under its dark hood a copper mask which caught the light in a startling ruddy flash—the setting sun.

Chandi turned to face it, back to the audience. His arms came up in the broad, embracing gesture.

CHANDI:
> *Heya hey heya!*
> *Heya heya!*
> *Beautiful the day was in the Valley.*

The dark figure crouched slowly down, stooping and so hiding the sun-mask. The lights darkened further.

CHANDI:
> There are the stars, shining.
> There is nothing between the stars,
> the dark dancing.

Into the Continuing Tone the musicians suddenly began to weave the tune of the Heron Dance. Stooping and half-naked, stiffly and painfully, Chandi began to dance the dance which he practiced in splendor in the first scene: but all the motions and turns were reversed, so that the dance carried him across the stage to the right. The last of the dark figures joined him, following his movements like a shadow. Together they vanished into the darkness. In the almost completely darkened, high, large room the musicians held the Ending Tone until it died away very gradually into silence.

After the performance, I asked a member of the cast if they varied the action and dialogue much from one performance to the next, and she replied, "Well, only to fit the evening or the town. This summer we're playing this play Clayface's way." Clayface was the actor who played Chandi. She went on, "I saw *Chandi* in Wakwaha last year, with Wind Deer; he raged and railed and went mad. He's an older actor, he can do that. Clayface is young to play Chandi, so he does it this way, very gently. I think it works. Maybe it goes too fast at the end; but the dances he does at the beginning and the end, they're very fine!" I agreed with her.

I asked some of the audience if they had seen widely different interpretations of this play, and found that they had; the action can be handled quite differently: for instance the fire, suicide, and illness which successively carried off Chandi's wife, daughter, and son in this version can be one cataclysmic event, and the deaths could take place onstage if the actors want to harrow up the audience's feelings directly. The events of Chandi's "fortunate" and "unfortunate" years can be acted out and dwelt upon in any number of ways, and Chandi's response to them could be quite different from the complex tone of resignation that Clayface struck. However, Thorn said to me, "Even when his friends and the Four-House people answer his question, how to live well, still you don't know if their answers are right. . . ."

I asked Clayface—who offstage turned out to be not more than twenty-five, shy-mannered, soft-spoken, and not tall—if he thought Chandi died in hope or in despair. After thinking quite a while he replied, "In pain. That's why his friends are afraid of him. But we don't have to be, because it's a play. So, you see, that's what matters."

Pandora, Worrying About What She Is Doing, Finds a Way into the Valley through the Scrub Oak

LOOK HOW MESSY this wilderness is. Look at this scrub oak, *chaparro*, the chaparral was named for it and consists of it mixed up with a lot of other things, but look at this shrub of it right here now. The tallest limb or stem is about four feet tall, but most of the stems are only a foot or two. One of them looks as if it had been cut off with a tool, a clean slice across, but who? what for? This shrub isn't good for anything and this ridge isn't on the way to anywhere. A lot of the smaller branch-ends look broken or bitten off. Maybe deer browse the leafbuds. The little grey branches and twigs grow every which way, many dead and lichened, crossing each other, choking each other out. Digger-pine needles, spiders' threads, dead bay leaves are stuck in the branches. It's a mess. It's littered. It has no overall shape. Most of the stems come up from one area, but not all; there's no center and no symmetry. A lot of sticks sticking up out of the ground a little ways with leaves on some of them—that describes it fairly well. The leaves themselves show some order, they seem to obey some laws, poorly. They are all different sizes from about a quarter of an inch to an inch long, but each is enough like the others that one could generalise an ideal scrub-oak leaf: a dusty, medium dark-green color, with a slight convex curve to the leaf, which pillows up a bit between the veins that run slanting outward from the central vein; and the edge is irregularly serrated, with a little spine at each apex. These leaves grow irregularly spaced on alternate sides of their twig up to the top, where they crowd into a bunch, a sloppy rosette. Under the litter of dead leaves, its own and others', and moss and rocks and mold and junk, the shrub must have a more or less shrub-shaped complex of roots, going fairly deep, probably deeper than it stands aboveground, because wet as it is here now in February, it will be bone dry on this ridge in summer. There are no acorns left from last fall, if this shrub is old enough to have borne them. It probably is. It could be two years old or twenty or who knows? It is an oak, but a scrub oak, a low oak, a no-account oak, and there are at least a hundred very much like it in sight from this rock I am sitting on, and there are hundreds and thousands and hundreds of thousands more on this ridge and the next ridge, but numbers are wrong. They are in error. You don't count scrub oaks. When you can count them, something has gone wrong. You can count how many in a hundred square yards and multiply, if you're a botantist, and so make a good estimate, a fair guess, but you cannot count the scrub

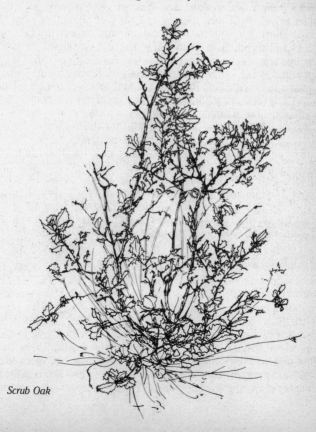

Scrub Oak

oaks on this ridge, let alone the ceanothus, buckbrush, or wild lilac, which I have not mentioned, and the other variously messy
and humble components of the chaparral. The chaparral is like
atoms and the components of atoms: it evades. It is innumerable. It
is not accidentally but essentially messy. This shrub is not beautiful, nor even if I were ten feet high on hashish would it be mystical,
nor is it nauseating; if a philosopher found it so, that would be his
problem, but nothing to do with the scrub oak. This thing is nothing to do with us. This thing is wilderness. The civilised human
mind's relation to it is imprecise, fortuitous, and full of risk. There
are no shortcuts. All the analogies run one direction, our direction.
There is a hideous little tumor in one branch. The new leaves, this
year's growth, are so large and symmetrical compared with the
older leaves that I took them at first for part of another plant, a
toyon growing in with the dwarf oak, but a summer's dry heat no
doubt will shrink them down and warp them. Analogies are easy;
the live oak, the humble evergreen, can certainly be made into a
sermon, just as it can be made into firewood. Read or burnt. *Sermo*,
I read; I read scrub oak. But I don't, and it isn't here to be read, or
burnt. It is casting a shadow across the page of this notebook in the
weak sunshine of three-thirty of a February afternoon in Northern
California. When I close the book and go, the shadow will not be on
the page, though I have drawn a line around it; only the pencil line
will be on the page. The shadow will be then on the dead-leaf-thick
messy ground or on the mossy rock my ass is on now, and the
shadow will move lawfully and with great majesty as the earth
turns. The mind can imagine that shadow of a few leaves falling in
the wilderness; the mind is a wonderful thing. But what about all
the shadows of all the other leaves on all the other branches on all
the other scrub oaks on all the other ridges of all the wlderness? If
you could imagine those even for a moment, what good would it
do? Infinite good.

Dancing the Moon

Told to the Editor by Thorn of Sinshan.

 The World is danced at the dark of the moon after the equinox of the rains; and the second time the moon comes full after that, we dance the Moon.

Sometimes when the dance begins the weather is still raining and cold, but usually the dry season has begun and the nights are getting warmer. Sometimes the grasses are still making seed and sometimes they're ripe and beginning to dry. Always the sei (lantern flower, calochortus) are in flower. Lambs and fawns are weaned but still going close beside the ewes and does. The birds are mating and nesting. The quail call in the daytime and the small owls at night. The creeks are running lively in their courses. It's a pleasant time of year, and a good time to make love.

At the World Dance people get married; that's a wakwa of sorting out things, getting things right and flowing on the two sides of the world; that's a wakwa of lasting and staying. The Moon Dance doesn't do anything like that. It goes the other way. It goes out and apart, undoing, separating. You know the heyiya-if comes in to the center and at the same time it's going out from the center. A hinge connects and it holds apart. So under the Moon there are no marriages. No households. Under the Moon there are no children. If a woman conceives in the dancing, usually she aborts the fetus; if she bears the child she does so because she meant to, she wanted a child with no father, a moon child.

Children don't like the Moon Dance. There are frightening things in the other dances, the White Clowns at the Sun, the mourning fire at the World, people getting crazy drunk at the Wine; but children have a part in all those wakwa, the giving at the Sun, the Last Day of the World, the singing at the Wine. But in the Moon dancing, nothing is for children. It's all backwards, it's a reversal, you see. It's sex without anything that belongs to sex—responsibility, marriage, children. Because young people are the most sexual, adolescents can't dance it. Because it's a women's dance, in the House of the Ewe, men are in charge of it and have it their way. Everything's turned round. The full moon reflects the sun's light, reverses it, not making daylight but making the dark light. The full moon rises at sunset and sets at dawn.

Well, so the children stay indoors, and adolescents too, or they go off somewhere together for the first night of the Moon at least and maybe for the whole time. Bay Laurel boys go off camping; and Blood Lodge girls spend the night together in a house or up in the hills in a summerhouse if the weather's dry. They stay apart, boys together and girls together. They look after themselves and keep apart. And they look after the little kids.

And man-living women and woman-living men don't usually dance the Moon; they go off to summerhouses, or look after the children indoors. Unless they're willing to make love with other-sexed people. That's part of the backwardness, the reversal: Moon dancing is supposed to be sex without conception, so only people who can conceive are supposed to dance it. Women usually stop dancing the Moon when they're around fifty, sometimes a long time before that. Of course old men always dance it, they make a big point of it. So there's always more men than women under the Moon.

Sometimes forest-living people come in for the Moon. And people come from other towns. Sometimes there's a man or woman dancing that you never saw before, you don't know where they live or who their mother was. You have to ask them, "In what House do you live?" so that you don't find yourself and that person committing incest.

Talking about it this way is strange. The Moon is all license and incontinence—but there are all these rules you have to keep in mind! It's because it's a backward-time, I suppose. And also, it isn't simple for a woman to live a man's way. You ask some man to tell you about the Moon, when I'm done; he might tell you a different story! But I don't know; there are just as many rules for the men.

A man could tell you more than I can about what they do before the moon comes full. For the fourteen days before it, all the men that want to dance do some sweating and singing. They use the old sweathouse down where Sinshan Creek goes round the outside of Adobe Hill there. After sweating they run out and jump in the irrigation reservoir. In the big towns up-Valley they have sweathouses built aboveground. In Kastoha and Chukulmas they heat the sweathouses with steam from hot springs. Here they just have a fire in the rock-pit and then pour water on it, you know. They do that any time of day, and they go naked to and from the sweathouse. And after sweating and bathing they come and sing in the common place. The songs are mostly matrix words. I don't know them; only men sing them. They sing deep down in their chests, in their bellies. It sounds like thunder far away, or like rain, or like thresher engines, very deep and soft. The women don't come out to listen to that singing. They listen from inside the houses or the workshops, doing whatever they're doing. They don't act like they're listening.

[A man of Sinshan, Fourth Quail, sang us two of the men's songs sung before the Moon; he said there was no harm in writing them down, "but writing down matrix words makes about as much sense as writing down dance-steps!"

BEFORE THE MOON SONG I

Meyan meyan
barra amarraman
ah, eh, eya meyan

BEFORE THE MOON SONG II

Ehe ene ene
ehi meyan heyu

Fourth Quail sang these without accompaniment, in the deep, "inward," chest-voice described by Thorn. As performed by a group, with repetitions and part-singing, each song would last several minutes.]

So for five and five and four days the men bathe and sing; and they don't have sex with anybody, they stay continent, married or unmarried. Sometimes women tease them, but it's better not to; they'll get back at you under the Moon.

On the day before the night of the full moon the women who want to dance go bathe at the reservoir, all together. If you don't want to dance that year you might talk about it and say, "I'm staying with the children tonight in such a house," or, "I'm sleeping tonight with the girls who haven't come inland." Even so, the men may come to the house and sing and call to make you come out and dance. There's always some silly woman who says she's not going to dance and doesn't want to dance and hates the Moon, but doesn't mean it; she just wants the men to come to her house and call her, so that everybody hears them calling her. And then she comes out, of course. Nobody comes out who doesn't want to.

After the sun goes behind the ridge, women and men both start coming out of the houses into the common place. And the music starts down inside the Obsidian heyimas. The musicians come up, and come along the path to the Hinge of the town and sing there, and then come on along the path into the common place, singing and drumming and playing all the time. Oh, the Moon music isn't like any other music! You can't stay still, you have to come out and dance. It gets running in your bones, the drumming, and the men singing down soft. There's a matrix word in the Moon songs: abahi. They sing that over and over, abahi, abahi, and the drums going syncopated in and out, abahi, abahi. And it's getting darker, and the moonlight's beginning to show behind the digger pines on the top of the ridge. By moonrise you're dancing in a line with the other women, just stepdancing in place. The men are beginning to make a line that moves forward gyring and reverses and goes around the women's line. Then the men's line breaks up, and four or five of them break through the women's line, break it apart, split it. You go on dancing in two lines, and then they break the lines again, and again, until each woman is dancing alone. Then the men may encircle a woman, or begin to pairdance with one. And it goes on like that. There's no set pattern of how it happens. You can pairdance for a while, and then he goes off to another woman or group, and some other man or men come facing you or circling you, and begin dancing with you. The women don't move from place; unless a man takes your hand you stay put; only the men move and choose.

The music keeps on—the musicians are mostly adolescents, Obsidian people, they don't dance the Moon yet, but they play it!—

and when the moon's getting higher the women begin to sing. They sing abahi, or just he-eh, or trill very high like night-crickets. That's when the men start getting excited. Some of them come out naked to start with, but when the women start that trilling, pretty soon the men are all dancing naked, and they've all got erections, too. And they start taking hold of the woman they're dancing with, instead of just facing her. They take your hands, or your shoulders. If more than one man is dancing with you, they begin to press against you from behind, and brush up against you, and maybe one has one of your hands and another the other. And then they begin to unfasten your clothes. If you don't want your clothes to get danced on all night, you don't wear much to begin with, because by the time it comes off it'll lie where it falls, most likely.

So then some couple begins having sex, usually standing up, and they and the people near them set up the coyote singing. It's called that because it sounds a little like coyotes, I guess, but it's more like a kind of music made out of the noises human people make making love. The musicians coyote-sing and keep drumming, keeping up the dance beat. Some people dance all night. Others have sex, and dance again, and have sex again with somebody else, and dance again; or make love to somebody once and go home; or however they like. A woman isn't supposed to go home so long as a man is with her or waiting for her, but actually, if you've had enough, or don't like the man, you can always get away—it's night, and there's so many people. There are stories about men staying at a woman, forcing her to keep having sex, usually in revenge because she had teased them, but I never knew anything like that to happen; those are romantic tales, men tell them. What isn't allowed is to go away together, to have sex anywhere that night but outside, in the common place, where the others are. If some man tried to follow a woman home, she'd set up a yell and the others would find out. But it doesn't happen. After all, it is a dance danced together.

The first Moon I danced, that was the best one. Before it I was a little frightened. It was a warm, windy night, the rains were over, the crickets were already singing, the moonlight looked like white water in pools on the grass. Oh, that was a good Moon! But sometimes it's raining. They put up the big awning on poles over the common place, and people come out and dance, but making love isn't so good—it's wet and cold and you can't see who's there alongside you, in the dark. The way I like it is when you can just see them in the moonlight, so you know who they are, and yet they aren't who they are on any other night, because they are under the

Moon. But when it's cloudy, it's like having sex with strangers, among strangers. Some people may like that, but I don't. I like the Moon when the moon shines.

Anybody who wants to can dance the Moon every night or any night while it wanes—nine nights. The first night, the Full Moon, is usually the big dance, but if it's raining then and then clears up, one of the Following Nights might have more people dancing. And men often go to another town to dance, on the Following Nights. If you go out to dance on one of those nights you're likely to find yourself with a man you don't know. You have to find out what House he lives in, of course, but if that's all right, then you'd do wrong to refuse him. If you come out to dance the Moon you don't choose and refuse.

On those Following Nights the music doesn't come down from the heyimas till late twilight, and usually the musicians go off to bed sometime not too late. Men decide all those things. Men of the Obsidian are in charge of the wakwa; they see that it's performed appropriately and without trouble. People getting drunk are usually the only trouble. It seems like there's always some old hunter who can't keep his penis up, so he drinks wine for lust, but then he can't get it up at all, so he drinks more and gets crazy, and the men in charge of the wakwa have to dip him in the reservoir or shut him into an empty barn till he quiets down. There used to be a woman here in Sinshan, Marigold of the Serpentine, who always drank at the Moon, and didn't stay put like you're supposed to; if there wasn't a man with her, she'd go get one. I suppose every boy in Sinshan who was too shy to go to the woman he really wanted, got sucked into that old whirlpool at one Moon or another. But it wasn't any harm to him, and Marigold certainly had a good time! At the Wine, she used to go around saying, "I drink all through the Moon, why can't I fuck all through the Wine?" And I expect she pretty well did, too. She was old when she stopped dancing the Moon— seventy or more. And she died soon after.

Anyway, however much or little dancing has gone on during the nine nights of the Moon, on the tenth night the reversal is reversed. It begins the dark of the moon. The women begin gathering on the common place, and the musicians come there when the sun is down behind the ridge. The women sing the Dark of the Moon songs, walking up to the Hinge and to the Obsidian heyimas.

The men are waiting for them there in the dancing place. They wear beautiful clothes that night, mostly black, black shirt and trousers, with a white vest embroidered in black, or a black vest embroidered with silver—some of those Moon Dance vests are

ten lifetimes old, they say. The men are all bareheaded and barefoot. Some of them draw a wide band of charcoal right across their
face, from the upper lip to the lower eyelids and from ear to ear.
They look magnificent. They stand in a gyring line facing the
women, and when the women stop singing the men begin. They
sing very deep, the way they did before the Moon. It's all matrix
words, only reversing that matrix word "meyan" makes "na yem,"
river shore, so those songs are called Shores of the River. The men
stand singing and the musicians drum. The women stand in their
line and listen. They are silent and don't dance.

When the Shores of the River have been sung, the women go
down into the Obsidian heyimas, to the Blood Lodge, one after
another, and wash their hands and eyes at the Moon Basin, and
then go on home. The men stay in the dancing place and have a
drum-singing, if they want; or they go down and bathe in Sinshan
Creek; then they come home. The Moon has been danced.

There are some things done during the Moon that aren't part
of the sacredness, they're just customs. In Sinshan, if a man wants
a woman to dance with him that night, he comes in the daytime
and gives her a sei flower. We had to laugh once in my household
when a quite old man in Up the Hill House gave my mother a
whole bunch of sei, twenty or thirty of them. She said, "How could
I not dance with a man like that!" Down in Madidinou, where I
lived when I was married, they don't give flowers that way, but they
go swimming together in the River, in the afternoon.

DARK OF THE MOON SONGS

Sung by women on the last night of the Moon Dance.

> The black ewe leads,
> her lamb follows.
> The sky closes.
> > Hey heya hey,
> > Obsidian House,
> > its door is shut.

> First House Woman
> suckles the lamb
> in the dark fold.
> > Hey heya hey,
> > Moon's House door
> > is black, is black!

Bloodclot, bloodclot,
black lump of blood,
black sacred lump,
I bleed you out.
Shining, shining,
whiteness shining,
shining whiteness,
white shining moon!
I give consent,
this blood consents,
this blood is black.
It bleeds itself.
I bleed this blood,
this clot, this lump,
this light, this life,
shining, shining.

More about the Moon Dance

A WOMAN IN CHUMO

Men love women best before they've had sex together, I think, and
women love men best after. So men aren't at home in marriage the
way women are, as a rule. So the Moon turns the rule around. Men
are at home, that month. There's no marriage, that month.

   When I wasn't married, I liked dancing the Moon, but when I
was married I was always glad when it was over. I'd come out to

sing the Dark of the Moon songs on the tenth night and see my husband in the men's line, wearing Obsidian black, looking fierce and handsome, and I'd be glad he was coming back into the house that night. He never seemed to be sorry to come, either; but he never said anything about it. He had his modesty. You know how men are.

A MAN IN KASTOHA-NA

Women make Moon veils, very fine and long and full. When they come out onto the common place they have those veils over their heads and wrapped around them and floating out behind them, and they keep part of the veil over their face if they like, so you can't tell who they are. They are white and full in the twilight and the moonlight, like reflections of the moon.

They always wear those Moon veils here; I didn't know the other towns don't dance the Moon with veils. You can lie on the veil while you're fucking and pull it over you if you like. They wash them out in the morning. All through the Moon all the washlines have white veils blowing on them—haven't you seen that?

Sometimes the women keep their face hidden, they really want you not to know who they are; that's good, that's right, the way it should be. You have to take care and notice, though, because she'll give you a sign, while you're dancing together, if she and you are of the same House, you know. Then you go off to another woman.

A YOUNG MAN IN CHUKULMAS

Oh, yes, the girls here wear veils, and the older women too, so you can't tell them apart, they're all just women. Only when you get very close, you do know them.

The girls who haven't danced the Moon before, they hide in their households. You have to go in. You sing outside awhile and call to them to come out, but they don't come out. So you have to go in. You sing,

> "Meyan, hey, meyan,
> I am coming in!"

They hide, they're waiting inside there, with the veil on. You take their hand and they come out with you to the common place. They always hide their face.

[In response to a question:] I don't think anybody has sex for the first time at the Moon—I don't know anybody who did. You come inland before it, that year, before you dance it the first time. That would be embarrassing, to make love the first time with all the others around. The older men are always showing off how great they are anyhow.

The Moon is very difficult when you're in love. You and a girl are in love and maybe you and she came inland together, you know, and then comes the Moon. Are you going to dance it? You can't stay with one person at the Moon. Maybe her feelings will be hurt when you go off with other women. But maybe she wants to dance it, and you don't want her to. A lot of love-matches get broken apart, around the Moon. I don't know about marriages.

POEMS

THIRD SECTION

Sinshan

A SIXTH HOUSE SONG
From the Madrone Lodge of Sinshan.

Coming down, going down
from the Grass to the Moon.

This house is falling,
its walls keep coming down
into creeks running downward,
into roots going downward.

From the Grass to the Moon
running down, hanging down.

The willow by the well rises falling,
the fallen apricot on Sinshan Knoll
lifts one branch in flower.
This house is built of falling.

A MEDITATION ON QUAIL FEATHER HOUSE

By Fox's Gift of the Blue Clay of Sinshan

How long has it been here,
the house of my household,
Quail Feather of Sinshan?
I go down to Ounmalin.
The house stays where it is.
I go up-Valley to the Mountain
and come back to the house.
I come and go, it stays.
I go in and out, it's both.
The mortar dries, the boards split,
the roof starts letting in the rain.
People rebuild the house.
It stays. People get born in it.
They die in it. It stays.
Maybe there was a fire.
They rebuilt it.
It keeps on staying here,
this house, Quail Feather,
the name of a house.
the shadow of a house.

THREE SHORT POEMS

Given to the Obsidian heyimas of Sinshan by Mooncarder.

IN FIRST HOLLOW

A great whicker of air,
the flicker's wingbeats.
The hawk of Sinshan cries
like a dream going away.

A NINTH HOUSE DAY

Between my eyes and the sun
windless clearness.
A buzzard moves
high up in this house
of the still air.
On the rock wall
a lizard does not move.
There is no roof.

THE VALLEY OAK
(FOURS)

No one has built
so beautiful
a house as this
great heyimas
deep-towering.

THE CRYING HAWK AT SINSHAN

By Ire of Sinshan. The meter is "klemchem."

What have you taken
    in your hard hands?
What are you breaking
    in your hooked lips?
Your eye is golden.
    You feed your child
    with my children.
Hawk, what do you hold?
    You fly crying,
    crying, crying,
    over the fields
    all day, grieving
    over the hills.
Hawk, what have you killed?

FIVES IN THE SECOND HOUSE

From the Blue Clay heyimas in Sinshan.

I know where she stepped,
that one with stick legs,
incense-cedar legs,
in the wet grasses.
I know where she lay,
pressing down the grass.
The wet dirt got warm
under her softness,
round belly, bent legs.
I know where her ears
stuck up thoughtfully
out of the grasstops
like two wet brown leaves.
I do not know, yet,
what she was thinking
while she looked at me.

TO GAHHEYA

By Stone Telling of the Blue Clay of Sinshan.

Old stone, hold my soul.
When I am not in this place
face the sunrise for me.
Grow warm slowly.
When I am not alive any more
face the sunrise for me.
Grow warm slowly.
this is my hand on you, warm.
This is my breath on you, warm.
This is my heart in you, warm.
This is my soul in you, warm.
You will be here a long time
facing the sunrise

with the warmth in you.
When you roll down,
when you break apart,
when the earth changes,
when the rockness of you ends,
we will be shining,
we will be dancing shining,
we will be warmth shining.

ON SECOND HILL

By Ire of Sinshan.

Whenever I come to this place
always somebody
always somebody
has been walking here,
has walked here before me.

The trails in the grass are thin and crooked,
hard to follow, leading
to the sacred of this place.
The flicker knocks the oak
five times, four times.

Who came here
before me, before sunrise?
Before the flicker?
Whose paths?

Their feet are narrow and divided,
their legs slender.
They walk
in a sacred manner.

THE PRIESTS OF THIS RELIGION

From an oral performance by Giver Ire's daughter of Sinshan.
The English title is an invention of the Editor.
The Poet called it goutun onkama,
a morning-twilight song.

The male of the great horned owl
in a voice like blowing into a hollow jar
sings the five-note heya
in the twilight of morning
in a sacred manner:
     hoo, hoo-oo, hoo, hoo.

The small frog whom he is hunting
in the creek-bottom among shadows
sings the four-note heya
in a fearless and contented voice:
     kaa-rigk, kaa-rigk.

THE TRAMPLED SPRING

From an oral performance by Giver Ire's daughter
of the Blue Clay of Sinshan.

Just over the hill
    from the heyimas
    from the heyimas
just over the hill from the heyimas
    of Sinshan
    of Sinshan
just over the hill
is the trampled spring.
Who dances, who dances?
Who dances there?
They dance, they dance there,

so that's where, that's where,
that's where the dancing is.

Stamping and dancing,
trampling and dancing.
with sharp feet
they cut the water
out of the ground,
with thin legs
they shoot the water
up from the ground,
jumping and dancing,
they trample the water
into rising,
into oozing and welling,
making mud under the grass,
making noises of water
beginning to flow, under the grass,
making flashing of water, shining of water
beginning to run, running down,
with the sound and flash of water running
to the creek from the trampled spring
  where they dance, trampling
  where they dance, springing,
  where they dance, stamping,
in secret, in sacred, in danger,
in the house of the puma,
just over the hill
  from the heyimas
  on the hunting side
just over the hill from Sinshan.

COMING HOME TO UP THE HILL HOUSE

By Little Bear Woman.

My heart dances, dances,
along these paths it dances,
through these doors it dances,
in these rooms it dances
with the dust motes in the morning sun.

In words is the dancing,
in singing is the dancing,
in sleeping is the dancing,
in sweeping is the dancing,
cleaning up this old sunlit house.

This is a long dancing:
The silence in these rooms,
the quail calling outside,
the sunlight coming in the windows,
all the years it has been this way.

Grandmother's sister sweeping this floor,
father gazing out this window,
mother writing at this table,
I a child and my children
waking mornings in this old sunlit house.

THE WRITER TO THE MORNING
IN UP THE HILL HOUSE IN SINSHAN

By Little Bear Woman.

Those who want fighting, let them smoke tobacco.
Those who want excitement, let them drink brandy.
Those who want withdrawal, let them smoke cannabis.
Those who want good talking, let them drink wine.
I don't want any of those things at this moment.
Early in the morning I breathe air and drink water,
because what I want is clarity and silence
and one thin line of words on the white paper
drawn around my thought in clarity and silence.

A SONG TO UP THE HILL HOUSE IN SINSHAN

By Little Bear Woman.

House, this place,
house, this place,
I am getting old living in you.
House, these rooms,

house, these rooms,
my mother was young living in this place.
Northwest door,
southwest door,
maybe my daughter's granddaughter will get old here,
inside these rooms,
in this house.
Maybe I will come in sometimes after dying
by the southwest door,
by the northwest door,
of this house, this place,
into this house, this place.

Buckeye

THE BLACK-CAPPED CHICKADEE

By Turning of the Blue Clay of Sinshan.

He is wise and very brave.
He sits on the branch,
preens and cleans his feathers,
picks his lice,
sharpens his beak,
will not let me pass.

What can I say?
He sings
    a long soft trilling
    thrice and turns his back.
He guards the silence.

I have come in.
I sit by the spring
with a dry heart.
The white azalea
flowers for the hummingbird.

I cannot read the writing
on the sparrow's breast,
though she comes close
for me to read it.

The water is silent,
drunk by tree roots.
It wells out in three places
from the rocks and sinks into its channel.

Beautiful the small speckled grasses
across the blue-green rock
glazed like porcelain.

The guardian chiks above the gate of moss,
the doorway of this house of silent water.

My heart is dry because I'm old,
but how many years
has the wild azalea flowered here?

How long has the water run?

It will rain tomorrow
and I will not come up here.
I will listen to the rain
and think of the birds
careful and fearless
in the bay and sweetshrub,
in the branches of the great azalea,
in the branches of the trees
that drink the water of this silence.

SINSHAN CREEK

By Peak of the Yellow Adobe and the Finders Lodge of Sinshan.

Thinking of the small water flowing
over stones under streambanks
under oak, alder, willow, madrone,
and the long-leaved laurel, the bay laurel,
thinking of the shallow water
softly going onward over gravel
where the creek curves outward
from the knoll's slope under the bay laurels,
and recurves back inward
to the little enfolded valley,
thinking of that water
in a dry autumn, in a foreign country,
I would cry out loud and cower
for longing, for the smell of the bay laurels.
My sleep would be that water and my soul
a stone in the running of that water.

GANAIV WAKWANA SINSHANSHUN

By the Ire of Sinshan.

I am at this place.
I am at this place now
where the water comes out of the rocks.

This is the water,
this is the spring of water
between the dark rocks,
between the blue rocks.

I am at this place now.
I am at the beginning of water.

With me at this place
the hummingbird with grey breast, green tail, red throat,
the hummingbird at this place
hunting, drumming.

I am at this place
where the water comes from darkness
with the winter hummingbird
that hangs bright-eyed over the water
not moving, drumming.

EIGHT LIFE STORIES

THE LIFE STORY was a story told by many people in the Valley. Biography and autobiography were written down and given to the heyimas or the lodge as an offering, a gift of life. Commonplace as most of them were, they were a "hinge" or intersection of private, individual, historical lived-time with communal, impersonal, cyclical being-time, and so were a joining of temporal and eternal, a sacred act.

The longest section of this book, Stone Telling's story, is an autobiography. In this section, a group of shorter life stories make a choir of Valley voices, men and women, old and young.

The Train, by seven-year-old Enough of Sinshan, is typical of the short autobiographical offering: it relates an event very important in the life of the author, in full confidence that this importance will be felt by the reader—that it will be, in our terms, meaningful.

She Listens (or *Listening Woman*) was offered to the Serpentine heyimas in Sinshan when the author took her middle name, the name by which she would be known all her adult life, until or unless she took or was given a last name.

Like many naïve autobiographies without literary pretensions, it is written in the third person.

In *Junco,* the author uses the third person to refer to himself when he is writing in the past tense, and uses the first person in the present tense. This record of a vision quest by a spiritual athlete presents a failure as the central event of a life.

The Bright Void of the Wind, given by Kulkunna of Telina-na to his heyimas, is a record of what we would call an out-of-body or afterlife experience; it presents a dying as the central event of a life.

Having had his life saved by the doctors (living and dead) of the Doctors Lodge, Kulkunna went directly on to join them; he felt he had a debt to pay. Towards the end of Stone Telling's story we see the other side of the weaving: a doctor who saved a life was thereafter, literally and in all respects, responsible for that life—as responsible as the parents who had conceived it. Debt and credit in the Doctors Lodge was a mortally serious business.

White Tree is the only straight biography in this group. When a friend or relative thought an untold life worth telling, they might do so, as here, after the death of the subject of the piece.

The Third Child's Story, signed by Spotted Goat of Madidinou, though told in the first person, may be a vengeful biography pretending to be autobiography; or may be pure fiction; or something between the two. The loose free-verse triplet structure was used for lamentations, satires, and scurrilities.

The Dog at the Door records a vision which began as a dream and then was consciously followed, using the technology of meditation provided by the heyimas. In our terms it is a mere mental excursion, a fantasy, not even rationalised. To its author and readers in the Valley it was the sufficient record of a life. The author, who gave it to the Red Adobe heyimas in Wakwaha, did not sign it.

Finally, in the longest of these pieces, *The Visionary,* Flicker of Telina-na recounts her life with considerable candor and realism. Copies of this work were kept both in her heyimas in Telina and in the Archives in Wakwaha. She may have been asked to write it by her fellow scholars on the Mountain, as a kind of guide for other people burdened with her gift; for she tries to describe what was more often left unstated, the emotions and relationships of a person pursuing (willingly or unwillingly) the career of visionary, and the place of a "great vision" in an ordinary life.

The Train

By Enough of the Serpentine of Sinshan.

This is the first offering I have made by writing. Heya hey heya heya heya. This is the first name my mothers gave me: Enough. I have been living in the Third House of Earth since the time of the Moon Dancing seven years ago. This is the name of the house where my mothers' hearth is: Blue Walls of Sinshan. After the Wine I went away from Sinshan with my cousin Poppy and my maternal aunt Gift. That was the first time I went away from Sinshan. We went to the other side of the Valley to those other mountains. We walked down onto the flat of the Valley and walked and came to the River. We crossed across the River on the ferry and the ferryman brings it across pulling on a rope and then he goes back across without you. He keeps chickens with green tails. Then we went on a little way and we came to the Line. It smells like some kinds of soap and also like something burnt. It is like a very wide ladder lying on the ground that comes from so far away in the northwest and so far away in the southeast you can't see either end. On both sides of it the grass is all cut down and there are beautiful smooth rocks inside it. We went across it by stepping on one of the rungs. We went up on a hill with thistles and under some oaks we sat down and ate some pickles and eggs. While we were there there was a noise far away like a drum. Gift said look and we looked and while the noise got very loud the Train came! I was afraid. At home when I heard that noise people said was the Train I always thought it was stone people walking heavily. The noise is much louder when you are close to it. It made rolls of smoke and it was like houses moving. On one of the parts that was more like a cart there was a person with a red hat sitting that waved their hand at us. I did not wave my hand because I was holding Gift's and Poppy's hands. I was excited. Gift said it was the Train with wine for the Amaranth people. The bluejays all started yelling on that hill when the Train came and the ducks flew up from down by the River and made the air get dark and I could smell them. The Train's direction of going was southeast. It went on. We went on that thistle path. We went to the Old Lake and stayed with our mothers' brother there fishing. Then we came home after four days with the fish. Heya Serpentine!

She Listens

*Given to the Serpentine heyimas of Sinshan
by She Listens of Chimbam House.*

Phoebe had seen nothing but what other people see and she did
not go to the heyimas very often or sing Blood Lodge songs or talk
with old people. She went on a day to her household's gathering
place on Black Ridge by Herou to gather chia seed. She got tired
working in the sun and went up into the chaparral to lie down and
sleep awhile. She lay down where the ground was clear and there
was no poison oak under a big madrone tree with five trunks. The
crickets stopped after a while. There was no noise of anything anywhere. She thought an earthquake. She sat up. In front of her a
woman was standing who was golden red down the left side of her
face and hair and body and arm and leg, and twisted black down
the right side, and her right leg was black and dry and had no foot
on it. She stood there. She looked at Phoebe with the bright eye
and the burnt eye. She said, "Take off your clothes!" The girl began
to cry. "Look at yourself whole and soft and all alive!" Madrone
Woman said. The girl tried to hide on the ground covered with
madrone leaves. "You are a fool and must marry to grow wise,"
Madrone Woman said, and she took a branch of live madrone with
her red hand and struck the girl across the breasts with it, making

Manzanita

scratches, and took a dead branch with her black hand and struck the girl across the belly with it, drawing blood. Then she turned away and became branches and sky. Phoebe crawled away crying and went down the hill road with her basket of chia seeds and came to her house in Sinshan. Her mother was sitting on the balcony. She said, "What has happened to you, daughter?" Phoebe stood there and cried. Her mother said, "I see you have been where I have to go. I have to go there. My heart is no good any more and I have to begin dying. I could not tell you that, but now I see you can hear me. Perhaps you met a Four-House person. Perhaps they spoke to you."

The girl said, "It was the Madrone. She did not say anything about you. She told me to get married."

The mother said, "That is what I tell you too."

The girl kept crying. The mother comforted her.

Soon after that the young man named Vine of the Yellow Adobe came from his household to live in the girl's household. They were married at the World Dance. The mother was well for that, but then began to get weak, and died nine days before the Moon. Her name came then to the girl. Her name now is She Listens.

Heya madrone
Heya madrone
Heya madrone
Heya madrone.

Junco

*Given to the Yellow Adobe heyimas of Chukulmas
by Junco of Tile House.*

He did not want to talk with stones or walk with the puma when he went up on Ama Kulkun in his twentieth year, that young man called Sungazer, who has become this old man writing.

He made no offerings as he left Wakwaha on the high road, and did not stop to sing or to be silent at the Springs of the River. He did not ask the deer or the bear, the oak or the poison oak, the hawk or the snake to help him or advise him. He did not ask help of the Mountain. He climbed straight to the summits and went to the northwest height. The wind was blowing.

He made a house there of lines on the ground drawn with a rock in the dirt, and standing up inside that house he said aloud: "I do not want the beings, the souls, the forms, the words. I want the eternal truth. I will do what I must do, I will fast, I will sacrifice, I will give my life, if I may see before death what lies behind life and death, behind word and form, behind all being, the eternal truth."

The wind was blowing, the sun was shining. The young man began his fast. Four days, four nights he stood there in the house of lines. That was the beginning.

The gyre of the buzzard, the history of the rocks, the silence of the grass, they were all there, but he would not have them, desiring the eternal truth.

He went down on the fifth day to get water at the Breathfeather Spring. He drank, and filled a clay jar that had been left as an offering at the spring, and went back up to the summit to stand in the house of lines. Each day for three days he drank some water from the jar. On the fourth day the water was gone, and he could not stand up at all any longer. He stayed crouching in the house of lines, saying in his mind, "I give my life, let me know the truth."

People from Wakwaha brought him water. People from his House came and told him that what he was doing was a mistake. A woman came from the Yellow Adobe of Wakwaha and said, "Because you stand on top of the mountain do you think you are greater than the mountain?" She left food in a bowl, but he did not touch it. He drank the water when the people had left him alone. It made him weak, and he could not crouch any longer. He lay down, and as soon as he lay down dreams came into his mind. He would not have them. He struggled to stay awake and kept saying in his mind, "Give me the truth, I give my life."

He began to hear his name: "Sungazer! Sungazer!"

It was a name that others had given him; he had not chosen it. Now he thought that he must do what his name said. He looked up and gazed at the sun.

It was a day of still air without cloud or wind. As he gazed at the shining of the sun, wheels began to come into his seeing, black wheels and very bright wheels, turning one within the other. The wheels rolled around and across the sun, and rolled across the world when he looked away from the sun.

A bluejay came inside the house of lines, walking, and said, "You will burn out your eyes."

Sungazer said, "I will do what I must do."

He went on looking at the sun. He felt very sick, and when the sun set and the dark was there, in the dark he saw the bright wheels and the black wheels still turning everywhere around him.

An owl came nearby and said many times, "You will be blind."

The young man tried to weep but the tears had been burned out of his eyes. He crawled on the ground among the turning wheels, crying out. Everything began talking to him, saying, "Go down, go down now!" He could feel the Mountain twitch the way a horse shudders its skin to twitch off a fly. He could feel the earth rolling like a wheel. When daylight began he could see a little, and he went down the mountain, crawling on all fours. He drank at Breathfeather Spring. After he had rested and drunk there for a while he gained strength and could walk. He heard everything still saying, "Go down!" and so he went down to Wakwaha-na, and still everything said, "Go down!" He went on down along the River to Kastoha-na, and there still everything said, "Go down!" He did not know how to go down below the Valley, until he thought of the caves at Kestets. He knew them as a vintner. He went there along

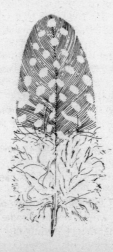

the old road and went into the caves, past where the wine is stored, back to where the springs seep out of the rock in the dark. There was no light there, but he saw the bright wheels turning under the ground. He began dancing there, stamping and rocking. The blood ran out of his nose and eyes. He danced and cried out, "Let me know the truth!"

A person began dancing with him, facing him. Although there was no light in the caves, Sungazer could see the person, who did not look like anyone he knew, nor like a man, nor like a woman. The person said dancing, "Do you know enough to know?"

Sungazer answered, "I have learned the teachings, I have learned the songs, I have lived on the Coast since I was a child, I have fasted, I have danced, I have given, I have given everything!"

"Yes, yes, yes, yes," the person said, dancing. The voice grew higher, speaking. The person kept shrinking, dancing. Sungazer could not see very clearly. The person kept looking smaller and smaller, dancing, until finally something like a mouse or a big spider was there, and ran away into the dark of the small caves.

People from the Wine Art of Kastoha came into the caves then, and they came around Sungazer and carried him out. He could not walk. They gave him water to drink, and then some milk, and the pulp of an apricot to eat. He drank and ate. They carried him on a hay-cart to Chukulmas, to his mothers' house, and left him there to get well.

But in the evening he got up and left Tile House and went out of town on the hunting side. He went as far as he could to a lonely place, a side canyon of Blue Creek Canyon, and there he tore and knotted his shirt into a rope and tied himself with it to a digger pine so that he could stand up with his back against the tree. He said, "Now I will die of hunger and thirst unless I am given one glimpse of the eternal truth."

He made this promise again and again all night.

As the day began he saw somebody coming up the canyon through the chaparral and digger pines. His eyes were still burnt and dim, and the light was not clear yet. He thought it was somebody from town coming to find him and make him stop fasting, and so he called out, "Don't come here! Go back!"

The person stopped there down by the creek and then turned around and began to go away. Then the young man thought it might be a person from the Four Houses bringing him what he had asked for, and he called out, "Come back! Please come back!" But the person was gone.

Standing tied to the tree, Sungazer said, "I am going to die now."

All at once a bright person stood before him, clear as glass, shining. The shining person spoke to him: "Take the gift!" That voice seemed to ring and shine, but the person was not there. The young man stood waiting in silence. The air was still. Clouds were across the sun and there was an even light. There was no sound. Nothing moved. Nothing happened. A junco flew alone across between two pines, alighting on a branch. The young man waited for the gift, for the truth. Bluejays began to quarrel and yell in the top of the tree he was tied to. The young man waited. It began to rain.

When the rain fell on his hair and face and arms, the young man knew that nothing would happen, that that was what was to happen, but he was angry. He thought, "Then I will go on and die." He bowed his head to keep the rain from wetting his lips, and stood there tied to the tree.

It rained a few big drops and ceased, and after a while the sun came out. That afternoon the young man went blind. Some time after that people from his house and heyimas, looking for him, found him. He was partly alive then, and did not know anything for a long time while the Doctors Lodge kept and healed him; and after he began to regain his mind and strength the healing went on until the winter. The doctors brought him back to life except for the sharpness of his eyesight, which was gone, so that I can see things only by looking sidelong at them. Straight before me I see nothing.

Sungazer later married Plum Flower of the Obsidian and lived in Built Too Quick House, where they had a daughter and a son. Sungazer worked with the Wine Art of his town, and sang with the Doctors Lodge. Last winter his wife died. Since that time I am Junco.

The Bright Void of the Wind

By Kulkunna of the Red Adobe of Telina-na.

Thirty years ago, I am told, an illness that had been in me for a long time grew stronger, taking consciousness from me, causing convulsions, and finally making my heartbeat and my breathing stop. Of this I remember nothing, but I remember what happened:

I was inside a dark house, strangely shaped, without rooms. The walls of the house were thin, and wind and rain beat against them. I stood in the middle of this house. High up in the walls were some narrow, small, dim windows. I could not see through them. I wanted to see out, to know what part of town this house was in, and said angrily, "Where is the doorway? Where is the door?" Groping along the walls then I found the door and opened it.

At once the wind blew it wide open with a rush and bang, and the house shrivelled up behind me like an empty bladder. I stood in a tremendous place of light and wind. Under my feet was only light and wind, the force of the wind bearing me up.

As soon as I saw that, I thought I must fall unless I found something to stand on: and I began falling. I sought for any place to set my foot or hold with my hand in the wind. There was nothing. I fell, and was terrified. I closed my eyes in fear, but it made no difference: there was no darkness there. I fell, and there was nothing I could do. I fell, like a feather falling from a bird in flight. The wind bore me, and I fell drifting. I was like a feather. There was no need to fear.

As I began to feel this and understand it, I began to know the greatness of the wind, the brightness of the light, and joy.

But along with that knowledge I felt a pulling, which grew stronger. The brightness shook, dimmed, and darkened; the wind grew smaller and weaker, becoming sounds, breaths, and voices.

Then I was back breathing through my nose and mouth, hearing in my ears, feeling in my skin, living in my heartbeat. For a while I could not yet see with my earthly eyes, and so was able to see with my mind's eyes that all my senses could perceive was themselves, that they were making the world by casting shadows on the bright void of the wind. I saw that living was catching at shadows with hands of light. I did not want to come back to that. But the doctors' art made me come back, pulling at me, and their singing drew me back, calling me home. I opened my eyes and saw an old man, Blackfern of the Black Adobe Lodge, sitting beside me singing. His voice was thin and husky. He looked into my eyes with his eyes, singing:

> "Walk here now, walk here.
> It is time to walk here now!"

I understood that it was time that I go on walking on the earth, and not time that I return to the shining. So with regret and pain, with difficulty and labor, even as the fire-covering song of *Going Westward to the Sunrise* says,

> It is hard, it is hard.
> It is not easy.
> You must go out—

even so, I became my ashes. I became my dark body and its illness once again.

For many nights and days I was helpless, but when at last I recovered health I was stronger than I had ever been, and by careful diet and learning I have remained well.

I had lain many days in the doctors' care before I asked why I did not see Blackfern, and, saying his name aloud, remembered that he had died, an old man, when I was still a child.

When I ceased to be a patient I began to learn to be a doctor. To those who taught me skills and songs I gave the song Blackfern gave me across the wind, thirty years ago. It has been useful in healing people in shock and in the crises of fever.

White Tree

By Ewe Dance of the Obsidian of Sinshan.

He was born in the House of Yellow Adobe early in the rainy season. His mothers' household was in Up the Hill House in Sinshan. That was a new house then; his mother and her mother and sister and their husbands had built it during the year before this man was born. His first name was Twenty-One Days.

His disposition was mild and unsociable, his mind active and thoughtful. He was not much inclined to words.

He was well educated in his household and heyimas, took part in the ceremonies of his House in due time, and became a member of the Planting Lodge at thirteen years old, a member of the Bay Laurel Lodge a year later, when he put on the undyed clothing. During his adolescence he learned arboriculture with his mother's brother, a scholar of the Planting Lodge and of the Yellow Adobe, and with orchard trees of all kinds.

When he had lived nineteen years he went up to Wakwaha to the Sun. He lived there at the Yellow Adobe heyimas learning and singing until the World was danced. After that he went alone on the Mountain.

When he came down from the Mountain he came to Kastoha-na, where he lived in a household of people of his House, studying the way the trees grew there, as the orchards of Kastoha were the richest and most beautiful anywhere in those times. Presently he took his middle name, Fairweather, and put on dyed shirts, and went to live in the household of a Serpentine woman, Hill of Hill House in Kastoha. She was a forester, working mostly with the oaks that are cut for fine carpentry. For some years he worked with her in locating, selecting, cutting, and replanting forest oaks. He joined the Wood Art.

Whenever he was back in Kastoha he worked at crossbreeding varieties of pear. In those times none of the Valley pears was very good, all were subject to cankers, and most needed irrigation to bear well. To obtain varieties of trees, he travelled with the Finders to Clear Lake and the Long Sound, and through the Exchange he asked people in the north for help. Some seedling pear trees were sent to him from orchards in a place called Forty Forks River far in the north, and were brought to him by some of the traders from those people trading smoked salmon for wine. By crossbreeding the northern trees with a pear tree he had found growing wild above the oak forests between Kastoha and Chukulmas, he came upon a strong, small, and drought-hardy tree with excellent fruit, and he came to Sinshan to plant some of the seedlings. Now this is the brown pear grown in most orchards and gardens, and people call it the Fairweather pear.

During these years when he was travelling and Hill was often in the forest they did not live together for long at a time. They had no children together. After a while Hill decided to leave her marriage and her household and be a forest-living woman. Fairweather went to live in the household of an Obsidian woman, Black Ewe of Magpie House in Kastoha. She had one daughter. She and Fairweather had one son.

Fairweather began to study with the apple trees of the Upper Valley orchards, working at crossbreeding to help the mountain apples resist the edge-curl disease. He was also doing a great work of many years with the soils and earths of the foothills of the Mountain and the trees that grew in the various soils, learning where and how they grew. But as he was in the midst of this work, Black Ewe began to be ill with the vedet, which affected her hearing and then her sight.

They moved from her mothers' household and came with their daughter and son to Sinshan, where they lived for some years in Old Red House. They worked with the Doctors Lodge, Black Ewe learning how to be ill and Fairweather how to care for her when she needed help. He worked as an orcharder and took part in all ceremonies of his House and the Arts and Lodges of which he was a member. He could not continue learning the earths of the Mountain foothills. Black Ewe lived nine years in pain, deaf and blind.

After she died her daughter returned to the grandmother's household in Kastoha-na. Fairweather and his son lived in a room in the Yellow Adobe household of Chimbam House, where he had cousins. At that time his last name came to him from the Planting Lodge at the Wine Dance: White Tree. He continued to work in the orchards of Sinshan, planting, tending, pruning, cleaning, fertilising, weeding, and picking. He became a member of the Green Clown Society, and danced the Wine and the World and the Moon till he was eighty-one. He died of pneumonia after working in the plum orchards of Sinshan in the rain.

White Tree was my father's father. He was a kind and silent old man. I am writing this for the library of his heyimas in Sinshan and copying it for the library of his heyimas in Kastoha, so that he may be remembered for a while when pear trees are planted or orchards praised.

TRANSLATOR'S NOTE:
p. 290. . . . *he learned arboriculture with his mother's brother . . . and with orchard trees of all kinds.*
We would be more likely to say that he learned *from* his uncle *about* orchard trees; but this would not be a fair translation of the repeated suffix *oud,* with, together with. To learn *with* an uncle and trees implies that

learning is not a transfer of something by someone to someone, but is a relationship. Moreover, the relationship is considered to be reciprocal. Such a point of view seems at hopeless odds with the distinction of subject and object considered essential to science. Yet it appears that White Tree's genetic experiments or manipulations were technically skilful, and that he was not ignorant of the theories involved, and it is certain that he achieved precisely what he set out to achieve. And the resulting strain of tree was given his name: a type case, in our vocabulary, of Man's control over Nature. This phrase, however, could not be translated into Kesh, which had no word meaning Nature except *she*, being; and anyhow the Kesh saw the Fairweather pear as the result of a collaboration between a man and some pear trees. The difference of attitude is interesting and the absence of capital letters perhaps not entirely trivial.

The Third Child's Story

By Spotted Goat of the Obsidian of Madidinou.

My mother didn't intend to conceive me,
    she was too lazy to abort me,
    my first name was Careless.
Her House was Obsidian,
    her town was Madidinou,
    her household was in Spotted Stone House.
The people of Madidinou are like gravel,
    like sand,
    like poor dirt.

My father's House was Blue Clay,
    he lived in Sinshan,
    in his mothers' household.

The people of Sinshan are like thistles,
    like nettles,
    like poison oak.
My mother's husband's House was Blue Clay too,
    he lived in Madidinou,
    in her household.

I am a superfluous person,
    a low-quality person,
    my soul is small.
I did not learn to dance well,
    or to sing well,
    or to write well.
I don't like farming,
    I have no skills,
    animals run away from me.

My older sister and brother were stronger than me
    and never waited for me
    and never taught me anything.
My mother's husband was their father,
    he cared only for them,
    he never taught me anything.
My mother's mother was impatient,
    she thought I should not have been born,
    she said I wasn't worth teaching.

I didn't dance any wakwa till I was thirteen,
    nobody in the heyimas would teach me the songs,
    nobody would teach me the dances.
I put on undyed clothing when I was fourteen,
    when some Blue Clay people from Sinshan took me
        on the Salt Voyage,
    but I didn't see any visions.

When I was fifteen a Blue Clay girl kept pestering me,
    she kept hanging around,
    she made me come inland with her.
She got pregnant,
    we got married,
    she miscarried the child.
She put my clothes outside her door,
    I had to go back to my mothers' household,
    they didn't want me in that house.

I had to work all the time for my mother's husband farming,
    for my mother at the power plant,
    for my grandmother doctoring animals.

There was a Serpentine girl wearing undyed clothing,
    that I kept following around
    until she came inland with me.
Her parents said we couldn't be married in their household,
    that she was too young to get married,
    that they didn't want me living there.
So she and I went to Telina-na,
    we lived with some Serpentine people,
    we worked at different things there.

The people of Telina-na are like flies,
    like mosquitoes,
    like gnats.
They think they're great-souled because their town is big,
    they think they're important because their town has big dances,
    they think they know everything because their town has big
    heyimas.
They think what they do is right,
    and other people are ignorant,
    and everybody should do what they say.

I kept getting into fights there,
    those people picked fights with me,
    the young men picked on me.
I was always being hurt,
    I got knocked down,
    my front teeth got loosened.
They didn't fight fair,
    so I used a knife,
    I split the belly of one of those young men.

They made a big fuss,
    they sent me back to Madidinou,
    they sent the Serpentine girl back too.
She went to her mothers' house,
    but I didn't go to my mothers' house,
    I went to a summer place in the hills.
It was cold there,
    it was lonesome,
    it rained all the time.

I got sick there,
>   I got chills and fever,
>   I nearly died there alone.
I went to Sinshan,
>   my father's mother took me in,
>   I stayed in Up the Hill House.
They kept telling me I had behaved unwisely,
>   I should learn more,
>   I should be more mindful.

I went down with them to fish at the Mouths of the Na,
>   we spent a long time fishing in those dangerous salt marshes,
>   we didn't catch much along those dreary beaches.
They said I was pestering a young girl there,
>   but she was pestering me,
>   she was always hanging around me.
I went back up the River,
>   but that girl followed me,
>   she came inland with me.

We tried to stay in Ounmalin,
>   but people there said the girl was too young,
>   they said she ought to go home to Sinshan.
The people in Ounmalin are spiteful,
>   meddling,
>   and provincial.
They interfered with us,
>   and some Blue Clay people took the girl back to Sinshan,
>   and I went alone to Tachas Touchas.

In Tachas Touchas there was not much to do,
>   there was no household to live in,
>   there weren't any friendly people.
The people of Tachas Touchas are like scorpions,
>   like rattlesnakes,
>   like black widow spiders.
An old Red Adobe woman in Tachas Touchas kept pestering me,
>   she made me live in her household,
>   she made me get married to her.

I lived there a long time,
    working hard for that old woman,
    for ten years I worked for her household.
Her daughter was a grown woman
    who had a daughter growing up there,
    and that girl began pestering me.
She lived there in her grandmother's house,
    she was always hanging around there,
    she made me have sex with her.

She told her mother and grandmother about it,
    they told the heyimas,
    the heyimas people told the whole town.
People came and shamed me,
    they humiliated me,
    they drove me away.
None of them ever wanted me,
    none of them ever trusted me,
    none of them ever liked me.

There's no use going to a town where I haven't been yet,
    all the towns are just the same,
    people are all just the same.
Human people are small-souled,
    selfish,
    and cruel.
I'll live here in Madidinou, where I'm not wanted,
        or trusted,
        or liked,
    I'll live here in my mothers' house where I don't want to live
        and they don't want me to live,
        doing work I don't like;
    I'll live here to spite them nine years more,
        and nine more years after that,
        and nine more years after that.

The Dog at the Door

*A record of a vision, given to the Red Adobe
heyimas in Wakwaha as a written
offering, not signed.*

I was in a town that was in the Valley yet was not one of the nine
towns of the Valley, a place strange to me. I knew that I lived in a
house in this town, but could not find it. I went to the common
place and then to the dancing place, thinking I would go to the Red
Adobe heyimas. In the dancing place there were not five heyimas,
but four, and I did not know which was mine. I said to a person
there, "Where is the other heyimas?" The person said, "Behind
you." I turned around and saw a dog running away between the
high roofs of the heyimas. This much I dreamed asleep.

Waking, I followed that dog. I came to a deep well lined with
stone. I set my hands on the coping, looked down into the well, and
saw the sky. I stood between the sky above and the sky below and
cried out, "Must all things end?"

The answer was: "They must end."

"Must my town fall?"

"It is falling now."

"Must the dances be forgotten?"

"They are forgotten."

The air became dark and earthquake shook the walls. Houses
fell down, dust obscured the mountains and the sun, and a terrible
cold came into the air. I cried out, "Is the world at its end?"

The answer was: "There is no end."

"My town is destroyed!"

"It is being built."

"I must die and forget all I have known!"

"Remember."

Then the dog came to me in the dust and darkness and cold,
carrying in its mouth a small bag woven of grass.

In the bag were the souls of the human beings of the world,
small like dill or chia seeds, very small and black.

I took the bag and went along beside the dog. As the sky began to clear and the air grew pale, I saw that the mountains had
fallen. Where they had been, where the Valley had been, there was
a great plain. On this plain I walked with the dog northeastward

among many other people. Each of them carried a bag like the one I carried. Some held seeds and some held little stones. The stones in the bags made a whispering as they moved together, saying, "In the end is no end. To build with us, unbuild with us." Understanding them, having forgotten my way I remembered it, and so came walking past the willows of the River into my town, Telina-na, and past the Red Adobe heyimas, and to the door of my own house. But the dog was there at the door, snarling, and would not let me in.

The Visionary:
The Life Story of Flicker of
the Serpentine of Telina-na

My mother and aunt said that when I was learning to talk I talked to people they could not see or hear, sometimes speaking in our language and sometimes saying words or names they did not know. I can't remember doing that, but I remember that I could not understand why people said that a room was empty, or that there was nobody in the gardens, because there were always people of different kinds, everywhere. Mostly they stayed quietly, or were going about their doings, or passing through. I had already learned that nobody talked to them and that they did not often pay heed or answer when I tried to talk to them; but it had not occurred to me that other people did not see them.

I had a big argument with my cousin once when she said there was nobody in the washhouse, and I had seen a whole group of people there, passing things from hand to hand and laughing silently, as if they were playing some gambling game. My cousin, who was older than I, said I was lying, and I began to scream and tried to knock her down. I can feel that same anger now. I was telling what I had seen, and could not believe she had not seen the people in the washhouse; I thought she was lying in order to call me a liar. That anger and shame stayed a long time and made me unwilling to look at the people that other people didn't see or wouldn't talk about. When I saw them, I looked away until they were gone. I had thought they were all my kinfolk, people of my household, and seeing them had been companionship and pleasure to me; but now I felt I could not trust them, since they had got me into trouble. Of course I had it all backwards, but there was nobody to help me get it straight. My family were not much given to thinking about things, and except for going to school I went to our heyimas only in the Summer before the games.

When I turned away from all those people that I had used to see, they went on and did not come back. Only a few were left, and I was lonely.

I liked to be with my father, Olive of the Yellow Adobe, a man who talked little and was cautious and gentle in mind and hand. He repaired and re-installed solar panels and collectors and batteries and lines and fixtures in houses and outbuildings; all his work was with the Millers Art. He did not mind if I came along if I was quiet, and so I went with him to be away from our noisy, busy household. When he saw that I liked his art he began to teach it to me. My mothers were not enthusiastic about that. My Serpentine grandmother did not like having a Miller for son-in-law, and my mother wanted me to learn medicine. "If she has the third eye she ought to put it to good use," they said, and they sent me to the Doctors Lodge on White Sulphur Creek to learn. Although I learned a good deal there and liked the teachers, I did not like the work, and was impatient with the illnesses and accidents of mortality, preferring the dangerous, dancing energies my father worked with. I could often see the electrical current, and there were excitements of feeling, tones of a kind of sweet music barely to be heard, and tones also of voices speaking and singing, distant and hard to understand, that came when I worked with the batteries and wires. I did not speak of this to my father. If he felt and heard any of these things he preferred to leave them unspoken, outside the house of words.

My childhood was like everybody's, except that with going to the Doctors Lodge and working with my father and liking to be alone, perhaps I played less with other children than many children do, after I was seven or eight years old. Also, though I went all over Telina with my father and knew all the ways and houses, we never went out of town. My family had no summerhouse and never even visited the hills. "Why leave Telina?" my grandmother would say. "Everything is here!" And in summer the town was pleasant, even when it was hot; so many people were away that there was never a crowd at the wash house, and houses standing empty were entirely different from houses full of people, and the ways and gardens and common places were lonesome and lazy and quiet. It was always in summer, often in the great heat of the afternoon, that I would see the people passing through Telina-na, coming upriver. They are hard to describe, and I have no idea who they were. They

were rather short and walked quietly, alone, or three or four one after the other; their limbs were smooth and their faces round, often with some lines or marks drawn on the lips or chin; their eyes were narrow, and sometimes looked swollen and sore as if from smoke or weeping. They would go quietly through the town not looking at it and never speaking, going upriver. When I saw them I would always say the four heyas. The way they went, silently, gripped at my heart. They were far from me, walking in sorrow.

When I was nearly twelve years old my cousin came of age and the family gave a very big passage party for her, giving away all kinds of things I didn't even know we had. The following year I came of age and we had another big party, though without such lavishness, as we didn't have so much left to give. I had entered the Blood Lodge just before the Moon, and the party for me was during the Summer Dance. At the end of the party there were horse games and races, for the Summer people had come down from Chukulmas.

I had never been on horseback. The boys and girls who rode in the games and races for Telina brought a steady mare for me to ride, and boosted me up to her back and put the rein in my hand, and off we went. I felt like the wild swan. That was pure joy. And I could share it with the other young people; we were all joined by the good feeling of the party and the excitement of the games and races and the beauty and passion of the horses, who thought it was all their festival. The mare taught me how to ride that day, and I was on horseback all night dreaming, and the next day rode again; and on the third day I rode in a race, on a roan colt from a household in Chukulmas. The colt ran second in the big race when I rode him, and ran first in the match race when the boy who had raised him rode him. In all that glory of festival and riding and racing and friendship I left my childhood most joyously, but also I went out of my House, and got lost from too much being given me at once. I gave my heart to the red colt I rode and to the boy who rode him, a brother of the Serpentine of Chukulmas.

It was a long time ago, and not his fault or doing; he did not know it. The word I write is my word; to myself let it be brought back.

So the Summer games were over in our town and the horse-riders went off downriver to Madidinou and Ounmalin; and there I was, a thirteen-year-old woman, and afoot.

I wore the undyed clothing I had been making all the year before, and I went often to the Blood Lodge, learning the songs and mysteries. Young people who had been friendly to me at the games remained friends, and when they found I longed to ride they shared the horses of their households with me. I learned to play vetulou, and helped with caring for the horses, who were stabled and pastured then northwest of Moon Creek in Halfhoof Pasture and on Butt Hill. I said at the Doctors Lodge that I wanted to learn horse doctoring, and so they sent me to learn that art by working with an old man, Striffen, who was a great doctor of horses and cattle. He talked with them. It was no wonder he could heal them. I would listen to him. He used different kinds of noises, words like the matrix words of songs, and different kinds of silences and breathing; and so did the animals; but I never could understand what they were saying.

He told me once, "I'm going to die next year around Grass time."

I said, "How do you know that?"

He said, "An ox told me. He saw this. See?" He showed me that when he held out both his arms rigid they had the sideways shaking or tremor of sevai.

"The later it begins the longer you live with it," said I, as I had learned at the Doctors Lodge; but he said, "One more World, one more Wine, the ox told me."

Another time I asked the old man, "How can I heal horses if I can't talk with them?" It seemed I was not learning much from him.

"You can't," he said. "Not the way I can. What are you here for?"

I laughed and shouted, like the man in the play,

> "What am I here for?
> What was I born for?
> Answer me! Answer!"

I was crazy. I was lost without knowing it, and did not care for anything.

Once when I came to the Obsidian heyimas for a Blood Lodge singing, a woman, I thought her old then, named Milk, met me in the passage. She looked at me with eyes as sharp and blind as a snake's eyes and said, "What are you here for?"

I answered her, "For the singing," and hurried by, but I knew that was not what she had asked.

In the summer I went with the dancers and riders of Telina to Chukulmas. There I met that boy, that young man. We talked about the roan horse and about the little moon-horse I was riding in the vetulou games. When he stroked the roan horse's flank I did so too, and the side of my hand touched the side of his hand once.

Then there was another year until the Summer games returned. That was how it was to me: there was nothing I cared for or was mindful of but the Summer and the games.

The old horse-doctor died on the first night of the Grass. I had gone to the Lodge Rejoining and learned the songs; I sang them for him. After he was burned I gave up learning his art. I could not talk with the animals, or with any other people. I saw nothing clearly and listened to no one. I went back to working with my father, and I rode and looked after the horses and practiced vetulou so that I could ride in the games in Summer. My cousin had a group of friends, girls who talked and played soulbone and dice, gambling for candy and almonds, sometimes for rings and earrings, and I hung around with them every evening. There were no real people in the world I saw at that time. All rooms were empty. Nobody was in the common places and gardens of Telina. Nobody walked up-river grieving.

When the sun turned south the dancers and riders came again

from Chukulmas to Telina, and I rode in the games and races, spending all day and night at the fields. People said, "That girl is in love with the roan stallion from Chukulmas," and teased me about it, but not shamefully; everybody knows how adolescents fall in love with horses, and songs have been made about that love. But the horse knew what was wrong: he would no longer let me handle him.

In a few days the riders went on to Madidinou, and I stayed behind.

Things are very obstinate and stubborn, but also there is a sweet willingness in them; they offer what they meet. Electricity is like horses: crazy and wilful, and also willing and reliable. If you are careless and running counter, a horse or a live wire is a contrary and perilous thing. I burnt and shocked myself several times that year, and once I started a fire in the walls of a house by making a bad connection and not grounding the wire. They smelled the smoke and put out the fire before it did much harm, but my father, who had brought me into his Art as a novice, was so alarmed and angry that he forbade me to work with him until the next rainy season.

At the Wine that year I was fifteen years old. I got drunk for the first time. I went around town shouting and talking to people nobody else saw: so I was told next day, but I could not remember anything of it. I thought if I got drunk again, but a little less drunk, I might see the kind of people I used to see, when the ways were full of them and they kept my soul company. So I stole wine from our house-neighbors, who had most of a barrel left in bottles after the dance, and I went down alone by the Na in the willow flats to drink it.

I drank the first bottle and made some songs, then I spilled most of the second bottle and went home and felt sick for a couple of days. I stole wine again, and this time I drank two bottles quickly. I made no songs. I felt dizzy and sick, and fell asleep. Next morning I woke up there in the willow flats on the cold stones by the river, very weak and cold. My family was worried about me after that. It had been a hot night, so I could say I had stayed out for the cool and had fallen asleep; but my mother knew I was lying about something. She thought it must be that I had come inland with some boy, but for some reason would not admit it. It shamed and worried her to think that I was wearing undyed clothing when I should no longer do so. It enraged me that she should so distrust me, yet I would say nothing to her in denial or explanation. My father knew that I was sick at heart; but it was soon after that that I set the fire, and his worry turned to anger. As for my cousin, she was in love with a Blue Clay boy and interested in nothing else; the girls with whom I gambled had taken to smoking a lot of hemp, which I never liked; and though the friends with whom I rode and looked after the horses were still kind, I did not want to be with humans much, or even with horses. I did not want the world to be as it was. I had begun making up the world.

I made the world this way: that young man of my House in Chukulmas felt as I felt; and I would go to Chukulmas after the Grass, this year. He and I would go up into the hills together and become forest-living people. We would take the roan stallion and go to Looks Up Valley, or farther; we would go to the grass dune country west of the Long Sound, where he had once told me the herds of wild horses run. He said that people went from Chukulmas sometimes to catch a wild horse there, but it was country where no human people lived. We would live there together alone, taming and riding the wild horses. Telling myself this world, in the daytime I made us live as brother and sister, but in the nights lying alone I made us make love together. The Grass came and passed. I put off going to Chukulmas, telling myself that it would be better to go after the Sun was danced. I had never danced the Sun as an adult, and I wanted to do that; after that, I told myself, I would go to Chukulmas. All along I knew that if I went or if I did not go it did not matter, and all I wanted was to die.

It is hard to say to yourself that what you want is to die. You keep hiding it behind other things, which you pretend to want. I was impatient for the Twenty-One Days to begin, as if my life would start over with them. On the eve of the first day I went to live at the heyimas.

As soon as I set foot on the ladder my heart went cold and tight. There was a long-singing that night. My lips got numb and my voice would not come out of my throat. I wanted to get out and run away all night, but I did not know where to go.

Next morning three groups formed: one would go over the northwest range into wild country in silence; one would use hemp and mushrooms for trance; and one would drum and long-sing. I could not choose which group to join, and this distressed me beyond anything. I began shaking, and went to the ladder, but could not lift my foot to climb it.

The old doctor named Gall, who had taught me sometimes at the Doctors Lodge, came down the ladder. She was coming to sing, but the habit of her art distracted her and she observed me. She turned back and said, "Are you not well?"

"I think I am ill."

"Why is that?"

"I want to dance and can't choose the dancing."

"The long-singing?"

"My voice is gone."

"The trances?"

"I'm afraid of them."

"The journey?"

"I can't leave this house!" I said loudly, and began to shake again.

Gall put her head back with her chin sunk in her neck and looked at me from the tops of her eyes. She was a short, dark, wrinkled woman. She said, "You're already stretched. Do you want to break?"

"Maybe it would be better."

"Maybe it would be better to relax?"

"No, it would be worse."

"There's a choice made. Come now."

Gall took my hand and brought me to the doorway of the inmost room of the heyimas, where the people of the Inner Sun were.

I said, "I can't go in there. I'm not old enough to begin the learning."

Gall said, "Your soul is old." She said the same to Black Oak, who came from the gyre to the doorway: "This is an old soul and a young one, stretching each other too hard."

Black Oak, who was then Speaker of the Serpentine, spoke with Gall, but I was not able to listen to what they said. As soon as we had come into the doorway of the inner room my hair lifted up on my head and my ears sang. I saw round, bright lights coming and going inside the room, where there was no light but the dim shaft from the topmost skylight. The light began to gyre. Black Oak turned to me and spoke, but at that time, as he spoke, the vision began.

I did not see the man Black Oak, but the Serpentine. It was a rock person, not man nor woman, not human, but in shape like a heavy human being, with the blue, blue-green, and black colors and the surfaces of serpentine rock in its skin. It had no hair, and its eyes were lidless and without transparency, seeing very slowly. Serpentine looked at me very slowly with those rock eyes.

I crouched down in terror. I could not weep or speak or stand or move. I was like a bag full of fear. All I could do was crouch there. I could not breathe at all until a stone, maybe Serpentine's hand, struck my head a hard blow on the right side above the ear. It knocked me off balance and hurt very much, so that I whimpered and sobbed with the pain, and after that I could breathe again. My head did not bleed where it had been struck, but began swelling up there.

I crouched recovering from the blow and the dizziness, and after a long while looked up again. Serpentine was standing there. It stood there. After a while I saw the hands moving slowly. They moved up slowly and came together at the navel, at the middle of the stone. There they pulled back and apart. They pulled open a long, wide rent or opening in the stone, like the doorway of a room, into which I knew I was to enter. I got up crouching and shaking and took a step forward into the stone.

It was not like a room. It was stone, and I was in it. There was no light or breath or room. I think the rest of the vision all took place in the stone; that is where it all happened and was; but because of the human way human people have to see things, it seemed to change, and to be other places, things, and beings.

As if the serpentine rock had crumbled and decayed into the red earth, after a while I was in the earth, part of the dirt. I could feel how the dirt felt. Presently I could feel rain coming into the dirt, coming down. I could feel it in a way that was like seeing, falling down on and into me, out of a sky that was all rain.

I would go to sleep and then be partly awake again, perceiving. I began feeling stones and roots, and along my left side I began to feel and hear cold water running, a creek in the rainy season. Veins of water underground went down and around through me to that creek, seeping in the dark through the dirt and stones. Near the creek I began to feel the big, deep roots of trees, and in the dirt everywhere the fine, many roots of the grasses, the bulbs of brodiaea and blue-eyed grass, the ground squirrel's heart beating, the mole asleep. I began to come up one of the great roots of a buckeye, up inside the trunk and out the leafless branches to the ends of the small outmost branches. From there I perceived the ladders of rain. These I climbed to the stairways of cloud. These I climbed to the paths of wind. There I stopped, for I was afraid to step out on the wind.

Coyote came down the wind path. She came like a thin woman with rough, dun hair on her head and arms, and a long, fine face with yellow eyes. Two of her children came with her like coyote pups.

Coyote looked at me and said, "Take it easy. You can look down. You can look back."

I looked back and down under the wind. Below and behind

me were dark ridges of forest with the rainbow shining across them and light shining on the water on the leaves of the trees. I thought there were people on the rainbow, but was not sure of that. Below and farther on were yellow hills of summer and a river among them going to the sea. In places, the air below me was so full of birds that I could not see the ground, but only the light on their wings.

Coyote had a high, singing voice like several voices at once. She said, "Do you want to go on from here?"

Grandmother Mountain

I said, "I was going to go to the Sun."

"Go ahead. This is all my country." Coyote said that, and then came past me on the wind, trotting on four legs as a coyote, with her pups. I was standing alone on the wind there. So I went on ahead.

My steps on the wind were long and slow, like the Rainbow Dancers' steps. At each step the world below me looked different. At one step it was light, at the next one dark. At the next step it was smoky, at the next clear. At the next long step, black and grey clouds of ash or dust hid everything, and at the next I saw a desert of sand with nothing growing or moving at all. I took a step and everything on the surface of the world was one single town, roofs and ways with people swarming in them like the swarming in pondwater under a lens. I took another step and saw the bottoms of the oceans laid dry, the lava slowly welling from long center seams, and huge desolate canyons far down in the shadow of the walls of the continents like ditches below the walls of a barn. The next step I took, long and slow on the wind, I saw the surface of the world blank, smooth, and pale, like the face of a baby I once saw that was born without forebrain or eyes. I took one more step and the hawk met me in the sunlight in the quiet air over the southwest slope of Grandmother Mountain. It had been raining, and clouds were still dark in the northwest. The rain shone on the leaves of the forests in the canyons of the mountainside.

Of the vision given me in the Ninth House I can tell some

parts in writing, and some I can sing with the drum, but for most of it I have not found words or music, though I have spent a good part of my life ever since learning how to look for them. I cannot draw what I saw, as my hand has no gift for making a likeness.

One reason it would be better drawn, and is hard to tell, is that there is no person in it. To tell a story, you say, "I did this," or "She saw that." When there is no I nor she there is no story. I was until I got to the Ninth House; there was the hawk, but I was not. The hawk was; the still air was. Seeing with the hawk's eyes is being without self. Self is mortal. That is the House of Eternity.

So of what the hawk's eyes saw all I can here recall to words is this:

It was the universe of power. It was the network, field, and lines of the energies of all the beings, stars and galaxies of stars, worlds, animals, minds, nerves, dust, the lace and foam of vibration that is being itself, all interconnected, every part part of another part and the whole part of each part, and so comprehensible to itself only as a whole, boundless and unclosed.

At the Exchange it is taught that the electrical mental network of the City extends from all over the surface of the world out past the moon and the other planets to unimaginable distances among the stars: in the vision, all that vast web was one momentary glitter of light on one wave on the ocean of the universe of power, one fleck of dust on one grass-seed in unending fields of grass. The images of the light dancing on the waves of the sea or on dust motes, the glitter of light on ripe grass, the flicker of sparks from a fire, are all I have: no image can contain the vision, which contained all images. Music can mirror it better than words can, but I am no poet to make music of words. Foam, and the scintillation of mica in rock, the flicker and sparkle of waves and dust, the working of the great broadcloth looms, and all dancing, have reflected the hawk's vision for a moment to my mind; and indeed everything would do so, if my mind were clear and strong enough. But no mind or mirror can hold it without breaking.

There was a descent or drawing away, and I saw some things that I can describe. Here is one of them: In this lesser place or plane, which was what might be called the gods or the divine, beings enacted possibilities. These I, being human, recall as having human form. One of them came and shaped the vibrations of energies, closing their paths from gyre into wheel. This one was very strong, and was crippled. He worked as blacksmith at the smithy, making wheels of energy closed upon themselves, terrible with power, flaming. He who made them was burnt away by them to a shell of cinder, with eyes like a potter's kiln when it is opened, and hair of burning wires, but still he turned the paths of energy and closed them into wheels, locking power into power. All around this being now was black and hollow where the wheels turned and ground and milled. There were other beings who came as if flying, like birds in a storm, flying and crying across the wheels of fire to stop the turning and the work, but they were caught in the wheels, and burst like feathers of flame. The miller was a thin shell of darkness now, very weak, burnt out, and he too was caught in the wheels' turning and burning and grinding, and was ground to dust, like fine black meal. The wheels as they turned kept growing and joining until the whole machine was interlocked cog within cog, and strained, and brightened, and burst into pieces. Every wheel as it burst was a flare of faces and eyes and flowers and beasts on fire, burning, exploding, destroyed, falling into black dust. That happened, and it was one flicker of brightness and dark in the universe of power, a bubble of foam, a flick of the shuttle, a fleck of mica. The dark dust or meal lay in the shape of open curves or spirals. It began to move and shift, and there was scintillation in it, like dust in a shaft of sunlight. It began dancing. Then the dancing drew away and drew away, and closer by, to the left, something was there crying like a little animal. That was myself, my mind and being in the world; and I began to become myself again; but my soul that had seen the vision was not entirely willing. Only my mind kept drawing it back to me from the Ninth House, calling and crying for it till it came.

I was lying on my right side on earth, in a small, warm room with earthen walls. The only light came from the red bar of an electric heater. Somewhere nearby people were singing a two-note chant. I was holding in my left hand a rock of serpentine, greenish with dark markings, quite round as if water-worn, though serpentine does not often wear round but splits and crumbles. It was just large enough that I could close my fingers around it. I held this round stone for a long time and listened to the chanting, until I went to sleep. When I woke up, after a while I felt the rock going immaterial, so that my fingers began sinking into it, and it weighed less and less, until it was gone. I was a little grieved by this, for I had thought it a remarkable thing to come back from the Right Arm of the World with a piece of it in my hand; but as I grew clearer-headed I perceived the vanity of that notion. Years later the rock came back to me. I was walking down by Moon Creek with my sons when they were small boys. The younger one saw the rock in the water and picked it up, saying, "A world!" I told him to keep it in his heya-box, which he did. When he died, I put that rock back in the water of Moon Creek.

I had been in the vision for the first two days and nights of the Twenty-One Days of the Sun. I was very weak and tired, and they kept me in the heyimas all the rest of the Twenty-One Days. I could hear the long-singing, and sometimes I went into other rooms of the heyimas; they made me welcome even in the inmost room, where they were singing and dancing the Inner Sun, and where I had entered the vision. I would sit and listen and half-watch. But if I tried to follow the dancing with my eyes, or sing, or even touch the tongue-drum, the weakness would wash into me like a wave on sand, and I would go back into the little room and lie down on the earth, in the earth.

They waked me to listen to the Morning Carol; that was the first time in twenty-one days that I climbed the ladder and saw the sun, that day, the day of the Sun Rising.

The people dancing the Inner Sun had been in charge of me. They had told me that I was in danger and that if I approached another vision I should try to turn away from it, as I was not strong enough for it yet. They had told me not to dance; and they kept bringing me food, so good and so kindly given that I could not refuse it, and ate it with enjoyment. After the Sun Risen days were past, certain scholars of the heyimas took me in their charge. Tarweed, a man of my House, and the woman Milk of the Obsidian, were my guides. It was now time that I begin to learn the recounting of the vision.

When I began I thought there was nothing to learn: all I had to do was say what I had seen.

Milk worked with words; Tarweed worked with words, drum, and matrix chanting. They had me go very slowly, telling very little at a time, sometimes one word only, and repeating what I had been able to tell, singing it with the matrix chant, so that as much as possible might be truly recalled and given and could be recalled and given again.

When I began thus to find out what it is to say what one has seen, and when the great complexity and innumerable vivid details of the vision overwhelmed my imagination and surpassed my ability to describe, I feared that I would lose it all before I could grasp one fragment of it and that even if I remembered some of it I would never understand any of it. My guides reassured me and quieted my impatience. Milk said, "We have some training in this craft, and you have none. You have to learn to speak sky with an earth tongue. Listen: if a baby were carried up the Mountain, could she walk back down, until she learned to walk?"

Tarweed explained to me that as I learned to apprehend mentally what I had perceived in vision, I would approach the condition of living in both Towns; and so, he said, "there's no great hurry."

I said, "But it will take years and years!"

He said, "You've been at it for a thousand years already. Gall said you were an old soul."

It bothered me that I was often not sure whether Tarweed was joking or not joking. That always bothers young people, and however old my soul might be, my mind was fifteen. I had to live awhile before I understood that a lot of things can only be said joking and not joking at the same time. I had to come clear back to Coyote's House from the Hawk's House to learn that, and sometimes I still forget it.

Tarweed's way was joking, shocking, stirring, but he was gentle; I had no fear of him. I had been afraid of Milk ever since she had looked at me in the Blood Lodge and said, "What are you here for?" She was a great scholar and was Singer of the Lodge. Her way was calm, patient, impersonal, but she was not gentle, and I feared her. With Tarweed she was polite, but it was plain that her manners masked contempt. She thought a man's place was in the woods and fields and workshops, not among sacred and intellectual things. In the Lodge I had heard her say the old gibe, "A man fucks with his brain and thinks with his penis." Tarweed knew well enough what she thought, but intellectual men are used to having their capacities doubted and their achievements snubbed; he did not seem to mind her arrogance as much as I sometimes did, even to the point of trying to defend him against her once, saying, "Even if he is a man he thinks like a woman!"

It did no good, of course; and if it was partly true, it wasn't wholly true, because the thing that was most important of all to me I could not speak of to Tarweed, a man, and a man of my House; and to Milk, arrogant and stern as she was, a woman who had lived all her life celibate, I did not even need to speak of it. I began to, once, feeling that I must, and she stopped me. "What is proper for me to know of this, I know," she said. "Vision is transgression! The vision is to be shared; the transgression cannot be."

I did not understand that. I was very much afraid of going out of the heyimas and being caught in my old life again, going the wrong way again in false thinking and despair. A half-month or so after the Sun, I began to feel and say that I was still weak and ill and could not leave the heyimas. To this Tarweed said, "Aha! About time for you to go home!"

I thought him most unfeeling. When I was working with Milk, in my worry I began crying, and presently I said, "I wish I had never had this vision!"

Milk looked at me, a glance across the eyes, like being whipped in the face with a thin branch. She said, "You did not have a vision."

I snivelled and stared at her.

"You had nothing. You have nothing. The house stands. You can live in a corner of it, or all of it, or go outside it, as you choose." So Milk said, and left me.

I stayed alone in the small room. I began to look at it, the small warm room with earth walls and floor and roof, underground. The walls were earth: the whole earth. Outside them was the sky: the whole sky. The room was the universe of power. I was in my vision. It was not in me.

So I went home to live and try to stay on the right way.

Part of most days I went to the heyimas to study with Tarweed or to the Blood Lodge to study with Milk. My health was sound, but I was still tired and sleepy, and my household did not get very much work out of me. All my family but my father were busy, restless people, eager to work and talk but never to be still. Among them, after the month in the heyimas, I felt like a pebble in a mountain creek, bounced and buffeted. But I could go to work with my father. Milk had suggested to him that he take me with him when he worked. Tarweed had questioned her about that, saying that the craft was spiritually dangerous, and Milk had replied in the patient, patronising tone she used to men, "Don't worry about that. It was danger that enabled her."

So I went back to working with power. I learned the art carefully and soberly, and set no more fires. I learned drumming with Tarweed and speaking mystery with Milk. But it was all slow, slow, and my fear kept growing: fear and impatience. The image of the roan horse's rider was not in my mind, as it had been, but was the center of my fear. I never went to ride, and kept away from my friends who cared for the horses, and stayed out of the pastures where the horses were. I tried never to think about the Summer dancing, the games and races. I tried never to think about lovemaking, although my mother's sister had a new husband and they made love every night in the next room with a good deal of noise. I began to fear and dislike myself, and fasted and purged to weaken myself.

I told Tarweed nothing of all this, shame preventing me; nor did I ever speak of it to Milk, fear preventing me.

So the World was danced, and next would come the Moon. The thought of that dance made me more and more frightened; I felt trapped by it. When the first night of the Moon came I went down into my heyimas, meaning to stay there the whole time, closing my ears to the love songs. I started drumming a vision-tune that Tarweed had brought back from his dragonfly visions. Almost at once I entered trance, and went into the house of anger.

In that house it was black and hot, with a yellowish glimmering like heat lightning, and a dull muttering noise underfoot and in the walls. There was an old woman in there, very black, with too many arms. She called me, not by the name I then had, Berry, but Flicker: "Flicker, come here! Flicker, come here!" I understood that Flicker was my name, but I did not come.

The old woman said, "What are you sulking about? Why don't you go fuck with your brother in Chukulmas? Desire unacted is corruption. Must Not is a slave-owner, Ought Not is a slave. Energy constrained turns the wheels of evil. Look what you're dragging with you! How can you run the gyre, how can you handle power, chained like that? Superstition! Superstition!"

I found that both my legs were fastened with bolts and hasps to a huge boulder of serpentine rock, so that I could not move at all. I thought that if I fell down, the boulder would roll on me and crush me.

The old woman said, "What are you wearing on your head? That's no Moon Dance veil. Superstition! Superstition!"

I put up my hands and found my head covered with a heavy helmet made of black obsidian. I was seeing and hearing through this black, murky glass, which came down over my eyes and ears.

"Take it off, Flicker!" the old woman said.

I said, "Not at your bidding!"

I could hardly see or hear her, as the helmet pressed heavier and thicker on my head, and the boulder pushed against my legs and back.

She cried, "Break free! You are turning into stone! Break free!"

I would not obey her. I chose to disobey. With my hands I pressed the obsidian helmet into my ears and eyes and forehead until it sank in and became part of me, and I pushed myself back into the boulder until it became part of my legs and body. Then I stood there, very stiff and heavy and hard, but I could walk, and I could see and hear, now that the dark glass was not over my ears

and eyes but was part of them. I saw that the house was all on fire, burning and smouldering, floor, walls, and roof. A black bird, a crow, was flying in the smoke from one room to the next. The old woman was burning, her clothes and flesh and hair smouldering. The crow flew around her and cried to me, "Sister, get out, you'd better get out!"

There is nothing but anger in the house of anger. I said, "No!"

The crow cawed, saying, "Sister, fetch water, water of the spring!" Then it flew out through the burning wall of the house. Just as it went it looked back at me with a man's face, beautiful and strong, with curly fiery hair streaming upward. Then the walls of fire sank down into the walls of the Serpentine heyimas where I was sitting drumming on the three-note drum. I was still drumming, but a different pattern, a new one.

After that vision I was called Flicker; the scholars agreed that it's best to use the name that that Grandmother gives you, even if you don't do what she says. After that vision I went up to the Springs of the River, as Crow had said to do; and after it I was freed from my fear of my desire.

The central vision is central, it is not for anything outside itself; indeed there is nothing outside it. What I beheld in the Ninth House is, as a cloud or a mountain is. We make use of such visions, make meanings out of them, find images in them, live on them, but they are not for us or about us, any more than the world is. We are part of them. There are other kinds of vision, all farther from the center and nearer to the mortal self; one of those is the turning vision, which is about a person's own life. The vision in which that Grandmother named me was a turning vision.

The Summer came, and the people came down from Chukulmas. My brother of the Serpentine did not ride his roan horse in the races; a girl of the Obsidian of Chukulmas rode that horse, and he rode a sorrel mare. The roan stallion won all races and was much praised. After that summer he would race no more, but be put to stud, they said. I did not ride, but watched the races and the games. It is hard to say how I felt. My throat ached all the time, and I kept saying silently inside myself, goodbye, goodbye! But what I was saying goodbye to was already gone. I was mourning and yet unmoved. The girl was a good rider and beautiful, and I thought, maybe they are going to come inland together, but it did not hurt or concern me. What I wanted was to be gone from Telina, to begin living the life that followed the turning vision, that followed the gyre.

So in the heat of the summertime I went with Tarweed upriver to the Springs of the River at Wakwaha.

On the Mountain I lived in the host-house of the Serpentine and worked mostly as electrician's assistant at odd jobs around the sacred buildings and the Archive and Exchange.

In the morning I would come outdoors at sunrise. All beyond and below the porch of that house I would see a vast pluming blankness, the summer fog filling the Valley, while the first rays of the sun brightened the rocks of the Mountain's peaks above me. I would sing as I had been taught:

> "It is the Valley of the puma,
> where the lion walks,
> where the lion wakes,
> shining, shining in the Seventh House!"

Later, in the rainy season, the puma walked on the Mountain itself, darkening the summits and the Springs in cloud and grey mist. To wake in the silence of that rainless, all-concealing fog was to wake to dream, to breathe the lion's breath.

Much of each day on the Mountain I spent in the heyimas, and at times slept there. I worked with the scholars and visionaries of Wakwaha at the techniques of revisioning, of recounting, and of music. I did not practice dancing or painting much, as I had no gift for them, but practiced recalling and recounting in spoken and written language and with the drum.

I had, as many people have, exaggerated notions of how visionaries live. I expected a strained, athletic, ascetic existence, always stretched towards the ineffable. In fact, it was a dull kind of life. When people are in vision they can't look after themselves, and when they come back from it they may be extremely tired, or excited and bewildered, and in either case need quietness without distractions and demands. In other words, it's like childbearing, or any hard, intense work. One supports and protects the worker. Revisioning and recounting are much the same, though not quite so hard.

In the host-house I fasted only before the great wakwa; I ate lightly, with some care of which foods I ate, and drank little wine, and watered it. If you are going into vision or revision you don't want to keep changing yourself and going in a different way—through starving one time, the next time through drunkenness, or cannabis, or trance-singing, or whatever. What you want is moderation and continuity. If one is an ecstatic, of course it's another matter; that is not work, but burning.

So the life I led in Wakwaha was dull and peaceful, much the same from day to day and season to season, and suited and pleased my mind and heart so that I desired nothing else. All the work I did in those years on the Mountain was revisioning and recounting the vision of the Ninth House that had been given me; I gave all I could of it to the scholars of the Serpentine for their records and interpretations, in which our guidance as a people lies. They were kind, true kin, family of my House, and I at last a child of that House again, not self-exiled. I thought I had come home and would live there all my life, telling and drumming, going into vision and coming back from it, dancing in the beautiful dancing place of the Five High Houses, drinking from the Springs of the River.

The Grass was late, in the third year I lived in Wakwaha. Some days after it ended and some days before the Twenty-One Days began, I was about to go up the ladder of the Serpentine heyimas when Hawk Woman came to me. I thought she was one of the people of the heyimas, until she cried the hawk's cry, "kiyir, kiyir!" I turned, and she said, "Dance the Sun upon the Mountain, Flicker, and after that go down. Maybe you should learn how to dye cloth." She laughed, and flew up as the hawk through the entrance overhead.

Other people came where I was standing at the foot of the ladder. They had heard the hawk's cry, and some saw her fly up through the entrance of the heyimas.

After that I had neither vision nor revision of the Ninth House or any house or kind.

I was bereft, and relieved. That terrible grandeur had been hard to bear, to bring back, to share and give and lose over and over. It had all been beyond my strength, and I was not sorry to cease revisioning. But when I thought that I had lost all vision and must soon leave Wakwaha, I began to grieve. I thought about those people whom I had thought were my kinfolk, long ago when I was a child, before I was afraid. They were gone, and now I too must go, leaving these kinfolk of my House of Wakwaha, and go live among strangers the rest of my life.

A woman-living man of the Serpentine of Wakwaha, Deertongue, who had taught me and sung with me and given me friendship, saw that I was downcast and anxious and said to me, "Listen. You think everything is done. Nothing is done. You think the door is shut. No door is shut. What did Coyote say to you, at the beginning of it all?"

I said, "She said to take it easy."

Deertongue nodded his head and laughed.

I said, "But Hawk said to go down."

"She didn't say not to come back."

"But I have lost the visions!"

"But you have your wits! Where is the center of your life, Flicker?"

I thought, not very long, and answered, "There. In that vision. In the Ninth House."

He said, "Your life turns on that center. Only don't blind your intellect by hankering after vision! You know that the vision is not your self. The hawk turns upon the hawk's desire. You will come round home and find the door wide open."

I danced the Sun upon the Mountain, as Hawk Woman had said to do, and after that I began to feel that I must go. There were some people living in Wakwaha who sought vision or ecstasy by continuous fasting or drug-taking and lived in hallucination; such people came not to know vision from imagination, and lived without honesty, making up the world all the time. I was afraid that if I stayed there I might begin imitating them, as Deertongue had warned me. After all, I had gone wrong that way once before. So I said goodbye to people, and on a cold bright morning I went down the Mountain. A young redwing hawk circled crying over the canyons, "kiyir! kiyir!"—so mournfully that I cried myself.

I went back to my mothers' household in Telina-na. My uncle had married and moved out, so I had his small room to myself; that was a good thing, since my cousin had married and had a child and the household was as crowded and restless as ever. I went back to work with my father, learning both theory and practice with him, and after two years I became a member of the Millers Art. He and I continued to work together often. My life was nearly as quiet as it had been in Wakwaha. Sometimes I would spend days in the heyimas drumming; there were no visions, but the silence inside the drumming was what I wanted.

So the seasons went along, and I was thinking about what Hawk Woman had said. I was rewiring an old house, Seven Steps House in the northeast arm of Telina, and while I was working there on a hot day a man of one of the households brought me some lemonade, and we fell to talking, and so again the next day. He was a Blue Clay man from Chukulmas who had married a Serpentine woman of Telina. They had been given two children, the younger born sevai. She had left the children with him and left her mothers' house, going across town to marry a Red Adobe man. I knew her, she was one of the people I had gambled with as a child, but I had never talked to this man, Stillwater, who lived in his children's grandmother's house. He worked mostly as a chemist and tanner and housekeeper. We talked, and got on well, and met to talk again. I came inland with him, and we decided to marry.

My father was against it, because Stillwater had two children in his household already and so I would bear none; but that was what I wanted. My grandmother and mother were not heartily for anything I did, because I had always disappointed them, and they did not want three more people in our house, which was crowded enough. But that, too, was what I wanted. Everything I wanted in those years came to be.

Stillwater and the little boys and I made a household on the ground floor of Seven Steps House, where their grandmother lived on the first floor. She was a lazy, sweet-tempered woman, very fond of Stillwater and the children, and we got on very well. We lived in that house fourteen years. All that time I had what I wanted, and was contented, like a ewe with two lambs in a safe pasture, with my head down eating the grass. All that time was like a long day in summer in the fenced fields or in a quiet house when the doors are closed to keep the rooms cool. That was my life's day. Before it and after it were the twilights and the dark, when things and the shadows of things become one.

Our elder son—and this was a satisfaction to my grandmother at last—went to learn with the Doctors Lodge on White Sulphur Creek as soon as he entered his sprouting years, and by the time he was twenty he was living at the Lodge much of the time. The younger died when he had lived sixteen years. Living with his pain and always increasing weakness and seeing him lose the use of his hands and the sight in his eyes had driven his brother to seek to be a healer, but living with his fearless soul had been my chief joy. He was like a little hawk that came into one's hands for the warmth, for a moment, fearless and harmless, but hurt. After he died, Stillwater lost heart and began longing for his old home. Presently he went back to Chukulmas to live in his mothers' house. Sometimes I went to visit him there.

I went back to my childhood home, my mothers' house, where my grandmother and mother and father and aunt and cousin and her husband and two children were. They were still busy and noisy; it was not where I wanted to be. I would go to the heyimas and drum, but that was not what I wanted, either. I missed Stillwater's company, but it was no longer the time for us to live together; that was done. It was something else I wanted, but I could not find out what.

In the Blood Lodge one day they told me that Milk, who was

now truly an old woman, had had a stroke. My son came with me to see her and helped her in her recovery; and since she was alone, I went to stay with her while she needed help. It suited her to have me there, and so I lived with her. It was comfortable for both of us; but she was looking for her last name and learning how to die, and although I could be of some help to her while she did that, and could learn from her, it wasn't what I wanted myself, yet.

One day a little before the Summer I was working in the storage barns above Moon Creek. The Art had put in a new generator there, and I was checking out the wiring to the threshers, some of which needed reinsulation; the mice had been at it. I was working away there in a dark, dusty crawl-space, hearing the mice scuttering about overhead in the rafters and between the walls. Presently I noticed with part of my attention that several people were in the crawl-space with me, watching what I was doing. They were greyish-brown people with long, slender, white hands and feet, and bright eyes; I had never seen them before, but they seemed familiar. I said, while I went on working, "I wish you would not take the insulation off the wires. A fire could start. There must be better things to eat, in a grain barn!"

The people laughed a little, and the darkest one said in a high, soft voice, "Bedding."

They looked behind them then, and went away quickly and quietly. Somebody else was there. I felt one little chill of fear. At first I couldn't see the person clearly in that twilight of the crawl-space; then I saw it was Tarweed.

"You never ride horses any more, Flicker," he said.

"Riding is for the young, Tarweed," I said.

"Are you old?"

"Nearly forty years old."

"And you don't miss riding?"

He was teasing me, as people had teased me once about being in love with the roan horse.

"No, I don't miss that."

"What do you miss?"

"My child that died."

"Why should you miss him?"

"He is dead."

"So am I," said Tarweed. And so he was. He had died five years ago.

So I knew then what it was I missed, what I wanted. It was only not to be shut into the House of Earth. I did not have to go in and out the doors, if only I could see those who did. There was Tarweed, and he laughed a little, like the mice.

He did not say anything more, but watched me in the shadows. When I was done with the work, he was gone. When I left the barn I saw the barn owl high up on a rafter, sleeping.

I went home to Milk's household. I told her at supper about Tarweed and the mice.

She listened, and began to cry a little. She was weak since the stroke and her fierceness sometimes turned to tears. She said, "You were always ahead of me, going ahead of me!"

I had never known that she envied me. It made me sad to know it, and yet I wanted to laugh at the way we waste our feelings. "Somebody has to open the door!" I said. I showed her the people who were coming into the room, the kind of people I used to see when I was a young child. I knew they were indeed my kin, but I did not know who they were. I asked Milk, "Who are they?"

She was bewildered at first, and could not see well, and complained. The people began to speak, and she to answer. Sometimes they spoke this language and sometimes I did not understand what they said; but she answered them eagerly.

When she grew tired, they went away quietly, and I helped her to bed. As she began to go to sleep I saw a little child come and lie down beside her. She put her arms around it. Every night after that until Milk died in the winter the child came to her bed to sleep.

Once I spoke of it, saying, "Your daughter." Milk looked at me with that whipping look in her one good eye. She said, "Not my daughter. Yours."

So I keep that house now with the daughter I never bore, the child of my first love, and with others of my family. Sometimes when I sweep the floor of that house I see the dust in a shaft of sunlight, dancing in curves and spirals, flickering.

NOTES:

p. 301. *vetulou*
A game a little like polo, played on horseback, with an openwork wicker ball scooped and thrown by long-handled wicker scoops; see the section "Playing" in the Back of the Book.

p. 301. *sevai*
Sevai means sheathed. It was a congenital degenerative condition, affecting the motor nerves and eventually involving the sympathetic nervous system. Evidently related to residual ancient industrial toxins in soil and water, in some regions of the planet it was not very common; in others it was. In the Valley as many as one in four human conceptions was stillborn due to sevai, and animals were similarly affected. As Flicker says, the later the condition declared itself the slower and milder its progress, but always tending inexorably towards incapacity, blindness, paralysis, and death.

p. 310. *scholar*
Ayash means both teacher and student, learner and learned person, as does our word *scholar*. The scholars of a heyimas were women and men with a religious or intellectual bent; they kept that House.

p. 311. . . . *living in both Towns* . . .
An unusual image for the two Arms of the World, the Five Houses of Earth and the Four Houses of Sky.

SOME BRIEF
VALLEY TEXTS

<hr />

OWL, COYOTE, SOUL.
From the Library in Wakwaha.

 Owl was flying in darkness. Its wings made no sound. There was no sound. Owl said itself to itself: "hu, hu, hu, hu." Owl hears itself; that makes sound be; sound comes into time then, four times.

Sound circles out on the waters of darkness, the airs of darkness, gyring outward from the open mouth of the owl. Like scum and broken twigs and wings of insects on pond water, things come to be, pushed by the circles moving outward. Near the owl's mouth the sound is strong and things move quickly and firmly and are distinct and strong. Moving outward the circles grow large and weak, and things out there are slow and mixed and broken. But the owl flew on and went flying on, listening, hunting, One is not all, nor once always. Owl is not all, but only owl.

Coyote was going along in the darkness very sad, lonesome. There was nothing to eat in the darkness, nothing to see, no way. Coyote sat down in the darkness and howled: "yau, yau, yau, yau, yau." Coyote hears herself; that makes death be; death comes into time then, five times.

Death shines. Death makes shining. Death makes brightness in water, brightness in air, brightness in being. Near Coyote's heart the shining is strong and things grow strong and warm and take fire. Farther outward things are burnt, weak, dim, and cold. Coyote went on and goes along, hunting live things, eating dead things. Coyote is not life or death, but only coyote.

Soul singing and shining goes outward towards the cold and dark. Soul silent and cold comes inward to the shining, to the singing at the fire. Owl flies without sound; coyote goes in darkness; soul listens and holds still.

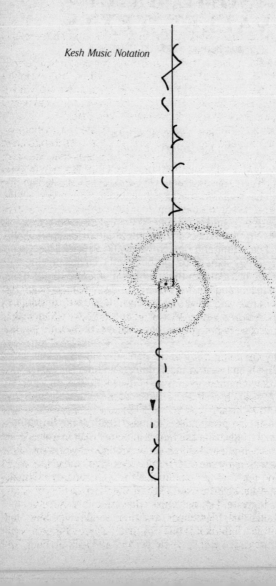

Kesh Music Notation

PERSON AND SELF.

*An offering by Old Jackrabbit of Telina-na
to his heyimas, the Serpentine.*

They say in the Grass singing: The universe is, and all there is is inside that house of houses.

Well, is the universe then a person? We speak as if to a person, saying, "Heya!" to a stone, saying to the sun rising, "Heya! Holy! I greet you!" We cry out as if to a person when alone in the wilderness we cry, "Bless me as I bless you, help me in my weakness!" Whom do we greet? Whom do we bless? Who helps?

Maybe in all things there is one person, one spirit whom we greet in the rock and the sun and trust in all things to bless and help. Maybe the oneness of the universe manifests that one spirit and the oneness of each being of the many kinds is a sign or symbol of that one person. Maybe so. People who say it is so call that person the self of all selves or the other of all others, the one eternal, the god. The lazyminded may say that inside the rock a spirit lives, inside the sun a fiery person lives, but these say that in the universe the god lives as a human lives in a house or a coyote in the wilderness, having made it, keeping it in order. These people believe. They are not lazyminded.

Some other people are better at thinking than at believing, and they wonder and ask who it is that we greet, that we bless, that we ask for blessing. Is it the rock itself, the sun itself, all things in themselves? Maybe so. After all, we live in this house which makes itself and keeps itself. Why should a soul be afraid in its own house? There are no strangers. The walls are life, the doors are death; we go in and out at our work.

I think it is one another whom we greet, and bless, and help. It is one another whom we eat. We are gatherer and gathered. Building and unbuilding, we make and are unmade; giving birth and killing, we take hands and let go. Thinking human people and other animals, the plants, the rocks and stars, all the beings that think or are thought, that are seen or see, that hold or are held, all of us are beings of the Nine Houses of Being, dancing the same dance. It is with my voice that the blue rock speaks, and the word I speak is the name of the blue rock. It is with my voice that the universe speaks, and the word I hear it speak when I listen is myself. Being is praise. I do not know what there is to believe.

So I think that, frightened, I will trust; weak, I will bless; suffering, I will live. I think it is this way: having asked for help, I will be silent, listening. I will serve no person, and lock no door. So I think I will live in the Valley as best I can, and so die here, coming in the open door.

A LIST OF THINGS THAT WILL BE NEEDED
FOUR DAYS FROM NOW.

Found on a scrap of husk-paper in a pasture near the heyimas of Ounmalin.

1. Very prickly round objects such as certain seedpods.
2. Some pieces of broken red unglazed pottery.
3. Fine copper wire rolled around a wooden spool.
4. Artificial or found cylindrical objects with at least one flared end, not pierced.
5. Writing or markings of ink on thick paper.
6. Small disks that reflect light.
7. Chia seeds, or dead ants.
8. A young donkey.
9. Rain.

CROWS, GEESE, ROCKS.

Some remarks made by an old man of the Serpentine of Kastoha-na, Walnut of Bridge End House, in conversation with the Editor, and recorded with his permission.

You can tell by the way crows walk that they're in touch with things you need to know. But they don't want to tell them.

When you see geese walking you'd think they didn't know anything, wouldn't you? But when you see them flying, or when you listen to them on the water in their flocks and towns, talking, and they still keep talking all the time they fly—they talk as much as people do, and know more about the other side of the hills— when you see them flying, that writing, then you wish you could read it!

Not all rocks are equally sensitive. Most basalt doesn't pay attention. It isn't listening. It's still thinking about the fire in the dark, perhaps. Serpentine rock is always sensitive. It's from both the water and the fire, it moved and flowed through other rocks to come to the air, and it's always on the point of breaking up, coming apart, turning into dirt. Serpentine listens, and speaks. Flint is a strange rock. It stays locked up. Sandstone is a rock for the hands, they understand one another. We don't have limestone here in the

Valley; the Finders bring pieces of it in. What I have seen of it is mortal and intellectual—it is a rock made out of lives. They say that where the land is made of limestone the rivers run through it in caves underground and don't come out into the shining. That would be strange. I'd like to see such caves. Granite from the Range of Light is a community of rocks, very beautiful and powerful. When the mica is in it, glittering, like light on the sea, that is a wonderful thing. Obsidian is glass, of course, and so are pumice and the ashrock from around Ama Kulkun. They have the character of glass, the edge and flow, and they hold light. They are dangerous rocks.

In general, rocks aren't living in the same way or at the same pace that we are. But you can find a rock, maybe a big boulder, maybe a little agate in a streambed, and by looking carefully at it, touching it or holding it, listening to it, or by a little talking and singing, a small ceremony, or being still and quiet with it, you can enter into the rock's soul to some extent and the rock can enter into yours, if it's disposed to. Most rocks live a long time. They've lived a long time before we pass them, and they'll live a long time after. Some of them are very old, grandchildren of the coming to be of the earth and sun. If there were nothing else to be known from them that would be enough, their long age of being. But there is much other knowledge in rocks, there are things that can be understood only with the help of rocks. They will help people who handle and study and work with them with pleasure and respect, with mindfulness.

THE BLACK BEETLE SOUL.
From the Library of the Black Adobe Lodge in Sinshan.

There are the souls that most people have heard about, and that superstitious people will tell you about, talking away; but the more the mind seeks to know certainly about the souls, the harder it gets to say anything about them at all. It is hard to know a soul; it is the knower knowing knowing. Images are knowledge of the soul. Words are images of images. The deepest of the souls has this image: it smells of the underground, and is like a beetle, a mole, or a dark worm. Sometimes it is called the black beetle soul, or the dark string, or the death soul. It is not a shadow or image of the body, any more than the body alive or dead is an image of it. It eats shit and shits food. While other souls and their body are awake it usually sleeps, and it is waking up while they go to sleep; they pass each other then, but do not turn their heads. While the body is dying, the death-soul is coming alive. It is what forgets. It makes mistakes, accidents, and many dreams. They say it inhabits the basements of the Nine Houses. It receives its body very tenderly at death and takes it into the dark. When rain falls on the ashes of the cremated body, the death soul may come up into the air. It is blind, and immensely wealthy. If you go down into its dwelling-places you will be given much. The problem is how to carry it back with you. When you speak to the deep soul you must shut your eyes; when you leave it you may not look back. When rain falls on a fire the death souls come into the air, darkening the air. The time they come is at the beginning of the rainy season, when the nights grow long and there is smoke in the air, the time when the house Rejoining is built. A vest or coat of moleskin is worn by people of the

Black Adobe Lodge when they sing or teach or dream. A black string may be tied around the dancer's arm or heart or head. A beetle may show them the way. There is no way to know this soul. It is the inmost. A person dies to it.

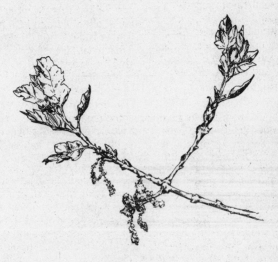

PRAISING THE OAKS.
A teaching from the Serpentine heyimas in Sinshan.

Five oaks, the Roundhead with the long acorn on the seaward slopes, the Furrowbark of our chaparral, the greybarked Longcup, the Great Oak of the mountains, the Tanners' Oak with buckeye blossom and acorn seed, they keep their leaves in the rainy season.

Four oaks, the Blueleaf that wants dry earth at its root, the lobeleafed Finewood of the hills, the blackbarked Redleaf of the high hills, and the Valley Oak, great-girthed, shady, praised by scriveners, that lives by the waters and on sunlit hills, they lose their leaves in the rainy season.

These are the nine noble and pleasant oaks, vigorous trees, sweet in the male and the female flower, towns of many birds and small animal and insect people, giving much shade, giving much food, great wealthy ones worthy of praise.

WORDS/BIRDS.
A Madrone Lodge text.

What works for words may not work for things, and to say that two sayings that contradict each other cannot both be true is not to say that opposites do not exist. The word is not the thing; word and thing have each their own way. It is true that a town is made of stone, clay, and wood; it is true that a town is made of people. These words do not deny each other at all. It is true that a bird's way and the wind blowing make a feather fall; it is true that finding that feather in my way I understand that it has fallen for me. Those words deny each other in part. It is true that everything that is must be as it is, and that nothing is but the play of illusion upon the void; it is true that everything is and it is true that nothing is. These words deny each other wholly. The world of our life is the weaving that holds them together while holding them apart. The world is the bridge between the walls of a canyon, the banks of a river in an abyss, and words are the birds that fly across and across. They cannot be in two places at the same time. But they can cross and come back. It takes all one's life long to cross the bridge to the other side. But the birds fly back and forth across the canyon, singing and speaking from one side to the other.

THE CATS HERE DON'T CARE
Some sayings, wise saws, and small stones
from the Valley.

Why are you making the house so clean?
Because there's going to be an earthquake.

If there was only one of anything, it would be the end of the world.

Judgment is poverty.

If there was only one of anything, it would be the end of the world.

When I'm afraid I listen to the silence of the fieldmouse.
When I'm fearless I listen to the silence of the mousing cat.

If you don't teach machines and horses to do what you want in their way they'll teach you to do what they want in your way.

To go again where you have gone: Increase. To go backwards: Danger. Better to come round.

Multitude, Diversity, Quantity, Exuberance.
Rarity, Purity, Quality, Chastity.

Nothing can make water better.

More than is needed is life.

The Valley is the House of Earth and the Left-Hand Way. The Mountain is the hinge of the heyiya-if. To enter upon the Right-Hand Way one goes up on the Mountain, and from it into the House of Sky, and looking back one sees the Valley as the dead see it.

To be singleminded is to be unmindful. Mindfulness is keeping many different things in mind and observing their relations and proportions.

To conquer is to be careless. Carefulness is holding oneself and one's acts in appropriate relation and proportion to the many other beings and intentions.

To take is to be joyless. Joyfulness is accepting the given, which cannot be earned by mindfulness nor deserved by carefulness.

The great hunter: one arrow in his quiver, one thought in his head.

Cats may be green somewhere else, but the cats here don't care.

All the mountains in a little stone.

Owning is owing, having is hoarding.

Like and *different* are quickening words, brooding and hatching. *Better* and *worse* are eggsucking words, they leave only the shell.

Care may be questioned with care, joy with joy.

Read what the worms write on the madrone leaf, and walk sideways.

Pandora Converses with
the Archivist of the Library of
the Madrone Lodge at Wakwaha-na

PANDORA: Niece, this is a beautiful library!

ARCHIVIST: In the town at the Springs of the River, it is appropriate that the library be beautiful.

PAN: This looks like a rare-book cabinet.

ARC: Old books, fragile ones. Here, this scroll—what strong calligraphy. And good materials. Linen paper; it hasn't darkened at all. This is milkweed paper, here. A good texture!

PAN: How old is the scroll?

ARC: Oh, four hundred years maybe, five hundred.

PAN: Like a Gutenberg Bible to us. Do you have a lot of such old books and scrolls, then?

ARC: Well, more here than anywhere else. Very old things are venerable, aren't they. So people bring things here when they get very old. Some of it's rubbish.

PAN: How do you decide what to keep and what to throw away? The library really isn't very large, when you consider how much writing goes on here in the Valley—

ARC: Oh, there's no end to the making of books.

PAN: And people give writings to their heyimas as offerings—

ARC: All gifts are sacred.

PAN: So the libraries would get to be enormous, if you didn't throw most of the books and things out. But how do you decide what to keep and what to destroy?

ARC: It's difficult. It's arbitrary, unjust, and exciting. We clear out the heyimas libraries every few years. Here in the Madrone of Wakwaha the lodge has destruction ceremonies yearly, between the Grass and the Sun dances. They're secret. Members only. A kind of orgy. A fit of housecleaning—the nesting in-

333

stinct, the collecting drive, turned inside out, reversed. Un-hoarding.

PAN: You destroy valuable books?

ARC: Oh yes. Who wants to be buried under them?

PAN: But you could keep important documents and valuable liter-ary works in electronic storage, at the Exchange, where they don't take up any room—

ARC: The City of Mind does that. They want a copy of everything. We give them some. What is "room"—is it only a piece of space?

PAN: But intangibles—information—

ARC: Tangible or intangible, either you keep a thing or you give it. We find it safer to give it.

PAN: But that's the point of information storage and retrieval sys-tems! The material is kept for anyone who wants or needs it. Information is passed on—the central act of human culture.

ARC: "Keeping grows; giving flows." Giving involves a good deal of discrimination; as a business it requires a more disciplined intelligence than keeping, perhaps. Disciplined people come here, Oak Lodge people, historians, learned people, scribes and reciters and writers, they're always here, like those four, you see, going through the books, copying out what they want, annotating. Books no one reads go; books people read go after a while. But they all go. Books are mortal. They die. A book is an act; it takes place in time, not just in space. It is not information, but relation.

PAN: This is the kind of conversation they always have in utopia. I set you up and then you give interesting, eloquent, and al-most entirely convincing replies. Surely we can do better than that!

ARC: Well, I don't know, aunt. What if I asked the questions? What if I asked you if you had considered my peculiar use of the word "safe," and if you had considered the danger of storing up information as you do in your society?

PAN: Well, I—

ARC: Who controls the storage and the retrieval? To what extent is the material there for anyone who wants and needs it, and to what extent is it "there" only for those who have the informa-tion that it is there, the education to obtain that information, and the power to get that education? How many people in your society are literate? How many are computer-competent? How many of them have the competence to use libraries and electronic information storage systems? How much real information is available to ordinary, nongovernment, nonmilitary, nonspecialist, nonrich people? What does "classified" mean? What do shredders shred? What does money buy? In a State, even a democracy, where power is hierarchic, how can you prevent the storage of information from becoming yet another source of power to the powerful—another piston in the great machine?

PAN: Niece, you're a damned Luddite.

ARC: No, I'm not. I like machines. My washing machine is an old friend. The printing press here is rather more than a friend. Look; when Mines died last year I printed this poem of his, thirty copies, for people to take home and to give to the hey-imas, here, this is the last copy.

PAN: It's a nice job. But you cheated. You didn't ask a question, you asked a rhetorical question.

ARC: Well, you know, people who live in cultures that have an oral literature as well as a written literature get a good deal of practice in rhetoric. But my question wasn't just a trick. How do you keep information yet keep it from being the property of the powerful?

PAN: Through not having censorship. Having free public libraries. Teaching people to read. And to use computers, to plug into the sources. Press, radio, television not fundamentally dependent on government or advertisers. I don't know. It keeps getting harder.

ARC: I didn't mean to make you sad, aunt.

PAN: I never did like smartass utopians. Always so much healthier and saner and sounder and fitter and kinder and tougher and wiser and righter than me and my family and friends. People who have the answers are boring, niece. Boring, boring, boring.

ARC: But I have no answers and this isn't utopia, aunt!

PAN: The hell it ain't.

ARC: This is a mere dream dreamed in a bad time, an Up Yours to the people who ride snowmobiles, make nuclear weapons, and run prison camps by a middle-aged housewife, a critique of civilisation possible only to the civilised, an affirmation pretending to be a rejection, a glass of milk for the soul ulcered by acid rain, a piece of pacifist jeanjacquerie, and a cannibal dance among the savages in the ungodly garden of the farthest West.

PAN: You can't talk that way!

ARC: True.

PAN: Go sing heya, like any savage.

ARC: Only if you'll sing with me.

PAN: I don't know how to sing heya.

ARC: I'll teach you, aunt.

PAN: I'll learn, niece.

PANDORA AND THE ARCHIVIST SING:

> Heya, heya, hey,
> heya, heya.
> Heya, hey, heya,
> heya, heya.
> Hey, heya, heya,
> heya, heya.
> Heya, heya, hey,
> heya, heya. .

(That is the five/four heya sung four times. It may be sung four times, or five times, or nine times, or as many times as you like, or not at all.)

DANGEROUS PEOPLE

A NOTE ABOUT THE NOVEL.

The Valley novel was a novel, not a romance; it was concerned with the daily lives of ordinary people in real places at some time not too far from the readers' present. Elements in it that we might categorise as fantastical or supernatural were nothing of the kind to the author and readers; indeed a common objection to novels voiced by non-novel-readers was that they were too realistic, without vision, "never going outside the Five Houses."

The novel generally contained some element of fact, being based on something that was known to have happened, or at least using real names of people who lived a few generations back. Like almost all Kesh fiction and drama, novels were set in a real town, in existing houses, or houses that were known to have existed. The invention of a tenth town, a nonexistent house, would have been felt to be a misuse of the imagination, a contradiction of reality rather than an augmentation of it.

The long novel *Dangerous People* by Wordriver of Telina-na was of course particularly popular in the town where it was written and set, but it was well-known all over the Valley in a handset edition that must have run to over a hundred copies, and was regarded with affectionate esteem. It is a pretty good example of the Valley novel. The construction of Chapter Two, which is the section translated for this volume, is exemplary of its kind: the pattern is of two people meeting, or "hinging," or "turning apart," one of whom is then followed to the next meeting with a different person, and so on (the pattern of the heyiya-if repeated). This pattern is not followed mechanically in a work as sophisticated as *Dangerous People*, but it is always present. The most unusual element of the book is Wordriver's use of ambiguity, red herrings, bum steers, and false witnesses in presenting and continually deepening the mystery of where Kamedan's wife has "in fact" gone, and with whom, and why.

My general practice has been to give proper names in translation; it seemed the right thing to do, since Valley names were meaningful, and their meaning was often quite vivid in people's minds. Translation may lend a false sense of familiarity, however, and may equally cause unnecessary strangeness. For instance, the name Kamedan means "coming into the cattails" or "he comes into the reed-bed"—too long and far too quaint for English; it would have to be abridged to Cattail or Reed. So in this one case I have left the names of the characters in their original form, to give the reader a different feeling, perhaps, of the people who used them. Wordriver's name in Kesh was Arravna.

Dangerous People

CHAPTER TWO

The dry season was well along into the heat, and the tarweed was blooming, about a month from ripe. When the moon was near full one night the little boy in Shamsha's household began talking in the dark. He said, "Take away the light, mother! Please, mother, take away the light!" Kamedan went across the room on hands and knees and held the child against his body, saying, "Your mother will be home soon, Monkeyflower. Please go to sleep now." He sang a rocking song, but the child could not sleep; he stared at the moon through the window and then cried and hid his face. Kamedan held him and felt fever coming into him. When the day began, Monkeyflower was hot and weak and dull-witted.

Kamedan said to Shamsha, "I think I should go with him to the Doctors Lodge." She said, "No need of that; don't fuss; my grandson will sleep this fever off." Never able to argue with her, he left the child asleep and went to the weaving lofts. They were warping the ten-foot power loom for canvas that morning, and he worked hard, not having the child in his mind at all for some while; but as soon as the warping was completed he started back to Hardcinder House, walking fast.

Near the Hinge of town he saw Modona going towards the hunting side with his deer bow. He said, "So you are here, man of the Hunters Lodge." Modona said, "So you are here, Miller," and was going on, when Kamedan said, "Listen, my wife, Whette, is in the hills somewhere on the hunting side, it seems. I keep thinking maybe she got lost. Please be careful when you shoot." He knew that they said that Modona would shoot at a falling leaf. He went on, "You might call aloud, in places where you're not looking for the deer. I keep thinking maybe she's hurt and not able to make her way back."

The hunter said, "I heard people saying that a person who had been in Ounmalin said that they had seen Whette there. No doubt they were mistaken."

"I don't think they could be altogether correct," Kamedan said. "Maybe they saw a woman who looked like Whette."

The hunter said, "Are there women who look like Whette?"

Kamedan was at a loss. He said, "I have to go home, the child is sick." He went on, and Modona went on his way, grinning.

Monkeyflower lay hot and miserable in the bed when Kamedan came to him. Shamsha told him there was nothing to worry about, and the other people in the household said the same, but Kamedan stayed around the house. Towards nightfall the fever cooled and the little boy began to talk and smile, and ate some food, and then slept. In the night, when the moon one day from full shone in the northwest window, he cried out, "O mother! come to me! come!" Kamedan, sleeping next to him, woke and reached out to him. He felt the child hot as a coal of fire. He soaked cloths in water and wrapped them around the child's head and chest and wrists, and gave him sips of cold water in which willowbark extract was infused. The burning lessened until the child could sleep. In the morning he lay sleeping soundly, and Shamsha said, "Last night was the crisis of the fever. Now all he needs is rest. You go on, you're not needed here."

Kamedan went to the lofts, but his mind would not turn fully to his work.

Sticky Monkeyflower

Sahelm was helping him that day. Usually he observed and followed Kamedan attentively, learning the art; this day he saw Kamedan making mistakes, and once he had to say, "I think that may be not altogether correct," to prevent Kamedan from jamming the machine on a miswound bobbin. Kamedan threw the switch to stop the power, and then sat down on the floor with his head between his hands.

Sahelm sat down not far away from him, crosslegged.

The sun was at noon. The moon was opposite it, directly opposed, pulling down.

The air in the high loft was still and hot, and the cloth-dust that always moved in the air while the looms were working hung still.

Kamedan said, "Five days ago my wife Whette left the Obsidian heyimas. In the heyimas they say that she said she was going up to walk on Spring Mountain. In the Blood Lodge the women say she was going to meet some dancers in a clearing on Spring Mountain, but didn't come. Her mother says she went to Kastoha-na to stay in her brother's wife's household for a few days. Her sister says that probably she went down the Valley, as she used to do before she married, walking alone to the seacoast and back. Modona says that people have seen her in Ounmalin."

Sahelm listened.

Kamedan said, "The child wakes in fever under the moon and calls to her. The grandmother says nothing is the matter. I don't know what to do. I don't know where to look for Whette. I don't want to leave the child, I must do something and there's nothing I can do. Thank you for listening to me, Sahelm."

He got up and turned the power of the loom back on. Sahelm got up, and they worked together. The thread broke and broke again, a bobbin caught and caught again. Sahelm said, "This isn't a good day for weavers."

Kamedan went on working until the loom jammed and he had to stop. He said then, "Leave me to untangle this mess. Maybe I can do that."

Sahelm said, "Let me do it. That kid might be glad to see you."

Kamedan would not go, and Sahelm thought it better to leave him. He went from the lofts to the herb gardens down by Moon Creek. He had seen Duhe there in the morning, and she was still there. She was sitting under the oak Nehaga, eating fresh lettuce. Sahelm came under the shade of the oak and said, "So you are here, Doctor." She said, "So you are here, Fourth-House Man, sit down." He sat down near her. She squeezed lemon juice on lettuce leaves and gave them to him. They finished the lettuce, and Duhe cut the sweet lemon in quarters and they ate it. They went down to Moon Creek to rinse their hands, and returned into the shade of Nehaga. Duhe had been watering, weeding, pruning, and harvesting herbs, and the air was fragrant where she was, and where the baskets she had filled with cuttings were in the shade covered with netting, and where she had laid rosemary and catnip and lemon balm and rue on linen cloth in the sun to dry. Cats kept coming by, wanting to get at the catnip as the sun released its scent. She gave a sprig to each cat once, and if the cat came back she threw pebbles at it to keep it off. An old grey woman-cat kept coming back; she was so fat the pebbles did not sting her and so greedy nothing frightened her.

Duhe said, "Where has the day taken you on the way here?"

Sahelm replied, "Into the broadloom lofts with Kamedan of Hardcinder House."

"Whette's husband," said Duhe. "Has she come back yet?"

"Where would she come back from?"

"Some people were saying that she went to the Springs of the River."

"I wonder, did she tell them she was going there?"

"They didn't say."

"Did any of them see her going there, I wonder?"

"Nobody said that," said Duhe, and laughed.

Sahelm said, "Here's how it is: she went five different ways at the same time. People have told Kamedan that she went to walk alone on Spring Mountain, to dance on Spring Mountain, to Kastoha, to Ounmalin, and to the Ocean. His mind keeps trying to follow her. It seems she said nothing to him about going anywhere, before she went."

Duhe threw an oakgall at the fat cat, who was coming at the catnip from the southeast. The cat went half a stones'-throw away, sat down with her back turned to them, and began to wash her hind legs. Duhe watched the cat and said, "That's strange, that story you tell. Are people lying, perhaps?"

"I don't know. Kamedan says the child wakes and cries in the night and the grandmother says nothing is the matter."

"Well, very likely she's right," said Duhe, whose mind was on the catnip and the cat, the hot sunlight and the shade, Sahelm and herself.

Duhe had lived about forty years in the Third House at that time. She was a short woman with large breasts, heavy hips, sleek, fine arms and legs, a slow, calm manner, a secretive nature, an intelligent and well-disciplined mind. The Lodge name she had given herself was Sleepwalker. A girl, now adolescent, had made her a mother, but she had not married the father, an Obsidian man, nor any other man. She and the girl lived in her sister's household in After the Earthquake House, but she was more often than not outdoors or in the Doctors Lodge.

She said, "You have a gift, Sahelm."

He said, "I have a burden."

She said, "Bring it to the Doctors, not the Millers."

Sahelm pointed: the old fat cat was approaching the catnip slowly from the southwest. Duhe threw a piece of bark at her, but she made a rush at the catnip nonetheless. Duhe got up and chased her down to the creek, and came back hot and sat down by Sahelm in the shaded grass again.

He said, "How could a person go five ways at once?"

"A person could go one way and four people could be lying."

"What would they be lying for?"

"Maybe in malice."

"Has Kamedan done something to bring malice against him?"

"Never that I've heard. But Modona is one of these people who tells where she went, isn't he?"

"I think Kamedan did speak of him."

"And besides malice there is laziness—it's easier to explain than to wonder. And besides malice and laziness there is vanity—people can't bear to admit that they don't know where she went, so they say authoritatively: She went to Spring Mountain, she went to Wakwaha, she went to the moon! Oh, I don't know where she went, but I know some of the reasons why people who don't know would say that they do know."

"Why did she herself not say, before she went?"

"That I don't know. Do you know Whette well?"

"No. I work with Kamedan."

"She is as beautiful as he. When they married, people called them Awar and Bulekwe. When they danced on the Wedding Night they were like those who dance on the rainbow. People watched in wonder."

She pointed: the old fat cat was sneaking along in the wild oats above the creekbed towards the catnip. Sahelm threw an oakgall which rolled between her front and hind legs, and she leaped in the air and rushed away down the creekbed. Sahelm laughed, and Duhe laughed with him. Up in Nehaga a bluejay screeched and a squirrel yelled back. Bees in the lavender bushes nearby made a noise like always boiling.

Sahelm said, "I wish you had not said she went to the moon."

Duhe said, "I'm sorry I said that. It was spoken without sense, foolishly. A bubble word."

"The child too is Obsidian," he said.

Not knowing that Whette's child was ill, she did not know why he said this. She was tired of talking about Whette, and sleepy after eating lettuce in the long, hot, late afternoon. She said, "Please keep the cats off for the next while, if you have nothing else you'd rather do, and I'll go to sleep."

She did not sleep altogether, but sometimes watched Sahelm from within her eyelashes and under her hair. He sat still, without motion, his legs crossed, his wrists on his knees, his back straight as a fir. Although he was much younger than Duhe, he did not look young, sitting still. When he spoke he seemed a boy; when he was still he seemed an old man, an old stone.

After she had dozed she sat up, rested, and said, "You sit well."

He said, "I was well trained to sit, to see, to listen. The teacher of my sprouting years in the Yellow Adobe heyimas of Kastoha told me to sit still enough long enough to see and hear every sight and sound in all the six directions, and so become the seventh."

"What did you see?" she asked. "What did you hear?"

"Just now here? Everything, nothing. My mind wasn't still. It wouldn't sit. It was running here and there all the time like the squirrel up there in the branches."

Duhe laughed. She picked up a duck's feather from the grasses, a down feather, lighter than breath. She said, "Your mind the squirrel; Whette the lost acorn."

Sahelm said, "You're right, I was thinking about her."

Duhe blew the feather into the air with a puff of breath and it floated back down into the grasses. She said, "The air's beginning to cool." She got up and went to see to the drying herbs, heaping them onto basket trays or tying them into bunches to hang. She stacked the trays, and Sahelm helped her to carry them to the storehouse the Doctors Lodge was using. It stood southwest of the northwest common place, a half-dugout with stone walling and cedar roof. All the back room of it was stored with herbs drying and dried. Duhe sang as she entered this room. As she stored and hung the herbs she continued to whisper the song.

Standing in the doorway, Sahelm said, "The smells here are strong. Too strong."

Duhe said, "Before mind saw, it smelled, and tasted, and touched. Even hearing is a most delicate touching. Often, in this Lodge, a person must close their eyes in order to learn."

The young man said, "Sight is the sun's gift."

The doctor said, "And the moon's gift as well."

She gave him a sprig of sweet rosemary to wear in his hair, and as she gave it to him, said, "What you fear is what you need, I think. I begrudge you to the Millers, man of Kastoha-na!" He took the sprig of rosemary and smelled it, saying nothing.

Duhe left the storehouse, going to After the Earthquake House.

Sahelm went to Between the Orchards House, the last house of the middle arm of town, where he was staying since Kailikusha had sent him away from her household. A Yellow Adobe family in Between the Orchards, having a spare room and balcony, had given them to Sahelm to use. He cooked dinner for the family that evening, and after they had cleared away he walked back inward and across towards Hardcinder House. The sun had set behind his back, the full moon was rising before his eyes, over the northeast range. He stopped in the gardens where he saw the moon between two houses. He stood still with his eyes fixed in a gaze upon the moon as it heightened and whitened in the dark blue sky, shining.

People from another place were coming in along the southeast arm there, three donkeys, three women, four men. They all carried backpacks and wore hats over their ears. One of the men played a four-note finger-drum slung on a cord round his neck as they walked along. A person up on a first-floor balcony greeted these strangers, saying, "Hey, people of the Valley, so you are here!" Other people came out on other porches and balconies to see so many strangers going by. The strangers stopped, and the man with the finger-drum tapped it with his nails to make a hard clear sound, playing a rain piece, and called out aloud, "Hey, people of this Telina-na town, so you are fortunately and beautifully here! We're coming in among you thus on four feet and two feet, twenty-six feet in all, dragging our heels with weariness, dancing on our toes for joy, speaking and braying and singing and piping and drumming and thumping as we go, until we get to the right place and the right time, and there and then we stop, we stay, we paint, we dress, and we change the world for you!"

A person called from a balcony, "What play?"

The drummer called back, "As you like it!"

People began to call out plays they wanted to hear. The drummer called back to each one, "Yes, we'll play that one, yes, yes, we'll play that one," promising to play them all, the next day, on the middle common place. A woman called from a window, "This is the right place, players, this is the right time!" The drummer laughed, and gestured to one of the women, who came out of the group and stood in the moonlight where it ran bright through the air and along the ground across the gardens between the houses. The drummer drummed five and five, and the players sang the Continuing Tone, and the woman lifted her arms up high. She danced a scene from the play *Tobbe*, dancing the ghost of the lost wife. As she danced she cried out again and again in a high faint voice. She sank down into a bar of darkness, the shadow of a house, and seemed so to vanish. The drummer changed the beat; the piper picked up her pipe and began to play a stampdance; and so calling and playing the players went on towards the common place, but only nine of them went.

The woman who had danced went along alone in the shadow of the unlighted house until she came beside Hardcinder House, among the big oleanders, white-flowered. There in the white light a man stood still with eyes fixed on the moon. So she had seen him standing with his back to the players while they played and sang and she danced the ghost's dance.

She stood watching him watch the moon for a long time from the shadow of the oleanders. She went then, following shadows all along, to the edge of Cheptash Vineyard, and sat down in the mixed dark and moonlight near the trunk of a long-armed vine. From there she watched the still man. When the moon was shining higher in the sky, she went along the side of the vineyard to the corner of the apricot orchard behind Generously Dwelling House, and stood awhile in the shadow of the porches of that house, watching him. He had not moved yet when she slipped away, still following shadow, towards the galleries on the common place where the others of her troupe had camped.

Sahelm stood still, head now held back, face lifted, eyes looking at the moon steadily. To him the blink of his eyes was a slow drumbeat. Of nothing else was he aware but the light of the moon and the drumbeat of the dark.

Kamedan came to him saying his name, late, when all lights in houses were out and the moon was above the southwestern range. "Sahelm! Sahelm! Sahelm!" he said. The fourth time he said his name, "Sahelm!" the visionary moved, cried out, staggered, and fell to hands and knees. Kamedan helped him to stand up, saying to him, "Go to the Doctors Lodge, Sahelm, please, go there for me."

"I have seen her," Sahelm said.

Kamedan said, "Please, go to the Doctors for me. I'm afraid to move the child, I'm afraid to leave him. The others are crazy, they won't do anything!"

Looking at Kamedan, Sahelm said, "I saw Whette. I saw your wife. She stood near your house. By the northeast windows."

Kamedan said, "The child is dying." He let go his hold of Sahelm's arms. Sahelm could not stand up, but fell again to his knees. Kamedan turned away and ran back to Hardcinder House.

He hurried into his household rooms, wrapped up Monkeyflower in the bedding, and carried him to the outer door. Shamsha followed, a blanket pulled round her and her grey hair over her eyes, saying "Are you crazy? The child is perfectly all right, what are you doing, where are you going with him?" She called to Fefinum and Tai, shouting, "Your sister's husband is crazy, make him stop!" But Kamedan was already out of the house, running to the Doctors Lodge.

No one was in the house of the Lodge but Duhe, who could not sleep under the full moon. She was reading in lamplight.

Kamedan spoke at the doorway and came in, carrying the child. He said, "This child of the First House is very ill, I think."

Duhe got up, saying as doctors say, "Well, well, well, well, let's see about this," slowly. She showed Kamedan a cane cot to set the child down on. "A choking? A burning? Fever, is it?" she asked, and while Kamedan answered, she watched Monkeyflower, who was half-awake, bewildered and whimpering. Kamedan said in haste, "Last night and the night before he was in high fever. In the daylight the fever goes away, but when the moon rises he calls to his mother over and over. In the household they pay no attention, they say nothing's wrong with him."

Duhe said, "Come away into the light." She tried to make Kamedan leave the child, but he would not go out of reach of him. She told him, "Please talk quietly, if you can. That person is sleepy, and frightened a little. How long has he lived in the Moon's House now?"

"Three winters," Kamedan said. "His name is Torip, but he has a nickname, his mother calls him Monkeyflower."

"Well, well, well, well," said Duhe. "Yes, a little person of gold skin and a pretty little mouth, I see the monkeyflower. There isn't any fever just now in this little flower, or not much. Bad dreams, is it, and crying and waking in the night, is that how it's been?" She talked slowly and softly, and Kamedan did the same when he answered, saying, "Yes, he cries, and he burns in my arms."

The doctor said, "You see, it's quiet here, and the light is quiet, and a person goes to sleep very easily. . . . Let him sleep now; come over here." Kamedan followed her this time. When they were on the other side of the room, near the lamp, Duhe said, "Now, I didn't understand well, please tell me again what's been wrong."

Kamedan began to weep, standing there. He said, "She doesn't come. He calls, she doesn't hear, she doesn't come. She's gone."

Duhe's mind had been in the book she had been reading, and then her attention had gone all to the child, so only as he wept and spoke did she bring into her mind now the things Sahelm had spoken of in the afternoon under Nehaga.

Kamedan went on, speaking louder, "The grandmother says that nothing's wrong, nothing's the matter—the mother gone and the child sick and nothing is the matter!"

"Hush," Duhe said. "Let him sleep, please. Listen now. It's not good carrying him about here and there, is it. Let him sleep out the night here, and you stay with him, of course. If medicine will help, we have medicine. If a bringing-in would be good for him, we'll hold a bringing-in, maybe for both of you; or whatever seems the right thing to do, in daylight, after talking and thinking and watching. Just now here, the best thing to do is sleep, I think. Since I can't do that when the moon's full in the sky, I'll be sitting on the porch by the door there. If he cried out in dream or waking I'll be here; I'll be awake, listening and hearing." While she spoke she was setting a mattress down on the floor beside the cane cot, and she said, "Now, my brother of the Serpentine, please lie down. You're as tired as your child is. If you want to go on talking, you see, I'm sitting here in the doorway; you can lie down and talk, I can sit here and talk. The night's cooling off at last, it'll be better for sleeping. Are you comfortable?"

Kamedan thanked her, and lay in silence for some while.

Duhe sang in undertone on a matrix word, making an interval and place for his silence. Her voice control was excellent; she sang always more faintly until the song became inaudible breath, and then stillness. After a while then she moved in her place by the door, so that Kamedan would know the song was done if he wanted to talk.

He said, "I don't understand the people in that house, this child's mother's house."

Duhe spoke enough that he knew she was listening. He went on, "When a Miller marries into a family whose work is all in the Five Houses, if they're conservative people, respectable, superstitious, you know, that can be difficult. Hard on everybody. I understood that, I understood how they felt. That's why I joined the Cloth Art, took up weaving, when I married. My gift is mechanical, that's how it is. You can't deny your gift, can you? All you can do is accept it and use it, fit it into your life with the others, people you live with, your people. When I saw how people from Telina were going to Kastoha for canvas because nobody was using the canvas loom or doing much broadcloth weaving here, I thought, that's the place for me, that's work they'll understand and approve of, using my own gift and my training as a Miller. Four years now I've been a member of the Cloth Art. Who else in Telina is making sheeting, canvas, broadloom linens? Since Houne left the lofts, I do all that work. Now Sahelm and Asole-Verou are learning the art with me, doing good work. I'm their teacher. But none of that does me any good in my wife's house. They don't care about my work, it's Miller's work.

I'm not respectable, they don't trust me. They wish she'd married any other man. The child, he's a Miller's child. And only a boy, anyway. They don't care for him. Five days, five days she's been gone without a word, and they don't worry about it, they say don't worry, what are you upset about, they say, oh, she always used to walk down to the coast alone! They make me a fool—the fool they want me to be. The moon rises and he cries out for her, and they say, nothing's wrong! Go back to sleep, fool!"

His voice had grown louder, and the child stirred a little. He fell silent.

After a while Duhe said in a quiet voice, "Please tell me how it was that Whette left."

Kamedan said, "I came into the house from working at the East Fields generator. They called me over there, there was a consultation; you know some work needs to be done there, and people in the Milling Art had to talk and decide about it. It took all day. I came home, and Tai was cooking dinner. Nobody else was home yet. I said, 'Where are Whette and Monkeyflower?' He said, 'He's with my wife and daughter. She went up onto Spring Mountain.' Pretty soon Fefinum came in with both the children, from the gardens. The grandmother came in from somewhere. The grandfather showed up too. We ate together. I went over up the Spring Mountain way to meet Whette coming home. She never came. She never came that night, or since."

The doctor said, "Tell me what you think about this, Kamedan."

"I think she went off with someone. Some person that walked with her. I don't think she meant to stay away, stay with them. Nobody's missing, that I've heard about. I haven't heard that any man is staying away somewhere or hasn't come home from somewhere. But it might not be far. She could be in the woods, on the hunting side, in the hills. Maybe at some summer place, up high. So many people are up in the hills this time of year, nobody really knows where anybody is. She might be staying with some people at a summerhouse. Or maybe she went on from where they were dancing, went on a ways to be alone, and got hurt. People can trip and fall, break an ankle, in those canyons. It's wild there on the south side and the southeast side of Spring Mountain. All those paths are bad, nothing but hunters' paths, it's hard not to get lost there. Once you get round on the wrong side of Spring Mountain it's very confusing. I ended up once coming into Chukulmas, when I thought I'd been going southwest all day! I couldn't believe it was Chukulmas—I thought I'd blundered into some town over in Osho

Valley, a foreign town, and I saw Chukulmas Tower but I kept thinking what's that doing here, I couldn't make sense of it. I had got turned around. It could have happened that Whette did the opposite thing, she meant to turn back here and kept going the wrong way, she might be over there, outside the Valley, with the Osho people, not sure how to get home. Or what worries me the most, you know—if she hurt herself—if she broke an ankle, and is where nobody can hear her— The rattlesnake. I can't think when I think of the rattlesnake."

Kamedan stopped talking. Duhe said nothing for some time. She said at last, "Maybe some people should be going up on Spring Mountain, calling out. Maybe there's a dog that knows Whette, and would help find her if she's there."

"Her mother and sister and the others say that would be foolish; they all say she went down the Valley to the Mouths of the Na, or up to the Springs. Fefinum is certain that she went downriver. She used to do that. Probably she's on the way home now. I'm a fool to worry this way, I know. But the child kept waking and crying to her."

Duhe did not answer. Presently she began to sing under her voice, a Serpentine blessing song:

"Where grass grows, go well, go easily.
Where grass grows, go well."

Kamedan knew the song. He did not sing with her, but listened to the song. She sang it very quietly and let her voice become fainter until the song became inaudible breath. After that they spoke no more, and Kamedan slept.

In the morning the little boy woke early and stared all around himself for a while, wondering. The only thing he saw that he knew was his father, sleeping beside the cot. Monkeyflower had never slept up on a cot with legs, and felt as if he might fall out of bed, but he liked the feeling. He lay still for a while, and then climbed down off the cot, stepped over his father's legs, and went to the door of the room to look out. There was a woman he did not know curled up asleep in the porch there, so he went the other direction, to the inner door, into the second room. There he saw a lot of beautiful glass jars and bottles and containers of various colors and shapes, many ceramic bowls and holders, and several machines with handles to turn. He turned all the handles he could reach, and then took down off the shelves first one colored glass jar and then another, until he had a great many of them on the floor.

There he began to arrange them. Some of them had something inside that made a noise when the jar was shaken. He shook all the jars. He opened one to see what was inside, and saw a grey, coarse powder, which he thought was sand. Another one had fine, white sand in it. A blue glass jar had black water in it. A red glass jar had brown honey in it; that got onto his fingers, and he licked them. The honey tasted bitter as oakgalls, but he was hungry, and finished licking his fingers. He was opening another bottle when he saw the woman stand in the doorway looking at him. He stopped doing anything, and sat there amidst all the jars and bottles arranged around him. The black water had run out of the jar and soaked into the floor. Seeing that, he wanted to piss, and did not dare to.

Duhe said, "Well, well, well, well. Monkeyflower, you get to work early!" She came into the pharmacy. Monkeyflower sat very small.

"What's this one?" Duhe said. She picked up the red jar. She looked at the child, took his hand, and sniffed it. "Sticky Monkeyflower, you are going to be constipated," she said to him. "When you become a doctor you can use all these things. Until you become a doctor you'd better not. So let's go outside."

Monkeyflower let out a wail. He had pissed on the floor.

Duhe said, "O Spring of the Yellow River! Come on outside *now*!" He would not get up, so she picked him up and carried him out to the porch.

Kamedan woke and came out on the porch. Monkeyflower was standing there, and Duhe was washing his buttocks and legs. Kamedan said, "Is he all right?"

"He is interested in becoming a doctor," Duhe said. Monkeyflower put up his arms and whimpered to Kamedan. Duhe picked him up and gave him to Kamedan to hold; the child was between them in the first light of the day's sun, hinging them. Monkeyflower held his father tight and would not look at Duhe, being ashamed.

Duhe said, "Listen, brother: instead of going to the lofts this morning, maybe you could go with Monkeyflower somewhere, do some work with him. Stay out of the sun in the middle of the day, make sure there'll be plenty of water to drink where you go. This way you will be able to judge for yourself if he's well or ill. I think he's been wishing to be with you, since his mother is away. You might come back by here with him towards the end of the day, and we can talk then about whether we might want to hold a singing, or a bringing-in, and about other things. We'll talk, we'll see. All right?"

Kamedan thanked her and left, carrying the child on his shoulders.

After Duhe had straightened up the pharmacy she went to bathe and eat breakfast in her household. Later in the morning she started across the arms to Hardcinder House. She wanted to talk to Whette's people. On the way, in the narrow gardens, Sahelm came to meet her. He said, "I've seen Whette."

"You saw her? Where?"

"Outside the house."

"Is she home, then?"

"I don't know that."

"Who else saw her?"

"I don't know that."

"Whettez—Whette?"

"I don't know that."

"Whom have you told?"

"No one but you."

"You're crazy, Sahelm," the doctor said. "What have you been doing? Moongazing?"

Sahelm said again, "I saw Whette," but the doctor was angry at him. She said, "Everybody's seen her, and each in a different place! If she's here she'll be in her house, not outside it. This is all crazy. I'm going to Hardcinder House and talk to the women there. Come if you want to."

Sahelm said nothing, and Duhe went on through the narrow gardens. He watched her go around the oleander bushes towards Hardcinder House. Somebody up on a balcony of that house was shaking out blankets and hanging them over the railing to air. The day was already getting hot. Squash blossoms and tomato blossoms were yellow all around in the narrow gardens, and the eggplant flowers were beautiful. Sahelm had eaten nothing but lettuce and lemon the day before. He felt dizzy, and began to separate and be in two times at one time. In one time he was standing among squash blossoms alone, in one time he was on a hillside talking to a woman wearing white clothes. She said, "I am Whette."

"You're not Whette."

"Who am I, then?"

"I don't know that."

The woman laughed and whirled around. His head whirled around inside itself. He came back together on his hands and knees on the path between tomato vines. A woman was standing there, saying something to him. He said, "You are Whette!"

She said, "What's the matter? Can you stand up? Come on out

of the sun. Maybe you've been fasting?" She pulled his arm and helped him up, and held his arm till they came into the shade of the drying-racks at the end of the narrow gardens by the first row of Pedoduks vines. She pushed him a little till he sat down on the ground in the shade. "Are you feeling better at all?" she asked him. "I came to pick tomatoes and saw you there, talking, and then you fell down. Who was it you were talking to?"

He asked, "Did you see someone?"

"I don't know, I couldn't see well through the tomato vines. Maybe some woman was there."

"Was she wearing white, or undyed?"

"I don't know. I don't know the people here," she said. She was a slender, strong, young woman with very long hair braided nine times, wearing a white shift belted with a many-colored woven sash, carrying a gathering basket.

Sahelm said, "I've been fasting and going into trance. I think I should go home and rest awhile."

"Eat something before you walk," the young woman said. She went and took some plums off the racks and picked some yellow pear-tomatoes from a vine. She brought these to Sahelm, gave them to him, and watched him eat them. He ate very slowly. "The flavors are strong," he said.

"You're weak," she said. "Go on. Eat it all, the food of your gardens given you by the stranger." When he was done, she asked, "Which house do you live in?"

"Between the Orchards House," he answered. "But you live in Hardcinder House there. With Kamedan."

"Not any more," she said. "Come on now, stand up. Show me where your house is between the orchards, and I'll go with you." She went with him to his house, and up the stairs to the first floor; she went with him into the room he used, laid out his mattress, and said to him, "Now lie down." While he turned away to lie down, she turned and left.

Coming away from that house she saw a man coming down into Telina between the Telory Hills, following the creek path from the hunting side, carrying a dead deer. She greeted them: "Heya, guest from the Right Hand coming, my word and thanks to you! And you, Hunter of Telina, so you are here."

He said, "So you are here, Dancer of Wakwaha!"

She walked along beside them. "Very beautiful, that Blue Clay person who gave himself to you. You must be a strong singer. Tell me all about your hunt."

Modona laughed. "I see you know that the best of the hunting is the telling. Well, I went up on Spring Mountain in the middle of the day, and spent the night at a camp I know up there, a well-hidden place. The next day I watched the deer. I saw which doe went with two fawns and which with one and which with a fawn and a yearling. I saw where they met and gathered, and what bucks were about alone. I chose this spike-horned buck to sing to, and began singing in my mind. In the twilight of evening he came, and died on my arrow. I slept by the death, and in the twilight of morning the coyote came by singing too. Now I'm bringing the death to the heyimas; they need deer hooves for the Water Dance; and the hide will go to the Tanners, and the meat to the old women in my household, to jerk; and the horns—maybe you'd like the horns to dance with?"

"I don't need the horns. Give them to your wife!"

"Such a being there is not," said Modona.

The smell of the blood and meat and hair of the death was pungent and sweet. The deer's head was near the dancer's shoulder, moving up and down as Modona walked. Grass seeds and chaff lay on the open eye of the deer. Seeing this, the dancer blinked and rubbed her eyes. She said, "How did you know that I'm from Wakwaha?"

"I've seen you dance."

"Not here in Telina."

"Maybe not."

"In Chukulmas?"

"Maybe so."

She laughed. She said, "And maybe in Kastoha-na, and maybe in Wakwaha-na, and maybe in Ababa-badaba-na! You can see me dance in Telina this evening, anyhow. What strange men there are in this town!"

"What have they done that you think so?"

"One of them sees me dancing where I'm not, another doesn't see me dancing where I am."

"What man is that—Kamedan?"

"No," she answered. "Kamedan lives there," pointing to Hard-cinder House, "though this man says that I do. He lives there," pointing along the arm to Between the Orchards House, "and has visions in the tomato patch."

Modona said nothing. He kept looking at her across the death, turning his eyes but not his head. They came to the narrow gardens, and Isitut stopped there, saying, "I came to pick tomatoes for our troupe to eat."

"If you players would like venison as well, here it is. Will you be here several days? It has to be hung."

"The old women in your household need the meat for jerky."

"What they need, I'll give them."

"A true hunter! Always giving himself!" said the dancer, laughing and showing her teeth. "We'll be here four days or five days, at least."

"If you want enough to go around, I'll kill a kid to roast with this meat. How many are you?"

"Nine and myself," said Isitut. "The deer is enough; all of us will be filled full with meat and gratitude. Tell me what to play for the feast you bring us."

"Play *Tobbe*, if you will," Modona said.

"We'll play *Tobbe*, on the fourth evening."

She was picking tomatoes, filling her basket with yellow pear and small red tomatoes. The day was hot and bright, all smells very powerful, the cicadas shrilling loud near and far continuously. Flies swarmed to the blood on the hair of the deer's death.

Modona said, "That man you met here, the visionary, he came here from Kastoha. He's always acting crazy. He doesn't go across into the Four Houses, he just walks around here staring and jabbering, making accusations, making up the world."

"A moongazer," said Isitut.

"In what House do you live, woman of Wakwaha?"

"In the moon's House, man of Telina."

"I live in this person's House," Modona said, lifting the deer's head with his hand so that the death seemed to look forward. The tongue had swollen and stuck out of the black lips. The dancer moved away, picking from the tall, strong-smelling vines.

The hunter asked, "What will you be playing this evening?"

From behind the vines Isitut replied, "I'll know that when I go back with the tomatoes." She moved farther away, picking.

Modona went on to the dancing place. Outside his heyimas he stopped, set the death down on the earth, and cut off the four hooves with his hunter's knife. He cleaned and strung them, tied the string to a bamboo rod, and stuck this in the earth near the southwest corner of the heyimas roof so that the hooves would dry in the sun. He went down into the heyimas to wash, and talked to some people there. He came back up the ladder and walked down the west steps of the roof, looking for the dead deer. It was not where he had set it down.

He walked clear round the heyimas roof, and then around the dancing place, hurrying and staring. Some people greeted him, and he said to them, "There's a death walking four-legged around here. Where's it gone?"

They laughed.

"There's a two-legged coyote around here," Modona said. "If you see a spike-horn buck walking without hooves, let me know!" He went off at a run, across the Hinge, to the middle common place. The troupe of players from Wakwaha were all sitting around in the shade of the gallery and the booths, eating flat bread, sheep's-milk cheese, and red and yellow tomatoes, and drinking dry Betebbes. Isitut was with them, eating and drinking. She said, "So you are here, man of the Blue Clay. Where's your brother?"

"That's what I'd like to know," he said. He looked around the booths and gallery. A cloud of flies was in one place behind the gallery, and he went to look there, but it was dog turds they were clustering on. The deer was nowhere there. He came back by the players, speaking to them: "So you are here, people of the Valley. Has any of you seen a deer's death go by this place?" He made his voice sound easy, but there was an angry look in his body and face. The strangers did not laugh. A man answered politely, "No, we have not seen such a thing."

"It was a gift to you. If you see it, take it, it's yours," the hunter said. He looked at Isitut. She was eating, and did not look at him. He went back to the dancing place.

This time he noticed some marks in the dirt at the foot of the southwest side of the roof of the Blue Clay heyimas. He looked with care and saw that farther on there were dry grass stems broken, pointing away from the heyimas. He went on in that direction.

Clear over at the bank of the River, down under the bank, he saw something white. He walked towards it, staring. The white being moved. It rose up and faced the hunter. It stood over the deer's death, which it had been eating. It showed its teeth and cried out.

Modona saw a woman in white clothes. His head whirled in itself and he saw a white dog.

He stooped and picked up rocks and threw them hard, shouting, "Get away! Get off that!"

When a rock hit the dog in the head she shrieked and ran away from the death, downstream, towards the dwelling-houses.

This dog's mother was hechi, her father dui, and she was unusually tall and strong; her coat of hair was white, with no other color, and her eyes were bluish. When a puppy she had been befriended by Whette, and they had played together and gone together whenever Whette went outside the town. Whette had called her Moondog. After marrying Kamedan Whette had seldom called the dog to walk or guard, and nobody else knew her well; she would not have anything to do with any human being but Whette, and kept alone even in dogtown. She was getting old now and had lost keenness of hearing; lately she had been getting thin. Hunger had given her the strength to drag the death from the heyimas down to the River, and she had eaten most of one haunch. Bewildered by the pain where the rock had struck her between eye and ear, she ran up into Telina, between the houses, to Hardcinder House.

Inside Shamsha's household the people heard a clawing and a crying at the outer door, which was closed to keep out the day's heat. Fefinum heard the voice crying and said, "She's back! She has come back!" Speaking, she cowered down in the corner of the room farthest from the door.

Shamsha jumped up and said, talking loudly, "Children playing on the porches, it's a shame, it's never quiet here!" She stood in front of her daughter, concealing her from Duhe.

Duhe looked at them, went over to the door, and opened it enough to look out. She said, "It's a white dog, crying here. Whette used to walk with this dog, I think."

Shamsha came to look. "Yes, but not for years now," she said. "Let me drive her away. She's crazy, coming here, trying to get inside the house like that. Old and crazy. Get away, get off, you!" She took up a broom and poked it out the door at Moondog, but Duhe kept the broom from striking the dog, and said, "Please wait a minute. It seems to me the dog's been hurt and wants help." She went out to look more closely at Moondog's head, having seen blood on the white hair about the eye. Moondog cringed and snarled at first, but feeling that the doctor was not at all afraid, she held still. When the doctor's hands touched her she felt great authority in them, and she made no objection while Duhe examined the wound the rock had made between her left ear and eye.

Duhe spoke to her: "What a beautiful old woman-dog you are, though a queer color for a dog, better for a sheep; and you haven't been overeating recently, to judge by your ribs. Now what happened, did you run into a branch? No, this looks more like a rock was thrown at you and you didn't dodge it; that's not so smart, old woman-dog. Shamsha, may I please have some water and a clean cloth to wash this injury with?"

The old woman brought a bowl of water and some rags, grumbling. "That dog is worthless, of no account."

Duhe cleaned the wound. Moondog made no protest, and stood still and patient, trembling a little in the hindquarters. When Duhe was done the dog wagged her tail several times.

"Please lie down now," the doctor said.

Moondog looked into her eyes, and lay down with her head on her outstretched front legs.

Duhe stroked her head behind the ears. Shamsha was inside the room, Fefinum had come near the door to watch. Duhe said to them, "She may have some concussion of the brain. That was a hard blow."

Shamsha asked, "Will she go into fits?"

The doctor said, "She might. More likely she'll sleep it off, if she's allowed to stay in a quiet place where she isn't disturbed. Sleep is a wonderful healer. I didn't have much of it myself last night!" She came back indoors, bringing the bowl and rags. Fefinum kept her back turned, and started cutting up cucumbers for pickling. Duhe said, "That is the dog who used to go along with Whette, isn't she? What did Whette call her?"

Shamsha said, "I don't remember."

Fefinum said without turning round, "My sister called her Moondog."

"It seems she came here to find Whette, or to help us find Whette," said Duhe.

"She's deaf, blind, and crazy," Shamsha said. "She couldn't find a dead deer if she fell over it. In any case, I don't understand what you say about finding my daughter. Anybody who wants to talk with her can go up to Wakwaha, they don't need a dog to show them the way upriver."

While the women were talking, Monkeyflower and Kamedan

came up the stairs onto the porch, hearing the women's voices behind the open door. Kamedan looked at the dog and went in without speaking. Monkeyflower stopped and looked at the dog for some time. Moondog lay with her head on her front legs and looked up at him. Her tail thumped on the porch floor quietly. Monkeyflower said in a low voice, "Moondog, do you know where she is?"

Moondog yawned with anxiety, showing all her yellow teeth, and shut her mouth with a snap, looking at Monkeyflower.

"Come on, then," Monkeyflower said. He thought about telling his father that he was going to find his mother, but all the adults were talking inside the house, and he did not want to be in there among them. He wanted to see the doctor again, but was ashamed of having peed on her floor. He did not go in, but went back down the stairs, looking over his shoulder at Moondog.

Moondog got up, whining a little, trying to do what Duhe had told her to do and what Monkeyflower wanted her to do. She yawned again and then with her tail down and wagging a little, her head down, she followed him. At the foot of the stairs he stopped and stood waiting for her to show him the way to go. She waited awhile too, to see what he wanted, and then set off towards the River. Monkeyflower came along, walking beside her. When she stopped he patted her back and said, "Go on, dog." So they went on out of town, northwestward, into the willow flats along the River, and along beside the water, going upstream.

NOTES:
p. 349. *She never came that night, or since.*
Kamedan's account differs in several respects from the account of the evening of Whette's disappearance as recounted by the narrator in the first chapter of the novel.

p. 352. *Whettez—Whette?*
Sky Mode and Earth Mode: "Whette in a vision, or Whette in the flesh?" The dialogue in this passage is in four-syllable meter.

p. 357. *This dog's mother was hechi, her father dui . . .*
Breeds of dog; see "Some of the Other People of the Valley" in the Back of the Book.

Pandora Gently to the Gentle Reader

 WHEN I TAKE you to the Valley, you'll see the blue hills on the left and the blue hills on the right, the rainbow and the vineyards under the rainbow late in the rainy season, and maybe you'll say, "There it is, that's it!" But I'll say, "A little farther." We'll go on, I hope, and you'll see the roofs of the little towns and the hillsides yellow with wild oats, a buzzard soaring and a woman singing by the shallows of a creek in the dry season, and maybe you'll say, "Let's stop here, this is it!" But I'll say, "A little farther yet." We'll go on, and you'll hear the quail calling on the mountain by the springs of the river, and looking back you'll see the river running downward through the wild hills behind, below, and you'll say, "Isn't that it, the Valley?" And all I will be able to say is, "Drink this water of the spring, rest here awhile, we have a long way yet to go, and I can't go without you."

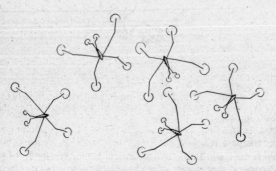

STONE TELLING

▊▊

PART THREE

 I HAD THOUGHT Tsaya House in South City very rich and splendid, but it was much less so than Terter House. Because the Condor households keep without giving, their furnishings are numerous and complicated; and because the servants and slaves that work for the household all live there, the people are also numerous, and their relationships complicated. Terter House was a village in itself, a nomad tribe settled down and staying in one place. Since I seldom got outside of its walls, I took it to be as prosperous and thriving as it seemed, once I realised that the Dayao counted wealth as what they had, what they kept.

The closer a True Condor is by birth to The Condor, the more power and dignity he has and reflects upon his household. The Terters were cousins in the second degree of The Condor through the male line. Terter Gebe had been a chosen companion of The Condor in youth and an adviser to him for many years, and was still in favor with The Condor's son, who would become the next Condor. But the father had become jealous of his power as that son grew older and had turned against the son and so against Terter Gebe, and the mirror of the Terters' glory had become clouded.

As well as I could understand from the talk of the Daughters, some of whom were shrewd and knowledgeable people for all that they were shut inside so many walls, since they had settled in Sai the Condors had purposed to glorify One by increasing their wealth and power by taking land, life, and service from other people. For three generations their armies had done this in the Volcano countries. But the people living there were few and elusive; the coyotes and wild horses, the humans and the rattlesnakes, none of them made very good slaves; and all the land wanted to grow was bunch grass and rabbit brush and sage. So the present Condor had ordered his soldiers to go south and west till they found rich, fertile

361

lands and places worth "winning." My father, Terter Abhao, was one of the soldiers and then one of the chiefs of those armies that were sent out to discover such places. He had gone the farthest southwest of all, first to Clear Lake and then to the Valley of the Na. His army had not destroyed and made war as they went, but had gone along like traders or like the Pig People, staying here and there for a while, sometimes asking for food and sometimes stealing it, learning the ways and properties of the various countries they went through and stayed in. From his first journey to the Valley, that time when he married my mother, he returned to Sai saying, "The Valley of the Na is the most beautiful place we have seen." His father, Terter Gebe, went to The Condor and said, "The armies should go south and west, making a way clear, so that soldiers, tyon, and women can be sent to make a new City in the Valley for the glory of One."

The Condor followed that plan at first, making war with the people that lived southwest of the Black Lava country; but because the Volcano country people had dispersed rather than stayed to fight and because everyone praised and flattered him continuously, telling him that the Mirror of One could do anything, he believed that his armies could do whatever he told them to do. So he sent one army northwest into the Six Rivers country to subdue the river towns, and another down along the Dark River to bring in tribute from the people there, and then another one, under my father's command, far to the southwest again to conquer the Valley and bring back cartloads of Valley wine on roads that the enslaved peoples were to make. They were to build a great bridge across the River of the Marshes and another across the Dark River. When they told me that, I thought of my father trying to make that bridge across the little Na.

Terter Gebe and Terter Abhao had both told The Condor that his soldiers and people could not do all this at once and "win" all these vast lands and various peoples, but must move more slowly out from their center; but The Condor took such counsel as offensive to the One-Spirit in himself and paid them no heed. When his son argued for them, he took this as an excuse for anger and had his son locked up in a part of the great house they lived in, the Palace; there he had lived for years, as far as the women knew. Some of them believed he had died of poisoning, others that he was alive but had been given poisons that had weakened his wits till he was docile and imbecilic. Terter Zadyaya Bele would hear no such talk, and punished the talkers; The Condor could do no wrong, nor could the Son of the Son be in any way defective. She knew perfectly well, however, that the household she had married into was in disgrace.

When my father left the Valley the second time, he had expected to return to it within the year with a very large army, all the True Condors and all the soldiers, to found a new City there. Instead, The Condor had sent him south to conquer the Valley with an army of one hundred and forty men.

Sinshan Mountain

By this time most of the human peoples that lived in the lands between the City and Valley were ready to go to war with the Condor soldiers as soon as they saw them. My father had spent six years getting back to the Valley. When he got to Clear Lake he had made a more or less safe way that far, but he had forty men left of his one hundred and forty. Many had been killed in wars and ambushes, others had run away to become dirt people. My father had gone alone to the Valley, to Sinshan, when he knew that he would never be going there again. He knew that he had to come back to Sai and show The Condor that he had gained little and lost much. Those who take power must take blame, and he was ready to do so.

At first, things were not so bad as he and the other Terters had feared. The Condor was of course displeased, but the bad news had already come to him little by little through messengers and through the Exchange—which only he, in all the City, was allowed to use: it was in his house, the Palace. Meanwhile his advisers had been putting new plans in his head, and he was intent on these rather than on his defeats.

I do not understand why the soldiers allowed him, who never left his house, to make all these plans and arrange for so many people to be killed; but that is how it was there.

The plans were still all for war, but now instead of sending out men with mere guns, they were to have more destructive and terrible weapons still. I heard about these plans when I lived with my husband.

I should tell here about getting married.

Living in Terter House I became ill. My skin became pale and I could not sleep at night, while in the daytime I was always sleepy and had fits of shivering. If I had been home I would have slept and sung in the heyimas for four or five days, or asked the Doctors Lodge for a bringing-in. If I had been home I would not have been ill. In Sai, I was ill because I was living indoors all the time, outside the world. When I saw my father I would ask him to take me out of the house. Twice he did that: he brought the dear sorrel mare and rode his dun gelding, and we went for the whole day out into the snowy, black wilderness of the lava beds. The second of those times, he took me down into one of the caves in the lava, long tubes where lava had flowed like water through the rock, now cold and black as fear itself. The winds in winter scraped that barren land, but it was beautiful, and even when I was so cold I cried, it was better to be in the wind than in the warm rooms of Terter House. Even in that black desert I was closer to the Valley than I was indoors. Indoors I felt stranger all the time.

When I was ill, the Condor's Daughters were kinder, and Terter Zadyaya Bele had a room curtained off where Esiryu and I could stay by ourselves. We talked there while we spun or sewed. I could talk about my home and so be there in the mind. I told Esiryu about Spear, and she told me about a young man who had gone as hostler with the army to the Six Rivers country. We talked often about those young men, telling each other what they were like and what they might be like when we saw them again.

My illness worried my father, but so did many other things. I knew that he regretted having brought me to the City. My presence was not a good thing for him. Other Condors said, "Men fuck animals, but they don't bring the cubs home, they don't bring dirt persons into the house." Terter Zadyaya told me directly that so long as I lived in it, Terter House could not be as glorious as it had been.

I said, "Then send me away. Let me go back to the Valley. I know the way!"

She said, "Don't talk foolishness."

"Then what is it you want me to do? To die?" I said.

She said, "I want you to do nothing—to be quiet for once. Let Terter Abhao be. He cannot be troubled with a girl's wants and follies. He is a great warrior."

I had heard that song before.

She went on, "You are a human person now, not an animal. If you will behave as such, a husband can be found for you."

"A husband!" I said, shocked. "But I'm still a virgin!"

"I'm glad to hear it," she said.

I was entirely confused, and said, "But what does a virgin want a husband for?"

Then she was shocked. "Be still!" she said. "Dirt!" She went out of the room, and did not speak to me or look at me again for a month.

My father was sent at about the time of the World Dancing in the Valley to the Six Rivers country to help an army there come back to Sai through hostile regions. It was a dangerous journey and there was no question, I saw, of my going with him. Spring and summer passed and he was still gone.

The times of the great dances came and passed one by one, and there was no dancing.

I tried to sing the Two Quail Song and the other songs of the Summer. My voice sounded wrong, alone and in that place. When it came towards the time of the Water I thought about the bowl of blue clay in my heyimas and about the spring of Sinshan Creek under the azalea and sweetshrub on the steep ridge of digger pines and dark firs and red madrone. I tried to sing the Water songs of my House, in that dry land. I thought of the blind woman, now dead, Cave, who had seen me here. I went nearly crazy with grief then. I took out the feather of the great condor that I had kept in my pouch, put it on the tiled hearth of the electric heater of the room, and set

fire to it. It burned with a stink, shrivelling. Where it was I saw a man in Condor warrior's clothing lying head downward in a steep canyon among fireweed and dead thistles, his mouth and eyes open, dead: it was my father. I began to cry with an owl's hooting, and could not stop.

A doctor was brought to me, a man, who gave me some poison to make me sleep. When I woke up the next day very tired and confused, he came back and felt my pulse and examined my body. He was half respectful because I was a Condor's Daughter, and half jokingly contemptuous because I was a woman; and when he found that I was menstruating he became nervous and disgusted, as if I bore some dreadful infection. I was most uncomfortable when he touched me, but I tried to be still. I was so terrified by what I had seen in the Four Houses that I wanted only to be still and hide. I thought I should tell Terter Zadyaya so that she could tell my grandfather, and so I asked to see her. She came and stood across the room in the doorway. The doctor stayed to listen.

"I saw a very bad thing in the mind's eye," I said. She said nothing. I had to go on. I said, "I saw Terter Abhao lying dead in the mountains." Still she said nothing.

The doctor spoke to her: "The girl is very nervous; this is mere womb-sickness. Nothing a young husband wouldn't cure!" And he smiled at her.

Terter Zadyaya went away without speaking.

Within that same month, one of the other Daughters told me that Terter Zadyaya was arranging a marriage for me with a True Condor of Retforok House. She praised him to me as a handsome man and of a good disposition. "He never beats his wife," she said. She wanted me to be happy about the marriage. Another woman, a spiteful one, said, "What kind of man would marry a dirt person to try to get close to The Cordor!" She meant that he was marrying me to become related to the Terters. Esiryu got to work and told me everything she could find out about this man, Retforok Dayat. He was the youngest of four sons, and neither a soldier nor a One-Warrior and so not of great account, but the Retforok family was wealthy. He was thirty-five years old—the Dayao were always particular about people's ages, because they had a numerical system of lucky and unlucky days that started with your birthday—and had five children. I was to be what they called his pretty wife. After their first wife had had a lot of children, Condor men often took a second wife, a pretty wife. A pretty wife did not have to give the husband's family goods and money, as a first wife did, and was not expected to have children, or at most one or two. I thought I was

lucky. Since Zadyaya had spoken of marriage I had been afraid.
Condors' wives were expected to have babies continuously, since
that is what One made women for; one of the Daughters of Terter
House had seven children, the eldest of them ten years old, and for
this incontinence she was praised by men and envied by women. If
they could have borne in litters, like himpi, such women would
have done so. I suppose this is again part of the Dayao being at war
with everyone else. Himpi have big litters, after all, because most
of them get killed young.

If I had to be a wife, then, I was glad to be a pretty wife; and
since I had seen my father dead and did not know how to get away
from Sai, I thought it best to marry. As a motherless and now father-
less daughter I was entirely without power in Terter House. As a
Condor's wife I might have some strength in Retforok House. Really
I did not care very much what I did at that time. Having lived for a
year with people who believed that animals and women were contemptible and unimportant, I had begun to feel that what I did was
indeed unimportant and could not be mindful or worthy of respect.

So I was married to that man, as a Condor's Daughter, wearing
all pure white clothes, which the Dayao use to mean that the wife is
a virgin. The clothes were beautiful and the wedding was cheerful.
It went on all day long, with musicians and round dances and acro-
bats and masses of good food and drink. I drank honey brandy and
got drunk. I was drunk when I went to Retforok House with my
husband, and drunk when we went to bed. We stayed in that bed-
room five days and nights. My fear and grief and shame and anger
all came out into sexual passion. I would not let him go, I filled him
up and emptied him out like a pitcher. I learned fucking from him
and then taught him his lessons back in forty different ways. He
was crazy for me and could not stay away from me for a day, all that
year long. Since I had little happiness I wanted pleasure, and took it
as often as I could.

My husband's first wife, Retforok Syasip Bele, was afraid of me
at first, through jealousy of course, and because people had told
her that I was an animal person, dangerous and crazy, like a wild
dog. She was afraid I would hurt her children. She was not stupid at
all, only ignorant. She had never been anywhere but the women's
quarters of two houses in Sai, and had been having a baby every
second summer since she was seventeen. When she found that I
did not bite, and did not eat babies, and even talked her language,
she began to make me welcome, and to see that both Esiryu and I
were treated well by the other women of the house. She was a
talkative, funny woman, not very thoughtful but quick and percep-

tive. She told me she was glad I was there for Dayat to fuck, because she was tired of his appetite and never interested in having sex when she was nursing, anyhow; but she said, "When I want another one, you'll have to send him across the passage, one night, at least!"

I said, "Another baby!"—disbelieving.

"These are all girls but one," she said.

I said, "Well, at least you could get pregnant by some man you liked?" That made her stare in disbelief, and then she laughed and said, "Ayatyu, you really are dirty! I don't like any men in this household, anyhow. We've got the best of the lot, I think." I agreed with her. Our husband was not a bully, and was good-natured and good-looking. She said, "But don't you let him know you even think about other men, he's very sensitive about that." And she told me that a woman who slept with a man not her husband would be killed by the husband's family. I did not believe that. Of course people kill each other out of jealousy and sexual rage, I knew that; but that was not what Syasip meant. She said, "No, no, you would be killed in public, to get the shame out of the house. You belong to Dayat, don't you see? You belong to him, and I belong to him, that's how it is."

I thought of my father saying in the common place of Sinshan, "But she belongs to me!" Now I had two eyes to see him with.

Early in the spring my husband said, "Ayatyu, good news from the west. Terter Abhao is back with the Victorious Army."

I said, "My father is dead."

Retforok Dayat laughed and said, "He's at the Palace now."

This too I did not believe, until I saw my father. He came to Retforok House to see me. He looked gaunt and fearfully weary, but he was not lying with his back broken, head downward, in a canyon in the wilderness. Still when I saw him here I saw him there also, as in images painted on glass placed one behind another.

We talked with pleasure and tenderness. He said, "I'm glad you have married, Ayatyu. Is it all right for you in this house?"

I said, "Yes, it's all right, and Dayat is kind. Is there any way I might go home?"

He looked at me and away, and shook his head.

"If you could take me as far as South City, I could go alone from there; I know the landmarks," I said.

He considered it only a moment before he said, "Listen, Ayatyu, since you chose to come here it can't be undone. If you run away from your husband, you put me into shame and disgrace. You belong to the Retforoks now. Better stay with them. You're well out of my house; things are not going well for us there. Make this your home. Put the Valley out of your mind!"

"My mind is not that small," I said. "It holds the Valley and the City and still I don't know where the end of it is. But it's only you that can make the City my home."

"No," he said, "I think only you can do that."

That was fairly said. And I continued to live as Dayat's pretty wife, knowing that what my father had said was true: he was living in disgrace, and any further disgrace brought upon him would endanger him. What I could do for him was to behave quietly and with patience until The Condor and his advisers no longer wanted somebody to blame for the loss of the war in the Six Rivers country.

It sounds strange when I say that disgrace could put a person in danger of his life; disgrace and shame are quite bad enough by themselves, among us in the Valley; but there, where every relationship was a battle, they were deadly. Punishment was violent. I have said that I was told that a hontik could be blinded for writing or reading, a woman killed for having sex; I did not see such things happen, but every day I did see or hear about violent punishments, striking children, beating slaves, locking up disobedient hontik or tyon; and later on, as I shall tell, it grew worse. It was frightening to live in this kind of continuous war. The Dayao seemed never to decide things together, never discussing and arguing and yielding and agreeing to do something before they did it. Everything was done because there was a law to do it or not do it, or an order to do it or not do it. And if something went wrong it seemed never to be the orders, but the people who obeyed them, that got blamed; and blame was usually physical punishment. I learned caution daily. I learned, whether I wanted to or not, how to be a warrior. Where life has been made into a battle, one has to fight.

The Retforoks were not in disgrace; indeed they had become favorites of The Condor. The chief of our household, Retforok Areman, and his youngest brother, my husband, Dayat, went often to the Palace, that tall house where The Condor lived. My husband, who liked talking as well as he liked sex, told me all about what he did and saw and heard there. I liked to listen, because it was interesting, although very strange and often as horrible as a ghost story. He told me what had happened to the son of The Condor: when he tried to escape from the part of the Palace where he had been walled in he was betrayed by people who had pretended to help him, and as punishment for disobeying the Law of One he was killed. The manner in which he was killed Dayat described at length. No mortal hand could kill the Son of the Son, so he was tied down and a strong current was run through his body until his heart and brain stopped; thus the electricity killed him in accordance with the Law of One. All his wives, kept women, children, and slaves were also killed. I said, "But then who will be the next Condor?" and Dayat told me that there was a second son, still a young child and still alive.

He told me also about the weapons the Dayao were building. The armies going out from Sai now were not making war to gain land, but to take copper, tin, and other metals from towns and peoples that had any store of them; and they made slaves of the Sensh, who worked the iron mines where Cloud River comes into the Dark River, and took all the iron the Sensh had used to trade with us and other people. The instructions for the materials needed and the making of the Great Weapons came, as well as I could tell, from the Exchange; and the Dayao were very skilled artisans in metal and

machinery, and excellent engineers, who could follow such instructions with understanding. I am not sure that their understanding of the use of the Exchange was very good, since no one but The
Condor and his High One-Warriors were permitted to learn the use
of it at all, and restricted knowledge is perverted knowledge, as
they say at the Library; but having little skill with the matter myself, I cannot be certain. In any case, the gathering of materials to
make the Great Weapons and the making of them took four years.

During that time I became pregnant twice. I aborted the first
pregnancy, because my husband had raped me when I told him I
did not want him and though I had no contraceptive. A Condor's
Daughter would go on and have the child of a rape, but I did not. It
was easy to get abortifacient from the tyon, who aborted more often
than they bore, and Esiryu helped me. Two years later, when I was
twenty-one years old, I wanted to become pregnant. Esiryu and
Syasip were good friends, but I was always bored, because there
was nothing to do but spin and sew and talk, always indoors and
always among people, never alone and therefore always lonely. I
kept thinking that a child would be like the Valley. It would be part
of me and I part of it; it would be beloved home. Maybe that part of
my soul that was like a tight string stretched between the City and
Sinshan would loosen and come back into my body if the child
consented to come into my womb. So I ceased to use the contraceptive, and after three months Dayat and I opened the door to the
child. It took that long because neither he nor I were living so easily
or eating so well as before, and though he still liked to talk to me he
did not have so much energy for fucking. Being a favorite of The
Condor was as difficult a life as being in disgrace with him. And all
the wealth of Sai was now going to The Condor's one purpose of
getting the materials and making the Great Weapons. Everything
was sacrificed to that. The Dayao were a people of true heroes.

The first of the Great Weapons was a hut made of iron plates
mounted on wheels that ran inside linked metal treads so that it

could climb a rough course clinging to it like a caterpillar without getting the wheels stuck. The wheels were turned by a powerful motor inside the hut. It was so strong that it could push over trees and houses, and mounted on it were guns to fire large shot and fire-bombs. It was huge and magnificent, making a noise like continuous thunder when it moved. It was displayed to the people of the City outside the walls. I came veiled with all the women of the Retforoks. We saw it push through a wall of bricks, thundering and shaking through the ruins it made, huge and blind, with a thick penis-snout. Three Condors inside it emerged from it like maggots from an ear of corn, small and soft. It was named Destroyer. It was to lead the army, making a path for the soldiers called The Way of Destruction. I went into my corner in Retforok House and lay there on the red rugs, imagining the Destroyer pushing against the oak trees named Gairga in Sinshan, pushing them over, pushing against High Porch House, pushing its wall in, pushing against the roof of the Blue Clay heyimas, pushing the roof in. I imagined its metal treads, caked with adobe, crushing cornstalks and cattle and children into the dirt, grinding them as millstones grind. I kept thinking about the Destroyer even after it broke through the roof of a hidden cave a few miles south of the City and destroyed itself with its own great weight, thrusting and wedging itself into the lava tube. Even then I dreamed of it moving in the cave, pushing the earth in, crushing darkness.

The Condor then set his purpose upon the machines called Nestlings. They were flying machines, condors with engines. The Dayao did not use balloons, but they knew how to make and fly light gliders, soaring off the cliffs above the black lava fields on the summer thermals like the buzzards and condors. Such gliding was a sacred sport, much prized and enjoyed by the young warriors. So there was great excitement over the planning of a self-powered flying vehicle. Dayat, however, did not share it. The Retforoks had worked and planned for the Destroyer, and when it came to grief they fell out of favor, and no longer went daily to the Palace, though they were not punished. Dayat was rather sore and gloomy, and sneered at the plans for the Nestlings. and the people building them. They required much less metal in their construction than the Destroyer, but they needed a good deal of fuel, and that was, Dayat said, a fatal weakness in them. The Condor had sent an army clear to the Range of Heaven to trade for petroleum fuel; it took them nearly a year to go and return, and then there was enough only for one Nestling to fly for a few days. But they began to make fuel out of alcohol from grain and shit, and two Nestlings that carried two men in them began to fly to Kulkun Eraian and back. The first day they did this was a holiday in Sai. Again we women all came out in our veils, and even the hontik cheered and danced when the Nestlings came flying over on their stiff black wings. That day I saw The Condor. He came out onto the balcony of the Palace to see his Nestlings fly over him. Women were not supposed to make him unclean with their eyes by looking at him, but I did not care about that, and was careful only not to be seen seeing him. He was dressed in golden cloth and wore a gold and black Condor helmet with the beak-mask, so I did not see the man at all, but only casings and surfaces, nothing of what was within. To be The Condor is to be outside.

The child was staying inside me that day, but thinking about coming out into the Second House. A few more days and it decided to be born and make me a daughter's mother. She was small, strong, and elegantly formed. Whenever I saw her pink flower-cunt I said heya in my heart, for if she had decided to be a son, that son would have "belonged" to my husband and been a Condor. Since she had decided to be a girl she was unimportant and did not matter to anyone but me and Esiryu and Syasip. Her family name was Retforok, and their priest named her Danaryu, which means Woman Given to One. The sound of it is pretty, and I used it before my husband and the others, but when I was alone with her I called her by one of the names quail have in Sinshan: Ekwerkwe, Watching Quail, the one of the covey who perches on a branch and watches out while the others are feeding on the ground, in the rainy season, before the birds pair off. Her eyes were bright like the eyes of a watching quail, and she was plump, and her hair made a little topknot, like a quail.

The rest of us were not very plump. The food in Sai was poor and scant in those years. One had ordered The Condor to make the City in the lava beds to be safe from enemies, but nothing much grew in that black desert, and they had to bring food in from places where food was. As they kept breeding, having as many children as possible, they kept having to go farther to get food, and many tyon and hontik that had used to grow crops, or herd, or hunt, were employed on the great labors of making the Weapons and supplying them with fuel. Grain that animals and humans would have eaten was eaten by the machines. The One-Warriors paraded through the streets of Sai in sacred procession, singing,

"Our food is Victory,
Battle is our wine,
In One we win all things!
One is our wealth!
There is no death!"

But I held mortality in my arms and suckled her, gave food to her, the person who was born because she would die, Watching Quail. And she fed my soul with her being, her needing. If One is anything other than a word, what can it be but food?

The sacrifices the Dayao were making were to win them wealth and comfort when the Nestlings went out to war. The trouble with the plan was that all the human peoples living anywhere near Dayao country had already moved away or, if they remained, stayed to make war, not to give tribute of food, slaves, or anything else. Anyone could see this, and as life got harder in Sai, the advice of the Terter family to move as a whole people southward into more prosperous lands began to be spoken of again. The old restless spirit of the Dayao was still in them, and many of their ways were better fitted to a nomad life than a settled one. Some of the Retforok women talked about going under the Condor's wing to the south where there would be plenty to eat, grass and trees and cattle and new things to see, and the men listened; though the talk of women was supposed to be ignorant, foolish babble, they listened. But since the Dayao did not talk decisions over in public council, as people usually do, there was no way for disagreements to come together into agreement. So ideas became opinions, and these made factions, which diverged and became fixed opponents.

The Retforok Condors were among the faction that said the City must remain where it was, where the finger of light had pointed, and only the soldiers would follow the fire-track of the Nestlings when they went to war. And though the women kept talking of their wish to find a better place to live, they were also frightened of moving, since most of them had lived their whole life inside the City, inside the houses, inside the rooms. They were as ignorant of other places and people as I was when I first went to Kastoha-na. Even the soldiers were ignorant about how other people lived and thought, though they had been among them for years. In the Finders Lodge they say that trading and learning go together, as do ignorance and war. And I think also, because the Dayao said that everything belonged to One, they forced themselves to think in twos: either this, or that. They could not be among the Many.

Before Ekwerkwe was a year old, there began to be trouble among the enslaved people who worked in the fields and mines and workshops, and even some of the farmers, the tyon, had begun to steal off to become forest-living people, or back east into the Basin to live with the jackrabbits in the sagebrush. At a mine up in the Crater Lake country a group of hontik men killed the Condor soldiers who were commanding them, and went off into the Silver Mountains. I knew about this because The Condor ordered that ten hontik of the City be killed as punishment or payment for the deaths of the ten Condors killed at the mine. This was fair, if all Condors were one and all non-Condors the other: either this, or that. The ten hontik men were tied to posts in front of the Palace at the end of the wide, beautiful street. The One-Warriors prayed aloud to One, and Condor soldiers armed with guns shot the men dead while they stood there tied. I did not see this, but was told about it. It was called the Execution of the Law of One. When I heard about it, I felt my head turning. I saw the sunlight in the common place of Kastoha-na, but it was not my mother I saw there: I saw the black vultures stooping to tear at their own bellies, pulling out their own entrails and eating them. I ran into the room where Ekwerkwe was and took her in my arms, and we sat on the floor in the corner for a long time till the vision and the sickness passed. But from that day I had no more heart to be a woman of the Condor or to follow their way. I was living among people who were going the wrong way. All I sought was to get my daughter and her mother away from them, to any other place.

It was a long time before I could do that, for Sai was more and more like an ant-hill against which another ant-hill is making war, closed and desperate. When The Condor sent the Nestlings out to drop fire-bombs on the forests and villages of the Ziaun people southwest of Kulkun Eraian, several other peoples joined with the Ziaun to fight the war. They had made plans ahead, meeting and talking and communicating news through the Exchange. They could not hurt the Nestlings when they flew, as they went above the range of guns, and the field from which they flew and to which they returned was protected by a great number of Condor soldiers; so one person, probably a man or woman who had been a hontik slave and knew where things were and how to behave and talk, came at night and set fire to the fuel storage tanks. They exploded. The person was burned to death, but the Nestlings were left without fuel. While more was being made, The Condor sent young warriors on gliders to fly over the Ziaun villages, but the gliders were easy to shoot down, and none returned. So much of the harvest of that autumn, not only grain but potatoes, turnips, and so on, went to make fuel for the Nestlings that the storehouses of the City were emptied out; they used the seed grain. All the songs were about the glory of dying for One. All the men of the Dayao were intent to kill all that they could kill, and the women to praise them for it.

One day early in the autumn of Ekwerkwe's third year it was possible for me to visit Terter House with another Retforok woman who had relatives there. We had asked to do this many times, and at last the Retforok men gave us permission and ordered several slave men to accompany us. Ekwerkwe walked beside me from Retforok House between the blind walls of the City street to Terter House. That was the only time she ever walked that way.

Terter Gebe had died the year before, and my father was the chief of his household, but he had been living hidden indoors like a Dayao woman so as to remain forgotten by The Condor and the One-Warriors, who were *executing* people called enemies of the Condor every day now, tearing out their own bowels. Terter Abhao had not seen his daughter's daughter for two years.

He was in the room where I had been taken to see Terter Gebe years ago. He looked old, being very pale and entirely bald, and stooped in his bearing. My heart sank when I saw him, for I had hoped that he might not be as sick as all the other men in this place. He looked sick, but when he looked at Ekwerkwe his smile was from the Valley, it seemed to me.

"So this is Danaryu Belela," he said when she went to him. She was not afraid of him; she liked all men, as little girls often do.

I said, "This is Danaryu to Da," that is One, "but also she has a first name of her own, Ekwerkwe. That's the quail that calls its name when it sees danger, and then the covey runs, or rises up and flies."

He looked at me.

The child patted his hand to get his attention and said, "I'm Ekwerkwe."

"That is a good name," he said. "You, Ayatyu, how is it with you?"

"I'm bored," I said. "There's nothing to read here." I used our Valley word for read.

He looked at me again awhile. "Owl," he said, in the Valley language, and smiled again. "Do you get enough to eat? You're very thin."

"My stomach can fast, but my mind is starving," I said. "Father, we made half a journey together, once."

He nodded his head very slightly. He watched the child for a while, and talked to the other people in the room, Condors and Daughters of his house and Retforok House. Presently he said to me, no one else hearing, "When they remember me, you might be remembered too."

I saw that place in front of the Palace in his face, the stakes and the bloody pavement.

"After all, the child!" he said.

My heart gave a great leap, and I said, "You will come—?"

He shook his head and said, "Wait."

Presently, when the Retforok people were making ready to leave, he said, "This night Ayatyu Bele will sleep here; I have not seen my grandchild for so long."

The Retforok women were uneasy, and fussed; the eldest of them said, "Great Condor, the woman's husband the Condor Retforok Dayat might be displeased, since he did not give permission for her to stay," and another of them said, "It is only a granddaughter," and another one, malicious, said, "The Great Condor Terter Abhao might ennoble Retforok House by visiting it sometimes."

There is no way that men could make women into slaves and dependents if the women did not choose to be so. I had hated the Dayao men for always giving orders, but the women were more hateful for taking them. I felt as if all the anger of all my years in Sai was swelling up in me, and that I could no longer keep it back; but fortunately my father—always a good general—said, "Well, the Great Condor Retforok Dayat will not be displeased with the woman if she stays here a few hours longer. I will have her sent home after dinner tonight." They could not argue much over that, and so they left me, and Esiryu with me. The moment they were gone my father sent for this man and that woman and made us ready to depart. In the little time we had, all he could do was send two men of his household with me and Ekwerkwe and Esiryu; he could not take us himself or send soldiers with us as he had hoped to do. I said, "Will they send men after us?" and he said, "Early in the morning I will go out with a patrol, and they will follow me, thinking I took you as I brought you."

We had dressed as tyon, and were standing in the hallway of Terter House. I said to my father, "Will you come ever?"

He was holding the child in his arms. She was sleepy and rested her head against his neck. He spoke with his head bowed to the child's head, so that I do not know if he spoke to her or to me. "Tell your mother not to wait, not to wait for me," he said. Then he stroked Ekwerkwe's hair with his big hand and carefully gave her to me to carry.

I said, "But you will be punished—you will be—" I could not say that word, the stakes and the ropes and the blood.

He said, "No, no. You ran away when you left my house. And I won't be here for punishment. I was ordered to take a patrol west to White Mountain; we'll leave a little early, that's all. I'll be out of trouble, over there."

Then I knew he was going to the canyon where I had seen him lying. But that is the kind of knowledge that cannot be said or used; so I embraced him and he held me and the child closely for a little while, and then we left him in that house.

We went out the back gate quietly in the early dark.

One of the men with us had been with us when I came from the Valley with my father, a capable, grave man named Arda. I did not know the other, Dorabadda, who had served with my father in the Six Rivers wars. They had the loyalty prized by the Dayao; they were like sheepdogs, trustworthy, tense, brave, and mindless, doing what another person thought, minding him.

The gate of the City was always guarded and people entering or leaving were questioned, but there was no trouble there. Dorabadda said that Esiryu and I were tyon belonging to some high official at the Palace, being sent back to the farms because "they're no good anymore, both pregnant," and there was a lot of joking about the One-Warriors, who are supposed to be lifelong celibates, and whom the soldiers detest and fear. Dorabadda talked easily and got us out without suspicion or delay. So we left Sai. The lights of the City glittered brilliant in the black plain and the dark air, a wonderful shining. All that night as we went slowly across the lava desert the City shone behind us. We passed the sleeping child among us; sometimes she woke for a while and looked into the darkness, watching. She had seldom seen the stars.

At the first lightening we left the great road and struck off across the lava plain, and at day's coming we took shelter in a cave and slept there all day long. We talked, and I learned a great deal I had not known living in Retforok House. Arda said that we would have to stay away from the villages and farms of the tyon, because they would very likely attack us to rob us or to kill the men and rape the women. I said, "But you're Condors, you give orders to tyon!" He said, "We did." So I found out that outside the walls of the City all that giving and taking of orders had ceased and there was only disorder. We travelled at night through all the Dayao lands, hiding, going on the desert ways.

Then it was, as they say, from the meat grinder into the chopping bowl. Leaving the farmlands of the Dayao, we came into the countries of the victims and enemies of the Dayao.

When we came to Dark River, Arda said we could travel by day, and I said, "Then you should go home, Arda, Dorabadda. Go tell Terter Abhao that you left his daughter on the way to her home, and all was well with her."

Arda said, "He ordered us to take you there."

I said, "Listen. You are good friends of mine now, but if you stay with me you'll do me harm. With you, Esiryu and Ekwerkwe and I are Dayao. Without you, we are two women and a baby, not having a war with anybody."

The men, following their orders, refused to go back. I refused to go on with them. I did not want them killed for us, or to be killed because I was with them. Since I would not even get up from where we had camped by the river, they had to talk about it, and we talked about it for hours. They found it very hard to disobey my father, or to listen to a woman; but they saw it was true that their presence put us in more danger than their absence. At last they decided, on Dorabadda's suggestion, to follow us, an hour or so behind us, as if they were pursuing us. It was a good solution to the disagreement, except for one fault: it left them still in danger. They would not count that as of any weight in the matter; so we embraced them and left them by the river. We went on, Esiryu and Ekwerkwe and I, following along the northern shore of the Dark River towards the high hills.

We came into the country of the people who call themselves Fennen. We were careful now to do just the opposite of what we had done at first: we travelled in broad daylight and in the most open ways, and if we came near any human place we made noise and spoke aloud so they would hear and see us coming. We spoke with people by sign language and the little TOK that I had learned in Sinshan; Erwerkwe's prattle was better than ours, since babies all speak the same language and everybody understands it. On the fourth evening after we had parted from Arda and Dorabadda, a family living in a wooden house by the great springs at Wallwell took us in for the night, sharing sweet milk and acorn mush with us and giving us warm beds. I slept sound and well for the first time since we had begun travelling, but in the morning waking I heard the people of the household talking outside and by the sound of their voices knew something bad had happened. By TOK and signs I found what it was. They had killed one of our friends from ambush; hearing them talk Dayao, they had shot without waiting to hear more. One was dead, the other had escaped them. I do not know whether it was Arda or Dorabadda that was killed, nor do I know whether the other got back safe to Sai. When I left that City of The Condor no word, nothing ever came to me from that place again.

I could not help crying for the grief and guilt I felt, and Esiryu tried to make me stop, fearing that the Fennen people would guess that we were Dayao women; Esiryu lived in great fear every hour of our journey. But the mother of the Fennen household, seeing my tears, wept too, and said to me in signs and words that there was too much war, too much killing going on, that the young men of her house were sick and carried guns, like crazy people.

We went on, very slowly, for Ekwerkwe's legs were very short. Though it was autumn, it seemed that the days grew brighter as we went.

Down near the confluence of the Dark River with the Great River of the Marshes, at a hilly place that is called Loklatso on the maps in the heyimas, we met some people coming northeastward. I saw a person on the side of a hill, and thought he was a dream, a ghost, a Four-House person: I knew his face. He was my cousins' stepfather, Changing Always of Madidinou, who had taken the Warrior Lodge name Maggot. I had known this man all my life. I did not know the men with him, but they were dressed in Valley clothes, and were short and slight and round-limbed, with round faces, Valley faces, and wore their hair in Warrior Lodge braids; and one of them called back to the others in my language, the language I had heard only my own souls speak in dream for seven years: "Some women are coming!"

I came on towards them and called out, "Changing Always! So you are here, my cousin's husband! How is it in Madidinou?" I did not care if they were ghosts or living, Warriors or friends—they were from the Valley, from my home, and I ran to them and embraced Maggot. He was so amazed that, Warrior though he was, he let me do so, and then peering into my face said, "North Owl?"

I said, "Oh, no, no, no longer—I am Woman Coming Home!"

So my name for the middle of my life came to me.

We camped that night with the men from the Valley in a willow grove of the hills of Loklatso, and talked a long time. I asked them to tell me all they could about Sinshan and the Valley, and they asked me to tell them all I could about the Dayao, for they were going to Sai. The slave mind that I had learned to have in Sai was still in my head, thinking like a slave, and after we had been talking awhile I began to lie to them. I was afraid they might force us to go with them as guides and translators. They asked me to do so once, and I said no, and that was all right, but then they asked me again, and then again, and by then I distrusted and feared them as I did Dayao men, and as I had never distrusted or feared Valley men.

At first I had told them plainly what I knew: that the way to Sai might get more dangerous for them every step, and that the Dayao people were living in great disorder, in violence and hunger.

Maggot listened with a Warrior face, that expression that had always exasperated me, of one who has superior knowledge; and he told me, "The Condor have great weapons. Flying engines and fire-bombs. They have great power, the greatest in this part of the world."

I said, "That is true, but also they are killing each other and starving!"

One of the others, a man from Telina-na whose name I do not remember, said to Maggot, "A woman; running away," and shrugged.

A younger man, that one's son, wearing undyed clothes, asked me, "Have you seen the Great Condor One fly?"

I said, "There is a man called The Condor, but he doesn't fly, he doesn't even walk. He never comes out of the house he lives in."

I did not know whether the young man meant The Condor or was trying to talk about the Nestlings, but it did not matter. They did not want to hear what I could tell them, any more than I wanted to hear why they were going to Sai. But I saw that Maggot, for all his superior look, was beginning to be uneasy; and I stopped telling them that the Dayao were a sick people destroying themselves. I began to behave the way Dayao women behaved with men, smiling and agreeing with everything and pretending not to know about anything except their own bodies and babies. The thought of taking one step back on the road to the City made me act this lie. So Maggot would ask, "Are there any Condor armies on this road along Dark River?" and I would answer, "I don't know, I think we did see some soldiers somewhere but I don't know the names of places. Maybe we were in some pine forests then? Or near the volcanoes? But maybe they weren't Condor soldiers, maybe they were somebody else. And you know, we came onto this road just by luck, we were wandering for a month eating roots and berries, that's why we're so thin. I don't really know where we've been." All this so they would not take me with them for a guide.

When they asked about Esiryu, again I lied without plan or hesitation. Esiryu had kept as much out of sight as she could; she was in terror of the men. I said, "She left her husband, and had to run away. So did I," and then I said, "You know the Condor kill women who leave their husbands. And they kill the men they find with such women."

That was my best lie, because it was true. It did the trick. Next morning the Valley Warriors went on their way towards the City and let us go on southwestwards. When we parted I said to them, "Go carefully, be mindful, men of the Valley!" To the young man, who was of my House, I said, "My brother, in the dry land, think of the creek running. My brother, in the dark house, think of the bowl of blue clay." Those words Cave had given me were all I had to give him. Maybe they would be of use to him, as they had been to me.

I do not know what became of those men after we parted at Loklatso.

From Loklatso on, we were coming through countries that had not been much infected by the City's sickness. When I had come through them with my father and the soldiers years ago we had kept away from human settlements and travelled like coyotes. This time I travelled like a human person. At each town or farmstead we came to, they would speak to us. I knew very little TOK, and many of the people living in those places spoke only their own languages, but with signs and expressions everything needful can be said, and hospitality is the flowing of the River itself. Not all of them were generous of heart, but not one of them turned us away hungry. The children of the farmsteads and small villages were excited to meet a new child, one they did not know, and sometimes they were shy and hid away. But Ekwerkwe, meeting strangers every day and playing with children she had never seen, had become bold, and would go looking for them. They all shouted their different languages at her, and she shouted back words of Dayao and Kesh and Fennen and Klatwish, and they taught one another songs that they did not understand the words of. It was a very different journey with her from the journey north with my father! Only Esiryu found it hard. She was leaving home, not going towards it, and she was afraid of people: not cautious and mindful of difference, but afraid like a stray dog, expecting to be hurt. To a Dayao woman outside the walls of her father's or her husband's house all men are dangerous, because to Dayao men all women unprotected by a man are victims; they call them not women or people, but cunts. Esiryu thought of herself that way, as something to be raped, and so she could not give any trust to these strangers we stayed with. She always stood behind me, and I called her Shadow Woman. Often I thought that she should not have come, and that I had done wrong to bring her with me; but she would not have let me go without her; on that evening that we left Terter House, she had said she would sooner die than live there without me and Ekwerkwe. And her companionship was a great comfort and help to me on our journey. Though her fear sometimes infected and troubled my feelings, sometimes it made me braver than I really was, when I had to say to her, "See, there's nothing to fear from these people!" and go forward to meet them.

Going with the little quail's legs, ten miles was a good day's journey for us. We came on down to the rope-and-boat ferry at Ikul and crossed the River of the Marshes there with some Amaranth people taking gold home from the high mining country. We three went west across the marshes, then south along the foothills to the place called Utud where the Chiryan Road begins, and came through the hills on that road. That is wild country. Not a human person was on that road but ourselves. Coyotes sang all night, the crazy-old-woman songs and the high-moon songs, up on the high hillsides; the grass was full of mice; deer sprang aside, or watched us from the thickets, all day long; mourning doves called continually, and the air at evening would darken with the vast flocks of pigeons and other birds; always at noon we looked up to see the redwing hawk, circling. I picked up feathers on that way as we went and saved them, feathers of nine kinds of bird. As we walked there the first rain fell. I walked singing a song that came to me out of the rain and the feathers, the words given to me:

"There is no knowing,
only going on,
only going by, ah ya hey.
I am the great being,
the grass bowing."

When I came back into the Valley of my being I brought this song and the feathers of nine birds from the wilderness, the coyote's way; and from the seven years I lived in the City of Man I brought my womanhood, the child Ekwerkwe, and my friend Shadow.

We came down Buda Creek into Deep Valley, then down Hana-if Creek to the River, singing heya at every step. We were very hungry, having lived off seeds and gatherings up in the hills, and I had not been willing to use our time in gathering, which is slow work even when there is plenty; I had hurried us along. We turned downriver and came past the Geyser and the Baths to Kastoha-na.

We went to the Blue Clay heyimas there. I said to the people there, "I am Woman Coming Home, from Sinshan, of this House. This is Ekwerkwe, from the Condor's City, of this House. This is Esiryu, from the Condor's City, of no House, our friend." They made us welcome in that heyimas.

While we stayed there I spoke of the men we had met at Loklatso, and was told that there had been a meeting of the Valley people about the Warriors, and that that lodge had stopped being. Maggot and the others had said nothing about this.

The scholars of my heyimas in Kastoha said that I might do well to go up to Wakwaha and give to the Libraries and to the Exchange what I knew about the doings and intentions of the Dayao people. I said I would do that, but first I wanted to go to my own town.

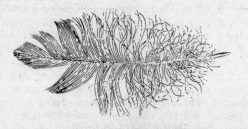

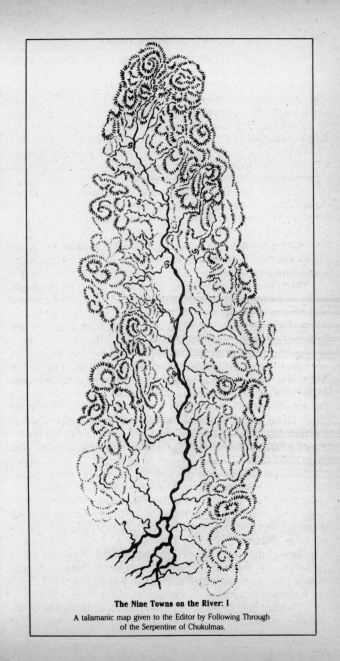

The Nine Towns on the River: I

A talismanic map given to the Editor by Following Through
of the Serpentine of Chukulmas.

So we walked down the southwest bank of the River along the Old Straight Road to beautiful Telina. There we slept at the heyimas and went on very early in the morning. It was raining thick, fine rain. We could hardly make out the grey hills across the Valley, and on our right the hills nearby coming down from the Spring Mountain, Sow Mountain, and Sinshan Mountain looked vast in the mist and moving rain.

> Going there, going there,
> Going where we went
> Dying into the Valley.
> Going there, going there,
> The rainclouds down the Valley.

We turned onto the Amiou path through Sinshan Fields, and came past Blue Rock and the outer paddocks, and crossed Hechu Creek on the cattle-bridge. The creek was already running lively in the rain. I saw the rocks, paths, trees, hills, fields, barns, fences, gates, stiles, groves, places that my heart knew. I told Ekwerkwe and Shadow their names, and said heya to each one. We came to the bridge over Sinshan Creek under the high alder and the oaks at the side of Adobe Hill. I said to Ekwerkwe, "There, do you see, in the path by the paddock gate, that place is where your grandfather, my father, Terter Abhao, stands for us now. There he came once on foot to me. There he came again for me, riding a great horse, leading a mare for me. Passing this place may we have him in mind in the days to come."

"There he is," Ekwerkwe said, watching. She saw what my memory saw. Shadow saw nothing.

We walked across the bridge into the town. It is only four steps long, that bridge.

As we turned right along Hard Canyon Creek, some children came by: I did not know them. That was strange! That made me go cold through my body and soul. But Ekwerkwe, who had learned to greet all strangers, let go my hand and looked at the children, greeting them in a small voice in their language. She said, "So you are here, children of the Valley."

Two of them ran away behind the smithy. Two were courageous and stood to face the foreigners. One of them said, in an even smaller voice than Ekwerkwe's, "So you are here," but she did not know what to call us.

"In what household do you live, children of the Valley?" I said, and after a while the boy, who was eight or nine, motioned with his head to Chimbam House. Then I thought of Ready's baby, born the summer before I left Sinshan. I said, "Perhaps you are a brother of my House, and live in Ready's household?" He nodded yes. I said, "Tell me, please, brother, are there Blue Clay people living now in High Porch House?"

He nodded yes again, but was still too shy to speak. So we went on, I with my new fear inside me. Why had I not thought that seven years had passed in Sinshan as well as in Sai? I had not asked Maggot nor the people in the heyimas in Kastoha and Telina about my household, because I had not been willing to think that any change had come to them.

We came to the foot of the northeast staircase that leads up to the balcony of the first floor. I looked at my companions: the little wet quail ragged and shining in the rain, the thin, bright-eyed Shadow standing wrapped, as I was, in a black cloak. My father had given us these cloaks the night we left; they were such as the soldiers wore. They were the color of the lava beds, the color of the Condor, the color of the night we left that City. I took mine off and folded it on my arm before I went up the stairs of my house. My feet knew the distance between the treads. My hand knew the rain-wet railing. My whole mind knew the smell of that rain-wet wood. My eyes knew the door frame and the door of oakwood standing ajar for the rainy wind to enter. The Bear had gone before me. The Coyote came with me. I said, "I was born in this house and have come back to it. Shall I come in?"

For many breaths no one replied. Then my mother, Towhee, came and opened the door wide, looking at us with frightened eyes. She had become small and strange-looking. Her clothes were not clean.

I said, "So you are here, my mother. Look here, this Ekwerkwe has made me her mother and you her grandmother!"

She said, "Valiant is dead. She has been dead a long time now."

She let us come in, but she did not touch me, and drew back when I would have touched her. For some while I think she did not understand who Ekwerkwe was, and that she was now the grandmother, for when I used the word, again she spoke of Valiant. She did not look at Shadow or ask about her; it was as if she did not see her at all.

My grandmother had died two summers after I left. My grandfather had gone back to Chumo after that, and had died not long after, people told me. Towhee had lived alone in the household for five years. Since the Lamb Lodge had stopped having meetings and

Soul Mountain

wakwa, she had stayed much alone, not coming to the heyimas, not dancing the great dances. In summer she went no longer to Gahheya meadow, but farther up the ridges, staying by herself. My grandmother's old friend Shell and my side-grandfather, Nine-point, had been mindful of her, but she did not want to be with people, neither human nor the sheep of our family nor even the old trees on Sinshan Ridge, the grey-leaved olives. Her souls had shrunk away and unmade themselves. That is the danger of going backward in the way she had done when she took back her child-name. She had not gyred, but had closed the circle. She was like the sticks of a fire put out by the rain. She neither wanted us to live with her in the household nor wanted us not to be there; everything was much the same to her. She would not let things change any more for her. I gave her a last name in my mind: Ashes. But I never spoke it until all her names were given to the fire in the Night of Mourning of the World Dance in the year she died.

Some people of Sinshan came to greet me with much kindness. Turning, who had been Cricket and had played the games of Shikashan with me, came hurrying and weeping to meet me, and later she made a song of my journey and return and gave it to me. Garnet, who had been Lark Rising when he played with us, had married an Ounmalin woman, but he came over to talk to me. Old Dada who never learned how to think kept giving me feathers to tell me he was glad I had come back; for days, whenever I went to the heyimas he was waiting around with his head down, holding out a chicken feather a little way towards me, and when I took it and spoke he would smile with his head bent down and go on along. Some of the older dogs remembered me and greeted me as a friend. But among the human people, there were some who were afraid of infection and would not come anywhere near me and Shadow, or even Ekwerkwe. Some very superstitious men blew at us whenever we passed them, so that they could not breathe in our outbreath. They believed their heads would turn backwards on their necks if they caught the Sickness of Man from us. Sinshan is indeed a small town. People in small towns have beliefs the way caves have bats. But there were also people of generous understanding in that small town, and what they offered me I was now able to take, without the fear and false pride of my adolescence.

My father was a no-House person, and my daughter's father also, so only through one grandmother was Ekwerkwe of the Valley and the Blue Clay. But nothing was said of that in the heyimas, and the children did not call her half-person. Truly I think some illness had gone out of the Valley that had been there when the Condor was there. There were people there who had been crippled, like my mother; but they were no longer sick.

Esiryu would not be called Esiryu, but took Shadow for her name, and for a long time it seemed she wanted to be a shadow, there and not there. She was tense and distrustful of herself and all other people. She did not know how to stroke the cat, and the sheep might as well have been wild dogs, to her; she took a long time to learn our Valley language, and she was bewildered by our ways. "I am an outsider, I come from outside, and you are all inside your world!" she said to me, when they were singing the Sun, and all around the common place and the dancing place the trees stood wonderfully flowering in winter with feathers, shells, gilt oakgalls, and carven birds. "Why are there children in the trees tying wooden flowers to them? Why do people in white clothes come to the windows to frighten Ekwerkwe at night? Why don't you eat

beefsteak? How can Jay and Stag Alone be married if they're both men? I will never understand anything here!"

But she was in fact quick to understand; and though a number of people returned her distrust, many came to like her for her good humor and honest generosity, and some even valued her because she was a woman of the Dayao, not in spite of it, saying, "This is the only woman of the Condor that came to us; she is her own gift." After she had lived a year in High Porch House she said to me one day, "It's easy to live in Sinshan. It's easy being here. In Sai it was hard; everything was hard; being was hard. Here it's soft."

I said, "The work here is hard." We were weeding cotton in Amhechu Field when she said that. "You never worked this hard in Sai. And I never worked at all there, except for that damned sewing."

"Not that kind of hard and soft," she said. "Animals live softly. They don't make it hard to live. Here people are animals."

I said, "Hontik."

"Yes. Here even the men are animals. Here everybody belongs to everybody. A Dayao man belongs to himself. He thinks everything else belongs to him, women, animals, things, the world."

I said, "We call that living outside the world."

"It's hard to live there," she said. "For the men, and the others."

I said, "But what about Valley men?"

She said, "Soft."

"Soft like jellied eels," I said, "or soft like pumas walking?"

"I don't know," she said. "They're strange. I'll never understand any of the men here!"

That, too, was not strictly true.

All the years I lived in Sai, before I was married to Dayat and after, from time to time my mind would turn to my cousin Spear, not with pain and anger as when I left the Valley, but with a kind of aching that was welcome to me because it was not like anything I felt there in Sai or ever would feel there. Although Spear had turned away from me, yet as children and again as adolescents we had sought each other's company, and our hearts had chosen each other, and even when he was so far away and I could not expect ever to see him again, still he was part of myself and part of the Valley, he was in my soul and familiar to my mind. Sometimes in the latter months of my pregnancy I had thought about dying, as a woman occupied with giving birth must do; and when I had thought about my own dying, that I might die there in the foreign place, outside the Valley, and go to that earth, such a dreariness would come into me that my heart sinks even now recalling it. At such bad times my help was sometimes to think of Gahheya meadow, the shadows of the wild oats against the rock, and sometimes to think of my cousin sitting on the bank of little Buckeye Creek looking for the thorn in his foot, saying to me, "North Owl! can you see this damned thorn?" And those thoughts were life to me.

Spear's sister who had been Pelican when we were children and now was Lily lived in their household in Madidinou with an Obsidian husband, but Spear had gone to live in Chukulmas at the time the Warrior Lodge stopped being. Late in the dry season, that year I came home, he came back to Madidinou to his sister's house. We met when he came to Sinshan to dance the Water.

I danced that year. I was dancing the deer-hoof music, the Water Shaking. I saw him standing with some Blue Clay people and Shadow and Ekwerkwe. After the dance I went over there. He greeted me, saying, "That's a good middle name that came to you, Woman Coming Home. Do you have to go away again so that it can go on being true?"

"No," I said, "I'm learning to be my name."

I saw that he had in his mind the last words I had said to him in the vineyards in the evening in late autumn years ago: that I had given him a name in my heart. He did not ask for that name now, nor did I give it to him.

After that night he came often to Sinshan. He was a member of the Wine Art, a skilled vintner, and worked in the wineries of both towns.

He had lived some years with a woman in Chukulmas, but they had not married. In Madidinou he lived as his sister's brother. When I kept meeting him in Sinshan, I saw that he was beginning to think about making our old friendship into a new one. That touched me, for I was grateful to him for having given me the memory to help me when I was afraid of dying in a strange country; and also it pleased my self-esteem. That had been hurt badly by his turning away from me, and it still craved satisfaction. But aside from that, I did not want him very much as a friend or lover. He was a handsome man with a straight back and a lithe walk, but I felt the Warrior still in him. He was too much like a Dayao man. Not like my father, who though a True Condor and soldier all his life was in mind and heart no warrior at all; Spear was more like my husband Dayat, who though he never fought with his body or weapons made all life into war, a matter of victory or defeat. Most men who had been in the Warrior Lodge and had stayed in the Valley had let a new name come to them, but Spear had kept his. When I looked at him now I saw that his eyes were restless and troubled; he did not look clearly at the world, as the puma gazes. That had not been the right name for him; Spear was better.

After I had made it clear that I was not interested in him except as my old friend and cousin, he still kept coming around, and Shadow was always glad to see him. That worried me a little. Bold, restive, strong-willed Esiryu, often in trouble for disobedience or insolence with her "superiors" in Sai, was the gentle Shadow in Sinshan, always hanging back and looking down. It was that behavior which suited Spear. Perhaps he was trying to make me jealous, but also he liked talking with Shadow. People who make life into a war fight it first with people of the other sex, I think, striving to defeat them, to win a victory. Shadow was too intelligent and too generous of soul to want to defeat Spear or any man, but all her education among the Dayao had fitted her to play the already-defeated one, the loving enemy. I did not like the way Spear began to strut when he walked with her. But she was growing stronger; there was more of the puma in her eyes than in his. I thought he might end up her hontik and never know it.

If Esiryu became another person as Shadow, so Ayatyu was becoming another person as Coming Home, but, as I had said to my cousin, I had to learn how to do that. It took me a long time.

In Sai I had been restless, longing for work to do. In Sinshan I found it. There was a great deal to do for the household. My mother had not kept up the house or the spinning or the gardens, and had let the family sheep go with the town flock. The pleasure of doing and making had died out of her with all other fires.

Maybe it was because I had seen what the passion of love did to my parents' lives that I kept shy of any man who might have brought such passion to my life. I was just beginning to learn to see and I did not want to be blinded. Neither of my parents had ever truly seen the other. To Abhao, Willow of Sinshan had been a dream—waking life was all elsewhere. To Willow, the Condor Abhao had been all the world—nothing had mattered but him. So they gave their great passion and their fidelity to no one, not truly to one another but to people who did not exist, a dream-woman, a god-man, and it was wasted, a gift to no one. My mother had gone out of her own being after that nonbeing, had spent all passion on nothing. Now nothing was left of it or of her. She was empty, cold, poor.

I decided I wanted to be rich. If my mother could not warm

herself at least I would keep her warm. Even that first year that I was home, I made a dance cloak to give to our heyimas. I wove it on Valiant's loom, which had stood unused in the second room of the household. As I wove I watched the silver crescent bracelet on my arm shine across the warp, forth and back.

Shell had looked after our ewes in lambing time, and at shearing had given the wool of them to the storehouses; there were still five sheep in the family, two wethers and three ewes. When I went to work with them I always took Ekwerkwe with me. She was ready to learn from them and the other animals of the pastures and the hills. In the City there had been nobody but human people, and her education had been grossly incomplete. On our journey to the Valley she had walked all the long way among the living Four-House people; she had tasted Coyote's milk. Now in the Valley she wanted to be with the sheep and in the barns with the milk-cows and in dogtown with the puppies, like the other children, all day long. She did not like the gardens and the gathering-places so well; the work there is slower and harder and the results are not so easy to see, except at harvest time. That learning comes slowly.

Ninepoint's household kept himpi, and they gave us four young ones from a litter. I built up the old pen under the balcony and gave Ekwerkwe the himpis' care, and she nearly smothered them with mindfulness at first and then forgot to give them water so that they nearly died, and she wept with remorse, and learned; she also learned to whistle like a himpi. The cat downstairs in High Porch House had kittens, and a couple of tabbies spilled over into our household. One day near our gathering trees I found a half-grown kid, lame and bleeding; wild dogs had killed the mother and mauled the kid. I doctored her as best I could, carried her down the ridge to town, and kept her penned till she recovered. As she was a stray, she became one of our household, and presently five of us were goats, very pretty tan-and-black longhairs, giving excellent mohair for weaving.

I had always liked potting more than any other skill, but with sheep, goats, and a good loom, it seemed that weaving was there to do; so I did it. I took what was given, since I wanted to give. The trouble with weaving was that I did not like to stay indoors. I had had enough of roofs, for seven years. But all through the dry season, from the Moon to the Grass, I had the loom outside on the balcony, and it was pleasant, working there.

Shadow, brought up as a "dressing-maid" in Sai, did not even know how to cook. She and Ekwerkwe learned that skill together. My mother got used to her company; she spoke very little to

Shadow, but came to like being with her and working with her. Shadow learned gardening with her and with Shell. After a while she began talking to women in the Blood Lodge, receiving instruction, and with women and men in the Blue Clay heyimas; and in her third summer in Sinshan, at the dancing of the Water, she became a Blue Clay person, living in my House, my sister, as she had been in love and loyalty since we met as adolescents in Terter House. Later on she joined the Planting Lodge. Once when we were spading the heavy black adobe of our garden plot at planting time, when the clay clogged the spade in masses so that one of us had to dig one spadeful and hand the spade to the other to clean while digging one more spadeful with a second spade, which the other then cleaned so that it could dig one more spadeful . . . while we were sweating at that in a fine, cold rain, she said to me, "My father was a tyon, a farmer. He sold me to Terter House when I was five to be trained as a maid, to be spared that work. Now look at me!" She tried to lift her foot, and it too was clogged and clotted with the sticky black dirt. "I am stuck in the mud," she said. She scraped a great weight of adobe off the shovel and handed it back to me, and we went on digging. We did not often talk about the City. Even for her, I think, those years now seemed like a feverish, restless night, which is long and dark and full of thoughts and emotions and miseries, a travail of the soul, but which will not let itself be remembered when the daylight shines.

I have forgotten to say that in the year I came home, after the Sun was danced, I left Ekwerkwe and Shadow and Towhee, and went alone to Kastoha-na and to Wakwaha to relate my story of living with the Dayao and to answer questions that people wanted to ask concerning them and their weapons and plans for war. At that time much information was given and taken at the Exchange concerning the Condor's armies; they told me that the Nestlings were flying again, and had set towns afire in the country southwest of Kulkun Eraian, but that there were no Condor armies outside the Condor's lands. While I was there, a message on the Exchange from the Six Rivers country said that people there had seen a Nestling fall out of the air on fire; and the Exchange itself confirmed this when the scholars asked it. So many peoples were using the Exchange, from the Basin and the Inland Sea up the coast and clear round to the Crater Lake country and north even of that, that everything the City's armies did was reported and known at once, they told me, and no one could be taken by surprise or left without aid if they asked for it. I listened to what they said and answered what they asked as best I could, but at that time I did not want to hear anything about the Dayao, but only to put them behind me; and so I left Wakwaha as soon as I could.

I went back with Ekwerkwe when she was nine years old, but we did not go to the Exchange. We went to the Springs of the River to dance the Water where the water begins to shine.

After I had been home two or three years, when the household was prospering and the day's work did not fill my whole mind, I began to listen more carefully in the heyimas, and to talk with my side-grandfather and with Shell, who were both thoughtful and magnanimous people. They had always been careful of me. Now they were getting old; it was time that I be careful of them, and take at last what they offered me. I was happy with the giving that flowed in and out the doors of our household now, and Shell and Ninepoint praised my wealth; but I knew they did not consider me wealthy, because I was so poorly educated in matters of history, poetry, and the intellect. I had no songs except the mud wakwa the old man had given me when I was a child at the Geyser, and the rain and feather song that was given me in the high hills coming home. Ninepoint said, "If you want it, I will give you the Deer Gyre, granddaughter." This was a very great gift, and I considered a long time before I accepted it, distrusting my ability. I said to Ninepoint, "That is a great stream to pour into a small bowl!" He said, "The bowl's empty, so it can hold a great deal." We took all that rainy season, meeting in the heyimas at early morning, to sing the Deer Gyre until I knew it. It is still the greatest thing in my keeping.

After that I began reading at the Archives of the Madrone Lodge, and later I went to the Madrone of Telina-na, and to the Blue Clay in Wakwaha, continuing my education. I had not much gift, but much was given me.

When Spear and Shadow married, that put two families in our two rooms of High Porch House, which was a crowd. Also I was not very comfortable living under one roof with Spear, whom I had once desired. I did not quite trust him or myself. Though I sang the Wedding Song for them with all my heart, still, old feelings can be there suddenly and swallow you up, like the caves in the lava fields. And I had not had a man in my bed since I left those black fields.

That spring I danced the Moon for the first time.

For the summer Towhee and Ekwerkwe and I went to Gahheya, while Shadow and Spear went across the Valley to a sum-mering place near Dry Falls. After the Water we were all together again in High Porch House, and I decided to go to Telina for a while. Ekwerkwe asked to come with me. We stayed in Hardcinder House. My half-uncle's wife, Vine, was ill with sevai, and going blind; she liked to talk about the old days with me. She had no daughters, so her house was very quiet now, that had been so noisy with children. She liked to tell Ekwerkwe how I had called her house a mountain, and how she had asked me to come stay with her in that mountain; and now, she said, "not only the Owl but the Quail has come to stay in the mountain!" Then Ekwerkwe, though she knew, would ask, "Who is the Owl?" So they got on happily, rattling along like two creeks in the rainy season.

While I was in Telina I went every day to the Madrone Lodge to read history. A person of the Serpentine of Chumo came there also, and sometimes we talked together. He had not been away from Chumo before, since he was somewhat lame from a boyhood fall, and it was hard for him to travel unless he got a ride on a horse or on a cart. He had not thought about travelling at all until he had lived about forty years. By then he had practiced for many years in the Doctors Lodge; he had a gift of healing, so great a gift that it burdened him beyond his strength. He had made so many life-debts in Chumo that he was worn out trying to pay them. So he had come to the Madrone in Telina to rest awhile, and went to the Doc-tors Lodge only to sing. He was a very quiet man but his talk was always interesting. Each time we talked I wanted to talk again.

One day he said, "Woman Coming Home, if we could make one bed, I would be in it; but I don't know where to make it."

I said, "I have a large bed in Sinshan, in High Porch House."

He said, "If I came into your household I would rather come as your husband. Maybe you don't want a husband, or this husband."

I was not sure, so I said, "Well, I'll speak to Vine. She was a girl in Chumo. She might like to have a Chumo man around her house for a while."

So he came into Hardcinder House to live with us, before the Sun. We both danced the Twenty-One days. Ekwerkwe slept with Vine, and I with Alder. What I felt was that if I wanted a husband, this was a good one; but maybe it was better that I not marry. My mothers had not been very good at being married, and I had already had one husband whom I had left without a word or a thought. Alder and I certainly got along well, and by marrying me he could leave his creditors in Chumo fairly and start fresh at the Doctors Lodge in Sinshan. That was a good reason for marrying. But I kept thinking about it. I was still the Condor's daughter and the Condor's wife, ignorant, poor of mind, only beginning to be a person. I was raw, and needed a lot of cooking yet. Though I had lived twenty-six years, I had lived only nineteen of them in the Valley. Nineteen is young to marry. I told Alder these thoughts. He listened carefully, without answering. That was a thing I liked very much in him and admired, his careful and silent listening. It was his gift and way.

Some days after I had spoke to him, he said, "Send me back to Chumo."

I said, "This is not my mothers' household. I can't send you out of it."

He said, "I can't leave you and should leave you. I am taking your strength. What I have to give you, you don't want or need."

What he meant was his need of me. He spoke with great passion and with as great restraint. What he said was true. I did not want his need of me. But there was more than that that was true. Once a waterskater had given me the gift I did not want or understand; I had taken it, and it might yet be my wealth. I said, "The husbands in our part of High Porch House don't seem to stay long; one of them kept going back to Chumo and the other went back outside the world. You needn't stay long. You can go back to Chumo when you like. Come for a while."

So we went to Sinshan to dance the World, but not the Wedding Night. Ekwerkwe stayed another month with Vine, and after that Shadow and Spear went to live in Plum Trees House, where a room on the second floor was empty since Shell's grandson had married Shopiwe of Up the Hill House. The other family on the first floor of High Porch House moved out of one small north room and let it come back to our family, so Alder and I slept there. In Sinshan we got along even better than in Telina. He never spoke of marrying, however, or behaved in any way that would remind me that he had said that if he came into my house he had wanted to come as my husband. I remembered it; but I kept thinking, "I will not be caught as my parents were caught. I will not let his need eat up my life. I must come to be myself by myself. When a man comes, under the Moon or in the sunlight, that I like as well as this man, I will have him if I wish." So it was. Only I did not meet any man I liked as well as Alder.

In the Doctors Lodge of Sinshan he conducted himself with caution, and I learned a good deal from watching his mindfulness. He knew that some smallminded people in that lodge would be jealous of his skill, and took care never to compete with them. And he did not want to pile up life-debts as he had done in Chumo in the pride of his art; so the people he asked the lodge for the care of were people who had mortal cancers or were sevai, those for whom there was little relief and no cure. At one time there were three such people in Sinshan, and he would go and sing and care for all of them. In the lodge an illnatured person said, "The Chumo man hangs around the dying like a buzzard!" He heard that, and was ashamed. He would not tell me why, but I saw something had shamed him, and found out from Woman Laughs what it was; I was angry for him, but to him I laughed. I said, "My husbands are all condors and buzzards!"

I had called him husband. He heard it, but he said nothing.

In the household, he got on very well with Ekwerkwe, and Towhee was as much at ease with him as with anyone. Sometimes in the evening he would sing, almost under his breath, one of the long songs of his art, and when my mother listened her face grew soft and deep, without strain. Though because of his lameness he had never gone with the flocks on Sheep Mountain, still he was a Chumo man, and the sheep trusted him; and the she-goat whom I had found on Sinshan Ridge would come to him whenever he was in the fields. As they were both lame, it was a funny sight, one

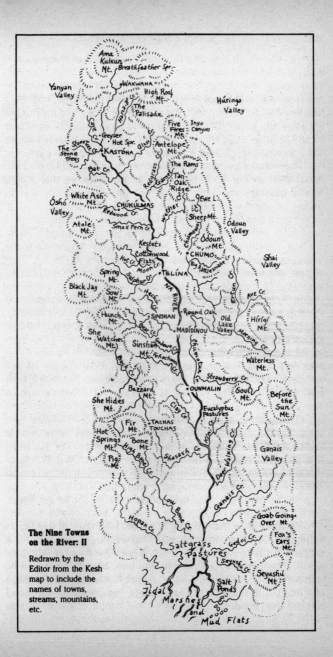

The Nine Towns on the River: II

Redrawn by the Editor from the Kesh map to include the names of towns, streams, mountains, etc.

hobbling along quietly after the other, and the rest of the goats of Sinshan trailing along behind.

When Ninepoint died I was the Deer Gyre Singer of my heyimas, and other responsibilities followed upon that. I felt quite wealthy enough, after a few years, and sometimes, like my mother, I wanted to go spend the summer away up in the hills away from human people. I did not do that, but I did walk in Coyote's house, always some time after the Summer dancing or before the Grass.

Sometimes a person would come across from Chumo to stay with Alder in our household. One of his creditors was a child whose inflamed appendix he had cut out when the boy was six years old. There was no denying his responsibility for that life. The boy was an adolescent now, and the mother would come with him to visit his side-father every season or so. She always said to Alder, "When are you coming back? So-and-so needs you, such-and-so asked me to ask you, when are you coming back to Chumo?"—all people who were alive because Alder had cured or healed them. He was fond of his side-son, whom he called Cutgut, an intelligent cheerful boy, but the mother always left him very cast down and uneasy. I could see him thinking about his life. At last, one day after they had been visiting and had left, he said, "I think I should go back to Chumo."

I had been thinking too, and I said, "Alder, those people are looking after one another in Chumo. Here there are people who need you now. How will the old man in Northwest House die, without you? How will this woman in High Porch House live, without you?"

He stayed in Sinshan, and our people sang the Wedding Song for us on the second night of the World that year. After that, he joined the Black Adobe Lodge and became a scholar of that learning. Twice he rode to Wakwaha for the Western Gyre. When my mother fell ill he cared for her, and when she began dying he went with her as far as it is appropriate to go. I came with him, following him like the lame goat, and my mother went on, and he and I came back together, into our house.

So there is no more history in my life after that; all that I could bring into the Valley from outside I have brought, all that I could remember I have written; the rest has been lived and will be lived again. I have lived in this place until I have become Stone Telling, and my husband Stone Listening, and my quail has become Shining; and in this house Acorn and Phoebe have made me the grandmother weaving at the loom.

NOTES:
pp. 395–396. *I was happy. . . . much was given me.*
"To be wealthy," "to give," are *ambad;* "to learn" is *andabad;* and "gift" in
the sense of talent or capacity is *badab.* Stone Telling does a little wordplay
to show that her education was not entirely wasted.

Messages Concerning the Condor

Most messages and notices coming into the Wakwaha Exchange
were held in short-term memory for about twenty-four hours and
then self-effaced, as they were of practical and immediate
significance—notifications from other peoples of the region of
goods and foods to trade, or changes in train schedules, announce-
ments of festivals to which strangers were welcome, weather reports from the City satellites, and warnings of impending flood,
fire, earthquake, volcanic eruption, or remote events which might
affect local conditions. Occasionally reports concerning human doings perceived as concerning the peoples of a large area were
printed out on paper for circulation and perhaps for preservation in
the Archives.

The following reports are of this latter kind. They were kept in
the Archives of the Madrone in Wakwaha. (Of course all such
records, along with all other data that passed through the computer
network either by human agency or as part of the City's process of
existence, were stored in the permanent Memory Bank of the City,
but the retrieval problem was considerable.)

DOCUMENT 1.

A notice concerning the Condor people, made and sent by
Shor'ki Ti' of Long Farms with Willows of the Rekwit People:

The annual council of the Farms of Rekwit agreed that a report should be made and sent to all the Exchanges in the westward drainage of the Range of Light and all drainages into the Inland Sea and all drainages into the Ocean southward of the mouth of the Ssu Nnoo. I was told to make the report since I proposed the idea. People in Rekwit think it important that we stop the Condor people from making trouble.

You can get a summary of information concerning this people from the Memory using Codes 1306611/3116/6/16 and 1306611/3116/6/6442. This is a synopsis of that summary: They call themselves Dayao or One People. They are related to people living in the Great Lakes area by language, and may have been sent west from that area a long time ago. They lived as nomads in the Grasslands and in the desert countries north of the Omorn Sea. About a hundred and twelve years ago they began to become civilised. A man named Kaspyoda took their power. They followed him west towards the Dark River country. He died near the Dry Lakes. His son took his power and started to give it back, but was killed by a cousin, a man named Astyoda, calling himself The Great Condor. He led the people down into the Lava Beds saying that a finger of light had pointed to the place where they should settle down. They made a town there. Their name for it is City. They have become entirely civilised, aggressive, and destructive. They have done much harm and will do more if we do not prevent them. A council is requested.

DOCUMENT 2.

A response to the notice concerning the Condor people from Shor'ki Ti' of Rekwit from Reads of the Serpentine of the Valley of the Na:

Your request is entirely appropriate. We have talked about it here and have seen that we have been self-concerned to an excessive degree, and have wanted mindfulness. Condor people, all men without women, have been coming into this Valley from the north for seventeen years. We have shared food and roof with them at request but have not worked, married, or danced with them. Nevertheless much infection has taken place. Cults have arisen. When a large group of Condor men stayed in the Lower Valley for a half-year, much dissension arose, superstitions were in-

creased, and trust was weakened. If fighting a war is necessary people will come from here to the fighting. If
quarantine is possible it would be better. We request the
peoples living northwest of us and near the Lava Beds, and
the Information Services of the Exchange, to notify through
the Exchange of any aggressive acts by the Condor people.

DOCUMENT 3.

From Vavats of Tahets concerning the Condor people:
   We have been fighting a war with these sick people for
two lifetimes.

From this point on there was a flurry and then a steady
crossflow of messages through the Exchanges of twenty-two different peoples of the region. Many of these were recriminatory or pan-
icky; the bitterest was from Wemewe Mag, a village southeast of
North Mountain:

Two years ago they killed eleven people and stole eight
women and all the horses. They come every winter and
take our food. If you try to fight them you had better have
guns and bullets. They do.

Ethical counsel from the Under White Mountain people, far
down the eastern coast of the Inland Sea, was not very well received. They advised: "Do not fight these sick people, cure them
with human behavior," to which Rekwit responded tersely, "You
come up north here and do that."

In the event, no war was mounted. If the Condor's City had
made an attempt to increase its territory or to move its people
southwestward, it would have met with concerted resistance by an
alliance of all the people of the region. But the Condor dreams of
empire were self-defeated.

The causes of this collapse may seem obscure, particularly
when the Condor people had all the resources of the Exchange to
call upon. For one thing, the Condor could in theory follow all the
discussions and plans of the other peoples in the Exchange. There
was no "classified information" in the Memory, and no way to seal
information off; a coded message was accompanied by the explanation of the code. It would appear that the Condor's use of the Exchange was very limited; only a priest caste was permitted to use it

at all, and they apparently drew upon it for information on material resources and technologies, without listening in much on the local section of the endless flow of worldwide message-sending. The Condor people seem to have been unusually self-isolated; their form of communication with other peoples was through aggression, domination, exploitation, and enforced acculturation. In this respect they were at a distinct disadvantage among the introverted but cooperative peoples native to the region.

Again it might be asked why they failed in their attempt to make powerful weapons of war, and why that attempt was so inept, when they had available in the Memory of the Exchange instructions for the production of every imaginable weapon from Greek fire through machine guns to hydrogen bombs, and beyond?

Tempting answers come to mind: the great City of Mind had decided long ago that such toys were not good for mankind, and would not release instructions for making them. . . . Or perhaps would release only garbled instructions, thus ensuring ineffective weapons. . . . But the City of Mind took no responsibility for its parent stock. If the humans got hold of nuclear weapons and blew up the planet, so be it; the deep-space stations of the Exchange would survive, each of them containing the Memory and capable of replicating the rest of the network, and indeed a good part of the universe—though, if humanity did dispose of itself, there is some question whether the computer would see fit to duplicate it. It was not the City of Mind, then, that kept the City of the Condor from success with its tanks and airplanes. Undoubtedly, if asked, it would have produced for the Condor a study of what we would call the cost-effectiveness of tanks, airplanes, missiles, or other elaborate weaponry, and demonstrated the hopelessness of the project, in the absence of the worldwide technological web, the "technological ecosystem," of the Industrial Age, and on a planet almost depleted of many of the fossil fuels and other materials from which the Industrial Age made itself. All that had been replaced by the almost ethereal technology of the City, on the one hand, which had no use for heavy machinery, even their spaceships and stations being mere nerve and gossamer, and on the other hand by the very loose, light, soft network of the human cultures, which in their small scale, great number, and endless diversity, manufactured and traded more or less actively, but never centralised their industry, did not ship goods and parts far, did not maintain roads well, and were not engaged in enterprises requiring heroic sacrifice, at least on the material plane. To construct, say, a battery to power a flashlight was not an easy matter, though at need it was done: the technology of the Valley was completely adequate to the needs of the people. To construct a tank or a bomber was so difficult and so unnecessary that it really cannot be spoken of in terms of the Valley economy. After all, the cost of making, maintaining, fueling, and operating such machines at the very height of the Industrial Age was incalculable, impoverishing the planet's substance forever and requiring the great majority of humankind to live in servitude and poverty. Perhaps the question concerning the Condor's failure to build an empire with its advanced weapons is not why did they fail, but why did they try. But it is not a question to which the people of the Valley could provide an answer.

Again, we may ask: since the Condor had access to the principal iron, copper, zinc, and gold mines of the Inland Sea area, and did not scruple to take what they wanted by force, why did they not use their superiority in metals not in a misguided effort to build anachronistic tanks and bombers, but in building up a good arsenal of guns, grenades, and other "conventional" weapons until they were invincible among the almost defenseless and poorly armed peoples about them? Then they might truly have made history!

To this I think the people of the Valley might have an answer, along the lines of "Very sick people tend to die of their sickness," or "Destruction destroys itself." This answer, however, involves a reversal from our point of view. What we call strength it calls sickness; what we call success it calls death.

Is it possible that the genetic changes worked by the residues of the Industrial Era upon the human race, which I saw as disastrous—low birth rate, short life expectancy, high incidence of crippling congenital disease—had a reverse side also? Is it possible that natural selection had had time to work in social, as well as physical and intellectual terms? Were the people of the Na Valley and Rekwit and Fennen and the Amaranth Coast and the Cotton Islands and Cloud River and Dark River and the Marshes and the Range of Light in fact healthier than I realised—healthier than I am capable of fully understanding, so long as I must look at them from

outside their world? In leaving progress to the machines, in letting technology go forward on its own terms and selecting from it, with what seems to us excessive caution, modesty, or restraint, the limited though completely adequate implements of their cultures, is it possible that in thus opting not to move "forward" or not only "forward," these people did in fact succeed in living in human history, with energy, liberty, and grace?

About a Meeting Concerning the Warriors

*Given to the Archives of the Madrone at Wakwaha
and to the Exchange by Bear Man of the Red
Adobe of Telina-na, a member
of the Doctors Lodge.*

A printed notice brought to all towns:
There is going to be a meeting of people at Cottonwood Flats on the 201st Day to talk about the Warrior Lodge. We will be there: Steady of Kastoha, Chooses and Redwood of Telina, Grey Horse of Chukulmas.

What Steady of the Serpentine of Kastoha-na said at the meeting:
People of the Warrior Lodge and people in the Lamb Lodge are not very likely to agree with what I am going to say. They will deny it, and we will have argument and dissension. Because many of us dislike argument and avoid dissension, we have not said what I am going to say, and in this we have been weak and careless. It is time now, in this place, to talk about these things aloud. I say this now:

The people of the Condor, those men who have come here from that people, are sick. Their heads are turned backwards. We have let people with the plague come into our house. We should not have done it and will not do it again. But listen! The people of the Warrior Lodge and some people in the Lamb Lodge have been infected. They are sick. Maybe they are willing to be healed, to be cured. If not, if they wish to live sick, then they will have to go where the sickness is, to the country those people came from in the Lava Beds north of Dark River, and stay there. That is what I say; that is what has been decided in talk with these people who came here with me, for whom I have been speaking.

Other things that were said by different people:

Four people are going to close the Valley?

Four people are going to open discussion.

Who is sick? People are sick who talk about driving people out of their houses, out of their towns, out of the Valley! That is sick-headed talk!

Yes, who is sick? People are sick who are afraid of fighting!

It is the nature of the sickness not to know itself. That ignorance is the sickness itself.

That argument eats itself! If not to know you're sick is sickness, how do you know you're not sick yourself?

Oh, you'll tell him if he is—you'll make him a Warrior and blow tobacco smoke at him and give him a sick name—Misery, or Stinks, or Diarrhoea!

Listen, you are talking foolishly. There is no use in anger. You cannot tell what sickness is until you have become well. Weakness calls itself strong, but strength calls itself weak, glory calls itself vile, and the peacemaker calls himself warrior. Listen: only the warrior can make peace.

Nobody makes peace. Peace is. Who do you think you are, to *make* peace? A mountain, a Rainbow Person, Coyote?

Calm down, you people. I want you to listen and hear me. I am not ashamed of being a Warrior. You want me to be ashamed of it, but it is not possible. I have found strength and knowledge I needed in the Warrior Lodge, and I would share it with you if you let me.

I too am not ashamed of being a Warrior! It is my pride! You people there, you're sick, you're dying and don't know it. You eat and drink and dance and talk and sleep and die and there is nothing to you, like ants or fleas or gnats, your life is nothing, it goes nowhere, it goes over and over and over nowhere! We are not insects, we are human people. We serve a higher purpose.

What? What purpose? Whose purpose? Listen to him! That's Big Man talking! That's a mouth on the back of a head talking! "I serve, I eat shit," that's Big Man saying "I'm better than anything else, I'll live forever, everything else is shit!"

Listen. If you wise people have thought that we were sick, why did you not ask us to come to the Doctors Lodge?

You know an unwanted cure won't cure.
You have to dance to be a dancer.
And you have to fight to be a Warrior!
Fight whom? Your mothers?

It was not the Warrior Lodge who agreed to let the Condor come here and stay here and come back again. When they come back, it is we, not you, who are ready to drive them away. Why are we Warriors? Because they made war! You let them come and go as they please, and now you talk about sickness, shaming your own people. But you did not listen to us. We have said all along that we would drive them away and keep them away. Now you say you want to do the same thing.

Yes, I say that, but I do not say it as a Warrior.

How are you going to meet the Condor, then? With songs and dances?

I don't put a fire out with a match, Warrior.

Only strength can defeat the strong, Speaker.

Warrior, if it is war you want, you must fight it with us, your own people, and the people of our fields and barns, and the wild people, and every tree of our orchards and vine of our vineyards and every stem of grass and every stone and grain of dirt in the Valley of the River. This is the first battle of that war. You have let yourself fall sick with the Sickness of Man, and you seek to make us sick: and now you must be the one to choose whether you will be killed or cured or driven out.

Steady said this, and many other people said:

The stones speak with that voice. The earth and the River speak in those words. The Lion speaks, the Bear is talking. Listen!

A description of what happened next:

After that speech of Steady's there was a pause for a while because other people were beginning to come to the meeting.

In the evening people came forward again to speak about the Warrior Lodge in praise or blame and to discuss what others said. After that the meeting went on for four days, many people coming and going with food from the towns and sharing the food with those staying at the Flats. Much was said about the human soul and mind, and sickness and sacredness. The things which were kept secret by the Warrior Lodge and the Lamb Lodge were all spoken of by members of those lodges and made plain and no secret. After hearing these things many people said that the minds of the Warriors were indeed diseased. Some Warriors came up and renounced their membership in that Lodge. Their speeches grew very passionate. Some Madrone Lodge people and Walks Along of the Serpentine of Wakwaha, the Speaker of that heyimas, said that it was better not to deny in public what one had done in secret, and that to be finished with a thing was simply to leave it and go on away from it. So the excitement was calmed down one way and another, and many people began joining in long drum dances, since there were so many gathered there, and the weather was pleasant, and there was a lot of emotion and feeling stirred up, and several very good drummers were present. But still there were more than a hundred men and women who held fast to the Warriors' way and wished to speak for it. For them, Skull of Telina-na said this:

Skull's speech:

You say that we are sick, mortally sick, dying of our sickness. You say that you fear our sickness. So it may be. Then I say this: Our sickness is our humanity. To be human is to be sick. The lion is well, the hawk is well, the oak is well, they live and die in the mindfulness of the sacred, and need take no care. But from us sacredness has withdrawn care; in us is the mind of the sacred. So all we do is careful, and all our effort is to be mindful, and yet we are not whole. We are not well, and we do not do well. To deny that is careless, mindless folly! You say that human people are no different from the other animals and the plants. You call yourself earth and stone. You deny that you are outcast from that fellowship, you deny that the soul of man has no house on earth. You pretend, you build up houses of desire and imagination, but you cannot live in them. In them is no habitation. And for your denying, your lying, your comfort-seeking, you will be punished. The day of punishment is the day of war. Only in war is redemption; only the victorious warrior will know the truth, and knowing the truth will live forever. For in sickness is our health, in war our peace, and for us there is only one, one house, One Above All Persons, outside whom there is no health, no peace, no life, no thing!

After Skull's speech.

To Skull's speech no direct answer was made. Some people wept, some were frightened, others very angry at hearing a person say what Skull had said. Feelings had run so high that Steady, Walks Along, Obsidian of Ounmalin, and others who were conducting the meeting preferred silence to response, lest there be violence. Only a singer of the Blood Clowns of Chumo began singing:

> "Outside the One there is nothing,
> nothing but women and coyotes."

Obsidian of Ounmalin told her to take the song away, and she did so, but many people picked it up and sang it later on. Then Walks Along spoke to Skull and the other Warriors, saying that she thought the open meeting had gone on long enough, and inviting the Warriors to come up to Wakwaha and go on talking and seeking what was best to do. The Warriors refused to come to Wakwaha, saying that they wanted to talk among themselves, not with other people. Steady said they should do as they chose.

Some Madrone Lodge people thought Steady and Walks Along were not being careful enough; they said that people who refused to talk to reach agreement and would talk only when other people agreed with them had better leave the Valley and go talk with the Condor, who agreed with them. This group and the people with Steady came to words, speaking hotly. The Warriors watched them argue, nodding and smiling.

The argument and the end of it.

Hawk Cries of Sinshan said, "If they will not talk they must go, and if they will not go they will be driven!" He lifted up the madrone staff he carried as speaker.

Steady in a passion of anger said, "If you drive them you go with them, driver with driven, beater with beaten!" He came towards Hawk Cries.

Walks Along said, "Sickness is speaking us."

They all heard that. Hawk Cries threw away his staff. Nobody said anything for a while. Presently Hawk Cries said, "They have gone."

Walks Along said, "Yes, I think they are going now."

Steady said, "I spoke ill. I will be silent now for a while." He went down to the River to wash and to be by himself. The others began also to go down to the River, or back to their towns, leaving the Warriors there where the meeting had been, by the cottonwood grove.

The next day the Warriors also went home to their towns.

That was the end of that lodge in the Valley. It was indeed gone.

Why I have written this.

Some of the men who had been Warriors went up to the Dark River country after that meeting, to live with the Condor people. Twenty-four of them went that year, and some more the next year, I am not sure how many. No woman went. There was a woman in

Sinshan who had gone to that country earlier with her father, who was a Condor man. She came back after several years. She wrote her life to tell about those people. I do not think much else has ever been written about that time when the Condor men came to the Valley and the Warrior Lodge came to be. I was a quite young man at the meeting at Cottonwood Flats, but I have thought about it a great deal all my life. We avoid talking about sickness when feeling well, but that is superstition, after all. Looking mindfully at the things that were talked about at the meeting, I have come to think that the sickness of Man is like the mutating viruses and the toxins: there will always be some form of it about, or brought in from else-where by people moving and travelling, and there will always be the risk of infection. What those sick with it said is true: It is a sickness of our being human, a fearful one. It would be unwise in us to forget the Warriors and the words spoken at Cottonwood Flats, lest it need all be done and said again.

POEMS

FOURTH SECTION

 THE POEMS in this section were more or less formally used in ceremonies or in teaching, in the heyimas or as part of the seven great wakwa.

MOON DANCE SONG

*Composed by Link of the Obsidian House of Ounmalin
and sung there as part of the men's ritual singing
before the Moon Dance.*

If you should ask me,
you should ask me where
she went, that girl
with fleecy hair.

If I should answer,
I should answer you,
that she lay down
under the moon.

EYEGEONKAMA

A part-song, sung by women before and during the Moon Dance, though not part of the formal ritual singing. Many different versions and improvisations go under the title and to the tune of the "yes-singing." This version is from Sinshan.

How far from lip to lip?
Wide enough for a word to get out.
How far from lip to lip?
Wide enough for a man to get in.
    If the word is yes, yes,
    if the word is yes,
if the lips part consenting,
    enter in me, yes, yes,
    enter in me, yes.

A SONG USED IN CHUMO WHEN DAMMING A CREEK OR DIVERTING WATER TO A HOLDING TANK FOR IRRIGATION

To the ousel, to the water ousel
may it go, may it go.
Tarweed, the corn roots
need this water also.
Buckbrush, the bean leaves
need this water also.
Way of the water's going,
we do not wish this!
Let it go to the water ousel,
to the waterskater.
Let the wild goose's wings
carry it upward.
Let the dragonfly larva
carry it downward.
We do not wish this,
we do not desire it,
only the water we borrow
on our way to returning.
We who are doing this

all will be dying.
Way of the water's going,
bear with us in this place now
on your way to returning.

COMING UPRIVER

*A Salt Journey song. Members of the Salt Lodge of the
Blue Clay House maintained the Salt Ponds—nine
diked enclosures on the mudflats east of the eastern-
most Mouth of the Na, in which evaporation and cry-
stallisation was controlled in a five-year continuous
cycle of drainage from pond to pond. Both crude and
refined salt were "in the gift" of the Blue Clay heyimas.
A month after the Water was danced, Salt Lodge people from all nine towns made a ceremonial journey
downriver to do any heavy repairs that might be
needed in the system of ponds and sluices, and to harvest the crimson brine shrimp which, dried and pow-
dered, were used as a condiment.*

Coming back, coming up from the mouths of the river,
to the left, in the southwest, blue mountains.
Coming back from the coast of the western ocean,
in the northeast, to the right, blue mountains.

From the flat shores, the beaches of the unborn,
walking back between mountains, coming upriver.
From the salt place, from the edge, from the empty place,
walking back between hills of dry grass, coming upriver.

THE INLAND SEA

Spoken as a teaching in the Serpentine heyimas
of Sinshan by Mica.

All there under the water are cities, the old cities.

All the bottom of the sea there is roads and houses,
    streets and houses.

Under the mud in the dark of the sea there
    books are, bones are.

All those old souls are under the sea there,
    under the water, in the mud,
    in the old cities in the dark.

There are too many souls there.

Look out if you go by the edge of the sea,
    if you go on a boat on the Inland Sea
    over the old cities.

You can see the souls of the old dead like cold fire in the water.

They will take any body, the luminifera, the jellyfish, the
    sandfleas, those old souls.

Any body they can get.

They swim through their windows, they drift down their roads,
    in the mud in the dark of the sea.

They rise through the water to sunlight, hungry for birth.

Look out for the sea-foam, young woman,
    look out for the sandfleas!

You might find an old soul in your womb,
    an old soul, a new person.

There aren't enough people for all the old souls,
    hopping like sandfleas.

Their lives were the sea-waves, their souls are the sea-foam,
    foam-lines on brown sand,
    there and not there.

TO THE PEOPLE ON THE HILLS

*Sung in Wakwaha to the Animals of the Blue Clay
on the Second Day of the World Dance.*

> On four feet, on four feet walking
> around the world, walking around
> on four feet, you walk
> the right way, you walk dancing,
> beautifully dancing you walk,
> carefully, dangerously you walk
> in the right direction.

A MADRONE LODGE SONG

*This song, with its matrix-words, takes about an hour to
sing. In some songs the matrix-words are "meaningless"
syllables or vowels, or are old words no longer in use; in
this one they are developed out of the song-words. For
instance, after the song is opened with the four-note* heya
heya, *the tune is first hummed: the* mmmmm *of hum-
ming is the first sound of the first word,* ma-invetun, *from
their houses, and it develops gradually into the syllable*
ma; *this is modulated gradually through the "Four-House*

vowels" backwards as ma-ún, ma-oun, ma-on, ma-un, to ma-in, and at last the whole first word/phrase, ma-invetun, is sung. Other key words of the song are similarly treated or "matricised."

The words and music of this song belonged to Mica of Sinshan and were given to us by him.

From their houses, from their town
rainbow people come walking
the dark paths between stars,
the bright tracks on water
of the moon, of the sun.
Tall and long-legged,
lithe and long-armed,
they follow the fog pumas
beside the wind coyotes,
passing the rain bears
under the still-air hawks
on the paths of sunlight,
on the tracks of moonlight,
on the ways of starlight,
on the dark roads.
They climb the ladders of wind,
the stairways of cloud.
They descend the ladders of air,
the steps of rain falling.
The closed eye sees them.
The deaf ear hears them.
The still mouth speaks to them.
The still hand touches them.
Going to sleep we waken to them,
walking the ways of their town.
Dying we live them,
entering their beautiful houses.

BONE POEMS

*From the Blue Clay teaching in that heyimas
in Wakwaha.*

The solution
dissolves itself
leaving the problem behind,
a skeleton,
the mystery before,
around, above, below, within.
O Clarity!

Don't break your handbones
trying to break mystery.
Pick it up, eat it, use it, wear it,
throw it at coyotes.

The bones of your heart,
there's mystery.
Clothes wearing the body,
there's a good clown.

Puzzlebits make whole puzzles.
Answers complete questions.
A whistle, though,
made from the heartbone,
plays the song the crow knows
and won't sing,
the song called Rejoining.

Oh, I am frightened,
I am afraid, afraid.
Each night I go in desolation
to a miserable place.
Is there no other way?

I wish I had died young, suddenly,
before I knew I had to make
the bones of my soul
out of cold rain and aching,
and walk into the dark.

From opaque rock
springs clear water.
The skull's hard cup
holds clarity.
Drink, traveller.
Be mindful. Drink.

TEACHING SONGS: ORDERS AND DANCES
OF THE EARTH AND SKY

Such songs were spoken or chanted to the tongue-drum,
often with much repetition of lines or words, as part
of children's education in the heyimas. They varied
from House to House and from town to town;
this set is from the Serpentine of Madidinou.

I. THE TOWN OF EARTH

Adobe, blue clay, serpentine, obsidian:
floors and walls
of the houses of the town of earth.
Cloud, rain, wind, air:
windows and roofs
of the houses of the town of earth.
Under floorboards, under cellars,
above roofs, above chimneys,
to the left of the right hand,
to the right of the left hand,
north of the future, south of the past,
earlier than east, later than west,
outside the walls:
the limitless,

the wilderness,
the mountains and rivers of being,
the valley of possibility.

II. THE ROUND TOWN

Ballround, earth-town.
Each street meets
itself at length.
Old are the roads,
long are the ways,
wide are the waters.
Whale swims west returning east,
tern flies north returning south,
rain falls to rise, sparks rise to fall.
Mind may hold the whole
but on foot walking we do not come
to the beginning end of the street.
The hills are steep,
the years are steep,
deep are the waters.
In the round town
it is a long way home.

III. THE COURSES.

Earth goes turning,
    earth goes turning spinning,
    spinning the day-course
    between shining and darkness.
What lies between south and north
is the axis of turning;
what lies from west to east
is the way of turning.
In shining and darkness, so,
turning in shining and darkness.

Moon goes turning,
    moon goes turning circling,
    moon circles the month-course,
    spinning the month-long moon's day,
    between shining and darkness
    circling the earth turning and spinning.
Crescent is dawn of the moon's day,
full moon full noon, waning the evening,
dark of the moon is the moon's night
that looks at the darkness, so,
turning in shining and darkness.

Earth and moon together,
together the two go turning,
    circling the sun,
    circling the year-course,
and the slanted axis of turning
making the winter and summer,
the rise and fall of the year-dance.
The dancers, the bright dancers,
    Ou, the bright sun-child,
    Adsevin, glory of morning, glory of evening,
the dancers, see the bright dancers,
    outward from earth, red Kemel,
    Gebayu and Udin,
    and the lost dancers in darkness
    seen by the eye no longer,
turning, circling the shining,
turning in shining and darkness.

NOTE: This description of the solar system might be acted out by young children taking the parts of earth, moon, and the five visible planets, spinning and circling appropriately around the singer, who played the sun.

    The next song was not danced or sung, but chanted or spoken to certain drum rhythms. Children learned the first section; the rest was not learned until adolescence; and so familiar and sacred were the words that often they were not spoken at all but "said on the drum"—the rhythms being as distinctive and familiar as the words.

III. THE GYRES

Around its center in an open gyre
earth turns, the day:
around the earth in an open gyre
moon turns, the month:

around the sun in an open gyre
earth turns, the year:
around its center in an open gyre
sun turns, the dance:
sun and the other stars in an open gyre
turn and return, the dance.

The dancing is stillness,
change without changing,
onward returning.
The dancing is making
mountains and rivers,
stars and the islands of stars
and the unmaking.
The dance is the open gyre
of the gyre of the gyre
of the dance in the valley.

To begin
is to return.
To lose the seed
is the flower.
To learn the stone
touches the spring.
To see the dancing:
starlight.
To hear the dancing:
darkness.
To dance the dancing:
shining, shining.

In the houses
they are dancing.
On the dancing places
they are dancing shining.

ASKING FOR A MESSENGER

*An old song, sung with the tongue-drum in the
Black Adobe Lodges.*

Quail, quail, carry
a word for me.

I cannot, I cannot,
I cannot cross across.

Chukar, chukar, carry
a word for me.

I don't know, I don't know
how to cross across.

Pigeon, pigeon, carry
a word for me.

I've returned already,
gone there and returned.
Your word is my feather,
my feather is your word.

A GRASS SONG

A Red Adobe song for the Grass Dance in Wakwaha.
The meter is "fives."

Very quietly
this is happening,
this is becoming,
the hills are changing
under the rainclouds,
inside the grey fogs,
the sun going south
and the wind colder,
blowing quietly
from the west and south.
Manyness of rain
falling quietly:
manyness of grass
rising into air.
The hills become green.
This is happening
very quietly.

CLOUDS, RAIN, AND WIND

A Grass Dance song.

From the house of the Lion that lies on the mountain,
footsteps of the dancers approaching,
hurrying: listen, the footsteps
of Bear dancers hurrying downwards
over the foothills towards us.
Coyote, Coyote follows them,
Coyote howling and singing!

THE ANT DANCE

*Sung and danced by children in all Valley towns
on the Third Day of the World Dance,
"Honey Day," along with the Bee Dance.*

A hundred hundred rooms in this house,
A hundred hundred halls in this house,
everybody running, running, running in this house,
everybody touching, touching, touching in this house,
Hey! little grandmothers!
Let me get out of this house!
Let me get out of here!
Hey! Let me out!

THE BEAR'S GIFT

*From the Black Adobe Lodge in Wakwaha: a teaching
poem. The meter is nine-syllable, a meter particularly
associated with Black Adobe verse.*

Nobody knows the name of the bear,
not even the bear. Only the ones
who make fires and cry tears know the name
of the bear, that the bear gave to them.
Quail and plumed grass, infant and puma,
all their lives they are wholly alive
and they do not have to say a word.

But those who know the name of the bear
have to go out alone and apart
across hollow places and bridges,
crossing dangerous places, careful:
and they speak. They must speak. They must say
all the words, all the names, having learned
the first name, the bear's name. Inside it
is language. Inside it is music.
We dance to the sound of the bear's name,
and it is the hand we take hands with.
We see with the dark eye of that name
what no one else sees: what will happen.
So we fear darkness. So we light fires.
So we cry tears, our rain, the salt rain.
All the deaths, our own and the others',
are not theirs, but our own, the bear's gift,
the dark name that the bear gave away.

A MARRIAGE

From the Madrone Lodge of Telina-na.

Seventh House Woman got up from the hillside.
With white arms, with white body, with white hair,
she got up from the grasses of the hillside
in early morning in the rainy season.
Where the hills fold together steep above the creek,
where the hillsides are open between the oaks,
facing the southeast, the white woman stood among the grasses.
The Sun took her hand.
                          So was the sacred thing done,
                          so, there, their hands touching,
                          their hands holding, there, so:
she took the Sun's hand
and became transparent, entering the Ninth House.

THE DEER DANCE

A very old and sacred song of the Blue Clay House.
Given for translation and inclusion in this book by
Madrone Red of the Blue Clay House of Sinshan.

In the Sixth House a deer walked
made of rain,
its legs rain falling.
        It danced in a spiral on the earth.
In the Seventh House a deer jumped
made of clouds,
its flanks clouds hanging.
        It danced in a spiral on the rocks.
In the Eighth House a deer ran
made of wind,
its horns wind blowing.
        It danced in a spiral in the valley.
In the Ninth House a deer stood
made of air,
its eyes still air.
        It danced in a spiral on the mountain.
In the spiral of the deer dancing
        a hawk feather has fallen.
In the Hinge of the Nine Houses
        a word has been spoken.

PUMA DANCE

*This song is taught in Sinshan to people preparing to
go up alone on the hills on a journey of the soul.*

I put down my southwest foot,
four round toes, one round pad,
in the dirt by the digger pine,
in the dust by the digger pine
    on the mountain.
I put down my northwest foot,
four round toes, one round pad,
in the dirt by the bay laurel,
in the dust by the bay laurel
    in the foothills.
I put down my northeast foot,
four round toes, one round pad,
in the dirt by the madrone,
in the dust by the madrone
    on the mountain.
I put down my southeast foot,
four round toes, one round pad,
in the dirt by the live oak,
in the dust by the live oak
    in the foothills.
I am standing in the middle
of the lion world
on the mountain of the lion,
in the hills of the lion.
I am standing in the tracks of the lion.

INITIATION SONG FROM THE FINDERS LODGE

Please bring strange things.
Please come bringing new things.
Let very old things come into your hands.
Let what you do not know come into your eyes.
Let desert sand harden your feet.
Let the arch of your feet be the mountains.
Let the paths of your fingertips be your maps
and the ways you go be the lines on your palms.
Let there be deep snow in your inbreathing
and your outbreath be the shining of ice.
May your mouth contain the shapes of strange words.
May you smell food cooking you have not eaten.
May the spring of a foreign river be your navel.
May your soul be at home where there are no houses.
Walk carefully, well loved one,
walk mindfully, well loved one,
walk fearlessly, well loved one.
Return with us, return to us,
be always coming home.

From the People of the Houses of Earth in the Valley to the Other People Who Were on Earth Before Them.

In the beginning when the word was spoken,
in the beginning when the fire was lighted,
in the beginning when the house was built,
    we were among you.
Silent, like a word not spoken,
dark, like a fire not lighted,
formless, like a house not built,
    we were among you:
        the sold woman,
        the enslaved enemy.
    We were among you, coming closer,
    coming closer to the world.
In your time when all the words were written,
in your time when everything was fuel,
in your time when houses hid the ground,
    we were among you.
Quiet, like a word whispered,
dim, like a coal under ashes,
insubstantial, like the idea of a house,
    we were among you:
        the hungry,
        the powerless,
   in your world, coming closer,
    coming closer to our world.
In your ending when the words were forgotten,
in your ending when the fires burned out,
in your ending when the walls fell down,
    we were among you:
        the children,
        your children,
    dying your dying to come closer,
    to come into our world, to be born.

We were the sands of your sea-coasts,
the stones of your hearths. You did not know us.
We were the words you had no language for.
O our fathers and mothers!
We were always your children.
From the beginning, from the beginning,
    we are your children.

THE BACK
OF THE BOOK

|||||||||||||||||||||||||||||||||||||||||||||||||||||

Húíshev	**wewey**	**tusheíye**	**rru**	**gestanai**
of-two-legged-people	[adj.] all	[s.n.] work	this [is]	doing things well, art

m	**duwey**		**gochey.**
and	[o.n.] all		shared, held in common

The Whole Business of Man is the Arts, and All Things Common.

—WILLIAM BLAKE

NOTE: As stated in the First Note at the front of the book, The Back of the Book consists largely of information. According to the distinctions proposed in the "Note Concerning Narrative Modes" on page 536, things from here on will be just as fictional, but more factual, although equally true.

Since accent marks give a bristly and forbidding look to a page of English print, they have been left out so far; but in The Back of the Book and the Glossary they are used to indicate long *i, o,* and *u* in Kesh words. Pronunciations are given on page 532, "The Kesh Alphabet."

Long Names of Houses

||||||||||||||||||||||||||||||||||||||||||||||||

OFTEN THE HOUSES of the nine towns of the Valley had quite long names, which I have sometimes shortened in translation, through cowardice. I was afraid that these long names—Rain Falling Straight Down House, Here With Its Back to the Vineyards House, Danced the Sun a Hundred Times House—might sound quaint, that they might sound "primitive." I was afraid that people who lived in houses with names like that could not be taken seriously by people who live in places with names like Chelsea Manors Estate, An Adult Community, or Loma Lake Acres East, a Planned Recreation Development. Though the adage runs the other way, the unfamiliar also risks contempt.

The length of some of these names might also make them seem improbable; would anybody actually say, "Do come see us, we live in Nine Buzzards Over the Mountain House in Kastóha-na!" In fact, they probably wouldn't, since anyone they talked to would very likely know where they lived. In the uncommon event of inviting strangers, they would mention the house's location or looks— "in the southeast arm, with red doors on the porches"—by way of address, as we might say, "2116½ Garden Court Drive, you take the second San Mateo exit going north and turn right at the third stop light and go two blocks."

Anyhow, the people of the Valley had no objection to long names. They liked them. Perhaps they enjoyed the fact that they had plenty of time to say them. They were not ashamed of having time. They lacked drive, that great urge to get done which powers us, sending us forward, ever forward ever faster, reducing San Francisco of the slow settlers to Frisco and Chicago of the even slower natives to Chi and the town of the mission of our lady of the angels becomes Los Angeles, but that takes too long so it becomes L.A., but jets go faster than we do so we use their language and call it LAX, because what we want is to move on quick, to go fast, get through, be done, done with everything. To get it over with, that's what we want. But the people who lived in the Valley and gave interminable names to their houses were in no hurry.

It is hard for us to conceive, harder to approve, of a serious adult person not in a hurry. Not being in a hurry is for infants, people over eighty, bums, and the Third World. Hurry is the essence of city, the very soul. There is no civilisation without hurry, without keeping ahead. The hurry may lurk invisible, contradicted by the indolent pose of the lounger at the bar or the lazy gait of the stroller along the hotel walkway, but it is there, in the terrific engines of the TWA or BSA supersonic planes that brought her from Rio, him from Rome, here to NY, NY for the IGPSA conference on implementation of GEPS, and will rush them back tomorrow, hurrying across the world of cities where there is no tense left but the present tense, every second and tenth of a second and millisecond and nanosecond clocked, the readout moving always a little faster, and the A rising. Mozart's A was a hundred and forty cycles a second, so Mozart's piano is out of tune with all our orchestras and singers. Our A is a hundred and sixty, because the instruments sound more brilliant tuned up higher, as they all rise like sirens towards the final scream. There is nothing to be done. There is no way to heighten the pitch of the instruments of the Valley, no way to abbreviate their institutions and addresses and names to capital letters, no way to get them to move ahead.

As their names tended to spread out and take time to say or write, so the houses themselves tended to take up room and elaborate themselves, a porch added on here, a wing there, so that the essentially simple plan might, over the slow lapse of years, burgeon and bulge and exfoliate like an old oak tree vastly gnarled and spacious. The basic plan was usually an oblong or a shallow V shape, the foundation being of half-sunk fieldstone on which two storeys in stone, adobe brick, or wood were built. Washrooms, workrooms, storage rooms, and such were in the basement. The first and second floors—they counted down from the roof—were divided into hearthrooms, kitchens, and sleeping rooms and porches, four or five rooms to a floor in the small houses, twelve or fifteen in the big ones. Such a house might contain one numerous household, or as many as five different households; generally two or three households shared a house, often for generations. Each family had at least one private entrance, so there might be several outside staircases to the upper and lower porches and balconies. It was on these porches that most of the life of the house went on, except in cold weather.

Many houses had no front and back: the front of the top floor might be the back of one ground-floor household and the side of the other—it depended on where your front door was. The foundation storey was often set out to get the light on the northwest side, and retired under the upper floor and balconies for summer shade on the southeast side, which gave such houses a lurching look; but they were soundly planned and built, and often stood for centuries.

A house was oriented to the local terrain and lightfall—hillslopes, other houses, trees, creeks, shade and sun patterns—and secondarily to the compass, the corners pointing N, E, S, W, which meant that the walls faced the preferred half-directions.

The siting of the house was determined by the ideal plan of the town—the heyiya-if figure. Each house made part of that pattern, an element of the Left Arm curving to meet the Right Arm of the five heyimas buildings at the Hinge of the Town—which was always running water or a well. The pattern was not neat or orderly (neither was the town), and nothing was in rows; yet the shape was there, and was felt, the interlocked curves springing from/ returning to the center. In Kastóha-na and Telína-na there were several Left Arms, for to build so many houses in a single curve would either have crammed them together or strung them out inconveniently.

The area within the loose curve of the houses, planted with some trees and perhaps containing a few sheds or booths, but mostly left open and mostly either muddy or dusty, was the *common place* of the town. The corresponding empty area within the curve of the five heyimas on the Right Arm of town was called the *dancing place*. But both places were common, and they danced in both.

One town of the nine did not quite fit this description. Tachas Touchas was (notoriously) settled by "people from outside"—from the northwest, traditionally. Certainly the village architecture showed a likeness to the styles of towns far north of the Valley on the west-running rivers of the redwood lands. The houses of Tachas Touchas were all wood, redwood or cedar, with shallow cellars, and no use of adobe. They stood so close that they shared rain-gutters, in a tight curve, all facing inward. The Hinge of the town was a lively falls in Shasash Creek, and the Right Arm was laid out and built conventionally. But the circle of dark, tall, steep-roofed houses under the sheer rise of Bone Mountain, black-green with fir, was somberly impressive and quite different from any other Valley town. Disapproval of the "tightness" of the town plan was frequently expressed outside it; inside it, the people of Tachas Touchas rebuilt, when, from century to century, a house must be

taken down and replaced, in their immemorial and peculiar fash-
ion; which perhaps did express or encourage a "tight," aloof, in-
turned quality in the character and manners of the townsfolk.

Wakwaha, at the other end of the Valley world, was also excep-
tional; being the Benares, Rome, or Mecca of the Valley, much visited by people from the other towns, its Left Arm included five long,
single-storey hostels, maintained by the Five Houses, where visi-

tors could housekeep for a few days or for months; and the Right Arm took in more area than the Left, containing not only the five great heyimas, but a dozen or more buildings of public and sacred use and significance, such as the Archives, the Conservatory, and the Theater. The Hinge of Wakwaha was one of the high sources of the Na, a beautiful steady spring rising from the volcanic rocks of a deep canyonhead of the Mountain. The site was a difficult one to put a fair-sized town on, but the steep, uneven ground and the sweep of the mountain slopes and canyon walls above and below the town gave it both grandeur and charm. Some of the houses of Wakwaha were very old, built of the stone they stood on and seeming to have grown from it; the madrones that shaded their roofs and walled courts were immense, but the walls had been there long before the trees. They had old, long names, these houses. Rising Up From Where the Quarrel Ended was one of them. Another was called Jackrabbit's Grandmother's Hole House. But then some equally old had very short names; there was a house called Wind, a house called High. And others had names that had lost their meaning over the years, worn away by the changing of the language— Angrawad House, Oufechohe House.

Though people in a small society may talk slowly, their language is likely to change quickly; even written, it keeps flowing, leaving the old spellings and usages high and dry. So the names of the nine towns, being old, had no translatable "meaning," except for Wakwaha-na, the town at the holy spring of the Na (but it could also mean the dancing way of the Na). Chúkúlmas probably meant Live Oak House originally, and the -mal- in Ounmalin is hill or hillock. The people of Tachas Touchas insisted, without offering evidence, that the name of their town in their forgotten northern tongue meant Where the Bear Sat Down. But why Sinshan and its mountain were Sinshan, or what Kastóha meant and why it changed, as it apparently had done, from Hastćha, and why the oldest house in Madídínou was called Madídínou Animoun, nobody knew. No doubt the etymologies could have been traced from data in the Memory Banks of the City of Mind, with a few weeks or months of work at the Exchange. But what for? Need every word be translated? Sometimes the untranslated word might serve to remind us that language is not meaning, that intelligibility is an element of it only, a function. The untranslated word or name is not functional. It sits there. Written, it is a row of letters, which spoken with a more or less wild guess at the pronunciation produces a complex of phonemes, a more or less musical and interesting sound, a noise, a thing. The untranslated word is like a rock, a piece of wood. Its use, its meaning, is not rational, definite, and limited, but concrete, potential, and infinite. To start with, all the words we say are untranslated words.

Some of the Other People of the Valley

I. Animals of the Obsidian

All domestic animals were considered to live in the First House, the Obsidian.

SHEEP.

The several strains of Valley sheep were all derived from crossing "foreign" breeds traded or stolen from neighboring peoples' flocks with the Odoun breed of the Upper Valley: a small, compact animal with loose, fine wool, dark legs and face, two or four short horns, and a pronounced Roman nose. The lambs were born dark, and about half had dark or mixed wool when adult. Every town kept sheep; individuals or households might have one or several sheep in the town flock, and sheepherding and care of the flock was in the charge of the town's Cloth Art. The towns of Chúmo and Telína-na ran large flocks on Sheep Mountain and in the Odoun Valley, northeast of Chúmo. To let the pasturage and soil recover and to fatten the sheep on saltgrass, these flocks were taken down the River to the floodplains at the Mouths of the Na in the middle of the rainy season, and not taken back up onto the hills until the weather began to get hot, between the Moon and the Summer dances. Mutton

and lamb were the festival meat of the Valley, and sheepskin leather and woolens of all grades and kinds were staple fabrics of use and wear. The sheep was not a symbol of passive stupidity and blind obedience as it is to us (and indeed the Valley sheep were both athletic and wily), but rather was regarded with a kind of affectionate awe, as an intrinsically mysterious being. The ewe was the sign and symbol of the Blood Lodge and of the First House, and sheep were called the Children of the Moon.

GOATS.

Goats were kept as commensals and for milk, in the Upper Valley towns; in Madídínou, Sinshan, Ounmalin, and Tachas Touchas they were raised for meat, leather, and wool. The Upper Valley towns, though liking goats for their mischievous intelligence, preferred not to keep them around in great numbers, saying, "One goat outnumbers three people, three goats outnumber thirty." As they were bred with various aesthetic and practical ends in view, there was a great variety of fancy strains and types, including several very small, fat, black or black-and-tan "short goats," the lop-eared, long-haired, cream-colored Ounmalin Milch Goat, and the pugnacious and handsome "mountain goat" that ran with the sheep on Sheep Mountain.

CATTLE.

The Valley cattle were mostly dun, cream, brindle, brown, and fawn color; they were small, with a moderate shoulder-hump, slender legs, incurved horns of medium length, dished brow, and large, oval eyes. In Telína-na a somewhat larger animal, often pure white, was much prized for work. The herds were primarily dairy herds, but a good deal of plowing and heavy hauling was done with oxen. They were not raised for beef, and if slaughtered were generally killed in the first year for veal. As a rule, each household had its cow or cows in the town herd, in charge of the Tanning Art; herding, feeding, and milking might be done by the family or by arrangement with the Art. Households going up into the hills to a summerhouse for the hot weather often took a cow along. Most cows and oxen were commensals, named, and counted and regarded as members of the household. A good deal of poetry was addressed to cows, some of it pointing out how much easier to get along with they are than human beings. The breed was mild, canny, and goodnatured, deserving the praise they got; only the bulls were of uncertain temper, and so were usually common property of the town or the Art, kept fenced in Penis Meadow.

HORSES, DONKEYS, AND MULES.

Since most human people of the Valley were not travellers and when they did travel usually went afoot, there being no long roads, horses were not kept for journeys. They were commensals, and rather extravagant ones. Riding was a sport, not a means of getting somewhere, and horses were seldom used to haul or work. There were not many of them in the Valley, and none of heavy stock; they were selected less for strength and patience than for "wit and beauty." The Summer games always included horse races and riding exhibitions, which might go on here and there up and down the Valley for a couple of months. There was a mystique of the horse, the stallion especially being considered sacred, uncanny, or venerable. The stallion was the cult symbol of men of the Obsidian, though Serpentine people, of the House of the Summer, were most often the breeders and trainers. In the Summer games men rode mares, women rode stallions; in the races the jockeys were adolescents of both sexes. White, black, or piebald stallions were sacred to the Obsidian, but the most prized colors were buckskin and red

A Portrait of Míbí

roan. The Valley horse was seldom as much as fifteen hands tall, fine-boned and short-barrelled, fast on a short track, and inclined to get fat. Unwanted colts were not killed but taken down the river and turned loose to join the wild herds on the grasslands and saltgrass flats west of the Mouths of the Na. These herds roamed the coasts of the Ocean and the Inland Sea. The horses in them were mostly scrubby, but sometimes a group of Bay Laurel boys or Obsidian men made an adventurous and enjoyable sacred journey to the wild horse country to catch an animal or two to recruit the Valley stock. The only large herds of horses in the Valley were kept by the Serpentine of Chúkúlmas. Lower Valley towns generally did not keep any horses at all.

All the towns kept donkeys. Like cows, donkeys were members of the household. They worked with people at hauling, carrying, pulling, plowing, and all donkeywork. Crippled people got about in little donkey-carts. Donkey colts trotted about loose with the cats, dogs, and children. The Valley donkey was the typical small burro, fine-legged, with a black cross on mouse-grey shoulders, and a dreadful voice. Donkey stallions, being notoriously irascible, were pastured in Penis Meadow with the bulls.

Mules, like horses, were mostly bred in Chúkúlmas. The small mule or hinny with a horse sire and donkey dam was sometimes used for riding, and for playing the game vetúlou, a kind of polo; mules with donkey sire and mare dam worked in harness, hauling, and in the fields. The Train was pulled mostly by mules. They were respected for their intelligence and reliability, and were handsome creatures, but since a mule needs nearly as much room and feed as a horse, the donkey remained the chief work-companion in most towns.

PIGS.

Pigs were not raised in the Valley, possibly as a result of cultural differentiation from the Teudem or Pig People, six or seven small nomadic tribes whose territory included the Ranges of the Valley and the Odoun and Yanyan valleys. The Kesh would barter with these tribes for pigskin, but felt all the prejudice of the householder against the nomad, and also considered that the Pig People went rather too far in identifying themselves as Farrows of the Great Sow.

DOGS.

Valley dogs were a motley lot. There was not much work for dogs in the towns, and strong feeling against letting dogs breed freely, since the pups must be either tamed or killed to prevent their joining the wild dog packs. Most male pups were gelded, and the principal job of the domesticated dog was as a guard against wild dogs: an ironic and unhappy role, but fortunately dogs do not have much sense of irony. The wild dogs were a real danger to people and livestock in the woods and fields; they ran in family packs of two to six and also in all-male "rogue" packs of fifteen to twenty, and could pull down any creature they hunted. Children who went out herding or gathering were taught to climb the nearest tree at once if they heard or saw wild dogs, and if possible they went out guarded by the household dog—often, in fact, with a whole cortege of hangers-on and trailers-along and wayside-sniffers.

The wild dogs ran rangy and large; the domesticated dogs were smaller, as a rule, but strong and stocky. There were no pure breeds, but the commonest types were the *hechí*, a sturdy, furry, chowlike watchdog, highly intelligent and serious, sharp-eared and bushy-tailed and usually tawny or reddish in color; the *dúí*, a long-legged dog with curly grey or black hair, very useful as a sheepdog, with a high forehead and a grave, sensitive disposition; and the *ou* or hound, short-haired, lop-eared, sociable, lazy, clownish, and keen. Hounds were allowed to run in packs on the hunting side of town, but the hunters kept a sharp eye on them lest they begin to fraternise with the wild dogs. The hounds were hunted with deer and small game only; when a wild dog, boar, or bear hunt was necessary, the hechí was the dog taken. Dogs were beloved commensals, but were seldom allowed indoors; and dogs hanging around among the houses of the town would be driven out by children, who were expected to keep them out of trouble in town as they kept the children out of trouble in the woods. A kind of subvillage of doghouses usually lined the approach to the Left-Hand Side of town, and there the puppies and children played freely.

CATS.

Since they don't foul the ways, cats had the freedom of the towns. The household cat was usually allowed to live indoors as mouser and commensal. Most Valley cats were shorthairs, of every conceivable color and marking, though black and tabby were favorites. As they were the main ally against mouse and rat depredations in the house, the granary, and the field, they were allowed to breed freely; if an excess-kitten problem arose it was solved by taking weaned kittens up onto the hunting side to fend for themselves. The forests were therefore well stocked with feral cats as well as the native bobcats (two or three times larger), all competing with the foxes and coyotes for the wood rats and innumerable voles and white-footed mice. Tales about giant crossbred wildcats—jet-black lynxes, monster tabbies—were earnestly vouched for, but never substantiated by actual eye witness. It was always somebody in another town who had seen one lurking near the chicken runs.

SMALL FRY AND BIRDS.

Chickens were always kept for eggs, meat, and company; the smaller towns had coops and runs here and there among the houses, while the big towns kept the smell and bustle of the poultry-yards off near the barns, but there was generally a hen in sight, anywhere in any town. Each town had its peculiar breed of poultry and defended its merits against all others. In Sinshan and Madídínou, people raised himpí, the little guinea-piglike animal with piebald fur, for meat; elsewhere himpí were kept only as pets, which put Sinshan and Madidinou at some moral disadvantage. Brush rabbits were sometimes kept and bred and fed with herbs for a finer meat than that of the wild rabbit, but the rabbit was a game animal, and rabbit-breeding was looked on as a kind of cheating, a bit contemptible. It appears that at some periods pigeons, geese, and ducks were kept in large flocks, and times when this practice was rare; sometimes, therefore, these birds lived in the First House as domestic animals, and sometimes in the Second House as wild game. But also, since most pigeons, ducks, and geese were neither hunted nor domesticated, but shared the woods and waters of the Valley in their immense flocks with the human inhabitants, and since they are not ground-dwelling birds, they were not considered to belong to any of the Five Houses, but rather to the Sky and the Wilderness. Because of these crossings and anomalies, the wild goose and the grey pigeon were the favorite pictorial image of the soul going from House to House, between Earth and Sky, between waking and dream or vision, between life and death. The vast migrations of the geese, when the River became "a river of wings and the shadows of wings," and the skeins of the geese crossing the sky daylong, were the beloved image of the passage and renewal of life. The wild goose, duck, and swan were drawn in the shape of the heyiya-if, and so was the flight-skein; the sounds of the geese calling as they flew, creaking and honking across the wind, were used in music.

PETS.

The word *commensal* has been used to avoid the condescending, patronising overtones of the word *pet*, and because it better translates the Valley term, which means people living together.

By the standards of the animal breeding and slaughtering industries of our society, all domesticated animals of the Valley were "pets," but those standards are questionable in every sense. At any rate, children and many adults "lived together" with various beasts beside the useful domestic companions: mice, wood rats, feral hamsters (a pest in the grainfields), crickets, toads, frogs, stagbeetles, and so on. Kingsnakes were not kept in the house, but were a much honored dweller beneath the house or barn, since they keep rattlesnakes away. The rare ringtail or "miners' cat" tamed easily and was sometimes kept as a treasured and sacred inhabitant of the Blue Clay heyimas. The young of the larger wild animals, game animals, most wild birds, and fish were never domesticated or made pets of. If a hunter in error shot a doe with nursing fawns, he killed the fawns, and then went through a ceremony in the Hunters Lodge to clear himself of guilt. A deer might consent to be killed and to be eaten, but not to be tamed. Deer shared the Second House of Life with human beings—not the First House, where the domestic animals lived. To coax or force them to live in a House not their own would be inappropriate or perverse.

THE HOUSE OF OBSIDIAN.

As the Kesh saw it, the domestic animals consented to live and to die with human beings in the First House of Life. The mysteries of animal–human interdependence and cooperation and the mystery of sacrifice were the central preoccupation of the animal rituals of the House of Obsidian. Such rites and teachings were also connected with those of the Blood Lodge. This lodge, into which all girls were initiated at puberty and to which all women belonged, was under Obsidian auspices: "All women live in the First House." The identification of woman and animal went deep throughout the sexual and intellectual teaching of the Blood Lodge (and where in our man-dominant culture that identification is used to devalue, this must not be assumed to hold for the Kesh: rather the opposite). Blood Lodge ritual and learning was passed on by the breath, not written down; but many of the women's songs of the Moon and Grass Dances grew out of it, and a whole body of mystical, satirical, erotic poetry—unfortunately, like most metaphysical poetry, very hard to translate—used its symbols and themes: the ewe, milk, blood sacrifice, orgasm as death spasm, impregnation as rebirth, and the mystery of consent.

～ら

II. Animals of the Blue Clay

In the world-view of the Valley people, all wild animals were Sky People, living in the Four Houses of Death, Dream, Wilderness, and Eternity; but those who allowed themselves to be hunted, who responded to the hunter's singing and came to meet the arrow or enter the snare, had consented to come across into the Second of the Earth Houses, the Blue Clay, in order to die. They had taken on mortality sacrificially and sacramentally.

By its mortality, the individual deer was related physically, materially, with human beings, and all other beings on earth; while "deerness" or The Deer was related metaphysically with the human soul and the eternal universe of being. This distinction of the individual and the type was fundamental in Valley thought, and even in the syntax of the language.

Most wild animals, most of the time, stayed over in the Wilderness: ground squirrel, wood rat, badger, jackrabbit, wildcat, songbird, buzzard, toad, beetle, fly, and all the rest, however familiar, beloved, or pestiferous, did not share a House of Life with human beings. The relationship is based essentially on who eats whom. Those whom we do not eat, or who eat us, are not related to us in the same way as those whom we eat.

On the northwest wall of a Blue Clay heyimas the figure of the deer was painted, on the southwest wall the brush rabbit, on the ceiling near the ladderway the quail. These were the Keepers of that House.

Only the deer, the brush rabbit, and the wild pig were regularly hunted by adults for food or for fur and hides and to control high population. All three species were numerous in the area, and in peak years were very troublesome to farmers, gardeners, and vintners. Pigs were a particularly fierce and persistent competitor for acorns, a valued gathering-crop. They were also dangerous, and so were always considered fair game.

The only other true game animal was wild cattle. Herds sometimes travelled down the grassy slopes west of the Inland Sea, and hunters went out after them, mostly for adventure and sport, since the Valley people had little taste for beef. The meat was treated like venison, and mostly dried for jerky.

Wild-dog packs were extremely dangerous to people and to domestic animals, and when a pack moved into the Ranges of the Valley it was systematically hunted down, usually by a group sent out from the Hunters Lodge; but the feral dogs were not usually spoken of as game. Nor were bears. The bear, the Rain Dancer, the Brother of Death, was the Keeper of its own House, the Sixth House. But when an individual bear began acting "crazy" or "lost," hanging around the pastures and fields near a town, or intimidating and stealing food from people in summerhouses up in the hills, then it was said to have "come into the House of Blue Clay," and might be hunted and killed, and its flesh eaten.

As for birds, quail was always called a game bird, and was a favorite figure in Blue Clay imagery and poetry, but in fact only young children ever seemed to hunt quail, though some people kept quail penned and fattened them to eat, or ate the eggs. Chukar and pheasant were especially prized for their feathers. Wild duck, wild goose, and several kinds of pigeon lived in and migrated through the Valley of the Na, especially the marshes of the lower river, in vast numbers. They were hunted and snared for food, and were also domesticated (see "Animals of the Obsidian").

The freshwater fish of the Na and the creeks were small and coarse, but since they were prized as food, along with crayfish and frogs, they were considered to live in the Second House. Ocean fish were more often traded for than caught, since few people of the Valley wanted much to do with boats or deep water. The Fishers Lodges of the Lower Valley sometimes gathered shellfish on the sea beaches, but the Pacific "red tides" plus residual pollution of the oceans made mussel-eating a risky business.

Fish were supposed to be prejudiced against men: "For her I rise, from him I hide." A good deal of the fishing in the Na and its tributaries was done, with hook and line and handnet, by old women.

Rules concerning hunting weapons in the Hunters Lodge were strict: guns might be used hunting bear, wild dog, and pig; otherwise the tools of the trade were bow and arrow, snare, and slingshot. Hunting was called "the art of silence."

Hunting for food and skins was primarily an occupation for children. All young children, and adolescent boys in the Bay Laurel Lodge, were allowed to hunt rabbit, possum, squirrel, wild himpí and other small game, and deer, and were praised for their successes. They were forbidden to hunt ground squirrel (still a carrier of bubonic plague), and only the older boys were given guns and allowed to join an exterminatory hunt of feral dogs or pigs. When girls became adolescent and joined the Blood Lodge, they stopped hunting. Women living in isolated summerhouses or the recluses called "forest-living" women might shoot or snare rabbit and deer for food, but they were exceptions to a norm. A man who spent much time hunting after he had outgrown the Bay Laurel Lodge and was of marrying age was looked upon as either childish or shiftless. Hunting, in general, was not seen as appropriate behavior for an adult.

All hunters were answerable to the Hunters Lodge and were subject to severe and continuous supervision. If a hunter—child or man—did not clean and skin his catch properly, distribute the meat, hide, etc., appropriately, and dispose of the waste, he would be lectured at or ridiculed as an incompetent. If a hunter killed excessively, or without a pretty good excuse of wanting food, hide, or furs, he would be in danger of getting a reputation as a psychotic, a "crazy" man, a "lost" man, like a dangerous bear. The Hunters Lodge exerted heavy social pressure upon individuals who overstepped these ethical restraints.

At the same time, since a certain degree of shame attached to hunting as an adult pursuit, the hunter got his reward of real understanding and admiration only within the Hunters Lodge, and, if he was a Blue Clay man, in his heyimas. For there the association of the House with the hunter and the hunted was not shameful, but sacramental.

Quail and Deer were celebrated over and over in the poetry, dancing, and art of the Blue Clay heyimas, and were identified with far more closely than any other animals, beloved in a way that even the domestic animals were not. It was a different intimacy. The game animals were the link between the Wilderness and the human soul; and the hunter, just in that he was somewhat less than fully human, was, with the animal he killed, both accomplice and sacrifice in a truly mysterious act. The meaning of the sacred as the dangerous, the holy as transgression, was implicit in Blue Clay animal dancing and in the hunters' songs.

> The walls of this House
>   are of blue clay,
> clay mixed with water,
>   clay mixed with blood,
> blood of the rabbit,
>   blood of the deer.
>
> Beating, beating,
>   this spring is red.
> Red is this spring,
>   beating, beating.
> You drink from it,
>   you start from it,
> Woman of this House,
> you start, Deer Woman!

I give you my arrow, my knife, my mind, my hands,
You give me your flesh, your blood, your skin, your feet.
You are my life. I am your death.
We drink from this spring together.

(There are more examples of hunting and fishing songs in the section "How to Die in the Valley.")

Kinfolk

THERE WERE FOUR KINDS of relatives in the Valley:

> People who lived in one's House: one of the five great divisions of the human and other beings of the Valley, the Obsidian, Blue Clay, Serpentine, Red and Yellow Adobes. The relationship was called maan.
> People who were related by blood (consanguines)—chan
> People who were related by marriage (affines)—giyamoudan
> People who were related by choice—goestun

The interrelationships of these four kinds of kinship could evidently get very complex; but there was no lack of time and interested people to figure them all out and keep them in order.

HOUSE KINSHIP.

Relatives within the House included creatures other than human beings: the chief ones being, in the Obsidian, domestic animals and the moon; in the Blue Clay, game animals and all springs and streams; in the Serpentine, stones and many wild plants; in the Adobes, earth and all domestic plants. To call an olive tree grandmother or a sheep sister, to address a half-acre field of dirt plowed for corn as "my brother," is behavior easily dismissed as *primitive*, or as *symbolic*. To the Kesh, it was the person who could not understand or admit such relationship whose intelligence was in a primitive condition and whose thinking was unrealistic.

The human groups in the Five Houses were, in anthropological lingo, matrilineal and exogamous: descent was through the mother, and you could not marry another member of your House.

The charts on pages 456 and 457 show some of the complicated interlinking of House and blood relationship. For instance, your mother's mother would always be of your House, and your father's father might be, but your father, his mother, and your mother's father could not be. Going down the generations, one might notice that a man is cut off from House relation with his own children. A woman's children were of her House, but a man's were not, nor were his grandchildren through his daughter, though his son's children might be. The two patterns interwove, not so much contradicting as complicating and enriching each other.

CONSANGUINEOUS KINSHIP.

The household, marai, typically consisted of a mother and her daughter(s), their husbands and children, and unmarried sons or other relatives on her side, living together in one set of rooms and sharing work as an economic unit.

When a household got too crowded, a daughter would move out with her husband and children and set up in a different set of rooms as a new unit; and thereafter the relationship between the two households was most importantly that of the House affiliation. But blood relationship was kept close track of, and the obligations of blood kinship were taken seriously. On the mother's side this ensured a double bond; on the father's side it could easily turn into a double bind.

Blood kinship was reckoned generally as it is in English, with some finer distinctions. These are the commonest kinship terms:

mother: mamou
father: bata, ta, tat
grandmother: homa
     mother's mother: ama
     mother's father: mavta
grandfather: hotat
     father's mother: tatvama
     father's father: tavta
daughter: sou
son: dúcha
grandchild: shepin
sibling: kosh
     sister: kekosh (*i.e.*, my mother's daughter, or the daughter of both my parents)
     brother: takosh (my mother's, or my parents', son)
     half-sister: hwikkosh (my father's but not my mother's daughter)

half-brother: hwikkosha (my father's but not my mother's son)

aunt (my mother's sister): madí or amasou

aunt (my father's sister): takekosh

uncle (my mother's brother): matai

uncle (my father's brother): tatakosh

(For great-aunt, etc., the word old, *ho*, is prefixed to these words.)

niece (husband's sister's daughter): madísou

niece (daughter of husband's brother or of husband's sibling): ketro

nephew (husband's sister's son): madídú

nephew (son of husband's brother or of husband's sibling): ketra

cousin (in maternal line, or of my House): machedí

cousin (in paternal line or of a different House): choud

There are other terms, which varied from the Upper to the Lower Valley, for the complicated relationships resulting from second or third marriages. Terms of pure House relationship, used to a person not necessarily related by blood, were made by prefixing ma (and the possessive adjective) to the term: marivdúcha, son of my House; makekosh, House-sister, and so on. Terms of both blood and House kinship were in continual use as salutations and endearments.

KINSHIP BY MARRIAGE.

The Kesh were matrilocal: a couple marrying were expected to live at least for a while in the bride's mother's household (which might involve some other relatives moving out). The custom was not rigid, and very commonly a young couple set up their own household in the same house or a different one or in a different town if their work took them there. The Kesh considered themselves as firmly rooted as trees and hills, but it was my observation that in fact many of them moved around for a great part of their grown life from one town to another.

When a marriage ended, the woman might stay in her mothers' household, or go back to it, but by no means was this a rule. The divorced man almost always went back to his mothers' household to live "as a son," handúcha. Children of divorced parents usually stayed with the mother, but if the father wanted to stay with them more than the mother did, he would go on living in his children's mother's mothers' household, bringing them up in that House.

The words giyamoud, married person; giyoudo, wife; giyouda, husband, were reserved for those who had publicly undertaken marriage at the Wedding Ceremony of the annual World Dance. For people who were living together unmarried, the term -hai, now, came in handy; haibí, "now-dear," was a temporary spouse; dúchahai, "son-now," a transitory son-in-law, and so on. Homosexual marriage was recognised, and homosexual spouses were distinguished, when such distinction was relevant, as hanashe and hankeshe, (living) in a man's or a woman's manner. There was no term for ex-spouse, nor any equivalent of our words bachelor and spinster. Marriage-relationship terms were, like the terms of House and blood kinship, much used in conversation; one addressed a relative by marriage as my aunt's husband, madív giyouda, or my brother's wife, takoshiv giyoudo, for instance, or just called them giyamoudan, in-law.

KINSHIP BY CHOICE: GOESTUN.

Two people might agree to undertake the obligations and privileges of relationship closer than House and descent gave them. Often this was simply adoption: an orphaned child at once became somebody's goestun child, always within the child's House. A baby of course had no choice in the matter, but an older child might; and sometimes children who were not orphaned opted to be the goestun child of another household (again within their House). Goestun siblings were usually friends of the same sex who wanted to assert and bind their friendship, rather like "bloodbrotherhood"; and sometimes friends of the same House but opposite sex undertook to be goestun brother and sister, asserting affection but reinforcing the incest ban. The goestun relationship was taken very seriously, and defaulting on it was held a most contemptible betrayal.

In Stone Telling's story, the man she calls her side-grandfather, amhotat, was a magoestun or stand-in grandfather. The House provided these stand-in relatives for people who lacked them—in this case, Stone Telling lacked any male relatives in her own House, the Blue Clay, having no maternal uncle, and no kin at all on the father's side, and so an older man of the Blue Clay asked to take that responsibility.

INCEST PROHIBITIONS.

Sexual relationship with any of the following was considered to be incestuous and was forbidden:

Any member of one's House
Anyone currently related by marriage to a blood relation
Any goestun relation
And the following blood relations: parent/child; grandparent/grandchild; sibling; uncle and aunt/nephew and niece; great-uncle and great-aunt/great-nephew and great-niece. First-cousin marriage was permitted with cousins and half-cousins on the father's side, but if a paternal uncle married a woman of my House his children would be my House siblings and so proscribed. My maternal aunt's children were of course of my House; my maternal uncle's children were not, but marriage with these cousins was unusual—"It is too close to the mothers." Second-cousin marriage was restricted only by House affiliation.

The Kesh gave no reason or justification whatever for incest prohibitions, neither religious, nor genetic, nor social, nor ethical. They said, "That is the way people are: that is how human people behave."

☺

CHARTS OF KINFOLK

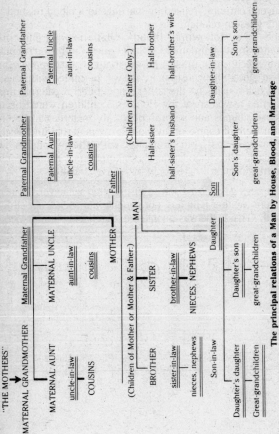

The principal relations of a Man by House, Blood, and Marriage

A relationship that must be in the man's House is CAPITALISED; a relationship that cannot be in his House is underlined. The other relationships may or may not be in his House.

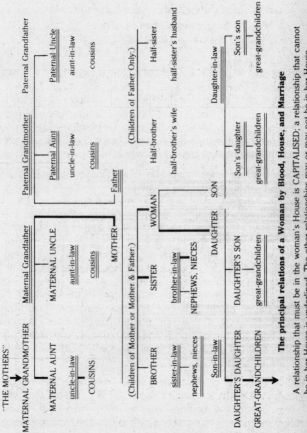

The principal relations of a Woman by Blood, House, and Marriage

A relationship that must be in the woman's House is CAPITALISED; a relationship that cannot be in her House is underlined. The other relationships may or may not be in her House.

Lodges, Societies, Arts

▬▬▬▬▬▬▬▬▬▬▬▬▬▬▬▬▬▬▬▬▬▬▬▬▬▬▬▬

*As explained by Thorn of Sinshan in response
to questions from Pandora.*

PANDORA: I don't think I understand when you say that a Lodge is
in one of the Five Houses.

THORN: Well, that just means that the meetings of the Lodge are in
the heyimas of that House, like the Planting Lodge always
meets in one of the Adobe heyimas. Or that if the Lodge people need things they ask that House for them, like Doctors
using Serpentine songs.

PANDORA: It doesn't mean that to be in that Lodge you have to have
been born in that House, then?

THORN: No. After all, all women join the Blood Lodge, don't they, it
doesn't matter if they're Obsidian people or not. And men
who aren't Blue Clay join the Hunters. And practically everybody belongs to the Planting Lodge. Although it's mostly
Adobe people who dance the Planting dances. The only
Lodge that's only for people of one House is the Salt Lodge, I
think. That's Blue Clay people only. And it only does one
thing—they keep up the salt ponds down by the Mouths of the
Na, and make the Salt Journey every year, and learn those
songs. Have you seen the salt ponds? The new ones are bright
red with the brine shrimp and the older ones are turquoise
blue with the algae and I always wonder how the salt comes
out pure white.

PANDORA: I hope to go down there soon. Now, how does a Lodge
come under the auspices of one of the Sky Houses, that don't
have heyimas to meet in?

THORN: It meets in its own place, a built lodge. The Madrone has an
archive building, a library, you know, and the Black Adobe
always has a lodge on the hunting side of town. The Finders
can use that lodge too, and the Bay Laurel boys meet there
when it rains. They're supposed to meet outdoors on the hunt-

ing side, in the open; but when it rains they always go to the Black Adobe earth lodge.

PANDORA: Are the Societies the same thing as the Lodges?

THORN: Well, not exactly. They're smaller, for one thing. And usually their speakers are people of the House they're connected with. But people of other Houses can join them. Except the male Clowns. Blood Clowns, you know, are women from any house, not just the Obsidian. But the White Clowns are Obsidian men, and the Green Clowns are Adobe men.

PANDORA: How does a person get to be a Clown?

THORN: You learn how. From the people who are Clowns already, in secret. It can take a long time.

PANDORA: What do the Societies do?

THORN: People in the Societies sing and learn. Each one has certain songs, certain ways of being, certain gifts.

PANDORA: They . . . learn with each other? [In English I would have asked, Are they schools?]

THORN: Some of them teach secrets. And the Oak Society is different from the others, it's got a lot of people in it, and it works with the Book Art and Madrone Lodge and the libraries in all the heyimas. The Oak is really more like an Art than a Society—it teaches reading and writing and bookmaking and inkmaking and copying and printing and all the skills that have to do with written words.

PANDORA: And the Arts, how closely are they connected with the Five Houses?

THORN: I don't really know how it's supposed to be. Here in Sinshan, women are likely to join one of the Arts that belongs to their House, but the men don't. And in the big towns I've noticed that the women don't either. An Art doesn't usually meet in the heyimas of its House, it usually meets in the workshop. But if something goes wrong, you know, some work isn't done, or is badly done, then the House takes responsibility for getting it right. And a person working in an Art can go to the House of that Art for help, if there's some kind of trouble. One reason it's dangerous to be a Miller is that the Millers Art doesn't have an Earth House—they are under the Sky. So if a Miller does anything wrong she gets everybody mad at her and hasn't got a roof over her head, as they say.

CHART OF LODGES, SOCIETIES, AND ARTS

THE FIVE HOUSES of EARTH

First OBSIDIAN	Second BLUE CLAY	Third SERPENTINE	Fourth YELLOW ADOBE	Fifth RED ADOBE
Blood Lodge ♀ (ritual and social)	*Hunters Lodge* ♂ *Fishers Lodge* ⚥ *Salt Lodge* ⚥	*Doctors Lodge* ⚥ (medicine and ritual)	*Planting Lodge* ⚥ (agriculture and ritual)	
Blood Clown Society ♀ *White Clown Society* ♂ *Lamb Society* ♀ (cult)		*Oak Society* ⚥ (writing, books)	*Green Clown Society* ♂ *Olive Society* ♂ (cult)	
Glass Art: windows, vessels, instruments *Tanning Art:* butchering, leather goods *Cloth Art:* spinning, weav- ing, dyeing, knitting	*Potting Art:* utensils, tiles, pipes *Water Art:* wells, aquifers, irrigation, sew- age, storage	*Book Art:* paper, ink, bindings, paints	*Wood Art:* carpentry, architecture *Drum Art:* musical instruments	*Wine Art:* viticulture, oenology *Smith Art:* mining, smelting, metallurgy, tools, wire

Lodges Belonging to All Five Houses:
> *Bay Laurel Lodge* ♂
>> (adolescent boys: scouting, athletic prowess, border-guarding, hunting,
>> ritual, and social)
>
> *Finders Lodge* ⚥
>> (exploration and trade outside the Valley)

THE FOUR HOUSES of SKY

Sixth	Seventh	Eighth	Ninth
RAIN	CLOUD	WIND	AIR
Black Adobe Lodge ⚥ (Earth lodge outside town. Funeral rites and burial)			
Madrone Lodge ⚥ (archives, records, history)			
		Toyon Society (cult)	*Mole Society* (cult)
Dancers of the Inner Sun ⚥			
Milling Art: windmills, water mills, turbines, electric power sources and motors, solar collectors, lighting, heating, refrigeration			

What They Wore in the Valley

‖‖

INDOORS, A BABY WORE a napkin or diaper; outdoors in the dry season, nothing. Little children wore clothing only for protection from the sun or the cold, or as ornament; what they wore was sketchy, usually cut down from somebody else's clothes or old bed-linen or what have you.

As they got older, in their "clearwater" and "sprouting" years, children generally put on some kind of modesty bit, a kilt or skirt, and they began to long for the kind of clothing adolescents wore; but if they put it on too soon they would be ridiculed by their age-mates and scolded by their household and heyimas.

Having reached puberty, the young adolescent was given a ceremony in the heyimas and a party at home, and a whole set of new clothes of a particular kind. The boys wore a heavy kilt to the knee, of white buckskin or white cotton or dark wool, and a white cotton shirt (cut like a kurta; sometimes collared and cuffed). In cold weather they might wear stockings and sandals, and in rough country, leather shoes. The girls wore a similar kilt or a gathered skirt, below the knee and above the ankle, of undyed cream, grey, or dark wool, an overblouse or shirt of white cotton, and stockings, sandals, or shoes like the boys. Both boys and girls might wear a fitted vest. Coats and shawls and knitted sweaters for cold weather were of no prescribed style, but they were never dyed. No dye color was used in any of these clothes for people "living on the Coast." They were made with care and of good material, often by their wearer, anxious to have everything about them exactly right. The lack of color gave them an austere elegance; young people living on the Coast stood out in any Valley crowd.

After they took a sexual partner—"came Inland"—young women and men often went on wearing the kilts and shirts of their time on the Coast, but they dyed them or wore colors with them.

As for the "native costume" of the Valley, it is rather hard to describe, because it varied so much according to time, place, and wearer. There were definitely styles, fashions; in wall paintings one could see figures dressed in clothes of a quite different cut than any being currently worn. For both women and men, shirts, full-cut overshirts, belted and unbelted shifts, kilts, and rather loose trousers were among the options; women sometimes added the gathered skirt. Underclothes were worn for warmth. Adults did not usually go naked in town, except men at the time of the Moon Dance, but everybody swam naked in the holding tanks, and in the household and at the summerhouse older people often went about without clothes. Coats for cold weather were made of sheepskin with the fleece, and of canvas; but people working outdoors in the rain often undressed rather than dressed for it, their theory being, "Skin dries quick."

The dancing clothes, costumes worn for the wakwa, were of course of conservative style and often of great beauty. The characteristic ceremonial garment was the sleeveless vest. Going down into the heyimas for singing or socialising or teaching or anything else, people generally put on a short, unbuttoned vest of fine make and finely decorated, kept for this purpose both by individuals and in the heyimas; and the men who danced the Moon, and both male and female dancers of the Summer, Wine, and Grass, wore magnificently ornate vests, some of them many generations old.

The principal materials of clothing were wool, cotton, linen, and leather.

Wool was entirely from Valley sheep. The most prized wool came from the Chúmo flocks and was spun in Chúmo and Telínana.

Cotton was raised in patches in the Valley, but most of it came from the southern shores of the Inland Sea. Wine was sent down annually on the Train to the port at Sed to be shipped in exchange for the cotton sent up from the south (see "Trouble with the Cotton People").

Flax was grown in the Valley, and more extensively north of the Mountain, in the Clear Lake region. It was bartered for with wine, olives, olive oil, lemons, and glassware, carried over the Mountain on the Train or by wagon and pack teams using the Line as a road.

Leather was made locally, using hides of cows, horses, sheep, goats, deer, rabbits, moles, himpí, and other small animals. Birdskins were tanned for ceremonial wear, and feather robes and vests were made as great gifts to the heyimas. Leatherworking was a very highly developed technology, and leathers of great variety were available for clothing, shoes, and other uses.

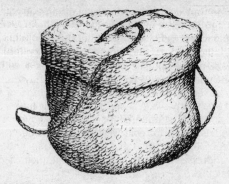

Raw fibers were mostly treated and prepared at the town workshop or manufactory under the direction of the Cloth Art. An individual might take a shearing from the family sheep or a quantity of homegrown flax or cotton to the workshop to clean, card, and dye; or a group might share the labor; or the individual or group might give the fleece or the bale to the Cloth Art to prepare. Much spinning was done on the powered machines at the workshop, and bulk weaving and broadloom was done on the big power looms by Cloth Art professionals, but most fine or ceremonial stuffs were homespun on wheels or with the drop spindle and woven at home. Wool was the great ceremonial material; it made the beautiful rugs of Chúmo and Chúkúlmas, and was knitted at home by men and women for stockings, shawls, and so on. Linsey-woolsey mixture was a favorite material for skirts, kilts, and trousers. Cotton and linen were also mixed for summer fabrics, both woven and knitted. The most prized material for everyday wear was cotton, and the technology was exquisitely refined; cotton fabrics ranged from massive canvases through soft heavy knits to gossamer voiles so fine they "let the moonlight through."

The Tanning Art looked after butchering, as well as the leather technologies of curing, tanning, and making harness, shoes, furnishings, clothing, etc., and the Cloth Art managed the preparation of raw fibers, including cleaning, carding, dyeing, and spinning, the technologies of fabric manufacture including weaving and powered knitting, and the production of some items—stockings, sheets, blankets, rugs—that were made in quantity and stockpiled. Important elements of the economy of each town and the Valley as a whole, the two Arts worked closely together. The tannery was always outside town, along with the slaughterhouse, but finished leather was brought in to the Cloth Art workshops to be made into shoes and clothing. Tanners and Clothiers were as a rule solid, prosperous, respectable people, who lived in the same house for generations, and considered themselves with complacency as pillars of the community.

Embroidery

What They Ate

THERE IS NO WORD in Kesh for famine.

Hunting-and-gathering is supposed to be a mode of subsistence incompatible with farming; when people learn to herd and farm they stop hunting and gathering, as a rule. The Kesh disobeyed the rule.

Their hunting was of very little real importance to their food supply; most of it was done, and most game was eaten, by children. (It may be asked how important hunting has ever been as a principal source of human food, except where there are no other sources of protein readily available; the intense symbolic value of hunting, especially to men, has disguised its practical triviality, so that "Man the Hunter" romantically dominates the scene, while the women who actually provide and prepare the food he lives on are not discussed.) As to us, hunting to the Kesh was a mixture of sport, religion, self-discipline, and self-indulgence. Gathering, however, was a major source of food. They gathered wild produce—acorns, greens, roots, herbs, berries, and many kinds of seeds, some requiring great patience to collect and process, and did so not at whim but methodically, going yearly in due season to the family's trees, the town's seed-meadows or cattail-beds. The question Why? might fairly, I think, be countered by the question Why not? The natural food supply was very rich, and they liked the taste and quality; and since large families, a large private food-supply, and a competitive attitude were all socially disapproved, there was no need or motivation to give up gathering for heavy farming. The essential factor is probably population size and growth, whether considered as cause or as effect. The city—the "opposite" of the farm—does not occur unless or until the land is heavily used for farming. Population explosions of any species depend upon excess food; the furrow ends in the street. The Kesh lived half in town and half in the wilderness. They had no streets, and their farms were, by our standards, gardens.

These were not particularly neat gardens, since a great many different people worked in them, with animal rather than machine assistants, or as assistants to animals rather than machines, and the patches and plots (except for the great vineyards of the Valley floor) were small and various. Indeed what they planted and prepared as food was various—surprisingly so for a people many of whose cultural styles were limited, resistant to borrowing, and "pure." For example, corn (maize) was the nearest thing to a staple grain they had, but they also gathered acorns, raised wheat, barley, and oats, and traded for rice. Rice and barley were mostly hulled and boiled whole; the other grains were variously prepared as groats, meal, or flour, and boiled, baked leavened, baked unleavened, and so on—giving a great variety of grain dishes, porridges, and breads.

In sum, the Kesh took or found or raised or grew food wherever convenient, and cooked and ate it with interest, respect, and pleasure. They were not a thin people. Small-boned, they tended towards the round rather than the angular, the easy rather than the lean.

Food is not something that lends itself to discussion in the abstract; it seems more sensible to give some recipes.

LÍRIV METADÍ, OR VALLEY SUCCOTASH

Wash about two cups of small red beans (the Valley metadí is very like the Mexican frijole), and cook till done (a couple of hours) with half an onion, three or four garlic cloves, and a bay leaf.

Simmer about a cup and a half of parched corn until thoroughly cooked, and drain (or in season use fresh corn cut off the cob, uncooked).

Simmer a handful of dried black mushrooms for half an hour or so, and keep them in their cooking broth.

When all these ingredients are done combine them, along with:

the juice and pulp of a lemon, or some preserved tamarind pulp

an onion chopped and fried in oil with some finely chopped garlic and a spoonful of cumin seeds

a large, mild green chile of the chile verde type, *or* a small, hot green chile (but *not* bell pepper), seeded and chopped fine

three or four tomatoes peeled and chopped coarsely

add, as seasoning, oregano, winter savory, and more lemon to taste

add dried red chile if you want it hot

To thicken the sauce, one dried tomato-paste ball was added; our equivalent would be two or three tablespoons of thick tomato paste. (If fresh tomatoes are not in season, double or triple the quantity of tomato paste.)

All this simmers for about an hour.

Serve with chopped raw onion to garnish, and a sour sauce or chutney made of green tomatoes or tomatillos, flavored with fresh or dry coriander leaf.

This dish, "too heavy for rice," was accompanied by cornbreads, either of the hoe-cake or the tortilla type.

HOTUKO, "OLD HEN," A RICE AND CHICKEN DINNER

Simmer a big, old, tough chicken with bay leaf, rosemary, and some wine until done. (Since most of us cannot get big, old, tough chickens, simmer a little, young, tough one.) Cool, and take the meat off the bones.

Save enough of the stock to cook the rice in; cook the rest down if it is thin, and then simmer in it, for five to fifteen minutes, until just barely done, some or any of the following:

a handful of blanched whole almonds

sliced celery, carrots, radishes, yellow or green squash, onions, etc.

a few leaves of spinach, Chinese cabbage, or other greens

whole mushrooms, fresh or dried

Add the chicken meat cut up, some chopped parsley, chopped fresh coriander or dry coriander leaf, and chopped green onions; season with cumin seed, coriander seed, a

little ground red pepper, and salt or lemon. Let it sit all day
or overnight for the flavors to "get used to one another."

Reheat gently and serve with rice cooked in the stock.

Serve any or all of the following as accompaniments:

   chopped hardboiled eggs
   toasted tarweed or chia seeds
   chopped coriander leaves
   green onions
   green tomato or tomatillo sauce or sour pickle
   hot red pepper chutney or pickle
   currant jelly
   dried currants or chopped raisins

These would be arranged in little dishes around the
main dish.

Most of the rice that came to the Valley was from the peoples of the
River of the Marshes, and was short-grained, cooking up rather
sticky. They prized and would trade their best wines for the rarer,
long-grained, very fine-flavored "sasí" rice grown farther south and
east of the Inland Sea.

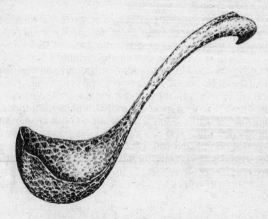

PRAGASÍV FAS—SUMMER SOUP

A hot-weather aftermath to a lamb feast.

Cook up in a piece of butter about egg-yolk size, about
half that much cornstarch (corn flour), and one egg yolk, stirring gently to make a thickening paste or roux. Cool this and

stir in about a cup of yogurt and about two cups of cold lamb broth (made from the bones, cleared of all fat). Flavor to taste with lemon juice and/or dry white wine. Serve topped with chopped mint leaves.

(For a hot soup, add cooked barley while heating gently, and use parsley or chervil instead of mint.)

DÚR M DREVÍ, "RED AND GREEN," A VEGETABLE DINNER

Peel one large or several small eggplants and slice "about as thick as my finger is." Sprinkle the slices with lemon juice and coarse salt, and let them sit while you prepare the rest for cooking:

slice a couple of fair-sized zucchini squash (unpeeled) the same way, and also sprinkle with lemon juice

a handful of parsley, the stems cut off

a couple of garlic cloves, chopped fine

a double handful of mushrooms—any delicate kind—fresh

Make a sauce of two cloves of garlic thoroughly mashed in a mortar or press, about two tablespoons of good olive oil, and a dash of ground red pepper, all stirred into two cups of yogurt until smooth and creamy.

Fry the zucchini fast and hot in light oil in an iron pan until the edges brown; pile it on one end of a platter. Using less oil, fry the eggplant very fast and hot till it turns vivid red-brown. Pile it on the other end of the platter. Stir-fry the mushrooms, garlic, and parsley gently and quickly just till the parsley wilts, and pile it in the center of the platter. Serve at once, along with potatoes boiled in their jackets. The yogurt sauce accompanies both the vegetables and the potatoes, poured over them or used as a dip.

Sliced tomatoes and black olives go well with this dish.

HWOVWON, "OAK-EGGS"

Acorn meal compares interestingly with corn meal and wheat flour. Before cooking, corn and wheat average 1 to 2 percent fat, 10 percent protein, and 75 percent carbohydrate. Acorn meal averages 21 percent fat, 5 percent protein, and 60 percent carbohydrate. Acorn meal was of course a staple food of the original human inhabitants of the area, though its use was abandoned by later people from cultures in which acorns were fed only to swine.

The Kesh planted oaks in and around their towns, and tended "gathering trees" in the woods and fields. The area was very rich in both species and numbers of oaks, and in a normal year there were vastly more acorns available than the human population could use. The Kesh favored the acorns from the Valley Oak and Tanoak. Gathering and processing were a communal activity under the supervision of the Serpentine, though of course a family that wanted an extra supply could provide it for themselves. After sorting and hulling, the acorns were ground, the millers using special stones, "acorn stones." Excess oil was saved for numerous uses. The meal, coarse or fine, was leached by submersion in cold or hot waters for a few hours up to several days, depending on the tannic acid content and the flavor desired. The meal or flour was usually parched or toasted before storage or just before use, to "sweeten" and bring up the nutty flavor.

Acorn meal soup, thick and variously flavored, was a daily winter food in many households. They called it doumfas, brown soup; it was often an infant's first food other than breast milk. Coarser meal was boiled to make a porridge or batter, which was eaten like polenta or rice, or baked as a heavy, dry, rich bread. Acorn flour was combined with honey and toasted seeds and wheat flour and baked as sweet cakes and wafers. Being oily, the flavor of acorn meal deteriorated in storage, and generally what was left after half a year or so was shared out to animals.

TÍS: HONEY

The Kesh were fond of sweets, and there were sugar-beet fields below Ounmalin; but they found the cultivation and processing of that crop arduous, and most of their sweetening came from honey. Like game animals, bees were considered to be visitors from the Sky Houses who consented to come into the Houses of the Earth, and indeed to live in the small houses provided for them there. Most bee-keepers were of the Red Adobe, and that House looked after the preparation, storage, and distribution of the honey. "Bee-towns," sets of hives, were numerous throughout the planting side of each human township. The hives were of wood, and the bee-keepers used removable wooden frames for the honeycombs, so that combs could be removed without destroying the hive or even dismaying the bees. Enough honey was made in the Upper Valley towns that it was used in trade with peoples to the north and east who were, apparently, less methodical in their bee-husbandry.

FATFAT—"CLOWN-CLOWN," A DESSERT

Clean about a quart of green gooseberries, red currants, or red huckleberries, with elder, madrone, or manzanita berries ad lib—any tart ripe berry—and stew gently. Stir up with honey to taste. Flavor with lemon rind or chopped kumquat if desired. Cool.

Scald one to two pints very heavy cream and beat until cooled and thickened. Mix with the fruit.

The scalded cream has a rich texture very different from our fluffy whipped cream; but you have to start with a heavier cream than we are likely to have available.

LÚTE: AMOLE

People in Chúmo stewed amole (or soaproot—*Chlorogalum pomeridianum*) with a little honey and ate it as a delicacy. People in the other eight towns used it as shampoo. The Kesh version of *De gustibus non disputandum* is, "He washes his hair with her dinner."

TABLE MANNERS.

They set the table with plates, dishes, bowls. cups, drinking glasses, and so on, often beautiful and in considerable variety, but not in great profusion, since dishes, after all, have to be washed. For soups and sloppy dishes they had spoons of china, wood, horn, and metal; otherwise they ate with their fingers. There was no tabu or "sinister" hand; it was presumed that you came to table with clean hands, and you could eat right-handed, left-handed, or with both hands—neatly. The various kinds of bread served as containers, supporters, and soppers. Meat was sliced or cut before serving, poultry was jointed. The table might be set bare or on a tablecloth or on mats of cloth or platted reed, bamboo, cattail, or grass; there was a bowl or two of water to wash the fingers in, and often a large cloth napkin was passed around at the end of the meal.

As the Kesh seldom used chairs, the tables were low. People sat on the floor, with the legs straight out, curled to the side, or crossed tailor-fashion, or they sat on the low chest-bench that ran along two or three sides of most rooms, and pulled a little stool-table up before them to eat from.

They counted three meals a day: breakfast, often of milk, bread or mush, fresh or dry fruit; a lunch of leftovers or uncooked food; and dinner, usually after sunset, hence early in winter and quite late in summer. They were, however, inclined to eat small amounts when hungry rather than to stuff in a great deal of food at a set time. This may be because food was both plentiful and handy; because no person was particularly privileged/obligated to prepare, dispense, or withhold food; and finally because heavy eating was considered embarrassing and gorging shameful, but greed could be satisfied more or less invisibly by casual but persistent snacking. As I remarked above, the Kesh were not a thin people.

Kesh Musical Instruments

THE INSTRUMENTS DISCUSSED HERE may all be heard on the sound recording that accompanies this book.

Instruments of professional quality, or for ceremonial use, were made by members of the Drum Art under the auspices of the Yellow Adobe House.

HOUMBÚTA.

The houmbúta or great horn was played in both theatrical and sacred music. Most scrupulous care was taken in selecting the madrone wood for the seven-foot-long conical body of the instrument, and each detail of the curing, shaping, and carving was essential to the capacity of the wood to gather, shape, and focus the sound of the breath. The funnel-like mouthpiece made of deer antler should be "like a lily that receives the warm rays of the sun"; though only five inches long, it was proportioned as a mirror image of the body and bell of the horn. The nine thin madrone slats forming the body were pitch-sealed and fiber-wrapped. The bell, nearly two feet long, was made of electrum, and was joined to the wooden body with pitch and fiber wrapping.

DOUBÚRE BINGA.

The name—"many vibrations"—described a set of nine brass bowls, kept in a box which opened out to form a platform on which the player arranged them in the heyiya-if pattern, five to the left and four to the right. The bowls varied in diameter from four to eleven inches, and their musical pitches spanned a major ninth. Tonal quality depended on the type of mallet—hard wood, soft wood, or cloth-covered—the part of the bowl struck, and the strength of the stroke. Seldom used solo, the instrument provided a rhythmic shimmering flow of tones which one musician described as "like the shining of the sun on running water, moving forward yet turning back. . . ."

YOYIDE.

This single-stringed instrument was about four feet long, and looked from the front like a sinuous teardrop. The beautifully re-curved bow was about two feet long, and strung with a combination of horsehair and human hair, which was believed to give the instrument its singularly sensitive tone.

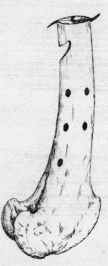

WEÓSAI MEDOUD TEYAHÍ.

Every Kesh child knew how to make a flute, and there seemed to be endless kinds of flute in the Valley, endblown and sideblown, with or without reeds, made of wood, metal, bone, and soapstone. The bone reed flute was one of the oddest: five or six inches long, it was made from the thighbone of a deer or lamb. The bore began at the smaller end of the bone, descended to the larger end, then

THE WILLOWS

QUAIL SONG

Fe - ho - chan am na pa - rad - tun am na fe-ho-chan am na

pa - ra - dan am na kaili-kú ge-le hú ge-le hú kailíkú

hú kaili - kú dí-ú hú kailí-kú ge-le dí-ú kaili-kú hú

pa - rad - tun am na fe - ho - chan am na

pa - rad-tun am na fe-ho-chan am na pa - ra-dan am na

kaili-kú ge-le hú ge-le hú -kaili-kú hú kaili - kú dí - ú

hú kaili - kú ge-le dí - ú kaili - kú hú pa-rad-tun am na

returned upward to the reed-holder: a cattail reed mounted between willow-wood fittings. The sound escaped from a bore in the
side of the bone. By applying subtle pressure to the reed-holder
the player could create stunning microtonal glides, and by sliding
the fingers on and off the five holes could produce strange, piercing, wailing, birdlike tones. Tabit of the Madrone and Yellow Adobe
of Wakwaha, who demonstrated the instrument said to us, said that
he had to keep it away from his cat, "who kept trying to get the bird
out of it."

TÓWANDOU.

This nine-stringed hammer dulcimer was actually two instruments
in one. The larger, half-moon-shaped, about five feet long, had five
strings; the smaller, with four strings, faced it. They shared the
soundingboard of cherry wood. The canoe-shaped body was of
finely carved and polished myrtle (bay laurel). The longest string of
the larger dulcimer, the "hinge string," was unbridged; the walnut
bridge of the other strings formed a gently heyiya-if curve. The
tówandou was much used to provide music for dancing and plays,
and its sound meant festival in the Valley. The finest instruments
were kept by the Yellow Adobe heyimas in each town; travelling
players or troupes used those or carried a smaller, portable version
of the instrument.

BOUD.

Everybody in the Valley played some kind of drum—usually a
small one with a wooden or stretched-hide head tapped softly with
the fingers or whole hand or with a rawhide-wrapped stick. The
drum accompanied singing, dancing, meditating, and thinking. It
was played many together or all alone. It was "the other heart" to
the Kesh.

Drums played by professional musicians were often large and
elaborate in construction. The wehosóboud, wood drum, might
have up to nine tongues or bars of different tone carved into its top,
and a set of a dozen different pairs of sticks and mallets; such a
drum was a melody instrument of considerable expressiveness.
Among the stretched-head drums, the ceremonial drum was most
impressive: a pair of large kettledrums (up to four or five feet
across, one larger than the other in the five to four ratio) were so
connected that when struck they rotated around a central pole,
which suspended them about three feet above the ground. This

majestic rotation controlled the pace of the drumbeat. These instruments, some of them very old, were never brought up from the heyimas; but even in informal, aboveground music-making their deep resonance and tempo might be sensed.

DARBAGATUSH.

The "handhitter" was an occasional instrument, providing a rhythmic accompaniment to a song or dance. It exploited the tendency of the bark of certain kinds of eucalyptus tree to come off in sheets or strips which curl up into tubes as they dry. Five to nine of these pleasant-smelling pieces, a couple of feet long, were chosen and lashed together with grass-stems at one end, and the bundle was held in one hand and hit against the open palm of the other to make a satisfying rattling clack. If the singing or dancing was by a fire, indoors or out, it was customary to burn the darbagatush when the music was done.

Darbagatush

Maps

|||||||||||||||||||||||||||||||||||||||||||||||||||||||||||||||||||

THE PEOPLE OF THE VALLEY drew maps—mostly of the Valley. They evidently enjoyed laying out and looking at the spatial relationships of places and objects they knew well. The better they knew them, the better they liked to draw and map them.

Children often drew maps of the fields and hills about their home town, often in incredible detail—a dot for every rock, a mark for every tree.

Small, schematised, symbolic maps of the Valley or a part of it were often carried by people going on a downriver journey to the ocean or upriver to Wakwaha. As most people knew every feature of the landscape, from mountains to molehills, within four or five miles of their home, and the entire length of the Valley was less than thirty miles, these maps were less guides than talismans.

The larger maps were remarkably accurate, considering that their function was mostly aesthetic or poetic; but then, accuracy was considered a fundamental element or quality of poetry.

Maps of the Valley were always drawn as charts of the Na and its confluents, and maps of areas within the Valley took the principal creek or creek-system as their axis. The source of the stream is at the top of the map. Compass directions may be noted, but the map is oriented to the flow of water, and "down" is the bottom of the page. There is often an element of perspective in the drawing of hills and mountains, but no foreshortening. Towns and other man-made features are usually marked with a symbol (the heyiya-if for towns); and the mapmakers did not like to write on their maps, it seems, for some have no lettering at all, and many have only an initial, or the most cryptic, crabbed indications, for the names of the towns, creeks, mountains, and so on. Since practically every feature of any interest or permanence had a name, the mapmakers may have followed a practical course in refusing to try to crowd them all onto the map.

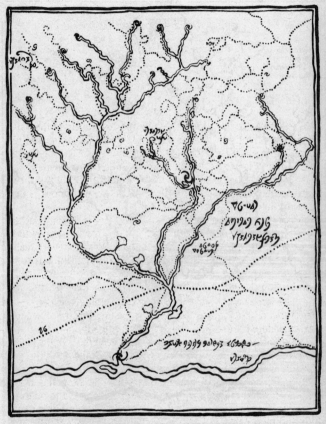

"Some of the Paths around Sinshan Creek"

A Kesh map of the watershed of Sinshan Creek, given to the Editor by Little Bear Woman of Sinshan.

Only Sinshan Mountain, Blue Rock, the Spring of Sinshan Creek, and a few other springs and hills are named on the map.

The note written on the lower right part of the map reads, "Northwestwards fifteen under toyon boulder. Before the Grass." Little Bear Woman had no idea what it referred to; she said the map "had been around the house for a long time."

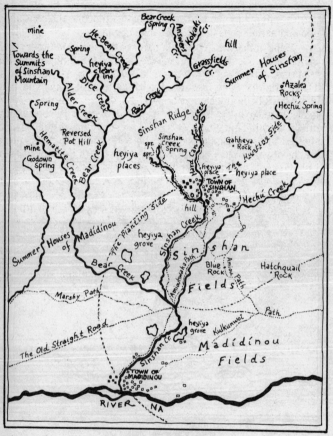

The Watershed of Sinshan Creek

This map is based upon and elaborates Little Bear Woman's map of the Sinshan and Madidinou region, including fewer paths and more place-names.

The Finders Lodge made and used maps of regions adjacent to the Ranges of the Valley, and of the area for some hundreds of miles around. Those were kept up-to-date both by the exploring parties sent out by the Finders, and by reference to the constantly updated aerial maps in the Exchange computers.

Maps of the whole continent and of the seas and other continents, and globes of the world, were used as teaching aids by the Madrone Lodge. Every town had at least a few of these world maps. They certainly came from the Exchange to start with, and they could have been updated at request; but the request was seldom made, to judge by the venerable fragility of most of the beautifully drawn and imaginatively decorated world maps displayed and shelved in the Madrone Lodges. The rest of the world was not a matter of very urgent concern to most people of the Valley. They were content to know that it was there. Most of them had a vague idea of global geography; their notions of global and continental distances were both inadequate and exaggerated. For most (not all), real geography included the Volcano country in the north and the desert mountains in the south; the Pacific Ocean was the west; to the east was the Inland Sea and its shores, the Range of Light, the Omorn Sea, and the remote Range of Heaven or Range of the Rocks. Beyond these, "the lands go on and on to the sea again, you know . . . and so on round till you come back to the Valley."

The World Dance

THE WORLD DANCE CELEBRATED human participation in the making and unmaking, the renewal and continuity, of the world.

While the people of the Valley danced the Sky Dance for all people and beings of the earth, the Sky People were dancing their part of the ceremony, the Earth Dance. The dead and the unborn danced on the wind and in the sea, birds in the air, the wild animals in secret places in the wilderness. ("Animal dancing is not like our dancing. We do not know their ceremonies. They dance their lives.") The linked spirals of these two cosmic dances formed the sacred image, the heyiya-if.

The World was danced during the dark of the moon after the equinox of spring. The ceremonies went on for three days, and on the evening of the third day the crescent moon would be first visible at sunset. The Madrone Lodge and the Black Adobe Lodge were in charge of the dance.

THE FIRST DAY OF THE WORLD.

The earthly performance of the World Dance began at daybreak, underground, in the Black Adobe earth lodges. These were underground chambers, always located outside town, on the hunting side. They were not as large as the heyimas of the Five Houses, so the dancers generally went in shifts, coming out after a few hours to make place for others. All the dancers of the First Day of the World were older people, "those whose children have children."

As with many of the ceremonies called dances, during long periods no actual dancing went on: the ceremony in the earth lodge was a long chanting, led by the trained singers of the Black Adobe and Madrone. The deep ceremonial drum underground beat a heartbeat rhythm without break from sunrise to sunset. Old people of the town waited near the lodge in silence, or returned home from the singing in silence; children were cautioned not to speak to their grandparents, who would not reply. The old people dancing fasted all day. They tied feathers in their hair, or wore a cape of thin, dark wool onto which feathers had been sewn: feathers not taken from birds raised or hunted, but found.

None of the words of the songs of the First Day were written down.

As the sun set, the steady drumbeat stopped. People would begin to gather in the dancing place, the open area in the curve of the five heyimas. They brought wood for fires—especially applewood, saved for the occasion: the apple was a tree connected with death.

At dusk the dancers came up from the Black Adobe lodge and into the dancing place. Those who danced this part of the ceremony had trained for it and were dressed for it, wearing black, tight-fitting clothes tied close at wrist and ankle, barefoot, their hair, face, hands, and feet smeared with white and grey ash. They were members of the Black Adobe and Madrone Lodges, and any townspeople who had asked to train with those lodges for the dancing. They came in file, singing. The words were archaic and the songs, complex and somber, using very wide intervals, had an eerie and depressing quality.

The dancers carried applewood torches, unlighted, upside down. When they were all gathered in the dancing place, the Speaker of the Madrone came from the west with a lighted torch: from it the dancers lighted their torches, and with them, dancing, lighted the fire that was laid ready in the dancing place. (If it was raining, high poles bearing a canopy would have been set up over the area; all the heyimas kept such equipment for rainy-season ceremonies.) The fire was not a roaring bonfire, but was kept small and hot. The dancers circled it in a shuffling line, carrying themselves in a kind of crouch, knees bent and arms raised and bent, the hands at about face level, shaking. All the other people attending stood or squatted in an outer ring. Most of the people of the town (or of that arm of the big towns) were there; all those who had lost a relative or friend to death since the last World Dance were there.

The Dead Singers kept up the shaking dance and kept the chant going, gradually increasing the tempo and raising the pitch, until suddenly one of the silent watchers in the dark outer ring called out the name of a person who had died during the past year. Others repeated the name in the rhythm of the chanting. The dancers picked it up. The name was repeated over and over, and all the various names the dead person had had were spoken and repeated, until the Dead Singers suddenly gathered in around the fire, chanting loud and fast and rocking their bent arms as if throwing or pushing something into the flames: and as suddenly ceased to sing, and crouched down, head bowed to earth and body trembling. And the mourners did the same. Then slowly and softly the insistent beat of the dance was taken up by one voice and another, the dancers got up and danced, the chanting increased in pitch and tempo, until another name was "thrown on the fire."

In the little towns of the Lower Valley there were years when nobody died, when there were no names to throw on the fire. The Ceremony of Mourning would be held, but only the dancers who had trained for it participated; the others sat in silence in the outer ring; the ceremony lasted only a couple of hours at most. In the big towns there were always deaths to be mourned, and there the ceremony became increasingly participatory and emotional as it went on. The first names thrown on the fire were usually those of older people; late in the ceremony it was the names of dead children that were spoken, and those born dead, who were all named at their burial so that they might be mourned at the Mourning. As the ceremony went on, the people in the outer circle joined in the rocking dance motions and in the chanting, and began to cry out as the names of the dead were spoken again and again, and to call to the dead, and to weep aloud. All rocked, all sang, all wept together, and sank back into the grieving silence together, and again were shaken by the growing beat and by the voices crying the names of the dead. The barriers of shame and self-containment were broken down, the fear and anger of loss made public, and these quiet people screamed aloud in their admission of pain.

When the last name had been thrown on the fire, the leaders of the dance began to slow and quiet the tempos, and the character of the chanting changed, the archaic words telling about places the souls of the dead may go in the Four Houses, and becoming a rain chant. The fires were allowed to die. At last the Speaker said, "The names have been spoken." The dancers brought water up from the Blue Clay heyimas and poured it on the fire, then formed in line and in silence and the dark returned to the Black Adobe lodge. The mourners marked their faces with the wet ash of the dead fire before going home. A traditional breakfast of milk, cornbread, and spring greens was eaten before they went to bed, or in the morning. The ashes of the mourning-fires were scattered on the plowlands next day by the dancers of the rite.

THE SECOND DAY OF THE WORLD.

People were likely to be worn out by the intense, passionate ceremonies of the previous night, and nothing got under way until well after noon. The five heyimas—the Houses of Earth—were in charge of this day's ceremonies of praise. Processions were made up of people between about seventeen and fifty or sixty years old, and the leaders were older adolescents and young adults who were "living on the Coast"—observing the period of sexual abstinence that was considered appropriate to their age. How many people joined the ceremony, and how elaborate it was, depended pretty much on these young leaders, and varied a great deal from year to year and from town to town; the following description is of a kind of ideal ceremony which was probably never fully performed in all its details.

People from the First House, the Obsidian, were supposed to go to the pastures and barns and poultry runs with songs for and about the domestic animals. These songs might be traditional, or composed by a poet-musician, or improvised on the spot, or a mixture; they were simple description, praise, without petitions for increase or any other demands. Often there was not much singing except for a few traditional choruses such as the Bull Song, which belongs in the category known as Lusty Folksong:

> Oh, the bull he rode the cow around
> the bull he rode the cow around
> the cow she bore the bull around

> the cow she bore the bull around
> aho ahey the bully bull

> Oh, the ram he rode the ewe around
> the ram he rode the ewe around
> the ewe she bore the ram around
> the ewe she bore the ram around
> aho ahey the ramrod ram

The processional visit around the barns and pastures often turned into a session of cow-riding, or sheepdog exercises, or donkey races, or an impromptu horse show. Children made collars for favorite animals, woven of grass and pennyroyal, and the livestock might get a sprig of pennyroyal stuck in their halter or their mane or their wool, or have their stalls decorated, or be given a treat such as an extra handful of oats; and the poultry and himpí got an extra feeding.

The Second House, the Blue Clay, sent people along the creeks of the hunting side of town to sing to the game animals. These songs were old and well-known, and it seemed that this procession was never scanted—somebody always went "singing to the deer."

The Third House, the Serpentine, sent people into the woods and hills to the various gathering-places and meadows used by the community. The speaker of the House was supposed to lead a long chant enumerating all the unsown crops, all the herbs, seeds, grasses, roots, fruits, barks, nuts, and leaves gathered for food or medicine or other uses by human beings.

The people of the Fourth and Fifth Houses, the Adobes, went into the orchards with a similar chant of praise to the trees, and into the plowlands to name and praise the sown crops of the town.

By early evening all these groups had returned to town, and people were making ready for the ceremony of the Second Night: the Wedding.

Like the Mourning, this was a community observance of a personal act. Couples who had taken to living together during the year did not call themselves married until they had danced the Wedding Night. Any married couple who wanted to participated also, reaffirming their bond.

The formality of the ceremony was slight. Everybody dancing the Wedding met on the dancing place, where singers from all the heyimas sang the Marriage Song—a very old, rather brief, joyous choral, never reproduced and never sung but in that place on that night—and if the weather was good and the musicians willing there might be some dancing afterwards; the Marriage Dance was a cheerful affair in ³/₄ time, with couples dancing down the line and under other couples' raised arms, as in our old line and square dances. After that everybody went home to the Wedding Dinner, at which hot wine and dirty jokes were traditional.

Two towns elaborated on this simple festival. In Chúkúlmas, bridegrooms were given a sedate and ceremonious dinner in their heyimas, and then sung to the house of their bride, where they would live henceforth, and only then was the Wedding Song sung for them. In Wakwaha, after the communal Wedding Song, the two Adobe Houses put on a sacred play, *The Wedding of Awar and Bulekwe;* and music, dancing, and other romantic, erotic, or mystical plays accompanied the ceremonial drama. People said, "You're not really married till you've been married in Wakwaha," and couples undertaking or celebrating a long-lasting marriage often went to dance the World at that town.

THE THIRD DAY OF THE WORLD.

Before dawn, in the darkness, the young adolescents—girls and boys up to fifteen or sixteen years old—got the little children up, and led them out onto the upper-storey balconies or the rooftop or any high place they could get onto. There they danced in place, not singing, with seed and deer-hoof rattles to keep the rhythm. The older siblings and cousins carried babies too young to walk, and taught the little ones the simple step-in-place of the dance. They faced southeast; and when the sun rose they greeted it with a whispered chant, the four-times-four heya. When the sun was clear of the hills, they went down and scattered out around the town and its gardens, the older children helping the younger ones, until everyone had found or had been given a feather and a stone.

Each child holding the stone in the right hand and the feather in the left—a cross-over or "marriage" of the usual ritual position of these two profoundly sacred things, the feather of the Right-Hand Houses and the stone of the Left—they regathered in the dancing place, and came as a procession to the Hinge of the town, between the dancing place and the common place. They halted there, and one little one was chosen to go forward towards the common place and cry out, "Let the children in!"

At this the adults, waiting in their houses, of which the doors must be kept shut till then, could open the doors and welcome in their children.

Breakfast in any household with children was a festival; and the rest of the Last Day of the World was for the children. The elements of reversal were playful: an adult speaking to a child was supposed to bow down or go on all fours, on penalty of being whacked with pine-branches by any child in sight. Green Clowns appeared and played tricks and performed juggleries. The Lower Valley towns staged mock wars, mudball and oakgall battles, which might go on in the fallow fields and around the hunting side all afternoon, and frequently resulted in black eyes and minor bruises. A particular kind of marzipan, ground almonds sweetened with honey, colored and shaped into beasts, birds, flowers, and faces, was handed out by every self-respecting household. The day, often called Honey Day, ended with a Bee Dance and an Ant Dance by the very young children. This had to be concluded before the sun set. As the sun got low above the ridges, adolescents, back up on the roofs and balconies, began to call out heya, heya.

Most people then went up to join them, or climbed a nearby hill; some of the older adolescents and adults would have spent the day climbing a nearby mountain. In Wakwaha, many would have gone up to the summits of Ama Kulkun. There they awaited the first sight of the new moon as it followed the sun down into the west. Clouds and rain of course often hid both sun and moon at that time of year; but clouds and rain were people of the sky, and the view was not what mattered, so long as one was up high, or looking up, skyward.

When sun and moon were down, the Speaker of the Obsidian House asked the moon to carry the blessing of earth and the people of earth through the Houses of the Sky. This single voice ended the three days of the World Dance. People might wait in silence for a while in the twilight, "watching for the rainbow people" on the mountain slopes or in the air, walking on the roads of the wind; but before dark they went down, went home, whispering the heya chant as they entered their own door.

THE DAY AFTER THE WORLD.

The three days of the World Dance involve a kind of time-reversal: the dance goes from mourning after death, through work and marriage, to childhood and infancy. The Day after the World carries this movement one stage further.

Anybody wishing to dance that day went early in the morning to the Black Adobe earth lodge, where the ceremonies had begun three days before. Members of that Lodge led the group—usually not many people—to certain places in side valleys or canyons, near springs or beside water. These places, often only a few paces in extent, and unmarked in any way, represented (reflected) places in the Four Houses, the Right-Hand World—places the reverse of graveyards: birthgrounds, where the unborn wait to be born.

The location and significance of the birthgrounds was part of the teaching of the Black Adobe Lodge.

At one of the birthgrounds, Lodge members would sing and teach to the other celebrants the song *Shining of the Sun,* which in both words and melody is related to the songs of *Going Westward to the Sunrise,* sung to the dying and the newly dead. The "matrix" of the song was the word hwavgepragú, shining of the sun; the other words might be sung in part, but rarely all together, as printed here (written out for us by Alder of the Black Adobe of Sinshan):

> You are coming,
> hwavgepragú.
> Surely you are coming,
> The way is short.
> The way is easy
> from town to town.
> Come when you want to.
> Come into sunlight,
> hwavgepragú, shining of the sun.

All oceans and sea-beaches were considered to be birth-grounds; the unborn were likely to be there. So there were always jokes when young women went down to the Mouths of the Na— "What did you come back with this time?"

The following teaching-piece is part of the teachings of the Black Adobe Lodges on the Day after the World.

The sands of all the beaches of all the coasts, the grains of sand of all the beaches of all the coasts of all the world, are the lives of the unborn, who will be born, who may be born. The waves of the sea, the bubbles of foam of the waves that break on the coasts of the seas of the world, all the flashes and gleams of light on the waves of the seas of the world, the flicker of sunlight on waves of the ocean, those are the lives of the Nine Houses of Life without end vanishing without stay forever.

The poem "The Inland Sea," p. 415, is related to these teachings also.

The Sun Dance

||||||||||||||||||||||||||||||||||||||||||||||||||||||||||||||||||||||||||

TWO OF THE SEVEN annual wakwa hedou, or Great Dances, were
danced by all nine Houses. In the World Dance of cosmic renewal
at the equinox of spring, Earth and Sky danced at the same time,
but not together: people of the Earth Houses offered all earthly
things to the use and for the blessing of the Sky people, who, dancing in their own places, received and returned the blessing to
Earth. The World ceremonies were referred to by scholars as "parting" or "sorting"—getting everything established, as it were, in its
own place. In the ceremonies of the Sun at the solstice of winter, all
that was parted was brought back together. All beings of both Earth
and Sky, of all planes of being, met and danced the Sun together.
This was not an easy business for ordinary mortals. The Sun was
considered the most arcane, intense, and dangerous of all dances.
Those who wished to participate fully in the mysteries and ceremonies, to dance the Inner Sun, trained for years; of an old person
dying, people said, "He's ready to dance the Inner Sun."

Most people participated only in the general ceremonies or
Outer Sun, and the extent of their participation was entirely a matter of choice. It was difficult to keep out of a townwide binge such
as the Wine Dance, and everyone joined in at least one of the
Nights of the World Dance, but the ceremonies of the Sun were
particularly attractive to people of introverted or mystical tempera-
ment, and might merely be observed from outside by many townsfolk. Children and adolescents had an important part, both active
and passive, in the advent period before the solstice, the time
called the Twenty-One Days.

During the Twenty-One Days, little children would find a
seedling tree or shrub in the woods, transplant it into a tub or
basket, and keep it hidden until, at the Sunrise, the morning of the
solstice, they presented it triumphantly to a beloved or admired
adult. Older children might do the same, or might have found and
nurtured a wild gathering tree (a nut tree or fruit tree or an ink oak)

493

unclaimed in the woods, or might have planted and tended a bearing tree in the town orchards, perhaps for several years, and this they would present at the Sunrise to an adult they wished to show love and honor to. Often the gift trees were decorated with oakgalls and nutshells painted in bright colors, with blown glass ornaments, and with feathers tied on the branches. These "featherwords" were wonderfully ornate and delicate little works of art.

Children and adolescents also saw to it that the trees growing in the common place and dancing place of the town were decorated, though the rain was often hard on the fine show. Apprentices in the Milling Art in the Upper Valley towns strung small lights on the trees, making a marvellous colored glimmering display, most splendid on the first night of the Twenty-One, but thinning out and darkening as the ceremonial period went on. Branches of juniper, fir, pine, and evergreen toyon with its bright red berries were put up over balconies and doorways and made into wreaths and garlands for the rooms. Special candles, often colored red and scented with bay laurel or rosemary, were made by the young people, and lighted nightly for the Twenty-One Nights; by the last of the nights they should have burned quite down.

The sacred or intellectual practices held in the five heyimas during the Twenty-One days were concerned with bringing the Left Hand and the Right Hand, the Earth and Sky, closer together until they should meet in the place and time of the solstice dance.

Attention was not focussed on the material and individual manifestations of being—the rocks, plants, animals, persons enumerated and celebrated in the World Dance—but on the generic and the spiritual: the aspect under which even living creatures still/already inhabit the Houses of Death, Dream, Wilderness, Eternity. The dead and the unborn were to be invited to the dancing. The people of the rainbow, the images of dream and vision, all wild creatures, the waves of the sea, the sun, and all the other stars, were to be part of that dancing. So the earthly, mortal, human dancers invited that part of their own being which was before and would be after their earthly life: their soul, or their souls. Not the "spirit," the essence of individuality, or not only the spirit; for individuality is mortality; but also the breath-soul, that which is shared with, taken from, given back to the wholeness of being; and the self that is beyond the self.

The practices and exercises of the Inner Sun involved breathing, as does yoga, but the theories and techniques resemble those of yoga only very remotely. The athletic austerity of yoga would not have been very congenial to the general Valley preference for "middling," ubbu; a closer parallel might be found in Chinese taoist practices.

The direct way, the royal road to communication or relationship with the Four-House World, was through dream or trance. The indirect but durable connection, the "low road," was through intellectual and physical discipline: the training of the Inner Sun. Inner Sun material was not written down; the teachings were transmitted orally or nonverbally through the long course of training mentioned above. None of that material is contained in the following description; I can discuss only the practices of the Outer Sun, as observed or as explained to me by participants and teachers.

Outer Sun exercises and rituals of the Twenty-One Days, then, were a progression farther and farther into a controlled condition of collective trance.

The means of achieving this condition were fasting, drumming, singing, dancing, and journeying.

Dream-quest journeys of the Sun were not solitary walks on the mountains, but were undertaken by a group of four or five, who went for several days or for the whole three-week period into remote wild regions, over on the "wrong" side of Ama Kulkun or other harsh ridge-and-canyon country outside the usual territory of Valley use. This exceeding of boundaries was an affirmation of the community to which the seekers returned, "as the child returns to the mothers' house, as the souls return from vision." These quests into the wilderness in winter were considered dangerous, not so much physically as morally or socially; as they were often undertaken under a sanction of complete silence, not a word to be spoken during the entire journey, the psychological strain must have been fairly intense.

Danger was also indicated in the "journeys backward," rituals in which the normal limits establishing the safety and decency of daily life were deliberately transgressed. Such transgressions were undertaken only under the guidance and direction of students of the Inner Sun—but rival disciplines arose, such as the Lamb and Warrior Lodges, with their own esoteric rites. The "journeys backward" were not called reversals, yahwe, except by the cults. They involved risk-taking and feats of physical endurance of the kind usually and carefully avoided by Valley people; drug-taking— purges, emetics, and hallucinogenics; extreme ascetic practices— fasting, sitting motionless, sensory deprivation; and, in the cults, self-mutilation and animal sacrifice.

The most sinister and extraordinary manifestation of the Twenty-One Days was the White Clown: a horrific figure, masked and cloaked in white, nine or ten feet tall, who singly or in groups stalked children in the woods and fields and even in the streets and ways of the towns. Whether or not the White Clowns did any physical harm, they were spoken of as if they did, and there were plenty of confirmatory legends and tales of the fate of children who met with White Clowns—regular ghost stories: "They found the child next morning, standing against the trunk of the apple tree. He was as cold as the rain and as stiff as the wood, and his eyes were staring and staring—but the pupils of his eyes had turned dead white."

The children, who had to reconcile their work of herding and gathering and so on, and their care of their gift-trees, with the real terror of these lurking monsters, went out when possible in pairs or groups all during the Twenty-One Days.

The other ceremonies of the period were held in the five heyimas, or jointly on the dancing place. Anyone could join the drumming and the dancing, dropping in and out of the group as they chose; the meters and simple steps were traditional. I would describe their character as restless yet monotonous, and curiously attractive; one was drawn in; time was obliterated. The dominant activity was the long singing. The words of a long singing were matrix syllables without rational meaning, with little or no "core" of meaningful words. A leader sang the chant, and those who joined her or him undertook to keep singing as long as the leader did. Such chants, held in one or several of the heyimas, might go on for days without a break, the fasting participants singing themselves through trance to total exhaustion. They might rest for four or five days and then repeat the long singing.

This is the text of a long singing held in the Yellow Adobe heyimas of Madídínou. It would not ordinarily have been written down, but the singer told me that writing it was considered unnecessary, not inappropriate.

> Heya kemeya
> ou
> imitimi
> ou-a ya

A scholar of the Inner Sun was the leader, keeping the beat from time to time on a one-tone wooden drum, and leading the chant. Each of the four phrases or syllables was chanted for no less than an hour at a time, and often several hours at a time, except the "imitimi," which was sung a relatively few times in succession, always in multiples of nine. The ability of the singers to follow the leader in the completely unheralded change to a new syllable or a new musical pattern was uncanny; two of them, evidently less gifted, did not sing, but maintained a barely audible keynote on the syllable *o*, and by spelling each other when they had to take breath maintained, or gave the illusion of maintaining, a perfectly steady unbroken sound, until they gave out after about eleven hours. The whole long singing lasted almost two days and two nights. When the leader's voice gave out, which was only towards the middle of the second night, he kept up the beat on the drum, and moved his

lips soundlessly in the chant, whispering aloud only when the matrix word changed.

Long singings that went on for more than a night or two had
several leaders, and might continue for four or five days and nights.
Most older adolescents and many adults participated in at least one
of the long singings.

Most people practiced some degree of fasting and sexual abstinence during the Twenty-One Days, and more did so and to a
greater degree as the period went on. The mood of the community
grew increasingly tense and somber—"stretched" was their word
for it.

On the day before the solstitial sunrise, all the groups of seekers arrived back home, if possible before nightfall, and scattered
families reunited, if they could, at the maternal household. Married
men often returned to their mothers' house for the Twenty-First
Night. The towns drew in as if under siege. At sunset all doors were
shut, all windows closed. The power sources had already been shut
down, mills stopped, machinery halted; insofar as possible, domestic animals were brought into the pens, barns, and byres; and at
sunset all lights and fires were extinguished. A hearthfire or a candle lighted before sunset might be allowed to burn out, but the
custom, well reinforced by the children and adolescents, with their
passion for tradition, was that no light should be relighted that
night. If the fire went out, it stayed out. The longest night of the
year was the darkest.

During the afternoon of that day people of the Inner Sun had
dug a hole or pit somewhere in the common place of the town, a
couple of feet across and fairly deep. After sunset, people came by
this small pit or grave, which was called "the absence," and
dropped into it a bit of ash from their hearthfire, or a bit of food
wrapped in a piece of cloth, or a feather, or a lock of hair, or maybe
a ring or a carving or a small roll of paper covered with writing, or
some other thing of personal value or significance. Nothing was
said or sung. People came by in a casual way to make this small
private sacrifice. The silent and irregular procession went on until
midnight or so. Each person returned alone in the dark to the dark
house, or to the silent heyimas, where one spark of an oil lamp
burned in the central room. Late in the night even that was put out.
Some time in the dark hours members of the Black Adobe Lodge
filled up the "absence" pit and swept over it to obliterate and dis-
guise its place.

Alder of the Black Adobe said: "It is like the memory of the town, there, under the surface where we walk in the common place, in the ground underfoot there, all the things that have been put there in silence in the dark, all the years, the forgotten things. They are put there to be forgotten. They are sacrificed."

The Twenty-First Night is passed in silence in the dark.

At the first sign of dawn, about cock-crow, one song is sung. Four or five adolescent girls, trained by the Inner Sun, go up onto a high roof, or a tower if the town has one, and there stand to sing the Winter Carol, once only.

Thorn said, "I always meant to stay awake and listen to the Carol when I was a small child, or to wake up and wait for it, but I never did. I begged my mothers to wake me up to hear it, but when they did it was over before I roused up enough to listen. But when I was older, and heard that song for the first time, it seemed I had known it since before I was born."

The words of that song are not written.

Early in the morning, hearthfires and heaters are relighted, and the underground heyimas are illuminated with festival lights until the sunrise—an event which, central as it is to the entire festival, is not formally observed at all.

Alder said, "At the center is the absence. It is so." Speaking, he held his hands facing each other, slightly curved inward, about an inch apart, the left thumb pointing down and the right thumb up.

The only event which might be said to mark the sunrise was a negative one: the disappearance of the White Clowns. At that sacred moment their power was broken, they vanished until next year, and the children were free of the lurking horror. The gift-trees were presented with much informal family ceremony. Some cooking had been done even during the fast in preparation for this morning, and during the Day of the Sunrise really heavy and impressive cooking got under way for the feasting which would be going on for four days in the houses and the heyimas.

In the heyimas, the Morning Dances of the Sun began some time after sunrise and were held each morning for four days (five every fourth year). The singers were people of the Inner Sun. Certain dances were performed by masked Inner Sun dancers, others were danced by anyone who had learned the dance.

Alder said, "If the dances are properly conducted and well danced, the sky people will be there dancing with the earth people. That's why you never take hands, dancing the Morning Dances of the Sun. Between each earth person and the next a place is left for a Four-House person to dance. So also the songs leave a silence after every line sung for the other voices to sing, whether we hear them or not; and the drums beat only every second note."

Fifteen-year-old Upstream Fish said, "The Morning Songs of the Sun aren't gloomy like the songs of the Twenty-One Days, they're mysterious, beautiful. They make your heart light, they make it easy to sing, they make you feel as if everyone singing, the living and the unborn and the dead, were all together in the Valley, that no one was lost, that nothing was wrong."

Thorn said, "Although I know it takes the singers of the Inner Sun years and years to learn and remake the Morning Songs, again, when I hear them sung I know that I know them. I know them as I do the sunlight."

In the afternoons of the four Sun Risen days, clowns came into town—not tall and white, but supernaturally fat, and dressed in green, with no mask, but fanciful beards and whiskers pluming and curling and trailing, made of white wool or tree-moss. The Sun Clowns often led, and tried to ride, billygoats, and they gave all kinds of little presents, mostly sweets, to the younger children. All

fasts were broken, and food was set out in every household for visitors. Thorn said, "A lot of people celebrate with grape brandy or hard cider, along with all that eating, so they get drunk, and there's a good deal of fooling around, but nobody gets angry or wild, because the children are having a good time, and because of the Four House people still being with us. You always set aside some of the food you serve or eat for them, and pour out the first draft of anything you drink. And in the heyimas they're still singing the half-silent songs."

Slowly during this four or five days of the Sun Risen, the two Arms of the World separated, the Four-House beings returning to their plane of existence, earthly people to the daily concerns of mortal life. Thorn said, "Working in the house, cleaning up or cooking, working in the workshops, people sing songs that go along with the rainbow people, as they go away, and keep going slowly farther away, back to their Houses. We sing those songs, and send our breath partway with them, breathing out." Alder said, "Breathing out, singing, we follow them, walking after them for a while, seeing the world as they see it, with the sun's eyes, that see only light."

About the Train

||||||||||||||||||||||||||||||||||||||||||||||||

THE MILLING ART and the Finders Lodge worked together on tracklaying, repair, and maintenance. Under professional direction, young people who were not Millers or Finders often worked for a season or two on the "Line" as an adventure. The leaders of these crews and the men and women whose chief work was driving the mule and oxen trains or the engine were notable, romantic, and "dangerous" characters.

The train tracks used and maintained by the Kesh ran from Chesteb, a depot south of Clear Lake, over Ama Kulkun to Kastóha, down the Valley past Telína and the great wineries south of it, then east through the Northeast Ranges to the port town of Sed on the Inland Sea coast in the territory of the Amaranth people; probably less than eighty miles in all.

The track was a single line, with short spurs to the lading warehouses and wineries, some twenty-two sidings along its length for passing or for holding cars, and turnaround loops for the engines at Kastóha and at Sed (and at Clear Lake by the town of Stoy, where there were connections to a north-running train line and to road haulage east).

The rails were of oak, heavily treated against decay, termites, and rodents; they were laid on cross-connected redwood sleepers in a creek-cobble roadbed. No metal was used in the rails, which were fastened in short sections by wood-pinned lock joints. The Wood Art, under Yellow Adobe auspices, provided these rails and was in charge of the ceremonial aspects of tracklaying and repair.

No tunnels were built; in hard grades and canyons on Ama Kulkun and the Northeast Ranges the looping switchbacks were innumerable. Trestle construction was massive, since it had to support a solid roadbed for animals hauling trains.

The cars or wains ran on hooped oaken wheels, two pair on a swivelled truck at each end of the car; the couplings were braided, laminated leather, sometimes reinforced with chain. Goods wains for heavy cargo were roofed boxcars; those carrying wine were insulated, with clamps and mountings to anchor the casks. There was one roofed boxcar fitted out with bunks, window panels, and wood stove, for people travelling by train—the height of luxury, according to the author of "Trouble with the Cotton People." Other wains were roofless and of light construction: a flatcar with socketed poles was common, the load lashed on under a canvas covering. No car was over nineteen feet long; axle width (standard since time immemorial on all roads in the region) was two feet nine inches (the Kesh meter or yard—the hersh). The wains were so narrow that they somewhat resembled boats, which was what the Kesh called them.

At the period this book is concerned with, two engines were in use in the Valley, one owned by the Kesh and the other by the Amaranth people. Both ran only between Kastóha and Sed. They were woodburning steam engines of (my guess) about 15 to 20 horsepower. The Kesh engine was built, maintained, and operated by members of the Millers Art in cooperation with other Arts and Lodges that used the train in their commerce with neighboring peoples. They called the engine The Grasshopper for its high-angled pistons, its jointed look, and probably for its habit of starting with a flying leap. It was built of pegged and fitted wood and riveted sheet iron; tubes were rolled up from the flat and seam-welded by hammering over a false core. The firebox and boiler sat up on little bolted legs well away from the carriage, and the high, narrow smokestack was topped with a complicated and unreliable spark baffle. The risk of forest fire in the dry grass and chaparral of the mountains was the main drawback to use of the engines; in dry years they were not run at all between the Water Dance and the beginning of the rains. At such times, and for short runs within the Valley, for single-wain hauls, and for all traffic north from Kastóha over the Mountain, the trains were pulled by oxen or mules: the tracks and roadbed served to make the hauling easier for those who did it.

A signalling system was maintained during periods of frequent operation (that is, more than once every nine or ten days). Lineswomen and men operated the signals, and travelling crews kept up the wood and water supplies along the line. The signals were connected to the Exchanges in Wakwaha, Sed, and other towns in the trade network, where schedules of runs and arrangements for shipments were made and posted.

Some Notes on Medical Practices

MOST OF THE LITTLE INFORMATION I have concerning Kesh medicine was given me in conversation by Alder of the Serpentine and the Doctors Lodge of Chúmo and of Sinshan. He said that a doctor did four things—prevent, care, cure, and kill.

Preventive medicine included immunisation, public and personal hygiene, teaching and advice about diet, work habits, work places, and exercise, counselling for psychic strain and distress, and a wide variety of kinds of massage, manipulation, music, and dance—"bodywork" in our terms.

Care or alleviation involved treatment of fevers, aches, infections, and communicable diseases, and the care of people suffering from handicaps and incurable disorders.

Curative practices included bonesetting, the use of a large and complex pharmacopoeia, therapeutic bodywork, and surgery. I do not have a list of surgical operations the Kesh considered feasible; Alder at one time or another mentioned having performed amputation, curettage, appendectomy, removal of an abdominal tumor, removal of skin cancers, and an operation to close a cleft palate. Anesthesia for a major operation was induced by herbal drugs taken for a period of days before and after surgery, and by "the lances," a system of thin bamboo needles inserted according to a body chart which—to this ignorant eye—looked a good deal like an acupuncture chart. (I did not hear about anything like therapeutic acupuncture.)

As our medicine makes no place for *killing*, considering itself in binary opposition to death, we have only the slightly suspect "euthanasia" to name practices the Kesh considered part of any doctor's work and a serious element of medical theory and morality: castration of animals; human abortion, which was considered neither a minor nor a reprehensible operation; and the killing of monstrous births, both human and animal.

There was no distinction by caste of the "veterinary" from the "doctor," though physicians usually specialised to some extent according to their knack and the community's need. There seemed to be no dentists as such, probably because most Kesh had good teeth and ate a low-sugar diet.

GEDWEAN: BRINGING-IN.

This most characteristic of Kesh medical practices could be called a "healing ceremony" if it's understood that a coronary bypass operation could also be called a "healing ceremony." Current high-technology medical practice in well-equipped hospitals includes the latter, Valley medicine included the former; both are cases of a specialised technology used by trained professionals, reflecting a certain moral stance and embodying certain judgments on the means and ends of medicine. Statistics comparing rates of alleviation, short-term cure, long-term cure, and failure would be interesting, but inappropriate.

Since each bringing-in was created for an individual in particular circumstances of illness or stress by a particular doctor or group of doctors, I can't give a general description; and a description of an actual bringing-in would violate Kesh standards of personal and sacred discretion. In the abstract, then: a bringing-in involved two parties, the goddwe or brought, and the dwesh or bringers. The goddwe—usually one person but sometimes a married couple or a child with a parent or sibling—lived for the four-, five-, or nine-day period of the gedwean in their heyimas or in the Doctors Lodge building. They were looked after attentively, given a special diet or fasting pattern, and followed a carefully prescribed regime of activity and rest; their body and face were marked or painted, and they wore special clothing, a long, loosely belted shift of wool challis. (Such a garment was the gift of a weaver to the Doctors Lodge in exchange—payment or prepayment—for medical attention. Contrary to the theory and practice of shamanistic and psychiatric curing, where the cost is an essential ingredient of the cure, Kesh doctors charged nothing; their practice was an integral part of the continuous exchange of services and goods that formed the Kesh village economy. The cost of successful practice *to the doctor* may be glimpsed in what Stone Telling mentions of Alder's patients in Chúmo and Sinshan.)

The dwesh or bringers, one of whom had to be a "singing doctor," worked out the treatment/ceremony, which might include: drug therapy, use of trance-inducing drugs, hypnosis through drumming and singing, massage, bathing, exercises, the teaching of symbols and figures drawn in sifted dust or painted or marked on the skin, and the discussion of the meaning of such symbols and also of songs, stories, and events in the life of the person being brought in; the performance of rituals, some of them traditional and some the private property of the doctor, obtained in vision or from another doctor as a gift; and the invention and performance of songs, dances, and drum patterns by patient and doctor together. The goddwe left the bringing-in with recommendations for further treatment if necessary and a routine to follow to maintain the healing effects of the gedwean itself.

Alder told me that he believed the beneficial effect of a bringing-in lay to a great extent in *attention*—the attention paid to the goddwe, who was the center of everybody's interest in a supportive, comforting, unstressed environment of warmth, rest, soft drumming and singing; and the attention which the goddwe must pay to his or her life and thinking and the mystical or intellectual or practical insights arrived at by the combined work of the people involved in the bringing-in. It was a pretty good example of what the Kesh meant by *uvrón,* carefulness, taking care.

Some people were brought in many times in a lifetime, others once or never. Some members of the Doctors Lodge would act as dwesh on request, others only in cases they considered serious;

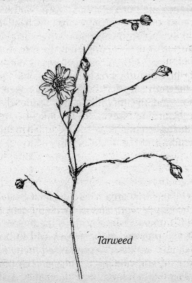

Tarweed

and though the former were liked for their response to a need for sympathy, it was the latter who were most respected. All doctors who performed bringings-in also had been goddwe, and were brought in from time to time, as training and as therapy.

DYING.

Fatally ill people, most of them sufferers from sevai, vedet, or cancer, came to live at the Doctors Lodge in a hospice routine called *hwagedwean,* continuous bringing-in. The alleviation of misery was set ahead of the prolongation of life, as a rule. If a patient asked for death and the family and close friends agreed, the issue was discussed by the Lodge. If the judgment was that death was appropriate, four doctors undertook to be present; euthanasia was performed as a ceremony, ritually, as were abortion and the killing of a monstrously defective birth. Euthanasia was performed with poison, given orally or injected; abortion was performed by curettage, preceded and followed by treatment with herbals; monstrous births, if they did not die of their infirmities at once, were starved, being looked after but not fed, until they died.

In response to my questions on this latter subject, Alder gave me this written statement: "People [human and animal] that we kill or let die when they are born are those with two heads or joined bodies, those born dúsevai [a baby born with advanced sevai: blind, deaf, and subject to muscle spasm which prevent it from suckling], and those born very terribly misshapen or without brain, without skin, or without another organ necessary to life. Such people born dying are let die. Human people born who cannot live are let die with care and singing the songs of Going Westward with them, and the mother names them so they can be mourned at the Mourning Fires of the Equinox. Animal people of the Obsidian House born unable to live are killed in the proper way with the due words, and the death is burned."

BIRTHING.

This seemed to be the only area where doctors specialised by sex. In animal practice there were almost as many men expert in attending on a difficult cow or ewe birth as there were women, but men doctors seldom presided at a human birth; and some women doctors—itatensho or "senders,"—specialised pretty exclusively in the care of pregnant and nursing women and as midwives. The complex and beautiful ceremonies of pregnancy and birth were directed by women of the Blood Lodge who were or who worked with women of the Doctors Lodge. Prenatal care and education was thorough, mostly embodied in ritual and ceremony. At the time of birth, hygiene was extremely strict. If the household of the mother failed to set aside a room for the birth and to have it ready and clean—down to scrubbed, sanded wood, fresh paint, boiled linens, and all the rest of a set of most exacting standards—the Lodge might insist that the delivery take place in their own building. The mother stayed in this clean, quiet, dimly lit room with the baby for a formal nine-day rest period; friends and family might come in to visit and sing, a few at a time. The father was in charge of welcoming, filtering, and sending away the visitors; a man of the father's House could act in his stead, if the father was absent or divorced or otherwise not given responsibility for the child. He or his stand-in was expected to help the new mother with her work and keep her from overdoing while she was nursing the baby, though in fact her household normally protected or overprotected a young mother until she had to insist upon her freedom to come and go and work as she pleased. Thorn, who was in training as an itatensho with the Doctors of Sinshan, said that difficult labor and delivery were unusual, but that many pregnancies ended in unavoidable premature or still birth or in severely defective birth, due, evidently, to genetic damage. The same was true of the large animals; less so of the smaller animals, who in their more rapid generations had discarded the worst injuries resulting from old environmental poisoning and other traumas affecting the gene pool of every species.

DISEASES.

This list of illnesses is imprecise, incomplete, and probably wrong in many places. I could not identify many of the conditions which Alder tried to describe to me, and we were never perfectly sure we were talking about the same thing. Viral and bacterial mutations will have occurred, changing the nature of many diseases, no doubt; but the main problem was one of vocabulary. Kesh theory of medicine and methods of diagnosis differed profoundly from ours. For example:

Though clearly aware of the role played by bacteria and viruses (the latter of which were utterly invisible to their microscopes) as agents of disease, they did not identify disease, or a disease, as an entity in itself. It was not something that *happened to* a person, but something a person *did*. The closest I could come to translating our word health into Kesh would be the word óya—ease or grace—or the word gestanai—living well, doing well, with a combination of inborn talent, luck, and skill. To translate our word disease or illness I would have to use the privative forms, póya—unease (not so far from the original sense of dis-ease) or difficulty or hardness; and gepestanai, living ill, doing badly, unlucky, unskilful. These Kesh words imply that the sick person is not a *patient* but an *agent,* not merely suffering an invasion from outside the body, but doing or being ill/ness. Curiously enough I think this view of illness involves less sense of guilt than does our image of a body victimised by malevolent forces from without. Implicit in it is an acceptance that we don't always do what we would like or hope or ought to do, and that living is not always easy. The practices of the Doctors Lodge were not in the service of an ideal of perfect health, permanent youth, and the eradication of disease; they tried only to ensure that living wasn't any harder than it had to be.

There were Doctors Lodge ceremonies for immunisation of infants at 9, 54, and 81 days old; of children at 2, 4, 5, and 9 years old; and of adults at request or need. Diseases which the Kesh doctors could prevent or mitigate by inoculation or immunisation are mentioned in the following list:

Tetanus, rabies, malaria, bubonic plague are the four diseases I feel I could identify with certainty. Immunisation existed for all these, and was given to infants and children, and to adults at need. Malaria was the scourge of the great inland marshes and estuaries, and though the immunisation was fairly effective it was not so completely so that the Kesh were very happy about travelling in the Great Valley marshlands. But then, they were mostly not very happy about travelling anywhere. Plague was still carried by ground squirrels, which were therefore never hunted and never handled, but no outbreak of plague had occurred in or near the Valley of the Na in living memory.

My inquiries for the symptoms of smallpox and tuberculosis left Alder unable to identify these diseases as such. We did seem to be talking about the same thing when I brought up the diseases or conditions of which the herpes virus is the agent: chickenpox, coldsore, genital herpes, shingles. Alder knew them all and considered them to be related, grouping them under the name chemhem. Chickenpox was as serious in children as in adults, and immunisation was mandatory and effective.

Venereal diseases—presumably varieties of syphilis and

gonorrhea—were mostly called fucksores or foreigners' misery—
the latter being fair enough, since none was endemic in the Valley.
Another reason for not travelling. Alder knew several treatments
but no methods of prevention except hygiene.

～〜

The rest of the diseases mentioned are identified only uncertainly:

Infants were immunised against something that sounded like
diphtheria, and against a rash which was certainly not measles, but
might have been a form of scarlet fever.

What Alder called "wet lung" was certainly some form of
pneumonia. Penicillin, or a fungal derivative like it, was effective in
treatment. I did not try to understand the immensely complex
pharmacopoeia, mostly derived from herbs.

Infectious hepatitis and some form of infectious jaundice were
fairly common; Alder said that liver disorders were among the least
tractable common illnesses. Hygiene was the principal tactic used
against them.

Passionately careful about their use of water and the condition
of their streams and wells, the Kesh knew of typhoid only through
books and the Exchange.

Cancers of the skin were quite common; other forms of cancer
certainly occurred but seem to have been less common than
among us, but here the differing approach and understanding may
have led me quite astray. Heart diseases, treated with drugs and
with gedwean, if not symptomatic of congenital heart defect, seem
to have been considered a liability of old age.

～〜

The diseases or conditions which burdened the Kesh and their
neighboring peoples with a load we don't have to carry were sevai
and vedet: congenital, intractable, degenerative disorders of the
nervous system. (Forms of both diseases were shared with humanity by all the large domestic animals, and it was said that elk had
died out in the whole Inland Sea drainage basin long ago because
they "were vedet.") As well as I could establish, both diseases expressed genetic (chromosomal) damage caused by long-lasting
toxic or radioactive wastes or residues of the military–industrial
era, widespread in soil and water, and leaching out uncontrollably

from the very highly contaminated areas. Vedet involved personality disorder and dementia; sevai usually led to blindness and other sensory loss, and degeneration of muscle control. Both diseases were painful, crippling, incurable, and fatal. Severity of onset and the length of the course of the illness depended very much on what Alder called the "thoroughness" of the condition: major damage led to nonviability in the womb; minor damage might not show up till late in life.

Late in life, in the Valley, would be over sixty. Life expectancy in our terms—averaged over the whole lifespan—would be short, not over thirty or forty, because so many children were born sevai or with other severe genetic abnormalities, leading to a high mortality in early infancy. But to a Kesh born óya and living gestanai, life generally went on well into the seventies, and old age was taken easily and lived, very often, with considerable skill and grace.

A Treatise on Practices

||||||||||||||||||||||||||||||||||||||||||||||||||||||

*From the instructional library of the Red Adobe
heyimas in Sinshan.*

Outermost: dim, coarse, cold, weak practices bring about a dead
body [truned]. The practices of hunting and of war want patience,
alertness, attention to detail, obedience, control, competitive ambi-
tion, experience, a dull imagination, a cold intellect. The butchering of animals and killing of plants for food are practices that want
patience, alertness, attention to detail, presence of mind, and great
carefulness. The danger to the killer is great. If the image of the
other's gift is lost the killer's mind is lost, if the image of pain is lost
the killer is lost. The image of the other's pain is the center of being
human. When by carelessness or wilfulness killing is practiced
with cruelty, this is beyond the outside, and cannot in any way ever
be brought in.

Outermost, the practices of hoarding and usury are intractable, insatiable, and to be compared to cancerous tumors.

Coming inwards, dim, coarse, cold, strong practices prepare a
dead body. The milling and shaping of wood and preparation of all
plants, roots, and seeds for food, the cutting up and smoking, drying, preserving, and cooking of meat of animal or bird or fish, the

burial of dead animals of the town, the burial and funeral of dead human beings, these are practices of which some knowledge is appropriate and needful to all, so that they are done mindfully, in an appropriate manner.

Coming inwards, those practices are coarse, bright, and strong, which chiefly exchange one thing for another. The practices of barter and exchange allow power to move in an appropriate manner from place to place; they imitate life strongly. The Millers' arts of the uses of the energies of sun, wind, water, electricity, and the combinations of things to make other things are all practices of exchange. They want vigilance and clarity of mind, a bright imagination, modesty, attention to detail and to implication, strength, and courage.

Coming farther inwards, coming directly in, the practices of impregnation, pregnancy, birth, and rearing and nurture bring in the living.

Innermost: warm, strong, fine, bright practices bring about living things and the diversity, complexity, power, and beauty of things. A bright imagination, a clear intellect, warmth, readiness, magnanimity, grace, and ease are wanted in the practices of gardening, farming, sharing food, caring for animals, cure, care, healing, and comforting, the arts of making order and cleanliness where people live and work, all dancing and delightful exercises, the arts of making beautiful and useful things, and all the arts and practices of music, of speaking, of writing, and of reading aloud or silently.

Playing

|||||||||||||||||||||||||||||||||||||||||||||||||||||||||||||||||||||||||||||||

TOYS MADE BY ADULTS for children were carved or sewn animals and dolls, miniature utensils and furnishings, blocks of shaped and sanded mill-ends, and balls of milkweed rubber, sheep-bladders, or stuffed sewn leather. Everything else children played with they made themselves or borrowed from the house or workshop. Most of their play was story-play, imitative of adult work and activities, including trance-singing, doctoring, death, birth, family quarrels, and all the soap-opera aspects of Kesh life. Children's games with rules included:

Many singing and dancing games, some quite complicated and pretty to watch. One called Múdúp (brush rabbit) was rather like hopscotch, the dancers following one another through a course or maze laid out ahead, and tossing and picking up beads or nutshells at certain points.

Ring-toss was played with a carved ring of light wood, always across a creek, in pairs or groups. Ring-toss songs were sung until somebody missed a catch, at which the song had to be started over; "winning" the game was getting to the end of the song.

Knife-toss or mumblety-peg was played very skilfully. A knife was often a child's most prized possession, "a real steel blade knife from Telína!"

Hish was a kind of badminton played with a feathered rubber-headed birdie (the hish, swallow) and long-handled, small-headed racquets strung with gut. Four people played, two on either side of a string or ribbon. The object of the game was to keep the "swallow" aloft in a regular swift pattern of exchanges. Hish was one of the Summer games, and adolescents and young men often went from town to town to play exhibition games. Grown women and older men seldom played hish, but often used the birdie and racquets to play without rules; in the dry season there was usually a hish court or two set up on the common place.

Horseshoes was played just as we play it.

For bowls, a heavy wooden ball was rolled on a smooth dirt lane towards five rocks placed in a V. Scoring was complicated, necessitating long, grave discussions. Old people played both bowls and horseshoes more often than most children did.

Archery, darts, and the throwing-stick were of course elements of hunting, but were played as games for their own sake and exhibited as skills in the Summer games. Most children had a small bow made for them and learned to make their own arrows. Their hunting of small animals cannot be called a game, although it did follow strict rules, and was not an indispensable contribution to subsistence.

Hide-and-seek was played a great deal in summer, as was a similar game which resembled Kick-the-Can—to free the prisoners, instead of kicking a can you threw a tall bamboo pole, and where it lit was the new base. Reverse hide-and-seek, or Sardines, was a great favorite with small children indoors in the rainy season.

Shinny or field hockey was played on a fallow field or in a barnyard with a leather ball and wooden sticks. Four teams played at once, of two to five players; the object was to get the ball through four goals in a certain order. A kind of soccer, the ball being kicked only, had similar rules, as well as I could determine. The polo game vetúlou was also of this type, but was played without teams, each horse and rider being a team to themselves. In all these games the team or pair which first completed the pattern was the winner, but the game was not over till all players had completed the pattern. Although the games were wildly active and risky, aggressive behavior disrupted them at once and absolutely. Excellence consisted in speed, skill, and teamwork in completing the pattern; the game was a metaphor of society, not of war. This dominance of collaboration over competition was true of all games except the gambling games.

Dice games were much played by older children, adolescents, and many adults. There were two kinds of dice, both six-sided: apap or zero-zero was played with a pair, each marked with one through five spots and a blank side; hwots was played with four dice, marked with six symbols—leaf, bone, eye, fish, spade, mouth—rolled for various winning combinations, like a more complicated version of our slot-machine fruitbasket. Other dice games, some involving eight-sided long dice, were borrowed from neighboring peoples. Stakes were mostly wooden counters or pebbles; playing for objects of real value was not socially countenanced, but was very common, and adults sometimes went on long gambling binges—especially at the summerhouses, where nobody was close by to disapprove. People did not actually own enough private property to be able to ruin themselves by gambling, but they could damage their reputation. So far as I know, gambling meant dice-playing only; the Kesh considered the other games to be matters of skill, not chance, and therefore not appropriate subjects for betting.

Among the sedentary games a favorite with children was jackstraws—a set of fine polished wooden sticks (or real straws, in the fields) dropped in a random heap, which had to be taken apart one by one, the player losing the turn by moving any straw but the first touched. A heavier set of polished sticks of olivewood was used for a whole group of games of pitch-and-toss, catch-on-the-hand, house-building, and so on, and some children did marvelous sleight of hand with such sticks.

Lettered wooden tablets about the size of dominoes, some of them beautifully made and decorated, served for a series of games the general object of which, like our anagrams, was word-building, or, in the more difficult versions, sentence-building. Such games might go on for hours, sometimes days. The object of the game might be to make a poem, or the players might engage in a "flyting" or "capping" series of insults and ripostes. Such contests—without the game pieces, spoken as free oral improvisation—were a feature of the Wine Dance. Direct competition and aggression was typically channeled by the Kesh into verbal expression, which was acceptable so long as it was controlled, and admired so long as it was witty.

Word games played orally included pass-along stories, each person in the circle telling "what happened next" and ending on a cliffhanger which the next person had to deal with and go on from. It seems that riddling as such did not exist in the Valley.

I saw no game like chess or any of the checkerboard games, nor any version of go; and the Kesh had no cards. Board games were of the Snakes-and-Ladders or Parcheesi type, very simple and mostly played by young children or adults with young children. In Tachas Touchas children went to the Red Adobe heyimas to play a

dice-roll game called Going to the Nine Towns the Hard Way, in which the traveller's way around the huge, ancient, wonderfully illustrated board was beset with rattlesnakes, wild dogs, angry millers, fireballs and thunderbolts, supernatural ground squirrels, and other dangers and reverses before they finally reached Wakwaha on the Mountain.

Some Generative Metaphors

|||||||||||||||||||||||||||||||||||||||||||||||||||||||||||||||||

Provided by the Editor as an exercise in cultural relativism, or in a fit of spring cleaning.

The Metaphor: THE WAR.
What it generates: STRUGGLE.
Universe as war: The triumph of being over nothingness. The battlefield.
Society as war: The subjection of weak to strong.
Person as warrior: Courage; the hero.
   Medicine as victory over death.
Mind as warrior: Conquistador.
   Language as control.
The relationship of human with other beings in war: Enmity.
Images of the War: Victory, defeat, loot, ruin, the army.

The Metaphor: THE LORD.
What it generates: POWER.
Universe as kingdom: Hierarchy from one god down. Order from chaos.
Society as kingdom: Hierarchy from one king down. Order from chaos.
Person as lord/subject: Class, caste, place, responsibility.
   Medicine as power.
Mind as lord/subject: Law. Judgment.
   Language as power.
The relationship of human with other beings in the kingdom: Superiority.
Images of the Kingdom: The pyramid, the city, the sun.

The Metaphor: THE ANIMAL.
What it generates: LIFE.

519

Universe as animal: Organic, indivisible wholeness.
Society as animal: Tribe, clan, family.
Person as animal: Kinship.
    Medicine as rest.
Mind as animal: Discovery.
    Language as relationship.
The relationship of human with other beings as animals: Eating.
    Interdependence.
Images of the Animal: Birth, mating, dying, the seasons, the tree,
    the diverse beasts and plants.

The Metaphor: THE MACHINE.
What it generates: WORK.
Universe as machine: Clock and clockmaker. Running and run-
    ning down.
Society as machine: Parts, functions, cogs; interrelations; produc-
    tion.
Person as machine: Use. Function.
    Medicine as repair.
Mind as machine: Information.
    Language as communication.
The relationship of human with other beings as machines: Exploi-
    tation.
Images of the Machine: Progress, ineluctability, breakdown, the
    wheel.

The Metaphor: THE DANCE.
What it generates: MUSIC.
Universe as dance: Harmony. Creation/destruction.
Society as dance: Participation.
Person as dancer: Cooperation.
    Medicine as art.
Mind as dancing: Rhythm, measure.
    Language as connection.
The relationship of human with other beings as dance: Horizontal
    linkings.
Images of the Dance: Steps, gestures, continuity, harmony, the spi-
    ral.

The Metaphor: THE HOUSE.
What it generates: STABILITY.
Universe as house: Rooms in one mansion.
Society as household: Division within unity; inclusion/exclusion.
Person as householder: Selfhood.
  Medicine as protection.
Mind as householder: Belonging.
  Language as self-domestication.
The relationship of human with other beings in the house: Inside/
    Outside.
Images of the House: Doors, windows, hearth, home, the town.

The Metaphor: THE WAY.
What it generates: CHANGE.
Universe as the way: Mystery; balance in movement.
Society as the way: Imitation of the nonhuman; inaction.
Person as wayfarer: Caution.
  Medicine as keeping in balance.
Mind as wayfarer: Spontaneity. Sureness.
  Language as inadequate.
The relationship of human with other beings on the way: Unity.
Images of the Way: Balance, reversal, journey, return.

Three Poems by Pandora,
Written Sideways from the Valley
to the City of Man

||||||||||||||||||||||||||||||||||||||||||||||||||||||||||||||||||||

THE HIGH TOWER

Noble the Tower built with stones of Will
on the rock of Law: eternal that habitation.
In the House of the One may dwell the
    multitudes.
But the heathen are cast out to die as animals.

So we said, very well then,
and came away from the Kingdom
to the fields of grass, where we made small
    houses.
We build with dirt and wood and water.
We live with the animals and plants,
eating and praising them, and die with them;
their way is our way made mindful,
a river running over stones and rocks.
We live in the low places
like water and shadows.
Our houses do not last long.
We have lost sight behind us
of the spiritual Tower.
We go on down along the river.

NEWTON DID NOT SLEEP HERE

I don't care if I am possible.
What are the bridges between us?
    Wind, the rainbow,
      mist, still air.
We must learn to step on the rainbow.
    (Even Old Jealousy
      called it a covenant.)
We must learn how to walk on the wind.
    What links us (O my sister soul)
      is the abyss between us.
We must learn the fog path.
    What parts us (O my brother flesh)
      is our kinship of one house.
We must learn to trust thin air.

NOT BEING SINGLEMINDED

No god no king no One no thing
that comes one at a time
no dupli repli multi identiplication
prolifer proliferation same after same
so no city. Sorry.
Here
is no away to throw to.
A way with no away.
Some people, not very many,
trying to keep a lot of things in mind,
going beside the water,
singing heya, hey, heya,
heya, heya.

Living on the Coast,
Energy, and Dancing

LIVING ON THE COAST.

This was the Kesh term for the period of sexual celibacy expected of all adolescents. For a long time I found this custom anomalous, uncharacteristic of the Valley culture as a whole. These people who sought a realistic and undemanding attitude towards sexuality, avoiding excess both of indulgence and of abstinence, whose style of control and self-control was one of ease, not of rigidity, seeking grace rather than rule, and whose children were at the center of their world—why did such people come down on adolescents with such an extreme demand so sternly enforced?

For a while I explained it to my own satisfaction by connecting it to the Kesh prejudice against early parenthood, which was very strong, as strong as their prejudice against bearing/siring more than two children, and no doubt related to it, rationally enough. Big families start with young parents. Whatever elements of reason lay at its root, however, the attitude was passionate: they considered early parenthood to be unwise, unhealthy, and degrading. Pregnancy in a girl under seventeen or eighteen was always aborted, I was told, and the same involved concerned the pregnancy, not the abortion. A boy in his teens who fathered a child was treated with such contempt by his townsfolk that he might be driven to exile or suicide.

But still, why celibacy? After all, due to genetic damage from ancient catastrophes, the rate of conception was rather low and the rate of full-term healthy birth very low, by our standards; and contraceptives (condoms, diaphragms, and sponges of milkweed rubber and other materials, and herbal spermicides compounded by the Doctors Lodge) were effective, available, and completely socially approved. Boys and girls by the age of ten knew all the uses of contraceptives, and most of them had used them—for children's sexual play was taken altogether for granted, indulged, and even encouraged. Along around the age of ten, however, the children themselves began to abandon sexual play, because they wanted to outgrow it, to imitate the celibate adolescents. But why, just as the sexual urge began to declare itself and reach power and potency, this ban, this unnecessary, absolute reversal?

When I finally saw the period of celibacy as a reversal I began to see it as fully characteristic of the culture of the Valley.

Explaining this will involve discussing a couple of key words, which were first discussed in the section on the *Serpentine Codex*.

HEYIYA.

The first element of this word, hey- or heya, is the untranslatable statement of praise/greeting/holiness/being sacred.

The second is the word iya. This means a hinge: the piece of hardware or leather that connects a door to the opening it closes and opens. Connotations and metaphors cluster thick to this image. Iya is the center of a spiral, the source of a gyring motion; hence a source of change, as well as a connection. Iya is the eternal beginning, the process of energy arising and continuing. The word for energy is iye.

Energy manifests itself in three principal forms: cosmic, social, and personal.

The cosmos, the universe, was usually referred to rather casually in Kesh as rruwey, "all this." There was a more formal and philosophical word, em, meaning extent-and-duration, or space-time. Energy in the physicist's sense, the fundamental power interconvertible with matter, was emiye.

Ostouud described weaving or the weave of a fabric, bringing together, relating, and so was used to mean society, the community of being, the fabric of interdependent existences. The energy of relationship, including both politics and ecology, was ostouudiye.

Finally personal energy, selfhood of the individual, was sheiye.

The interplay of these three forms of energy throughout the universe was what the Kesh called "the dancing."

The last of the three, selfhood or personal energy, ramified into another set of concepts, which I shall treat very summarily:

Personal energy was seen as having five main components, relating to sex, mind, movement, work, and play, each with an inward-coming and outward-going aspect.

1. Lamaye, sexual energy. Lamawoiye, the energy that goes into sex (Freudian libido?).

2. Yaiye, extraverted thought. Yaiwoye, introverted thought.

3. Daoye is kinetic energy proper. Shevdaoye is energy expressed in athletics, travelling, all bodily skills, labors, activities. Shevdaowoye, personal movement, is the body itself.

4. Ayaye, playing, learning, teaching. Ayawoye seems best translated as "learning without a teacher."

5. Sheiye, personal energy, considered as work: the basic activities of staying alive—getting and preparing food, housekeeping, the arts and work of life. Shewoiye, work directed inward, work towards personhood or selfhood, might be translated as soulmaking.

To be alive was to choose and use, consciously or not, well or ill, these energies, in a manner appropriate to one's stage of life, state of health, moral ideals, and so on. The *deployment of iye* was really the principal subject of education in the Valley, in the home and in the heyimas, from infancy till death.

Personal energy was of course a personal matter; the individual made the choices, and the choosing, wise or foolish, mindful or careless, was the person. But no choice could be made independent of the superpersonal and impersonal energies, the cosmic/social/self-relatedness of all existences. Another word very important in Kesh thinking, túuvyai, mindfulness, might be described as the intelligent awareness of this interdependence of energies and beings, a sense of one's place and part in the whole.

Now, finally, as all these abstracts might be applied to an actual life in the Valley: A baby existed more in terms of physical energy and relationship (emiye, ostouudiye) than as a person. As the child grew, its outward-going personal energy (sheiye) got going and began to differentiate, first into moving about and playing and learning (shevdaoye, ayaye), the proper activities of the young, not to be hindered or pent or, in Blake's term, curbed. More slowly, the energies of sex and mind (lamaye, yaiye) would develop and find expression, still mostly outward-going, extraverted. And in the years called "clearwater" for girls (nine or ten till regular menstruation) and "sprouting" for boys (ten or eleven till full puberty), personal energy proper, the person working, would emerge.

With adolescence all these outgoing, centrifugal, growing energies began to be doubled by the inward-coming, centripetal energies of the mature human being. The adolescent had to learn how to balance out all these forces and so become a whole person, a "person entirely," yeweyshe. The means of doing so with economy, intelligence, and grace was the *regulation of energies*. And here we come back round to the rule of celibacy, the reversal.

Children were *going towards* sexual potency. Adolescents, as they attained it, *turned from* it. At the time they became able to "work" as sexual beings they ceased to do so—consciously, by choice. All the outgoing energies were now to reverse, to come back in to the center, to work in the service of personhood, at its most vulnerable and crucial stage.

In this reversal the young "person-becoming" went elsewhere, to those inward places where the unborn wait to be born (the image is mental, and physical: what goes on in the head and what goes on in the testes and ovaries are not separable events). They went to live "on the Coast." When they had made that journey, when they had gone there, they were ready to come "inland," to come home.

Of course the understanding, willing choice was an ideal. In practice, most young people undertook celibacy out of mere social conformity, obediently, and because its rewards were considerable. One started living on the Coast with a celebration at home, a ceremony in the heyimas, and a whole wardrobe of new clothes; and the adolescent in undyed clothing was held in honor and treated with a notable tenderness. One was supported by the entire fabric of relationships, kin, House, bond, lodge, art, and town. And how long one lived on the Coast really was up to the individual. The celibate period might be only a year or so, or might go on into the

early twenties. All that was to be avoided was the extreme: early promiscuity or obsessive asceticism.

Living on the Coast, then, was the beginning of living mindfully. It was a "hinge" act. From it would arise the work of being a person, itself part of the work of relationship, and that part of the universal work, the river flowing, the dancing, the turning of the galaxies. Weyiya heyiya—everything hinges, is holy.

WAKWA.

The phrase translated as "regulation of energies," iyevkwa, is a technical term—Kesh psychotechnological jargon, heyimas language.

In ordinary talk, the element *kwa* turns up only in the word wakwa, a very common word and a very complicated one. It can mean: a spring, running water, the rising or the flowing of water, to flow, to dance, dancing, a dance, festival, ceremony, or observation, and a mystery, both in the sense of obscure or unrevealed knowledge, and in the sense of the sacred means by which mysterious being or knowledge may be approached and revealed. As Mica, my teacher, said to me, the word is a small bag to hold so many nuts.

An actual spring or current of water is usually specified as wakwana. The town at the headwater and principal spring of the Na River is Wakwaha: Springway. This word as an ordinary noun/verb, wakwaha, means the course of the water as it leaves a spring, the way it goes: a very potent image and concept in Kesh thought. It also means "danceway"—the way a dance is danced, the way a ceremony is ordered, the order of happenings in an event, the direction an action tends. The pattern or figure made by an event or process is wakwaha-if.

Wakwa as mystery takes two forms. Wegotenhwya wakwa, literally sent-behind-wakwa, means mystification, the occult: rites or knowledge deliberately hidden or unrevealed. Gouwakwa, the dark dance, means mystery itself: the unknown, the unknowable. To the sun rising, the Kesh said, "Heya, heya!" in praise and greeting. To the darkness between the stars they spoke also, saying, "Heya gouwakwa."

Love

||||||||||||||||||||||||||||||||||||||||||||||||||||||||||||||||||||

THERE ARE SIX Kesh words which can be translated as "love," or conversely one can say that there is no Kesh word for love, but there are six words for different kinds of love. At first I thought the Kesh distinctions were similar to the Islandian—that subtle and useful trilogy of *ania, apia, alia*—but the overlap of meaning is only partial. The following list is the best I can do.

1. *wenun:* noun and verb, to want, desire, covet ("I love apples.")
2. *lamawenun:* noun and verb, sexual desire, lust, passion ("I love you!")
3. *kwaiyó —woi dad,* heart goes to —: to like, to feel an impulse of warmth toward ("I like him very much.")
4. *unne:* noun and verb, trust, friendship, affection, lasting warmth ("I love my brother." "I love her like a sister.")
5. *iyakwun:* noun and verb, mutual connection, interdependence, filial or parental love, love of place, love of one's people, cosmic love ("I love you, Mother." "I love my country." "God loves me.")
6. *bahó:* as a verb, to please, to give pleasure or delight ("I love to dance.")

The principal distinction between 3 and 4 is one of duration—3 is brief, or a beginning, 4 is lasting or continuing. The distinction between 4 and 5 is more difficult. Unne implies mutuality, iyakwun asserts it; unne is lovingkindness, iyakwun is passion; unne is rational, moderate, social love, iyakwun is the love that moves the sun and the other stars.

Written Kesh

|||||||||||||||||||||||||||||||||||||||||||||||||||||||||||||||||||||||||||

READING AND WRITING were taken to be elements of human social existence as fundamental as speech itself. From the age of three or four a child learned to read and write at home and in the heyimas, and no Kesh was illiterate, except those with brain or vision dysfunction; the latter often compensated for their inability to read by developing their verbal memory to a fantastic degree.

The Kesh were less inclined than we to consider speaking and writing as one activity taking different forms. Anything we speak can be written down, and we seem to feel that it *should* be written down if it is of any importance: writing authenticates speech, and has taken priority over it. We now read what our speechmakers are going to say before they say it. The current uses of computers enhance and enforce this fitting of the word into the visual mode. The Kesh had a few kinds of writing that were never spoken or read aloud, but since they also had some very important kinds of speech that were never written down, they did not identify speaking and writing as forms or aspects of the same thing; to the Kesh they were two kinds of language, either of which might be translated into the other, if it was useful or appropriate to do so.

The alphabet in use while we were in the Valley had been developed several centuries earlier by a group of people in the Madrone Lodge of Wakwaha who were dissatisfied with the alphabet then in use. Either because it had been borrowed from another language or because Kesh had changed a good deal in sound, this ornate "fesu" alphabet was cumbrous and arbitrary, using 67 letters to represent the 34 phonemes recognised by the Kesh. The "aiha" (new) alphabet of 29 letters plus the Four-House and Five-House signs was pretty nearly phonetic (discrepancies are noted in the chart below). The design of the letters was severely chastened, and perhaps overrationalised. Scholars learned to read fesu out of antiquarian curiosity, but all documents of interest had long since been retranscribed into aiha writing.

530

Ink Pot

Pen and brush were the writing instruments. A steel pen in a wooden holder was the commonest (the Kastoha ironworks produced steel in quantity sufficient for pen-nibs, sewing needles, knifeblades, razors, and certain other fine tools and small machine parts). In the heyimas quill pens were used, since feathers were themselves considered to be words. The brush, of hair set in bamboo, was an alternative for those who preferred it. Most poets seemed to favor brush calligraphy, perhaps because it enlivened the rather monotonous aiha letters.

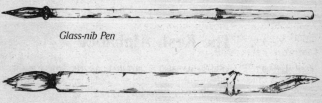

Glass-nib Pen

Brush/Pen

Pen ink was made of tannin from oak and walnut galls, ferrous sulphate (vitriol), and indigo, and was bottled in small, broad-based, grey ceramic pots of a pleasing shape. Brush ink, made from the soot of burnt pitch or oil mixed with glue and camphor, was shaped in cakes and sticks, like Chinese ink. Printing ink was a mixture of rosin, linseed oil, a pinetar soap, soot, and indigo.

Paper was made in a fascinating variety of weights and textures, using mixtures of fir and other wood pulp, cotton, linen, cattail and other reeds, milkweed, and practically any other fiber. In the paper workshop of the Book Art in Telína-na I saw a poem brush-written on a cloudy, filmy, unsized paper which the poet said he had made from dandelion clocks and thistledown, carded. The poem was less memorable than the paper, I thought.

The Book Art and the Oak Lodge of each town made and provided paper and ink, writing materials and printing materials, and the facilities for making and using them.

A poem or a set of poems might be written on one large sheet of paper, and short works were often written on scrolls rolled vertically on wooden rods. Books were made like our books, bound by gluing and sewing one margin of the sheets, and covered with calfskin leather or goatskin parchment or heavy cloth on paperboard. People who wrote a good deal generally made their own paper and blank books. Fine copies and printed editions of literary pieces were usually the work of copyists and printers in the Book Art, and were called *wudaddú*, "going back through," rendition, performance—the word used also for an oral recitation, the acting of a written play, or the performance of a piece of music.

Paper Duster

The Kesh Alphabet

KESH ALPHABET	ENGLISH ALPHABET	INTERNATIONAL PHONETIC ALPHABET
ⲣ	k	[k]
ʃ · f	g	[g]
⟨	sh	[ʃ]
Ƨ	ch	[tʃ]
Ꙅ	l	[l], [ɬ] (The two kinds of l in 'little')
Ӡ	n	[n]
⋁	s	[s]
⊿	d	[d], [ḍ], [ð]
⊽	t	[tˀ]
ꙅ	r	[ř], [ř], [dr], [ð] (See note below)

∂	f	[f]
ⱦ	v	[v]
ㄣ	m	[m]
ƙ	b	[b]
·	p	[p̓]
ʋ	w	[w], [ʷ]
∼ · ∽	hw	[hw] (As in English "what")
ʕ	y	[y], [ʸ]
ⱬ	h	[h], sometimes [x]
ઉ · б	o	[ɔ] (As in English "off")
᧒ · 9	ó	[o] (As in "oat" without glide)
𝒪𝒰	ou	[ow] (As in "go")
᧒ · ᧒	ú	[u] (As in "toot")
o	u	[ə]; [ʌ] (As in "the"; as in "but," "dumb")
᧒	e	[ɛ] (As in "yet")
᧒ · ᧒	a	[a] (As in "father")
᧒	ai	[aʸ] (as in "tie")
᧒	i	[ɪ] (As in "pit")
᧒	í	[i] (As in "meet")
᧒		Five-House sign, pronounced [z] (a suffix to words in the Five House mode, which is not used in most kinds of writing)
᧒		Four-House sign (there is no spoken sign)
∼ · ∼		Doubled letter sign, written over the letter.

Note concerning the Kesh *r*: depending on context it may be a trill, a flap (as in English "steady" or "Betty"), the fricative [ð] as in "then," or a stop [dr]; and as a final sound it is often very like American English "hard *r*" in "her."

It will be noted that the order of the aiha alphabet was a fairly orderly progression of the consonants from the back of the mouth forward to the lips, back through the semiconsonants from dental to glottal, and forward again through the vowels. The glides *ou* [ow] and *ai* [ai] were included as letters in the alphabet, the equally common glides *ei* or *ey* [ɛy] and *oi* or *oy* [ɔy] were not, for no reason anybody could cite. The symbol or letter (‿◡) signalling the Five-House or Earth Mode, sounded as [z], the Four-House or Sky Mode sign (◠), which represented no sound, and the doubled-letter sign written above the letter, were not included in the order of the alphabet as written or recited.

Text was written and read left to right, top to bottom; but clowns practiced reverse writing, bottom to top, right to left, the letters reversed.

There were no capital letters; punctuation and spacing separated sentences. Vowels were usually written larger than consonants.

PUNCTUATION.

In inscriptions and mural writing little punctuation was used except for a slanting stroke to divide sentences. In ordinary and literary writing, punctuation was careful and complex, including indications of expression and tempo which we use only for music. The principal signs were:

——	Equivalent to our period
⌐⌐	A "double period," roughly equivalent to a paragraph break
⋏	Equivalent to our comma, indicating a phrase within a continuing sentence
⋩	Equivalent to our semicolon, indicating a self-contained phrase within a continuing sentence

These four signs, like our punctuation, were syntactically meaningful and aided clarity. The next five concern dynamics and tempo:

/	Equivalent to our dash, signifying a pause. Repeated, a long pause; repeated more than once, a longer pause
<u>word</u>	Kesh underlining, just like ours, denotes emphasis or stress
word	The opposite of underlining: de-emphasis, a soft or even tone
⌢	Written over a word, a fermata: prolong the word. Written in the margin: rallentando: read this line or these lines slowly
⋀	Written in the margin: speed up, or resume normal reading pace

The Modes of Earth and Sky

‖‖‖‖‖‖‖‖‖‖‖‖‖‖‖‖‖‖‖‖‖‖‖‖‖‖‖‖‖‖‖‖‖‖‖‖‖‖‖

MUCH SPOKEN KESH was in a mode which occurs only once in this book, in a line of dialogue in *Dangerous People*. The Five-House or Earth Mode was indicated by a final *z*-sound added to the noun/verbs of the sentence, and was used when one was speaking to and of living persons and local places, in one of the present tenses or with the auxiliaries meaning "can," "be able," "must," in everyday informal conversation.

The Four-House or Sky Mode would be used in all discourse concerning Four-House people and places (those unborn, dead, thought, imagined, dreamed, in the wilderness, etc.) and in all past and future tenses, as well as with the auxiliaries of the conditional, optative, subjunctive, etc.; in the negative; in making abstract or general statements; and in all formal discourse and rhetoric and works of literature both written and oral. There was a letter of the alphabet for the [z] phoneme that indicated the Earth Mode, but, evidently, it was very seldom used. People who in real life would use the Earth Mode talking would keep to the Sky Mode in even the most realistic history or novel.

So in an actual conversation one would say, "Pandora, are you living in Sinshan now?"—Pandoraz, Sinshanzan gehóvzes hai ohu—the two proper nouns and the verbal both in the Earth Mode. But the same question in a play or any narrative would be— Pandora, Sinshanan gehóves hai ohu. The negative, whether colloquial or formal, would be: Pandora Sinshanan pegehov hai, "Pandora is not living in Sinshan now." And the past would always be in the Sky Mode: Pandora Sinshanan yinyegegohóv ayeha, "Pandora did truly live a little while in Sinshan."

Though my note on the narrative modes shows that the Kesh did not distinguish factual from fictional literature as we do, the precision of their use of these basic modes of the language indicates a clear awareness of the difference between the *actual* and the *imagined*.

A Note and a Chart Concerning Narrative Modes

THE PRINCIPAL MODE of our thinking is binary: on/off, hard/soft, true/false, etc. Our categories of narrative follow the pattern. Narrative is either factual (nonfiction) or nonfactual (fiction). The distinction is clear, and the feeble forms such as the "novelised biography" or the "nonfiction novel" that attempt to ignore it only demonstrate its firmness.

In the Valley the distinction is gradual and messy. The kind of narrative that tells "what happened" is never clearly defined by genre, style, or valuation from the kind that tells a story "like what happened." Some of the Romantic Tales certainly recount real events; some of the sober Historical Accounts concern events which we do not admit into the category of the real, or the possible. Here of course is the difference: where you stop, on what grounds you stop, and say, "Reality goes no further."

If fact and fiction are not clearly separated in Kesh literature, truth and falsehood, however, are. A deliberate lie (slander, boast, tall tale) is identified as such and is not considered in the light of literature at all. In this case I find our categories perhaps less clear than theirs. The distinction is one of intent, and we often do not make it at all, since we allow propaganda to be qualified both as journalism and as fiction; while the Kesh dismiss it as a lie.

The accompanying chart attempts to show these continuities and discontinuities.

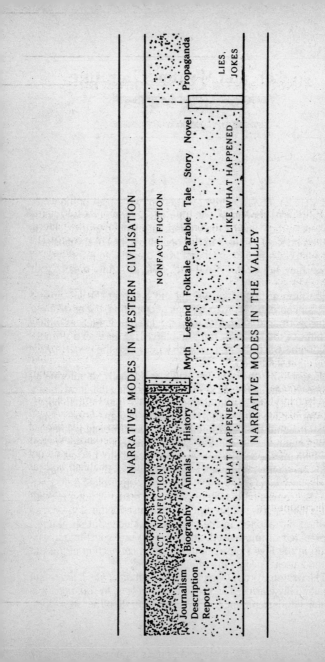

NARRATIVE MODES IN WESTERN CIVILISATION

FACT: NONFICTION

NONFACT: FICTION

Report Description Journalism Biography Annals History — Myth Legend Folktale Parable Tale Story Novel — Propaganda

LIES, JOKES

WHAT HAPPENED

LIKE WHAT HAPPENED

NARRATIVE MODES IN THE VALLEY

Spoken and Written Literature

|||||||||||||||||||||||||||||||||||||||||||||||||||||||||||||||||||||

SOME VALLEY TEXTS were unwritten in two senses of the word. In the first place they have not, after all, been written yet. In the second place they never were written: they were oral texts. Those of the second kind included in this book have thus been translated twice, from Kesh into English and from breath into print—and, if you like, they can be translated back from print into breath, your breath.

The Kesh distinguished writing and speaking, the written and the spoken word, not as two versions of one thing, but as different activities with a large area of overlap, different languages with a large but not total area of translatability. They saw as a primary distinction between the oral and the written text the *quality of the relationship* established.

Undoubtedly one can and will say (formally or informally) what one wouldn't write (or wouldn't say knowing that it was being recorded). The writer's solitude might look like maximum freedom, but the immediate relationship between speaker and hearer(s) may increase freedom by increasing trust. (A writer of course may remain anonymous as a speaker cannot, but anonymity or a penname, denying the self, denies even the possibility of trust.)

Between writer and reader, the text itself mediates. It may be properly seen as a communication rather than a relation. In Kesh terms, the connection between writer and reader is not a present one: it is made in the nonpresent, in the Houses of the Sky—and so all written narration is in the Four-House Mode. But speaking a text, prepared or improvised, and listening to it constitute a relationship in the Five Houses of the Earth, a connection of present contemporaries, "people breathing together."

The written word is *there,* for *anyone,* at *any time.* It is general and potentially eternal. The spoken word is *here,* to *you, now.* It is ephemeral and irreproducible. (We might question the latter word;

but mechanical reproduction, even the moving picture with sound, makes an image of but does not reconstitute the occasion, the time, the place, or the people there.)

The trust or confidence that can be established between writer and reader is real, though entirely mental; on both sides it consists in the willingness to animate, to project one's own thinking and feeling into a harmony with a not-yet-existent reader or a not-present and perhaps long-dead writer. It is a miraculous and entirely symbolical transubstantiation.

When the artist and the audience are together, collaboration on the work becomes mundane and actual; the work shapes itself in the speaker's voice and the listeners' response together. This powerful relationship can be, and in politics frequently is, abused: the speaker may appropriate the power to himself, dominating and exploiting the audience. When the power of the relationship is used not abused, when the trust is mutual, as when a parent tells a bedtime story or a teacher shares the treasures of the intellect or a poet speaks both to and for the listeners, real community is achieved; the occasion is sacred.

It would confuse things, however, to make a correlation of oral with sacred, written with secular literature, in the Valley: because the binary opposition sacred/secular was one they didn't make. There were indeed certain songs, dramas, instructions, and other oral texts connected with the great festivals and with sacred occasions or places, which they never wrote down or recorded in any way. For instance the Wedding Song, sung every year at the World Dance, known to every adult in the Valley, remained unwritten; it belonged "to the breath," they said. To reproduce such a text would be, in their view, most inappropriate, not because it was sacrosanct but because its oral/occasional/communal character was *essential*. (When it was indicated to me that to record or transcribe would be inappropriate, I honored the request. A particular and valuable exception was made for me in the case of the death songs called Going Westward to the Sunrise, printed in the section called "How to Die in the Valley," and discussed again below.)

We mostly seem to feel it appropriate and desirable that all spoken words, even office memoranda, recordings of private conversations, grandmother's tales, be saved on tape, stored in memory banks, transcribed, written, printed, preserved in libraries. Perhaps not many of us could say why we save so many words, why our forests must all be cut to make paper to mark our words on, our rivers dammed to make electricity to power our word pro-

cessors; we do it obsessively, as if afraid of something, as if com-
pensating for something. Maybe we're afraid of death, afraid to let
our words simply be spoken and die, leaving silence for new words
to be born in. Maybe we seek community, the lost, the irreproducible.

~⟋~

Kesh poetry might be written down, or might not. It might be improvised, memorised and recited, or read—but when read, even by
a reader quite alone in a room, it was read aloud. A good many of
the poems and songs in this book were not written down by their
authors or performers, but they were pleased to have us do so.
When poetry is a form of conversation, you might not try to record
it all, but you do appreciate having your fine points noted. Other
poems included here were written down by the author and given to
the heyimas, where they would be kept in the treasury or archives
for a while, and eventually sorted through and the paper recycled,
or the text recopied and taken home by somebody who wanted it,
or otherwise dispersed. Still others were performed aloud at Lodge
teachings or other ceremonies; some of these were common property, others were given "by the breath" by one individual (author or
owner) to another: these were property as gift.

I haven't tried to distinguish lyric poems from song lyrics.
When I asked to write down the words of an improvisation or to
record a song, the singer usually gave cordial permission, but not
always. As a fourteen-year-old boy said when I asked him to repeat
an improvisation so that I could tape it, "It was a dragonfly song,
you can't make it come back."

When writing down songs with a "matrix" of repeated syllables, the Kesh usually wrote only the syntactically meaningful
words and omitted the matrix, which often constituted both the
bulk of the song and the most deeply felt or meaningful part of it.
But that meaning was, in their view, carried by the music and by
the breath, and miscarried by the written letters. I think they were
right.

Instructions and descriptions of ritual and the order of a ceremony might be written or not written; I never found any consistent
pattern. A hermetic tradition and a strong resistance to hermetic
and esoteric practices ran side by side in the Valley. The reverse of
the situation of trust I spoke about above is that a secret is after all
best kept by the breath; to write a word is to publish it. In her life-
story, Stone Telling refers to the mysteries of the Lamb and Warrior

cults; though these had all been exposed, spoken aloud, long ago, she still could not bring herself to *write* about them.

The songs and instructions of Going Westward to the Sunrise were both esoteric and common, both written and unwritten. The songs, sung by and for a dying person, were held in reverence. They were learned only from a designated teacher, a member of the Black Adobe Lodge; and teaching and learning took place at a certain time of year in a certain place set aside, a house specially built, the typical temenos or holy ground. Yet there was nothing secret about the songs at all. All adults learned them, sooner or later; children heard them sung on the First Night of the World Dance. They were, in the fullest sense of the word, common property. Yet, though a learner might write them down to aid memorisation, or the teacher write them for a person who had difficulty hearing an oral text, such transcriptions were always burned on the last night of the teaching period. The songs were never copied from writing, and never printed. Their publication here is a privilege granted by my teacher of the Lodge Rejoining, Mica of Sinshan, after careful consultation with people of the Black Adobe Lodge of Sinshan and other towns.

As for narrative fiction, it might be entirely oral, story-telling of traditional or extemporised tales; or it might be retold or read aloud from a text—this was often the method of the librarians, the more or less professional tellers of tales in prose and verse. Some narrative forms were entirely written texts, never performed aloud: biography, autobiography, the Romantic Tales, were transmitted "by the hand" not "by the breath," in manuscript or in print. Their essential character was to be *there* for anyone. The same is true for the great novels of the writers Marsh, Cowardly Dog, and Mote, which are alas far too long to include in this book, though I did get in a chapter of Wordriver's *Dangerous People*.

Much of what I have said about written and spoken words applies, in a general sort of way, to music. The Kesh had an adequate system of musical notation, but they used it mostly for student exercises, as a guide to practice. They did not choose to write down the score of any composition, though they might make a note of a tune, or of certain harmonies, or of matters of technique such as a tonguing or "hinge breathing," etc., as a reminder. Music was transmitted in performance. But, most strikingly, they did not choose ever to record performance. They allowed the Exchange to make and store electronic recordings when it asked to, and we were able to record a certain number of songs and performances; but in this we were doing something which they never did, and

often it was tactfully indicated to us that replication of the music—
of music—was a mistake, perhaps a mistake concerning the nature
of Time.

Or to put it another way, what we consider both desirable and
necessary they tended to consider a weakness and a needless risk:
replication, multiplication.

"One note once only in the wilderness . . ."

Pandora No Longer Worrying

||||||||||||||||||||||||||||||||||||||||||||||||||||||||||||||||||||||||||||||

HERE AS THE CEREMONY begins to end and the heyiya-if opens out, Pandora takes hands and dances with her friends, and among them beautifully dancing are these:

Bart Jones, who first heard the first songs, the quail and the creek, and sang them to me so that I could hear my people.

Judd Boynton, who told me how to make rubber from milkweed and how to recycle the waste and how to power the washing machine, and who showed me also how a man may dance dying, as Yeats knew:

> "Soul clap its hands and sing, and louder sing
> For every tatter in its mortal dress!"
> —"Sailing to Byzantium"

And the Other Owners, who gave us those four months.

Jim Bittner, who provided *Heinrich von Offerdingen*, und andere Dingen.

Jean Nordhaus of the Folger Poetry Series, who enabled me to hoot and croak in the Folger Shakespeare Library.

Mrs. Clara Pearson of the Nehalem Tillamook people, who told the story which Kingsnake stole; and E. D. and Melville Jacobs and Jarold Ramsay, who recorded and reprinted it.

And those who make the music for the dancing: Gregory C. Hayes, who provided the time and the dancing place.

Masters of the Millers Art, working under the auspices of the Four Houses of the Sky, Douglas K. Faerber, Míbbí himself; and Kimberley Barry, whom I name Nówelemaha, Beautiful Stillness.

And the singers, listen to the names of the singers: Anne Hodgkinson Beyúnaheo, and Thomas Wagner Tomhoia, and Rebecca Warner Ódbahó Handúshe, Woman Who Delights in Birds; and Patricia O'Scannell, David Marston, Susan Marston, Malcolm

Lowe, and Meredith Beck. Híó dadamnes hanóya dónhayú koumushúde!

The Three Who Cared for the Cow, my Virginia, Valerie, Jane, they are at the center, there would be no dance without them.

And behold the Geomancer, whose name measures the Valley, who shaped the hills and helped me sink half California, who went on the Salt Journey, caught the Train, and walked every step with Grey Bull—Heya Heggaia, han es im! Amoud gewakwasur, yeshou gewakwasur.

GLOSSARY

IT WAS MY INTENTION in making this glossary to include all the Kesh words which occur in the text of the book or in the songs and poems in the recording that accompanies it. A number of other words were included for the pleasure of my fellow dictionary-readers and adepts of what an illustrious predecessor referred to as the Secret Vice.

Kesh Numbers

ap	0	chemchemdai . . .	26
dai	1	dídechem . . .	30
hú	2	dúsechem . . .	35
íde	3	bekelchem . . .	40
kle	4	gahóchem . . .	45
chem	5	chúmchem . . .	50
díde	6	chúmchemdai . . .	51
dúse	7	chúmchemchem . . .	55
bekel	8	chúmdíde . . .	60
gahó	9	chúmdúse . . .	70
chúm	10	chumbekel . . .	80
húchemdai	11	chúmgahó . . .	90
húchemhú	12	chúmchúm . . .	100
húchemíde	13	chúmchúmhwaihú . . .	200
húchemkle	14	chúmchúmhwaíde . . .	300
ídechem	15	chúmchúmhwaichúm.	1000
ídechemdai	16		
ídechemú	17	wedai: first	
ídechemíde	18	wehú: second, etc.	
ídechemkle	19		
klechem	20	hwaidai: once	
klechemdai . . .	21	hwaihú: twice	
chemchem	25	hwaíde: three times, etc.	

A

a   1. (prefix or suffix; indicates
masculine gender. See also *ta,
peke.*)
2. (interjection; indicates voca-
tive)

ach   redwood *(Sequoia semper-
virens)* tree or wood.

adre   moon. To shine (of, or
like, the moon).
adre wakwa   the Moon
Dance. To dance the Moon.

adselon   puma, mountain lion
(Felis concolor).

adsevin   Venus (planet); the
morning or evening star.

adgí (or) **aggí**   wild dog (feral
Canis domesticus).

aibre   purple, violet color.

aiha   young; new.

aió   eternity, endlessness, open-
ness. Eternal, endless, open.

al   ringtail, miners' cat *(Bassaris-
cus astutus).*

am   (usually precedes obj.) by,
beside, next to; along, alongside; very shortly before or
after, at nearly the same time
as.

ama   grandmother; female
ancestor in the mother's line.

amab   acceptance. To accept, to
receive.

amakesh   the Valley of the Na.

amavtat   grandfather (mother's
father).

ambad   giving, the act of giving;
generosity; wealth. To give; to
be rich, wealthy; to be generous.

ambadush   giver, rich person,
generous person.

amhú   (usually precedes obj.)
between, in between; (as noun)

skin, surface, interface; (as
verb) to be between, to be what
separates or defines.

amhúdade   waterskater (insect;
see also *taidagam*).

amoud   (usually precedes obj.)
together, together with, in the
same time or rhythm with.
amoud manhóv   (to be) a
member of the (same) family, to
live together.

an   (follows obj.) in; into; within.

anan   (follows obj.) into.

anasayú   madrone *(Arbutus
menziesii)* tree or wood.

ansai   rainbow, spectrum.

ansaivshe   Rainbow People.

anyabad   learning (rather "what
one needs or ought to know"
than "what is to be known").
To learn.

aó   voice. To voice, give voice,
speak, say.

ap   zero; blank.

apap   a dice game.

arba   hand; handling. To use the
hands, to handle.

arban   work, responsibility; to
look after, to work with.
arban hanuvrón   to take good
care of, to work carefully.

arbayai   "handmind," physical
work done with intelligence, or
the results of such work.

aregin   coast, shore, beach;
margin, edge.

areginounhóv   "to live on the
coast," *i.e.,* to be celibate.

arra word. To speak (a language in which there are words).

arrakou (or) **arrakoum** (or) **rakoum** poem; poetry; poiesis. To make or write a poem, poetry.

arrakush poet.

arsh (adj., pron., rel. pron.: subject of verb, agent) which; who; that/those which; he/she who.

asai (or) **asay** crossing. To cross.

asaika coming or to come across from the Five Houses to the Four Houses, or vice versa; hence, to die or to be born.

ashe man; male being. Masculine, male.

asole opal.

ast break, come apart.

aya learning; teaching; play; imitation, mimesis. To learn; to teach; to play; to imitate, to participate.

ayache manzanita *(Arctostaphylos spp.)* tree, shrub, wood.

ayash scholar, learner, teacher.

ayeha indeed, to be sure, truly.

B

badap gift (in the sense of talent, capacity).

bahó pleasure, delight. To please, to delight.

banhe acceptance, inclusion; insight, understanding; female orgasm. To include; to comprehend; to have orgasm (female).

baroi (or) **baroy** kind, kindly. To be kind.

bata (or) **ta** (or) **tat** father (biological father).

belai squash.

besh wall; shelter. To stand between, to shelter.
  beshan indoors.
  beshvou outdoors.

beyunahe otter *(Lutra)*.

bí (suffix; an endearment) dear.
  binye (suffix) dear little.

bibí dear, darling.

bínbín kitten, young of any species of cat.

bit fox *(Urocyon)*.
  bitbín fox cub.

bod clay pot, jar.

boled (precedes obj.) around, about (in spatial or temporal sense).

boleka return. To return, come back, turn back.

bósó acorn woodpecker *(Melanerpes formicivorus)*.

bou (suffix) out; out of, out from (see also *vou*).

brai wine.
  hwan (or) **suhwan** white wine.
  úyúma rosé wine.
  (About thirty kinds of wine were made in the Valley. The most famous were the red Ganais, Berrena, Tomehey, and Shipa; the rosé Mes made in Ounmalin; and the white Tekage from the foothills of the Mountain.)
bú great horned owl *(Bubo).*
búrebúre (a plural) many, a great many.
búta horn.
búye (may precede or follow obj.) near, near to, close to, nearly, in the vicinity of, around the time of; nearby.

CH

chan relation, relative, family member.
chandí wood rat, packrat *(Neotoma fuscipes).*
chebeshí lemonade.
chechení a people, people living together in a group larger than a household; townsfolk, society; social existence. (People of the household, commensals, are manhóvoud.) To live in a town or village, to live as a social being.
chemma the Five Houses of Earth; (as adj.) Five-House, of the Five Houses.
  chemmahóv to live in the Five Houses; *i.e.*, to be alive, exist, be.
  chemmashe Five-House being, Earth Person.
chenats doctor, expert in medicine, physician.
  geónkamats singing doctor.
  nóchenats silent doctor.

gearbanats handling doctor.
  dwesh bringer-in (see *gedwean*).
  chenatsiv hedom Doctors Lodge.
chep (precedes obj.) without (see also *poud*).
chewítú chukar *(Alectoris graeca).*
chey sharing, mutual ownership. To share, to hold in common.
  gochey shared, common, mutual, public
chiní eggplant.
chog leather.
chomadú boulder, rock larger than a small goat lying down.
choum town, village, place where more than one household lives.
chunú flesh, substance of an animal or plant while alive (see *truned*).

D

d, du (prefix; indicates the word is functioning as a direct object noun.)
dad going. To go.
dadam going along. To go along.
dade touch, the act of touching. To feel, touch, skim, go upon.
dagga leg; agent of locomotion on ground (see also *hurga*).
dahaihai jackrabbit *(Lepus californicus).*
dai one; single, singly; alone.
daihúda walking. To walk (on two feet; used of human beings, animals on their hind legs, and birds such as pigeons that walk).
  haida to hop on two feet.
  yakleda to walk on four feet.
  handesddade to crawl.

dadam   to walk or go on more than four or an indeterminate number of feet.

dam   earth, dirt, soil; the earth. **damshe** Earth People.

damsa   the world; the cosmos; the Nine Houses.

daó   moving, motion, action, activity. To move, to move about, be active.

delup   heart (the physical organ). To pulse, throb, beat (like the heart).

dem   width, breadth; to widen; wide, broad.

depemehai   (usually precedes obj.) far, far from; away; at a distance, at another time, a long way/time from.

dest   snake.

deyón   toyon *(Photinia arbutifolia)*, "California holly."

dídúmí   excess, superfluity, too much. To exceed, to be too much.

diftú   little, small (but not brief; see *inye*. A pebble is diftú, not inye).

dirats   blood. To bleed.

díú   rising, arising. To rise, rise up, go up.

díúha   southeast.

díúhafar   east.

doduk   rock, stone; a rock not too large or heavy to lift.

don   brindle, brindled, tabby.

dót   sheep.
dóto   ewe.
dóta   ram.
pedóta   wether.
mebí, omebí, amebí   lamb.

dou   (usually precedes obj.) up; upon; over (see also *stou; tai; oun*).

doubúre   (a plural) many, a good many.

doum   brown, or mixed color of dark, warm tone.

doumiadú ohwe   an artificial "dragon" enclosing several dancers which appeared during the Wine Dance; also called *damiv hodest,* Old Earth Snake. Earthquakes, as well as bodily tremors and reelings, could be ascribed to the movements of the Doumiadú ohwe underlying all the Coast Ranges.

dreví   green, or yellowish green.

dú   (may precede or follow obj.) through; throughout (an area or space).

dúcha   son.

dúchatat   half-brother, father's son.

dúdam   enclosure, enclave, cell, room (usually underground). To enclose, surround, contain.

duéde   clarity, transparency. To be transparent, clear.

dúi   a breed of sheepdog with very short curly hair.

dukab   (or **berka**) (or **tuk**) poultry; fowl.

dúme   calculate, figure out.

dúmí   fill up; reach the limit; attain; win a game or a race.

dúr   red.

dut   (pronoun, rel. pron., or adj.: object of verb) which, whom; that/those which, whom.

dwe   bringing. To bring, to fetch.

E

ed   sight, seeing. To see.

em   extent/duration; space/time.

emwey (or **emweyem**:   ever, forever, always, everywhere.

emwoum manifestation. To manifest, to be manifest.

ene maybe not. (Often used to mean "No.")

ense 1. (precedes obj.) after. 2. (follows obj.) then; next, next after.

eppe end, halt, stop, interruption. To stop, cease, leave off.

eppeshe death (of living being), cessation, destruction, end (of nonliving being). To cease being, to end; not to be.

er northwest.

erai (or) **farer** north.

erhwaha west.

eshe while; during; during the time that.

estun choice, option. To choose.

evai Society: so translated in this book. A group of people formally organised with a common interest and the activities of such a group, guild, or cult; also the place where they meet or work.

eye (or) **ey** yes.

F

farkí ground squirrel *(Citellus)*.

fas soup, broth, juice.

fat clown
 sufat White Clown.
 drevífat Green Clown.
 wediratsfat Blood Clown.

fefinum incense cedar *(Libocedrus decurrens)*.

fege tick, wood tick.

fehoch field, cultivated land, arable.
 fehochóvoud To farm, to cultivate

feitúlí a poisonous mushroom (an *Amanita?*).

fen cord, string.

fesent moving in line, following. To move or go in line, to follow after. One after another.

fía evaporation. To evaporate, to go into or become part of the atmosphere (used of water, smoke, breath, etc.).

finí a poetic contest of insults (fliting or flyting in the OED).

fíyóyú buckeye *(Aesculus californica)*, a wild horse-chestnut which blooms in May and loses its leaves in late summer.

foure beginning, start. To begin, to start.

fumó a substance, apparently a residue of industrial products or byproducts, perhaps of petroleum-based plastics, which occurs in small whitish grains or larger concretions, covering regions of the ocean surface and found on beaches and tidal flats, often to a depth of several feet; useless, indestructible, and poisonous when burning.

fún mole.

G

galik deer *(Odocoileus?* or similar, slightly larger new species).
 ogalik doe
 galika buck.
 galikaiha fawn.

gai 1. ready (for), prepared; resolved, resolute, determined. 2. socketed, fixed, settled, tightened.

gam buzzard, turkey-vulture *(Cathartes)*.

ganai creek, brook, stream. To run, flow (of a creek, or a small amount of water).

gat to hit, strike. Blow.

gawatse toad *(Bufo)*.

gebayú Jupiter (planet).

gedadha direction.

gedwean bringing-in; a medical treatment, described in the section "Notes on Medical Practices." To bring in.

gele running. To run on two legs. (To run on four legs: *yaklegele, yaklele, leste*.)

gettop skunk *(Mephitis)*.
gettop wevave: cloudy skunk (the description sounded like the Western Spotted Skunk, *Spilogale*, but the Kesh insisted that the animal danced upon its hands while emitting a sweet perfume that attracted dogs, wild dogs, and coyotes and made them dance too until they died of exhaustion; hence, perhaps, a mythical animal).

geved hanóya meditation. To meditate.

gewotun arban to plant, to garden.
gowotun (or) mane dam gowotun garden, planted plot.

gey fire. To burn.
houmgey forest fire.

geyí tone (in music).

gí patient, attentive, waiting; patience; a patient person.

gochey shared, common, commonly owned or used.

góli live oak *(Quercus agrifolia)* tree or wood.
golidun *(Q. wislizenii)*.

góra eating, drinking. To eat, to drink, to consume with the mouth.

gou dark, darkness. To be dark, to darken, grow dark.

goutun (or) **gedagoutun** twilight of morning.

gouwoy (or) **gedagouwoy** twilight of evening.

grut slug.

gunyú wild pig (domestic swine reverted to feral).

H

ha way; wayfaring, journey. To journey, travel; to go on a way or one's way.

hai now.

haip bite. To bite.

haitrou fear. To fear, to be afraid.

ham breath; air. To breathe.

hamdúshe bird.

han 1. in a . . . manner; resembling; like. 2. (suffix, indicates use of the word as adverb; may be translated *-like* or *ly*.) 3. so. Han (es) im So you are here, *i.e.*, Hello.

hannaheda stream, flow, flowing, continuous coherent onward motion. To run, flow, pour, stream (of any substance).

hanyó in such a manner that.

hat adobe clay or earth.
dúrhatvma the House of Red Adobe.
hwanhatvma the House of Yellow Adobe.

hechí a breed of domestic dog resembling a chow.

he action. To act, to do.

hedom Lodge: so translated in this book. A formally organised group of people learning, teaching, or practicing certain crafts, skills, rituals, bodies of knowledge, etc., and the practices and work of such a group, and the place or building where they meet and work.

hedou 1. great, major, important, notable. 2. the California condor *(Gymnogyps californianus)* or a closely similar species, but with a more northerly range and far wider distribution than at present.

heggai domestic dog (used when the breed or type is not specified.
hebbí (or) wí puppy.

hegou black.

hegoudo obsidian (volcanic glass).
hegoudovma the House of Obsidian.

hehóle a keepsake, treasure, object considered beautiful or sacred.
hehóle-nó an object, usually the size to be held in the hand and carried easily in a pouch or pocket, used as an adjunct to meditation or "sitting easily."

hem, helm [archaic] soul.

hemham breathsoul (one of the varieties of soul).

henni (interrogative) what? what is . . . ?

hersh 2 feet 9.2 inches: the basic unit of linear measurement in the Valley and in all cultures of the area except the northern Redwood Coast peoples. The hersh was subdivided into fourths, into fifths, into tenths, twelfths, and twenty-fourths, to give various "feet" and "inches," some of which were used preferentially in various professions (*e.g.*, paper

was measured in kekel, lumber in eyai, wool fabric in ótónehou, cotton in kumpetú).

hestanai Art: so translated in this book. A guild or society of people learning, teaching, and practicing a skill, craft, or profession, and the practice itself.

heve (or) **hevewaho** soul (used as a generic term).

heyimas the building (variously evolved from a basic pattern of five-sided underground room with four-sided pyramidal roof) where the activities of one of the Five Houses of Earth took place. The "Right Arm" of each Valley town consisted of the five heyimas laid out in a curve around the dancing place.

heyiya sacred, holy, or important thing, place, time, or event; connection; spiral, gyre, or helix; hinge; center; change. To be sacred, holy, significant; to connect; to move in a spiral, to gyre; to be or to be at the center; to change; to become. Praise; to praise.
heyiya-if a figure or image of the heyiya.

hilla enough (n. and adj.) To suffice, to be enough.

himpí a small animal resembling a large guinea pig, domesticated in the Valley; said to occur wild in the Range of Light.

híó (invariant verbal form used to form imperatives and optatives; may be translated *may, would that*.)
híó wóya (es) may you be easy, *i.e.*, goodbye.
híó dadam (es) hanóya go along easily, *i.e.*, goodbye.

hirai homesick, homesickness. To be homesick, to long for home.

hish swallow *(Tachycinata?)*.

ho age, old age, old. To be old.
hoo old woman.
aho, hota old man.

hohevoun spirit, deity, supernatural or non-natural object; god. To be divine, spiritual, supernatural.

honne rootlet, fine fiber.

hosó wood; timber.

houdada growth; bigness; swelling. To grow (in size), to increase, swell, swell up, get big.

houhwo Valley oak *(Quercus lobata)*.

houm big, large, long and wide, long-lasting.

hóv staying, dwelling, living (in a place). To stay, dwell, inhabit.
manhóv to live in a house, or in a House (hence to be).
hóvinye to visit, stay a while, be a guest, or visitor.

hoyfit raccoon *(Procyon lotor)*.

hú two.

húge division, separation, split, parting. To part, divide, separate two things, split in two.

húgele to run (on two legs).

húí two-legged being or person; human being, human. To be human.

huppaida hop, jump with two feet.

hur support, foundation; vehicle, that which carries. To hold up, carry, take, sustain.

hurga leg (of chair, table, etc.); pedestal, support.

HW

hwa sun. To shine (of, or like, the sun).

hwadíúha south.

hwaha southwest.

hwai time (time of day, at which an event occurs, a point in time, a length of time). To time, to measure time.

hwan yellow, golden.

hwapeweyo the dry season (approx. May–October).

hwavgedíú morning, forenoon.
hwavgodíú noon.
hwavgemaló afternoon.
hwavgomaló sunset, evening.

hwe 1. (precedes obj.) in front of, before (in place or time). 2. (after a verb) forward; truth.

hwefesent train, the Train.

hwerin horse.
ohwerin mare.
tahwerin, hwerina stallion.
pehwerin gelding.
klin foal.

hwette scrub oak *(Quercus dumosa)*.

(Spelled Whette as a name, to
conform to English spelling, in
the text.)

hwette súdrevídoun   *Q.
durata.*

hwik   half. To halve.

hwikonoy   mule; she-mule.
tahwik   he-mule.

hwo   oak (tree or wood).

hwovwon   acorn.

hwoi   help, assistance. To help,
aid, assist.

hwol   outbreath. To blow, to
puff.

hwots   a dice game.

hwu   an industrial residue,
occurring as fragmentary or
fibrous matter, mostly in earth
and as a water pollutant.

hwún   olive tree, wood, or fruit.

hwya   1. (follows obj.) behind,
in back of. 2. (after verb) back,
backwards..

hwyahwe   reversal. To reverse.
wehwyahwe   reversed, backward (adj.).

I

im   here.

íme   lip.
ímehú   lips.

imhai   here now, here and now.
rru imhaian   in this place at
this time.

in   (diminutive prefix. Little . . .)

inye   little, small, brief. (See also
diftú. Most small living creatures would be inye, not diftú,
except perhaps a tortoise, or
something small but notable for
longevity.)

irai   home; being home. To be
home, at home.
iraiwoi dad   to go home.

íríwin   Valley hawk, redwing or
red-shouldered hawk *(Buteo).*

íshavó   wilderness, wild places,
wild. To be wild.

íshavólen   feral cat *(Felis domesticus* gone wild).

ísítut   wild iris *(Iris spp.)*

íúgó   zenith; heights.

iya   hinge; connection; gyre;
source, beginning, center. To
connect; to originate.

iyakwun   love, mutual love,
interdependence; love of people, place; cosmic love.

iye   energy, power to work. To
work.

K

ka   coming. To come.

kach   city (not used of Kesh
towns).

kada   wave. To come and go; to
move as or like a wave or
waves.

kailíkú   Valley quail *(Lophortyx
californicus).*

kaiya   turn, turning. To turn,
turn round.

kakaga   dry streambed; arroyo.
(The bed of a running stream is
genakaga or nahevha.)

kan   the act of entering, coming
in. To enter, come in.

kanadra   duck (wild or domestic).

kaou   leaving, coming out, exit.
To leave, to come out.

karai   homecoming. To come
home.

ke   (usually prefixed) female,
woman, feminine gender.

kekosh   sister (see *kosh*).

kemel   Mars (planet).

kesh 1. valley, esp. the Valley of the Na River; variants of the latter: keshheya, amakesh, rrukesh, keshnav. 2. person, people, inhabitant of the Valley of the Na; variant: keshivshe. 3. the language of the human inhabitants of the Valley of the Na; variants: arrakeshiv, arrawekesh.

keshe, kesho woman, female person or being.

kevem sandal.

kinta war. To make war.
kintash warrior.
kintashúde the Warriors (Society).

klei, kley four-legged being or person; animal.

klema the Four Houses of the Sky; (as adj.) Four-House, of the Four Houses.
klemahóv, klemashe inhabitant of the Four Houses. To inhabit the Four Houses; hence, to be or to exist as such; hence also, in some cases, to be dead, to be not yet born, to be unreal, to be mythological, fictional, historical, or eternal. Klemashe is usually translated as Sky Person in the text.

kliltí chamise (Adenostoma).

kod corn, maize.

kosh sibling. The terms for biological siblings:
kekosh womb-sister.
takosh womb-brother.
souma half-sister, father's but not mother's daughter.
dúchatat half-brother, father's but not mother's son.
The terms for siblings of one's House (not necessarily related biologically):
makosh House brother or sister.
makekosh House sister.

matakosh House brother. (See the section "Kinfolk" in the text.)

koum craft; creation, making. To make, to shape, to form.
gokoum (n) shape, form.

kulkun mountain. (Ama Kulkun, Grandmother Mountain, is the dormant volcano at the head of the Valley of the Na.)

kwaiyó heart, in the metaphorical sense; emotional being, sensibility, feeling, feelings; intellect in the feeling mode, cognition informed by the senses, bodily knowledge. To think and feel, to know bodily or with mind and heart.

kwaiyó —woi dad to like.

L

lahe sleep. To sleep.

lama intercourse, fucking. To fuck.

lamawenun sexual passion or desire or love. To love, lust, desire.

lemaha beauty. To be beautiful.

lení cat (Felis domesticus).
olen tabby.
lena tom.
bínbín kitten.

leste to run on four feet (especially of small animals).

lim hair.

lír dream; vision. To dream, to have a vision.
lírsh visionary.

líyi like, seeming, seemingly.

lonel bobcat (Lynx rufus).

louswa sinking. To sink, to drain.

lúte amole. (Chlorogalum pomeridianum).

M

m, me and; also; as well as.

ma house (dwelling place), House (social/cosmic principle).

machumat towhee *(Pipilo spp.)*.

mal hill, knoll.

maldou ascent; uphill, upward. To ascend, to go up, to climb.

maló descent; downhill, downward. To descend, to go down.

mamou mother (biological).

mane (usually a partitive adj.) some; not all; a portion of.

manhóv the act or condition of living in a house or a House. To live in a house or House; to inhabit, to dwell.

manhóvoud community, commensality. To live with, together with.

marai household (the place and the people).

med cattails; bed of cattails or reeds.

meddelt left; Left-Hand (of the heyiya-if figure).

mehoi to listen, pay attention (to).

memen semen.

míp mouse (when the species is unknown or unspecified).
  aregímíp saltmarsh mouse *(Reithrodontomys)*.
  míbí fieldmouse or meadow vole *(Microtus spp.)*.
  útí deer mouse *(Peromyscus)*.

mo cow, cattle.
  amo cow.
  momota bull.
  mudí ox, steer.
  aihamo, aihama calf.

muddumada muttering, buzz. To mutter, to buzz, to simmer.

múdúp brush rabbit *(Sylvilagus)*.

mun clay.
  súmun blue or potters clay.

N

na river, esp. the River flowing through the Valley where the Kesh people live. To flow as or like a river.

nahai freedom. To be free.

nahe water.

nen for.

nó stillness; meditation. To be still, unmoving; to be quiet.

O

o (prefix or suffix indicating feminine gender)

ó, ók (usually preceding or prefixed to obj.) under; beneath; below; down.

ób (precedes obj.) to, toward (see also *woi*).

ógó nadir; depths.

ohu (interrogative, indicating the statement is a question; most often at the beginning, but may be anywhere in the sentence)

ohuhan how much? how many? how? in what way?

óló heron *(Ardea)*.

ólun bay laurel, myrtlewood *(Umbellularia californica)* tree, shrub, wood, fruit, or leaves (used as condiment).

om there; in that place.
  rrai om, rrai om pehaian then and there, in that place at that time (a narrative formula).

one maybe, perhaps.

ónhayú music. To be or to make music.

ónkama song. To sing.

onoy donkey.

opal frog *(Rana spp.)*.

ósai bone.

ou hound dog. To howl.

oud (usually suffixed to obj.) with, along with.

oudan (usually suffixed to obj.) with; within; among, amidst.

ouklalt right; on or of the Right Arm.

oun (follows or suffixed to obj.) on, onto.

óya ease. To be easy, to be at ease.
  wóyo easily.
  hanóya easily, with ease.
  geved hanóya sitting easily, *i.e.,* meditation, meditating.

P

p, pe (prefix indicating negative or privative)

paó achievement; sowing; ejaculation, male orgasm. To attain, achieve; to sow grain; to ejaculate, have orgasm (male).

parad meadow, uncultivated field, fallow.

pawon to hold, to carry in the hands or arms or next to the body.

pehai then (not now; at another time. Sequential *then,* next in order of events, is *ense*).

peham unbreathing, nonliving, dead.

peke (usually prefix) male, of masculine gender.

pekesh foreigner, person not of the Valley.

pekeshe man, male being.

pema foreigner, person without a House.

perru other; the other; another.

perrukesh valley (other than the Valley of the Na).

peshai drought.

peweyo piece, portion; region, area, place; era, time span.
  wakwav peweyo dancing place, sacred area.
  sheweiv peweyo, gochey peweyo common place, town plaza.

poud separate, separately; apart; alone.

póya difficulty, pain.
  wepoya hard, difficult, painful.

pragasí summer; hot weather.

pragú shining; brightness. To shine, to be bright.

púch thornbush, esp. chaparral pea *(Pickeringia montana).*

púl if not.

R

rahem souls (the various souls of one being, or the souls of many beings).

rava speech, language, tongue. To speak, with or without words, to talk (see *arra*).

recha hunt, hunting. To hunt. rechúde, rechúdiv hedom Hunters Lodge.

reysh line; anything very long, thin, and straight.
  húreysh the Line, tracks of the train.

rip rib, spoke, bar.

ro (reflexive pronoun) self.

rón care. To care; to take care, be careful.
  uvrón careful.

roy courage. To be valiant, brave.
  oweroy valiant (woman), a name.

rrai (dem. adj. or pronoun) that.

rru (dem. adj. or pronoun) this.

rrutouyó (or) **rrunenyó** because; because of; on account of.

rruwey cosmos, universe.

S

sa sky; Sky.

saham atmosphere.

sahamdaó wind. To blow, of or like wind.

sahamnó still air, windlessness.

sas (or) **dessas** rattlesnake *(Crotalus).*

saya (may precede or follow obj.) across.

sayaten to send a message, to communicate.
  sayagoten message.
  she sayageten,
  sayatensh messenger.

sei lantern flower *(Calochortus spp.).*

sense (may precede or follow obj.) following, succeeding; after; behind; later than.

seppí fence lizard *(Sceloporus).*

set level, even, plane, smooth. To smoothe, to plane, level off.

setaik (precedes obj.) preceding; in front of; before; earlier than.

sev grass, grasses.

sevai 1. sheath, case, envelope. To sheathe, to envelop. 2. a fatal degenerative illness. To be affected by this illness.

seyed eye.
  huseyed eye.

(SH listings follow S listings)

sitshidu winter; cold weather.

sobe conduct, behavior. To behave, conduct oneself.

sóde tree. To grow or form a shape or pattern like a tree.

sósóde wood, woods, forest, wooded country.

soun hummingbird *(Calypte anna).*

stad danger, peril, risk.

stanai art, skill, craft; to do or practice something with skill, to do (something) well.

stechab to offer.
  gostechab offering, thing offered.

stik falcon, sharpwinged hawk.
  yestik peregrine *(Falco peregrinus).*
  inyesti sparrowhawk *(F. sparverius).*

stou, dou (usually precedes or prefixed to obj.) over; up, up across; upon.

stre, sústre California jay, scrub jay *(Aphelocoma coerulescens).*

su white; colorless. Whiteness. To be white.

sú blue; blue-violet. Blueness. To be blue.

súdrevídó serpentine (rock).
  súdrevídóvma the Serpentine House.

sum head; top, summit.

súmun blue clay, potters clay.
  súmunivma the Blue Clay House.

susha grey, or a mixed color of light or cold tone; pale.

SH

sh (suffix, indicating agency; may be translated *-er*)

sha   grey, or a mixed color of dark, cold tone.

shahu   ocean.

malov shahu   the Pacific Ocean.

shai   rain. To rain, to fall like rain.

shaipeweyo   rainy season (approx. Nov.–April).

shansa   (a plural) some, some few, a few.

shasóde   digger pine *(Pinus sabiniana)*.

she   person; persons, people; being; self. To be a person, to exist (as a person or being).

sheiye   work, business, doing, industry. To work, to do, to act, to be active.

shestanai   artist, craftsperson, maker.

shewey   everyone, everybody; everything; (as a plural) all, every.

sho   as.

shókó   1. flicker (a woodpecker, *Colaptes*). 2. repeated multiple motions; sparkling, glimmering. To move or dance (of many people or objects), to sparkle, to glimmer or flicker.

shou   large, big. (But not necessarily long-enduring; see *houm*. A mountain would be houm; a big cloud would be shou. Most living creatures would be shou not houm.)

shun   (suffix) at.

T

ta   (prefix or suffix) male, of masculine gender, man.

tabetúpah   a miniature drama (a genre of oral literature).

tai   (prefix or suffix) above; upon.

taidagam   waterskater (insect; also *amhudade*).

taik   (precedes obj.) before; preceding; in front of.

tar   end, ending. To end, to finish, to come to the/an end.

tat (or) **bada**   father (biological).

tavkach   City of Man, *i.e.*, civilisation.

ten   to send.

tetiswou   bat (*Myotis* or *Pipistrellus*).

tibro   kingsnake *(Lampropeltis).*

tíodwa   blue-green, turquoise color.

tís   honey.

to   circle; wheel. To form or turn in a circle, to circle, to wheel or turn as a wheel. (If the figure or motion is broken or spiral, the word used will be *toudou* or *heyiya*.)

TOK   (not a Kesh word) a computer language taught to all human programmers by the Exchanges of the City of Mind, and used in spoken and/or written form as a lingua franca among human beings of different languages.

tom   ball, sphere; roundness; round.

tomhoi   completion, fulfilment, satisfaction; to complete, fulfill, satisfy; complete.

tóp   to keep.

tópush   keeper.

tótóp   hoard, treasure. To hoard.

tou   (prefix signifying the noun is the subject of the verb; also signifying the agent in a passive construction, where it may be translated as *by*)

toudou an open or broken circle or ring; a circling motion that does not return entirely upon itself. The motion of a millwheel is described by the word *to* (see above), but the motion of the water in and through the wheel is described by *toudou*.

tramad death; killing. To die; to cause to die; to kill.

tregai goose (*Anser* or *Branta*). **tregaiavarra** wild geese in flight-skein.

trum bear (*Ursus americanus?* Pictures and descriptions indicated a larger animal, but this might well be exaggeration; it was spoken of as always black or dark but with white or grey underparts.)

truned substance of a living creature after death—meat, corpse, wood, straw, etc.; body in the sense of dead body (living body is *chunú*).

tú through (a substance, hole, passage; see *dú*).

tun (suffix) from.

túpúde (a plural) some, more than a few, a good many.

uddamten, uddamtunten birth. To bear, to give birth.
uddamgoten born, to have been born.
uddamgotenshe one having been born, (hence) to be (of animate beings only).

úde 1. (a plural) a group of, a number of. 2. (affix signifying a group, grouping, herd, etc.; thus kintashúde, Warriors Society; galikúde, a herd of deer)

údín Saturn (planet).

údou open; opening: To open.

úl if.

úm empty, hollow, void. To empty.

úmí bee, honeybee.

unne love, trust, friendship, affection, loving kindness. To love, trust, to be a friend.

úrlele dragonfly.

ushud murder. To kill unjustifiably, without reason, in the wrong way, place, or time; to murder.

útí deermouse (see *míp*).

uv (prefix signifying use of the word as adj.; may be translated *characterised by, apt* or *able to, -ful*, etc.)

uvlemaha beautiful.

uvyai mindful.

úyúma rose (*Rosa californica*).

U

ubbu middle; middling. To be in the middle.

úbiú owl (usually the screech owl, *Otus asio*).
úbishí barn owl (*Tyto alba*).

ud, udde (prefix signifying the noun is the indirect object of the verb)

uddam womb. To be pregnant with.

V

v, iv (suffix signifying the possessive; may be translated *of, belonging to,* or with the possessive *'s, s';* also with the sense *made of, consisting of,* etc. Thus nahevna: river of water; navnahe: water of the river, river-water.)

vaheb salt.
vahevha the Salt Journey.

vahevhedom   the Salt Lodge.

vana   not yet; almost; not quite; nearly.

vave   cloud, especially cumulus and cirrus types of cloud.

ved   seat. To sit; to seat.
geved hanóya   sitting easily, *i,e.*, meditating, meditation.

vedet   a severe congenital disease.

ven   (suffix) to (especially to a place).

verou   quartz.

vesheve   fog, mist, low cloud, cloudiness. To cloud, to fog, to be foggy, misty, overcast.

vetúlou   a game played on horseback, with a wicker ball and scoops.

veya   (a plural) some, a couple, more than one but not many.

viddí   weakness. To be weak.

vodam   inland.
kavodam   to come inland, *i.e.*, to cease being celibate.

vón   shadow. To cast a shadow, to shadow.

vou   (suffix) outside, beyond; out, out of (see *bou*).

vúre   sand, sands.

W

wakwa   spring, source of water; ceremony, festival, rite, ritual, observance; dance; mystery. To spring, flow from a source, arise; to hold or participate in a ceremony or festival or observance; to dance; to be mysterious, to participate in mystery.

wakwana   spring of water, headwaters, source of stream.

we   (prefix signifying use of the word as adj; may be translated by *-y, -ish, -ian,* etc.)

wenha   to find, to discover.

wenhash   finder. Finder (plural: wenhaúde).

wenhav hedom   the Finders Lodge.

wenun   desire, want. To want, desire, covet, like, love.

weshole   mean, poor, stingy, wretched.

wey   all; whole, wholeness; entire, entirety.

weyewey   everything, all times and places.

wisúyú   willow *(Salix)* tree and wood.

wo   seed. To be a seed, seeds.

woi, woy   (suffix) to, towards (see also *ób*).

won   egg. To be an egg, eggs.

wotun   increase, maturation. To grow, mature, increase in being (for growth in size, enlargement, see *houdada*).

wu, wud   (prefix) again (signifies repeated action; may be translated *re-*).

wudun   exchange, transference, some forms of barter. To exchange. The Exchange (computer terminal[s] of the City of Mind).

wukaiya   return; repetition. To return; to repeat.

wurrai   story; fiction; invention; telling. To tell, tell a story, make up, invent.

wurrarap   recitation; report; telling. To tell, repeat, report, make a report, recite.

wuyai   reflection. To reflect; to return an image; to ponder.

Y

ya   (precedes obj. or prefix) by; by means of.

yabre   vine.
braiv yabre   grapevine *(Vitis vinifera).*

sódev yabre   wild grape *(Vitis californicus)*, used as root stock for the wine-grape grafts.

yai   mind; thought; thinking. To think, to give mind to.

yaivkach   the City of Mind, an autonomous computer network or organisation of artificial intelligence, represented in human communities by the terminals called *wudun,* Exchanges.

yakle, yakleda   to walk or go on four feet.

yaklegele, yaklele   to run on four feet.

yambad   (literally, *generously*) please. (Signifies the imperative mode when used with a verb, usually with híó.)

ye   (prefix signifying use of the word as adv.; may be translated -*ly*)

yebshe   to yield; to oblige.

yem   shore, bank of stream or river.

yí   note (in music).
    geyí   tone, played note

yik   boat. To boat, to go on water in a boat.

yó, yówut   in order to; in order that; so that.

yówai   coyote *(Canis latrans)*.
    yówayo   Coyote.

Z

z   (suffix, signifying that the word is in the Five-House Mode, used only in colloquial speech)

Stammersong

||||||||||||||||||||||||||||||||||||||||||||||||||||||

From the Library at Wakwaha.

I have a different way, I have a different will,
I have a different word to say.
I am coming back by the road around the side,
by the outside way, from the other direction.

There is a valley, there are no hills around it.
There is a river, it has no banks.
There are people, they have no bodies,
      dancing by the river in the valley.

I have drunk the water of that river.
I am drunk my life long, my tongue is thick,
and when I dance I stumble and fall over.
When I die I will come back by the outside road
and drink the water of this river and be sober.

There is a valley, high hills around it.
There is a river, willows on its shores.
There are people, their feet are beautiful,
      dancing by the river in the valley.

ABOUT THE AUTHOR

A resident of Portland, Oregon, URSULA K. LE GUIN was born in California, graduated from Radcliffe and earned her master's degree at Columbia University. One of the most distinguished authors of our time and winner of numerous awards, including the National Book Award, the Nebula and the Hugo, she has written many novels and short stories. Among her best known books are *The Left Hand of Darkness, The Disposessed,* and *The Earthsea Trilogy. Always Coming Home* was nominated for the American Book Award.